SAFETY

In the Classroom

- Read all of the directions. Make sure you understand them. When you see , be sure to follow the safety rule.

- Listen to your teacher for special safety directions. If you don't understand something, ask for help.

- Wear safety goggles when your teacher tells you to wear them and whenever you see 👓.

- Wear a safety apron if you work with anything messy or anything that might spill.

- If you spill something, wipe it up right away or ask your teacher for help.

- Tell your teacher if something breaks. If glass breaks do not clean it up yourself.

- Keep your hair and clothes away from open flames. Tie back long hair and roll up long sleeves.

- Be careful around a hot plate. Know when it is on and when it is off. Remember that the plate stays hot for a few minutes after you turn it off.

- Keep your hands dry around electrical equipment.

- Don't eat or drink anything during an experiment.

- Put equipment back the way your teacher tells you.

- Dispose of things the way your teacher tells you.

- Clean up your work area, and wash your hands.

In the Field

- Always be accompanied by a trusted adult—like your teacher or a parent or guardian.

- Never touch animals or plants without the adult's approval. The animal might bite. The plant might be poison ivy or another dangerous plant.

Responsibility

- Treat living things, the environment, and each other with respect.

California Topics

WHY IT MATTERS

Lassen Peak is an active volcano in your home state.

SCIENCE WORDS

composite volcano a volcano built from alternating eruptions of lava flow and pyroclastic materials

pyroclastic materials the rocks and ash that violently erupt from a volcano

shield volcano a volcano with a broad, slightly domed shape

cinder cone the smallest type of volcano, formed entirely by rock fragments

hydrothermal activity the action of underground water that is heated by magma

fumarole a vent in the ground that releases volcanic gases and steam

lahar a mudflow that results from volcanic activity

Lassen Volcanic National Park

Lassen Volcanic National Park is the site of one of the two most recent volcanic eruptions in the "lower 48" United States. The other is Mount Saint Helens in the state of Washington. At Lassen, there is a volcano that has year-round ice at its highest elevations. Because the roads are blocked by snow once the weather starts to get cold, a trip to Lassen will need to be in the summer.

EXPLORE

HYPOTHESIZE Why do volcanoes erupt? Why are some eruptions more forceful than others? Write a hypothesis in your *Science Journal*. How can you test your ideas?

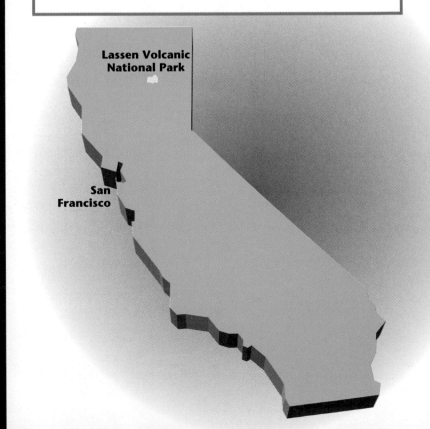

Lassen Volcanic National Park

San Francisco

What Is Lassen Peak?

Lassen Peak, which is 3,187 meters (10,453 ft) tall, is part of the Cascade Range. This mountain range runs from British Columbia, Canada, to northern California. Other mountains that are part of this range include Mount Rainier and Mount Saint Helens in Washington, Mount Hood in Oregon, and Mount Shasta in California. These are all part of a long line of volcanoes that encircle the Pacific Ocean in a "ring of fire."

Mount Saint Helens erupted as recently as 1980. The eruption and its mudflows killed 64 people and destroyed 100 homes.

Mount Saint Helens erupted as recently as 1980.

Types of Volcanoes

The Cascade volcanoes are all composite volcanoes, one of three volcano types. The two other types are shield volcanoes and cinder cones.

A **composite** (kam poz'-it) **volcano** is cone-shaped and tapers evenly from its wide base to its narrow peak. It is built from alternating eruptions of lava flow

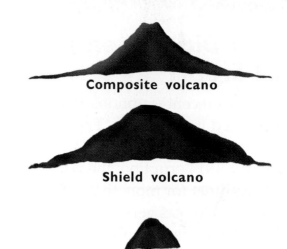

Composite volcano

Shield volcano

Cinder cone volcano

and pyroclastic materials. **Pyroclastic** (pi' rə klas'-tik) **materials** are the rocks and ash that violently erupt from the volcano.

A **shield** (shēld) **volcano** has a broad, slightly domed shape. It is built primarily from lava flows.

A **cinder** (sin'dər) **cone** is the smallest type of volcano. It is formed entirely by rock fragments. Cinder cones are usually less than 300 meters (984 ft) high.

Hydrothermal Activity

In areas where there is volcanic activity, hot magma(melted rock) lies not far below Earth's surface. The magma often heats groundwater, causing it to rise to the surface. This flow of heated water is called **hydrothermal** (hī' drō thûr'məl) **activity**.

Hot springs are one result of hydrothermal activity. Geysers are another. In a geyser, boiling water gushes upward, sometimes forming a plume of spray. Hydrothermal activity can also cause **fumaroles** (fū'-ma rōlz'), vents in the ground that release volcanic gases and steam.

When Did Lassen Peak Last Erupt?

The most recent eruptions at Lassen Peak started in May, 1914. They continued off and on for seven years. Before the 1914 eruption, the volcano had been quiet for more than 400 years.

The volcano was very active from 1914 to 1915. There were almost 150 eruptions during that time. Some of them sent clouds of ash as high as 3 kilometers (2 miles) above the peak.

In May, 1915, the nature of the eruptions changed. Lava began to flow onto the summit. An eerie red glow could be seen at night from as far away as 34 kilometers (21 miles).

On May 19, an avalanche of hot rocks spilled onto the snow of the peak. The hot rocks melted the snow and produced a lahar. A **lahar** is a mudflow that results from volcanic activity. The flow consisted of a mixture of the rocks, water, and soil. This lahar traveled for more than 15 kilometers (9 miles).

Blast Off

Two days later, the volcano blew its top! A pyroclastic eruption occurred. In a pyroclastic eruption, the magma has a high silica content and a relatively high percentage of gases. Rocks and ash are thrown upward and outward for long distances. The effect is similar to what happens when you drop a can of soda pop and then open it immediately.

In the pyroclastic eruption, one whole side of Lassen Peak was blasted away. Pyroclastic debris destroyed forests more than 6.5 kilometers (4 miles) away. The forests in this area are just now beginning to grow back.

A huge ash plume rose more than 9 kilometers (6 miles) above the peak. The wind carried the ash as far as 500 kilometers (310 miles) to the east.

Fortunately, when Lassen Peak erupted in 1915, not many people lived in the area. There were no deaths and no property damage. This eruption was considered moderate by volcano experts.

A pyroclastic eruption occurred at Lassen Peak on May 21, 1915. Above: Volcanic activity at Lassen Peak in 1915 produced this mudflow.

How Were Lassen Peak and Its Surroundings Formed?

The Dome

You have learned that Lassen Peak is a composite volcano. Geologists classify it further as a composite dome.

To get an idea of how the dome was formed, think of a tube of toothpaste. When you squeeze the tube, the toothpaste is forced up and out. If you didn't put it on your toothbrush, the toothpaste might just fall over onto the tube because it is so thick.

Lassen Peak formed in somewhat the same way. In eruption after eruption, the thick lava came up through the vent and flowed over the top. It cooled and hardened before it got very far. The dome was formed by the build-up of these flows over the years. The surface of the dome is rough and jagged because lava fragments broke off as the lava cooled.

The dome is made up mainly of dacite. Dacite is a volcanic rock that is usually light in color and contains 62 percent to 69 percent silica and moderate amounts of the elements sodium and potassium.

Chaos Crags

Chaos Crags is another result of volcanic activity in Lassen Volcanic National Park. These hills of rocks surround hidden lakes where snow and ice have melted.

The Chaos Crags area was formed from several eruptions that took place starting about a thousand years ago. First, volcanic activity formed a cone. Eruptions then hurled rocks over a wide area. Finally, cooling lava formed a dome that plugged the vent.

A quiet period was followed about 70 years later by another violent eruption that destroyed the dome. Pyroclastic materials were thrown as far as 10 kilometers (6 miles) from Chaos Crags. Then lava once again formed a dome and plugged the vent. This process was repeated many times.

Eventually, about 700 years after the last dome was formed, it collapsed. Avalanches moved the rocks and deposited them across a 3-kilometer (2 mile) area. This rocky area is called Chaos Jumbles.

This area has not yet been greatly affected by weathering or erosion. It is a good place to explore volcanic activity and do some rock climbing.

The Chaos Crags area is a result of eruptions that go back 1,000 years. [Inset] The dome of Mt. Lassen is similar to the domes of the other mountains of the Cascade Range.

What Other Evidence of Volcanic Activity Does the Park Have?

There are two major hydrothermal areas of Lassen National Park. The first area is about 3 kilometers (2 miles) from the nearest road. It is noted for its hot springs, mudpots, fumaroles, and mud volcanoes. You can follow a trail around but you have to be careful not to get too close. The water and gases have been heated by magma beneath Earth's crust.

The other hydrothermal area is called Sulfur Works. It is very easy to visit. It is located near the road that goes through the park. Boardwalks lead you right up to the bubbling mud pots. The clay here is tinted yellow, tan, or pink by iron oxides and other minerals.

Although this area is colorful, you may not like the smell. The air smells like rotten eggs. The sulfur in egg yolks is the same element responsible for the unpleasant smells in this area. The water contains hydrogen sulfide, which is noted for its pungent odor.

Scientists have noted that the hydrothermal areas of Lassen Peak have been getting hotter. They think that Lassen Peak and Mount Shasta

could join Mount Saint Helens as the next active volcanoes in the Cascade Range.

Cinder Cone

In the northeastern part of the park lies Cinder Cone. This nearly perfect example of a cinder cone can be reached only by adventurous visitors. The roads are unpaved in this part of the park. Scientists believe that this cone was formed between 400 and 450 years ago. Other cinder cones are also visible in this area.

Lava Tubes

In the Lassen Forest, just outside the park, there are lava tubes. A lava tube is formed when the outside of a lava flow hardens and hot lava continues to flow through it. When the internal flow of hot lava stops, a tubelike structure remains.

For scientists and visitors, Lassen Volcanic National Park is California's own laboratory for studying volcanoes.

Left: The Sulfur Works clays are made up of many different-colored minerals. Above: Cinder Cone is formed entirely from rock fragments.

Choose the letter of the best answer. Mark your answer on a separate sheet of paper.

1. Lassen Peak is part of which of the following mountain chains?
   A Sierra Nevada
   B San Gabriel Mountains
   C Rocky Mountains
   D Cascade Range

2. When was the last eruption of Lassen Peak?
   A about 20 years ago
   B about 80 years ago
   C about 200 years ago
   D about 1,000 years ago

3. Lassen Peak is an example of which kind of volcano?
   A composite
   B shield
   C cinder cone
   D none of the above

4. The Chaos Jumbles area near Lassen Peak
   A is a result of the most recent eruption
   B is becoming forested again
   C is covered with rocks from pyroclastic eruptions
   D is an area of hydrothermal activity

5. Hydrothermal activity provides evidence that
   A there is hot magma underneath the crust
   B a volcanic eruption is going to occur right away
   C lava is about to flow
   D there is sulfur in the ground

6. During the most recent years of volcanic activity at Lassen Peak, which of the following did *not* happen?
   A Ash plumes flew into the sky.
   B Lava flows buried the Chaos Crags.
   C Pyroclastic debris destroyed forests.
   D Lava flowed from the summit.

7. Look at the graph on page CA28. Which is the tallest mountain listed?
   A Lassen Peak
   B Mount Hood
   C Mount Saint Helens
   D Mount Rainier

8. According to the information on page CA28, which volcano has not erupted in the last 1,000 years?
   A Meager Mountain
   B Mount Shasta
   C Mount Hood
   D Mount Rainier

9. Which statement about composite volcano domes is accurate?
   A The mountains of the Cascade Range do not have domes.
   B The dome is a result of the build-up of lava.
   C Once a volcano has a dome, it will never erupt again.
   D The dome is very smooth.

Write the answer to the question below on your piece of paper.

10. Explain how a scientist might predict whether a volcano will erupt.

The Beaches of Point Reyes

Point Reyes extends out into the Pacific Ocean just north of San Francisco. It has been officially protected as a National Seashore since 1962. On Point Reyes there are 12 different beaches. How did the ocean cause differences in these beaches? How do the rocks differ from beach to beach?

WHY IT MATTERS

The variety of beaches at Point Reyes National Seashore shows how the ocean and tectonic activity have helped to form the landscape around you.

SCIENCE WORDS

wave a movement of energy through a body of water, such as the ocean

refraction the process in which waves meeting a curving shore tend to bend and lose energy

abrasion a process in which rocks rub against each other and break down into pebbles or sand

HYPOTHESIZE How do waves shape a shoreline? Does the angle at which the waves approach the shore make a difference? Write a hypothesis in your *Science Journal*. How can you test your ideas?

Point Reyes National Seashore

San Francisco

Why Are There Different Types of Shorelines?

Have you seen pictures of the California coastline? Have you traveled along it? If so, what kinds of coastline did you see? In southern California, there are many long stretches of sandy beaches. On the northern coast, many visitors might be afraid to drive on Highway 1 along the rugged cliffs high above the rocky shores.

These different shorelines are formed by waves. **Waves** are a form of energy. When you look out over the ocean and see the waves rushing toward the coast, the enormous body of water is not going anywhere. What you see moving is the wave energy moving through the water. A buoy floating near the coast does not change its location. It simply moves up and down as the waves pass by.

Coastline Shapes

Some coastlines are almost straight, but others have many narrow inlets. The shape of the coastline affects the energy of the waves as they hit land.

Where there are curves and inlets in the coast, the waves strike different points with different amounts of force. The parts of the land that stick out into the ocean the farthest are hit first and hardest. But where waves hit a curving shore, they bend in a process called **refraction**. They lose energy and strike the shore with less force.

Where there is a long stretch of coast without any inlets or curves, the waves come in with their full strength. These kinds of beaches usually have the surf that is attractive to surfers.

In some parts of California, cliffs along the seashore are made of soft rocks. Over time, the pounding of the waves will erode the rocks and turn curved shorelines into straight beaches. In other areas, however, the sea cliffs are made of hard rocks such as granite. These cliffs are better able to resist erosion.

The lighthouse at Point Reyes overlooks the Pacific Ocean.

What Is the Geologic Structure of Drake's Beach?

One of the most popular beaches at Point Reyes is Drakes Beach, a crescent-shaped body of water sheltered from the main force of the wind and waves. In 1579, Sir Francis Drake, a famous English explorer, may have anchored in this bay.

The fine sands and tide pools make the area fun to explore. You can go swimming in the bay. You can find red seastars in the tiny tide pools right in the sand or next to the sandstone rocks. The sand is dotted with these rocks when the tide is low.

The beach is backed by white cliffs. The rock of these cliffs was deposited in a shallow sea over ten million years ago. The sands were compacted and then uplifted by the movement of tectonic plates.

The cliffs are made up of several types of rocks with different colored layers. Two of the rocks in these cliffs are siltstone and sandstone. They are colored white, brown, and different tones of gray.

The waves, winds, and rains have worn away at these cliffs. Although the surf is not wild here, the sandstone is not very hard. The continued erosion has left the sides of the cliffs exposed. Scientists study the different layers of the cliffs to learn more about the geologic history of this area.

Drakes Beach is noted for its sandstone cliffs. Rocks protrude from the sand.

What Are the Other Beaches at Point Reyes?

Point Reyes has two other famous beaches. They are the Great Beach and Kohoe Beach.

The Great Beach

The Great Beach at Point Reyes National Seashore is over 16 kilometers (10 miles) long. Here there are no towering cliffs close to the road. You can walk to the beach directly from a car. To the left and right all you can see is beach and ocean. You may see someone taking a dog for a walk on a leash.

Left: The Great Beach is too dangerous for any water sports. Right: Kehoe Beach is at the northern end of the Great Beach.

When you first see the surf here, your reaction might be to tell your surfer friends to get their surfboards. However, surfing is not allowed on the Great Beach.

The waves of the Great Beach are too high for any water sports. It is too dangerous to go swimming in these waters. There are undercurrents and rip tides that could carry an unsuspecting swimmer far out into the ocean. Sharks have been spotted in these waters. This is a place to enjoy by watching the crashing surf.

The sand of this beach has a fine texture near the ocean, but it becomes coarse and pebbly as you move inland. Sands are created by two processes. The first is erosion, which can break down the rocks and other materials along the land as the waves hit the shore.

The second process is **abrasion**, in which the waves cause rocks to rub against each other. This action breaks the rocks down and creates smooth pebbles or fine sand.

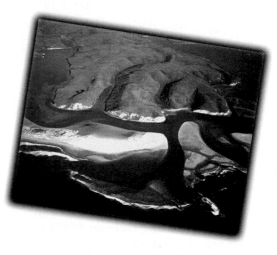

Kehoe Beach

Kehoe Beach is at the northern end of the Great Beach. It is noted for its giant dunes. A dune is a hill of wind-blown sand.

You will also see a stream on Kehoe Beach. The stream has cut out a small channel as it has worked its way through the sand.

Beyond the sand dunes are cliffs. Close to the dunes the cliffs are made of sandstone. Then they change abruptly to granite. Millions of years ago, tectonic plate activity caused a fault to form at this site along the cliffs. The sandstone that was originally sitting on top of the granite ended up next to it.

What Formed the Point Reyes Peninsula?

Point Reyes National Seashore is part of the Point Reyes Peninsula. The peninsula is a piece of Earth's crust located just west of the San Andreas fault.

Scientists have discovered that the siltstone in the cliffs at Drakes Beach is very similar to the siltstone found along the beaches of Santa Cruz just north of Monterey. They think that from about 60 million years ago until 15 million years ago, this area may have been located near Monterey in central California.

The same tectonic plate activity that formed the San Andreas fault is thought to be responsible for moving this chunk of land.

Right: The earth moved and this fence was split along the San Andreas fault. Below: McClures Beach is part of the newly formed coastline of Pt. Reyes.

The entire peninsula is thought to be "riding" at the edge of a tectonic plate. Along with the rest of the plate, it is traveling from southeast to northwest. Millions of years ago it was near central California. Millions of years from now, it may be located far to the north.

During the great San Francisco earthquake of 1906, the land along the fault in the Point Reyes Peninsula moved as much as 80 meters (25 feet). Over the span of millions of years, there may be many more earthquakes of that size in this area.

Choose the letter of the best answer. Mark your answer on a separate sheet of paper.

1. Which is the best description of a wave?

   A moving water

   B energy that moves through water

   C surf

   D breakers

2. Which beach in Point Reyes is next to a bay?

   A The Great Beach

   B Kehoe Beach

   C Drakes Beach

   D McClures Beach

3. When were the sands of the cliffs of Drakes Bay deposited in a shallow sea?

   A one thousand years ago

   B one million years ago

   C ten million years ago

   D one billion years ago

4. Which type of rock is *not* part of the Point Reyes headlands?

   A granite

   B sandstone

   C basalt

   D igneous rocks

5. How long is the Great Beach?

   A 2 miles

   B 20 miles

   C 10 kilometers

   D 10 miles

6. Why is the Great Beach dangerous for water sports?

   A the surf is extremely high

   B there are rip tides

   C the water is very cold

   D all of the above

7. According to the map on page CA29, which statement best describes Point Reyes?

   A Point Reyes has no inlets.

   B Point Reyes is mostly flat land.

   C Point Reyes is mostly steep hills.

   D Point Reyes is in San Francisco Bay.

8. According to the map on page CA29, Point Reyes Lighthouse is at the southwestern tip of the point. The lighthouse is

   A near the San Andreas fault

   B on an inlet

   C faces the Pacific Ocean

   D faces Drakes Bay

9. Which of the following is *not* a true statement about the Point Reyes Peninsula?

   A The San Andreas fault is its eastern boundary.

   B All the beaches are backed by cliffs.

   C An English explorer may have landed there in 1579.

   D Sand dunes can be found on some of the beaches.

Write the answer to the question below on your piece of paper.

10. Explain why scientists think that the Point Reyes Peninsula once sat next to Monterey.

WHY IT MATTERS

Every year, Santa Ana winds increase fire hazards in southern California.

SCIENCE WORDS

gradient a difference in air pressure

The Santa Ana Winds

The Santa Ana winds are hot, dry, powerful winds that occur every year in southern California. They begin far away, in the Great Basin region east of California. From about October to February, the conditions necessary for a "Santa Ana effect" are often in place.

HYPOTHESIZE Why are some winds warm and others cold? Write a hypothesis in your *Science Journal*. How can you test your ideas?

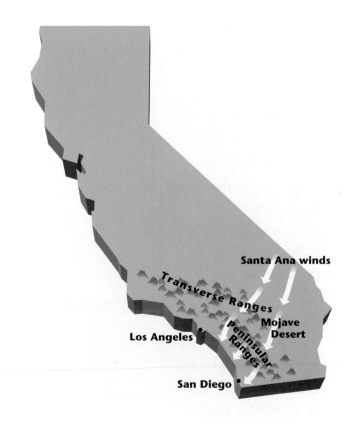

Santa Ana winds

Transverse Ranges

Mojave Desert

Peninsular Ranges

Los Angeles

San Diego

How Do Santa Ana Winds Start?

Winds are caused by differences in air pressure from one area to another. Air in an area of high pressure will flow toward an area of lower pressure. This process is the same one by which the air rushes out of an inflated balloon when it bursts. Scientists call the difference in air pressures the **gradient** (grā' dē ənt).

How does a gradient develop? For the Santa Ana winds, the process starts in the Great Basin. The Great Basin is the vast, dry region of plateaus and hills west of the Rocky Mountains. It extends westward all the way to the Sierra Nevada on the California border.

In the fall, areas of high pressure often build up over the Great Basin. Winds circle clockwise around the center of the high-pressure area. But when they begin to flow westward, the winds are blocked and turned south by the Sierra Nevada.

At the same time, a low-pressure area often forms just off the coast of southern California. The gradient between the areas of low and high pressure grows steadily greater. The winds in the Great Basin speed up and grow stronger.

Finally, the winds "break through" the mountain passes and rush down upon southern California. By the time they reach the coastal basins, they have become full-scale Santa Ana winds.

The conditions that produce Santa Ana winds start as far away as the Great Salt Lake in the Great Basin.

Why Are the Santa Ana Winds So Hot and Strong?

The desert air mass that produces Santa Ana winds is already warm and dry. As the winds flow toward southern California, they become even warmer and drier.

As they descend through narrow mountain canyons, the winds speed up due to what scientists call the Venturi Effect. Think back to a windy summer day when some windows were open in your house. You may have noticed that when you tried to close the front door, the wind howled and blew harder as the door shut. This is an example of the Venturi effect.

The narrow canyons pinch the rivers of air just as your front door squeezed the air entering your house. The Venturi effect causes the winds to move faster. Compression in the canyons also makes the winds hotter.

Finally, the winds pass through the Santa Ana Mountains just above Los Angeles. By this time, they are blowing at more than 80 kilometers (50 miles) per hour. Trees go down. Power lines fall. Property can be damaged. The Santa Ana winds can blow for days.

The greatest problem caused by the Santa Ana winds is the increased risk of fire. In Santa Ana season, the southern California forests are tinder-dry. The undergrowth is dead. This huge fuel mass is literally ready to explode at the first spark. If that spark is struck, the Santa Anas multiply the destruction many times by fanning and spreading the flames. In October, 1996, Santa Ana winds sent a blaze out of control. The fire destroyed 2,800 acres of trees and killed seven people.

Amazingly, not everyone dreads the Santa Anas. Those high-speed winds tumbling through canyons and over mountains create some spectacular soaring conditions for glider airplanes. In the right places, glider pilots can soar to 48,000 meters (30,000 feet). That's higher than the highest mountain on Earth, Mount Everest.

Brushfires are a problem during Santa Ana season. Top: Gliders take advantage of Santa Ana winds.

Choose the letter of the best answer. Mark your answer on a separate sheet of paper.

1. Where is the Great Basin?
   A in southern California
   B in northern California
   C east of California
   D south of California

2. When does the Santa Ana effect usually develop?
   A from about October to February
   B from about June to September
   C from about February to May
   D from about September to December

3. Wind blows
   A when two areas have the same air pressure
   B from an area of low air pressure to an area of high air pressure
   C from an area of high air pressure to an area of low air pressure
   D all of the above

4. Which of the following does *not* describe how Santa Ana winds form?
   A An area of high air pressure develops over the Great Basin.
   B The Great Basin fills with rainwater, which pushes out the air.
   C Great Basin winds blow clockwise.
   D Winds flow through the mountain passes toward southern California.

5. When air is squeezed through the canyon
   A it cools down
   B it expands
   C it heats up
   D none of the above

6. Which of the following is *not* a direct result of the Santa Ana effect?
   A floods
   B increased risk of forest fires
   C downed trees
   D good hang gliding conditions

7. Look at the fire safety diagram on page CA30. In order to make a home safer, how wide an area should be cleared on the non-slope sides?
   A 10 feet
   B 20 feet
   C 30 feet
   D 100 feet

8. According to the information on page CA 30, which fire was responsible for the loss of the most homes?
   A 1993 Kinneloa Fire
   B 1970 Malibu Fire
   C 1993 Old Topanga Fire
   D 1982 Malibu Fire

9. Which of the following is true about the Santa Ana winds?
   A They travel from west to east.
   B They travel at speeds of more than 80 kilometers per hour.
   C They accumulate moist air.
   D They are moist and cool.

Write the answer to the question below on your piece of paper.

10. When is the danger of fire greatest in the southern California mountains? Explain.

WHY IT MATTERS

The kelp forest is an underwater ecological community that is home to many different animals.

SCIENCE WORDS

kelp large marine algae, or seaweed

holdfast rootlike structure that holds kelp tightly to the ocean floor

upwelling the rising of cold water from the ocean's depths to replace warmer surface water that was driven offshore

The Kelp Forest

Large brown algae called **kelp** grow in huge underwater "forests" along the entire Pacific coast of the United States. One of the largest and best studied kelp forests is off the central coast of California, in Monterey Bay.

The kelp forest is similar in structure to any forest on land. The kelp is a tall plant, like a tree. Just as a tree is rooted to the ground, the kelp is attached to the ocean floor. The kelp has a "canopy" of leaflike fronds that sway in the waters just below the surface. The canopy shelters other life forms from sunlight and predators.

Many different species of plants and animals live in the kelp forest, and they depend on each other for survival.

EXPLORE

HYPOTHESIZE How does the mixture of warm and cold water currents in the ocean affect an ecoystem? Write a hypothesis in your *Science Journal.* How can you test your ideas?

Left: There is great biological diversity in the kelp forest. Right: The same processes that give the California coast great biological diversity affect our weather.

What Is It Like in the Kelp Forest?

Kelp attaches itself to the ocean floor with rootlike structures called **holdfasts**. Kelp stems called stipes rise from the ocean floor. The kelp often reaches all the way to the surface of the ocean, a distance of up to 75 meters (245 feet). Natural, gas-filled floats help the kelp to rise to the surface.

In the surface waters at the top of the kelp forest, yellowtail and other large fish look for smaller fish to eat. Small fish like the opaleye hide among the kelp fronds and are hard to spot.

Many small fish eat the kelp itself. As they eat, bits of kelp are dropped and sink to the ocean floor. Bottom dwellers such as the sea urchin eat them. These bottom dwellers also get food from eating the holdfast and other plant life. In turn, urchins are eaten by other bottom dwellers such as sea stars.

Also prowling these waters is a rare ocean-dwelling mammal called the California sea otter. These animals dive to 60 meters (200 feet) for food. They eat sea urchins, abalone, and crabs.

Ideal Growing Conditions

The kelp forests flourish because ocean currents bring water that is just the right temperature. The California current flows southward from Oregon to southern California, bringing cool water from the north. This cold current keeps the water temperature low enough for the kelp and the other organisms that live in the kelp forests to thrive.

During the spring, wind and Earth's rotation drive surface waters offshore. Cold waters from the deep ocean take their place. These waters bring dissolved nutrients from the ocean floor up near the surface, where many living things can take advantage of them. This process is called **upwelling** and is also responsible for California's coastal fogs.

How Do Kelp Forest Animals Interact?

This is a story about two animals that are about as different as they can be. However, they both live together in the kelp forest, and without one, the kelp forest could not survive.

The California sea otter is a mammal that is specially adapted to life in the water. Otters have webbed toes that make them good swimmers. They have thick fur that keeps them warm and also traps air so that they can float. However, an otter's fur cannot hold air unless it is clean, so it common to see otters grooming themselves.

The otter eats a lot. It can eat an amount equal to one-fourth of its body weight every day. The foods the otter prefers are abalone, crabs, and sea urchins. Also, otters are smart. They are one of the few animals that use tools. They use rocks to break open abalone shells.

The other animal in our story is the sea urchin. This animal is a relative of the sea star. The sea urchin lives at the base of the kelp forest, in cool, deep waters. Like the otter, the sea urchin eats a lot. If it does not get enough to eat by eating those bits of leaves that fall from higher in the kelp forest, it will start to eat the kelp plants themselves. It may start by eating the holdfasts.

About 100 years ago, the California sea otter was hunted until almost none were left. The loss of the otters brought change to the whole kelp forest. The urchins, with few otters to eat them, multiplied rapidly. However, their food supply stayed the same. Once the urchins had eaten all of the bits of leaves that were drifting down from above, they started eating the holdfasts of the kelp. This killed the kelp, and large parts of the kelp forest were destroyed.

California sea otters are now protected, and although they are still considered a threatened species, their population is growing. More otters are eating more urchins, and as a result, the kelp forest is recovering.

The California sea otter eats almost one-fourth of its body weight every day. [Inset] The sea urchin is one of the otter's favorite foods.

Left: Kelp forests protects beaches from erosion. Right: Kelp is used to make many products.

What If There Were No Kelp?

Sea urchins are not the only threat to the kelp forests. Another naturally occurring danger is the world-wide weather event called El Niño. Every few years when an El Niño occurs, ocean currents come up the California coast from the south. They bring water that is too warm for the kelp to survive, and much of the kelp forest dies. However, El Niños are part of a natural cycle. The following year, water currents return to normal, and the kelp forests grow back.

More dangerous to the kelp are two problems caused by people: pollution and erosion. These are particularly serious in southern California.

People pollute the ocean by dumping harmful chemicals and other substances into it. This pollution can damage the kelp forests. Eroded soil can also affect kelp. Rain washes the eroded soil, sewage, and trash into the ocean. As a result, the ocean's waters become muddy. Little sunlight reaches the kelp, and without sunlight, the kelp die.

What happens when the kelp forest disappears? Fish and other animals must leave the area to find food and shelter elsewhere. In addition, because the kelp provided a natural break-water, waves can now strike the beach with full force. The result can be erosion of beaches and coastlines.

It is not only the natural world that is affected when a help forest disap-pears. People are affected as well. Kelp is harvested to make about 1,000 different consumer products. For example, a chemical in kelp is used to make ice cream.

Where Can You See a Kelp Forest?

On the central coast of California, the city of Monterey stands on a peninsula at the south end of the Monterey Bay. Off the coast is Monterey Bay National Marine Reserve, which stretches from San Francisco south to Big Sur. Not only can divers see kelp forests in Monterey Bay, but visitors can see a kelp forest without even getting wet!

Monterey is the home of Monterey Bay Aquarium, which holds exhibits with thousands of species of marine animals, plants, and birds from around Monterey Bay. Included in the exhibits is an actual kelp forest. It is three stories tall and uses a surge machine to create waves that keep the kelp and animals healthy.

Many of the animals that live in the kelp forests in Monterey Bay are on display in the aquarium's kelp forest. The animals are fed by divers who explain to visitors how the fish are fed.

After you spend time at the kelp forest in the Aquarium, you can walk outside and see the bay. It is not uncommon to see sea otters and sea lions frolicking in the wild at the Aquarium's back door.

When people see animals and plants in an aquarium, they are often inspired to preserve them in the wild. Preservation efforts can help ensure the survival of the kelp forests and the many other plants and animals that live in them.

Left: At the Monterey Bay Aquarium, visitors can see a kelp forest without getting wet. Right: They can also see ocean animals from the aquarium terrace.

REVIEW

Choose the letter of the best answer. Mark your answer on a separate sheet of paper.

1. Kelp is a(n)
   A fish
   B crustacean
   C algae or seaweed
   D area of California

2. The part of kelp that attaches to the ocean floor is the
   A holdfast
   B canopy
   C frond
   D stipe

3. How do sea otters get their food?
   A They eat leaves off the kelp at the surface.
   B They swim to shore.
   C They hunt animals on the ocean bottom.
   D They eat fish near the surface.

4. If otters do not eat enough sea urchins, what happens?
   A Fish will leave the area.
   B Sea urchins will eat all the kelp.
   C Beaches will erode.
   D all of the above

5. How does the process called upwelling help plants and animals in the ocean?
   A It causes beach erosion.
   B It brings up dissolved nutrients from deep waters.
   C It brings sea urchins and sea stars to the surface.
   D It allows more sunlight to reach the kelp.

6. Why are kelp forests important to fishermen?
   A Kelp is used to make many products.
   B Fisherman want to catch only bottom-dwelling fish.
   C If there were no kelp forests, fish would leave the area.
   D Otters attract fish.

7. At the Monterey Bay Aquarium, artificial waves are used to
   A keep a kelp forest healthy
   B bring up nutrients from the ocean floor
   C reduce the number of sea urchins
   D study beach erosion

8. What natural event sometimes damages southern California's kelp forests?
   A beach erosion
   B pollution from sewage and harmful chemicals
   C upwelling of cold waters from the ocean depths
   D El Niño

9. Use the illustrations on page CA31. Which of these animals eat kelp?
   A yellowtails and sea otters
   B sea stars and sea otters
   C opaleyes and sea urchins
   D sea stars and abalone

Write the answer to the question below on your piece of paper.

10. Explain what may happen to a group of plants and animals if one species suddenly disappears. Use an example to support your ideas.

WHY IT MATTERS

California is the third largest oil-producing state in the country.

SCIENCE WORDS

fossil fuel a fuel formed from the decay of ancient forms of life

gusher an oil well in which the oil is pushed up out of the ground forcefully by natural underground pressures

crude oil oil that contains substances that need to be removed before the oil is useful

derrick a framework or tower built over an oil well

Oil Country

In 1859 the rush for oil began in Titusville, Pennsylvania, when oil was first pumped out of the ground. The rush for oil in California started in 1861 when the first well was dug in search of oil in Humbolt County, which is in northern California. Today, most California oil comes from the southern end of the state, from Kern and Los Angeles counties and from offshore wells such as the one shown in the photograph. Such wells are disguised as high-rise buildings. California is still a leader in the United States oil industry.

EXPLORE

HYPOTHESIZE How do people make the crude oil from fossil fuels into a useful energy source? Write a hypothesis in your *Science Journal*. How can you test your ideas?

Where Does Oil Come From?

Oil is a **fossil fuel**, or a fuel formed from the remains of ancient living things. Its history begins many millions of years ago. In that distant time, huge numbers of microorganisms lived in the oceans, just as they do today. When these organisms died, their remains were buried under sand and small particles of dirt that settled on the ocean floor. As time passed, more sand, dirt, and rock covered them.

As the weight of these materials grew, pressure and heat changed the remains of the microorganisms into oil and natural gas. These changes took place deep below Earth's surface over hundreds of thousands of years.

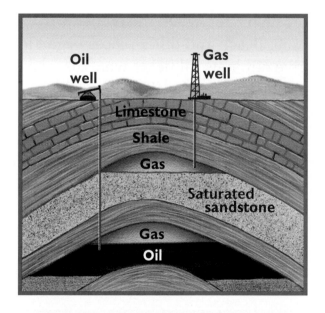

As the oil formed, it moved upward through holes in the rock. Large pools formed where the oil was trapped by solid rock. It is these pools that oil wells tap into. Sometimes natural underground pressures push the oil up

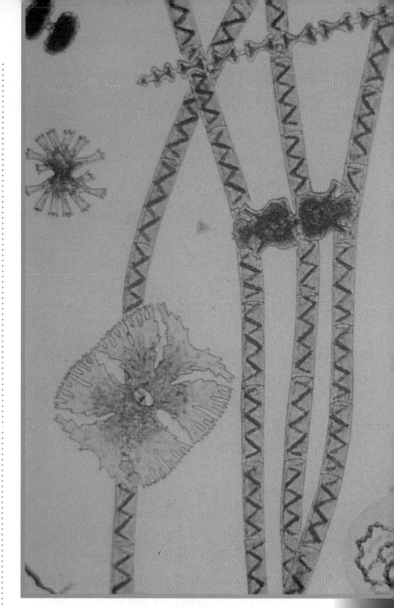

Above: Microscopic organisms such as these changed into oil and natural gas deposits. Left: Oil and natural gas move up through saturated rock layers. Gas is less dense than oil and moves above all deposits.

out of the ground forcefully. This kind of well is called a **gusher**.

The oil that is pumped up is called **crude oil**. Crude oil contains substances that must be removed before the oil can be used. The crude oil is sent through a pipeline to an oil refinery. There the crude oil is refined, or cleaned, and processed into usable forms. Then it is sold for a wide variety of uses.

What Is the History of Oil in California?

In the 1860's near Los Angeles, people noticed that there were pits of tar and areas where asphalt was seeping out of the ground. They concluded that there was oil beneath the surface. Drilling soon began and some oil was found, but not enough to earn the drillers a profit. This first oil rush quickly fizzled.

It was in the 1890s that the first really big oil discovery was made in California. Drilling began at a major oil field north of Los Angeles. From that time on, the growth of the California oil industry was dramatic. In 1893, 470,000 barrels of oil were produced. By 1910, yearly production had reached 73,000,000 barrels. This was 22 percent of the entire world production at the time. Until 1907 California produced only crude oil. That year, however, the state's first refinery was built. From that point forward, the crude oil could be turned into many useful petroleum products. These could then be shipped to markets in the Midwest and on the East Coast.

At first, California's principal petroleum product was heating oil. But in the early twentieth century, after automobiles were invented, demand grew for gasoline. That's when the market for California oil really took off!

In the 1920s, a new southern California oil boom began in Long Beach. Behind Long Beach is an area called Signal Hill. At that time it was being divided up into small housing lots. Then, in 1921, an exploratory oil well gushed, and the Long Beach oil boom was on! Prospectors began buying up the lots on Signal Hill. Soon the whole area was covered with wooden oil **derricks**. The lots were sold, divided, and sold again until finally there were derricks on nearly every tiny bit of land. By 1923, oil from Long Beach had helped make California the biggest oil producer of all of the states. In fact, California was producing 25 percent of the world's oil.

Much later, when the oil fields in Long Beach and other places began to give out, new oil fields were discovered off the coast. Oil wells were drilled in the ocean floor off Long Beach and Santa Barbara. An increasing share of California's oil comes from these offshore wells.

Today, California is the country's third-largest oil producer, behind only Alaska and Texas. It is a very important source of oil for the United States.

Oil is still produced in the Long Beach oil fields.

Choose the letter of the best answer. Mark your answer on a separate sheet of paper.

1. Fossil fuels would *not* include
   A oil for heating
   B logs for a campfire
   C gasoline for a car
   D natural gas for cooking

2. Based on how oil and natural gas are formed, you may conclude that
   A natural gas and oil are found mixed together
   B natural gas and oil are found separately, never together
   C gasoline is pumped from the ground
   D natural gas is not a fossil fuel

3. Which is a fact about oil in California?
   A Los Angeles was the site of the world's first oil well.
   B In 1923, California was the leading oil-producing state in America.
   C Signal Hill never produced oil.
   D There is no offshore oil drilling.

4. The word *gusher* means
   A an oil well that uses a pump
   B an oil well in which the oil is pushed out by natural pressure
   C a way to refine oil
   D a tool used to find oil

5. As early as the 1860s, people knew there was oil in California because
   A oil was found by offshore drilling
   B a "gusher" was found on Signal Hill
   C prospectors found oil in the north
   D there were places where asphalt seeped to the surface

6. A state that produces more oil than California is
   A Alaska
   B Oklahoma
   C Wyoming
   D Pennsylvania

7. Look at the table on page CA31. As of 1997, which of the following oil fields had the greatest number of producing wells?
   A Wilmington
   B Midway-Sunset
   C South Belridge
   D Hondo Offshore

8. When wells go dry, they are shut down. In a field of 60 wells, if one third go dry and are shut down, how many wells would still be operating?
   A 50
   B 40
   C 30
   D 20

9. Why have oil wells been drilled offshore?
   A Offshore wells are easier to drill.
   B Onshore wells are running out of oil.
   C There are no more onshore wells.
   D Both A and C

Write the answer to the question below on your piece of paper.

10. Explain why the invention of the automobile caused a greater demand for California oil.

CALIFORNIA DATA BANK

Topic 1

Volcanoes of the Cascade Range

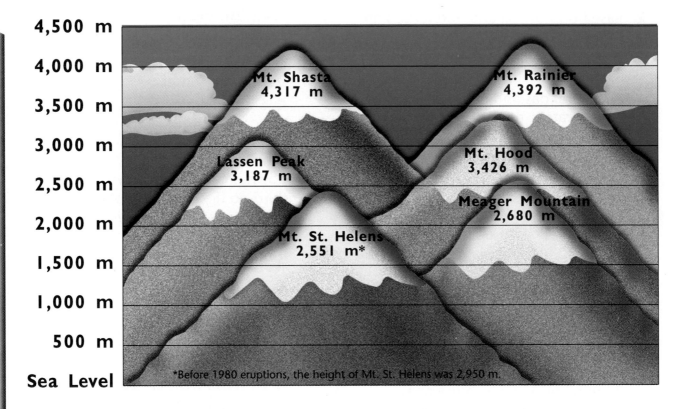

4,500 m
4,000 m
3,500 m
3,000 m
2,500 m
2,000 m
1,500 m
1,000 m
500 m
Sea Level

Mt. Shasta 4,317 m
Mt. Rainier 4,392 m
Lassen Peak 3,187 m
Mt. Hood 3,426 m
Meager Mountain 2,680 m
Mt. St. Helens 2,551 m*

*Before 1980 eruptions, the height of Mt. St. Helens was 2,950 m.

Volcano	State	Year of Last Eruption
Meager Mountain	British Columbia, Canada	About 350 B.C.
Mt. Rainier	Washington	1882
Mt. Saint Helens	Washington	1986
Mt. Hood	Oregon	1865
Mt. Shasta	California	1786
Lassen Peak	California	1917

Topic 2

Point Reyes
National Seashore

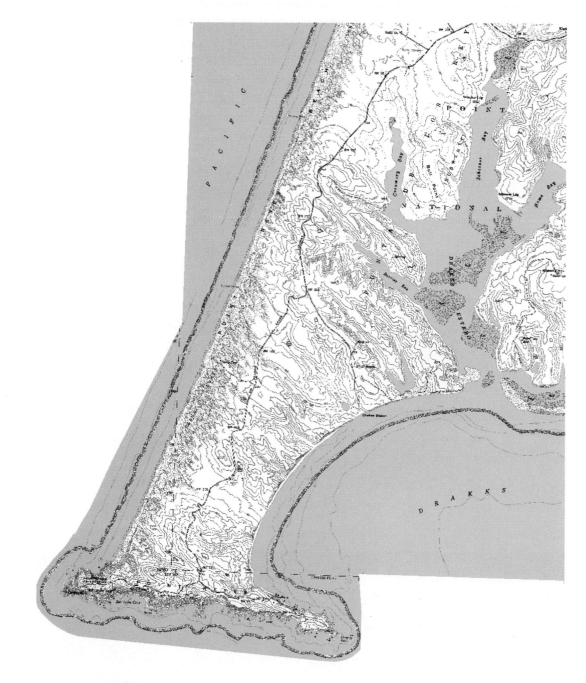

Scale: 1 : 24 000
Contour Interval: 40 Feet

Southern California Fires

PROTECTING HILLSIDE HOMES FROM FIRES

People who live in hillside areas where there is fire danger often create fire breaks. An area around the home is cleared of vegetation so that fire will not spread directly into the home.

The diagram shows the recommended clearing. The clearing on the sloped side of the house depends on how steep the hill is.

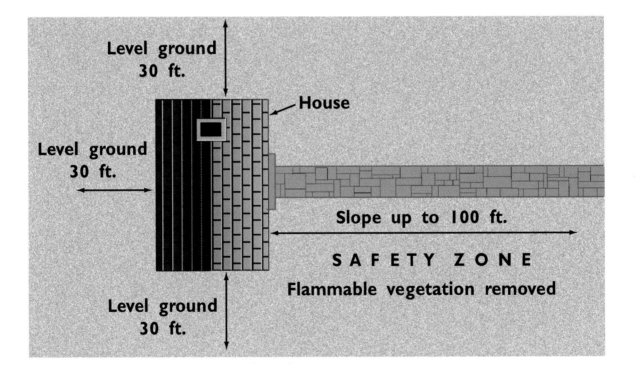

Year	Name of Fire, or General Area	Number of Homes Destroyed
1970	Malibu Fire	103
1978	Malibu Fire	230
1980	Mouth of San Gabriel Canyon	55
1982	Dayton Fire, Malibu	85
1993	Kinneloa Fire, Foothills of San Gabriel Mountains	121
1993	Old Topanga Fire	369

Topic 4
Kelp Forest Organisms

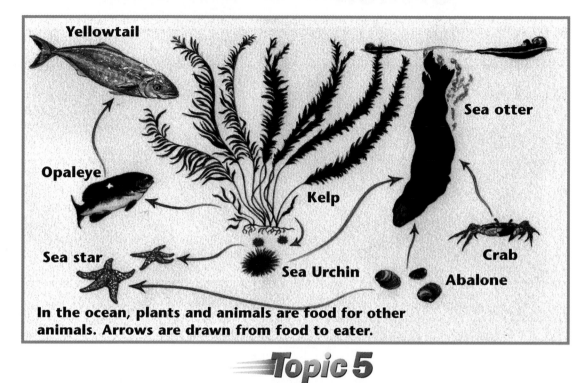

Yellowtail

Opaleye

Kelp

Sea otter

Sea star

Sea Urchin

Crab

Abalone

In the ocean, plants and animals are food for other animals. Arrows are drawn from food to eater.

Topic 5
Some California Oil Fields

Field	Year Discovered	Cumulative Production (millions of barrels)	Producing Wells (1997)
Wilmington	1932	2,497,454	1,376
Midway-Sunset	1894	2,419,886	10,954
Kern River	1899	1,618,839	8,363
Elk Hills	1911	1,119,280	1,034
South Belridge	1911	1,108,555	4,521
Huntington Beach	1920	1,099,597	377
Ventura	1919	945,295	445
Long Beach	1921	926,004	276
Coalinga	1890	849,212	2,021
Dos Cuadras Offshore	1968	241,686	131
Hondo Offshore	1969	187,415	42

Source: California Department of Conservation, Division of Oil, Gas, and Geothermal Resources

Physical Map of California

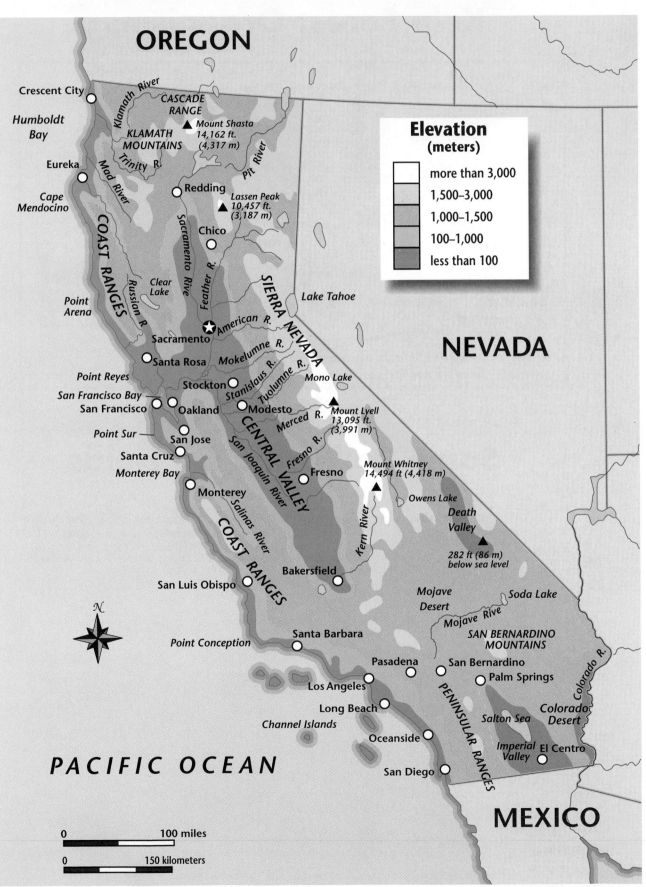

OREGON

Crescent City

Humboldt Bay

Eureka

Cape Mendocino

Klamath River

CASCADE RANGE

▲ Mount Shasta 14,162 ft. (4,317 m)

KLAMATH MOUNTAINS

Trinity R.

Pit River

Mad River

Redding

▲ Lassen Peak 10,457 ft. (3,187 m)

Chico

COAST RANGES

Clear Lake

Russian R.

Sacramento River

Feather R.

SIERRA NEVADA

Lake Tahoe

Elevation
(meters)

more than 3,000
1,500–3,000
1,000–1,500
100–1,000
less than 100

Point Arena

☆ Sacramento

American R.

NEVADA

Santa Rosa

Mokelumne R.

Point Reyes

Stockton

Stanislaus R.

Tuolumne R.

Mono Lake

San Francisco Bay

San Francisco

Oakland

Modesto

Merced R.

▲ Mount Lyell 13,095 ft. (3,991 m)

Point Sur

San Jose

CENTRAL VALLEY

Fresno R.

Santa Cruz

Monterey Bay

Monterey

San Joaquin River

Fresno

▲ Mount Whitney 14,494 ft (4,418 m)

Owens Lake

Death Valley

Salinas River

COAST RANGES

Kern River

Bakersfield

▲ 282 ft (86 m) below sea level

San Luis Obispo

Mojave Desert

Soda Lake

Mojave River

SAN BERNARDINO MOUNTAINS

Point Conception

Santa Barbara

Pasadena

San Bernardino

Palm Springs

Colorado R.

Los Angeles

Long Beach

PENINSULAR RANGES

Colorado Desert

Channel Islands

Salton Sea

Oceanside

Imperial Valley

El Centro

PACIFIC OCEAN

San Diego

MEXICO

N

0   100 miles

0   150 kilometers

McGRAW-HILL
SCIENCE

MACMILLAN/McGRAW-HILL EDITION

RICHARD MOYER ■ LUCY DANIEL ■ JAY HACKETT
PRENTICE BAPTISTE ■ PAMELA STRYKER ■ JOANNE VASQUEZ

NATIONAL
GEOGRAPHIC
SOCIETY

McGraw-Hill School Division

New York   Farmington

California
EDITION

PROGRAM AUTHORS

Dr. Lucy H. Daniel
Teacher, Consultant
Rutherford County Schools,
North Carolina

Dr. Jay Hackett
Emeritus Professor of Earth
Sciences
University of Northern
Colorado

Dr. Richard H. Moyer
Professor of Science
Education
University of Michigan-
Dearborn

Dr. H. Prentice Baptiste
Professor of Curriculum and
Instruction
New Mexico State
University

Pamela Stryker, M.Ed.
Elementary Educator and
Science Consultant
Eanes Independent School
District
Austin, Texas

JoAnne Vasquez, M. Ed.
Elementary Science
Education Specialist
Mesa Public Schools,
Arizona
NSTA President 1996–1997

NATIONAL
GEOGRAPHIC
SOCIETY

Washington, D.C.

CONTRIBUTING AUTHORS

Dr. Thomas Custer

Eric W. Danielson, Jr.

Edward J. Denecke, Jr.

Dr. James Flood

Dr. Diane Lapp

Doug Llewellyn

Dorothy Reid

Dr. Donald M. Silver

CONSULTANTS

Dr. Danny J. Ballard

Dr. Carol Baskin

Dr. Bonnie Buratti

Dr. Suellen Cabe

Dr. Shawn Carlson

Dr. Thomas A. Davies

Dr. Marie DiBerardino

Dr. R. E. Duhrkopf

Dr. Ed Geary

Dr. Susan C. Giarratano-Russell

Dr. Karen Kwitter

Dr. Donna Lloyd-Kolkin

Ericka Lochner, RN

Donna Harrell Lubcker

Dr. Dennis L. Nelson

Dr. Fred S. Sack

Dr. Martin VanDyke

Dr. E. Peter Volpe

Dr. Josephine Davis Wallace

Dr. Joe Yelderman

The Book Cover, *Invitation to Science*, *World of Science*, and *FUNtastic Facts* features found in this textbook were designed and developed by the National Geographic Society's Education Division.
Copyright © 2001 National Geographic Society
The name "National Geographic Society" and the Yellow Border Rectangle are trademarks of the Society and their use, without prior written permission, is strictly prohibited.

McGraw-Hill School Division

A Division of The McGraw·Hill Companies

McGraw-Hill School Division
Two Penn Plaza
New York, New York 10121

Printed in the United States of America

ISBN 0-02-277796-2 / 6

1 2 3 4 5 6 7 8 9 027/046 05 04 03 02 01 00 99

CONTENTS

UNIT
1

PLATE TECTONICS AND EARTH STRUCTURE

UNIT 2

SHAPING EARTH'S SURFACE

UNIT 3 — ENERGY

UNIT 4 ECOLOGY

UNIT 5 RESOURCES

REFERENCE SECTION

YOUR TEXTBOOK at a Glance

Begin each topic with an **Explore** question. Investigate further by doing an **Explore Activity**.

Topic 4
EARTH SCIENCE

WHY IT MATTERS

...cean shapes ...oreline where ...e live and play.

...CE WORDS

...the motion of sand ...he beach by the

...ce a steplike ...e a coast that ...cient shoreline

...of the sea at the

The Work of the Ocean

Picture yourself at the beach on a sunny summer day. Feel the sand between your toes. Did you ever wonder where the sand comes from? Have you ever returned to the beach in winter to find a lot of the sand washed away? Where did it go?

Many people like to live near the beach. Many more like to visit it when they can. Yet the beach and the shoreline are always changing. What causes that change? What does it mean for people who live near the shore?

EXPLORE

HYPOTHESIZE How do the ocean's waves shape the beach? Write a hypothesis in your *Science Journal*. How would you test your ideas?

Discuss an exciting **Science Magazine** or **National Geographic World of Science** magazine after each topic.

122

Brain Power

A vibrating guitar string can make sound waves that travel to your ear. How does that compare with what happens during an earthquake?

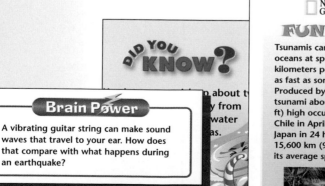

NATIONAL GEOGRAPHIC

FUNtastic Facts

Tsunamis can race across the oceans at speeds up to 900 kilometers per hour (560 mph)— as fast as some jet planes! Produced by an earthquake, a tsunami about 46 meters (150 ft) high occurred off the coast of Chile in April 1971. It reached Japan in 24 hours, a distance of 15,600 km (9,700 mi). What was its average speed?

 Flex your brain with questions about real-world facts.

EXPLORE ACTIVITY

EXPLORE ACTIVITY

Investigate "Current" Events

Find out what happens to beach sand when waves strike the shore at an angle.

MATERIALS
- drinking straw
- blue food coloring
- plastic cup
- rectangular aluminum baking pan
- wet sand
- several plastic spoons
- *Science Journal*

PROCEDURES

1. Obtain 2–3 cups of wet sand from your teacher. Use the plastic spoons to form it into a beach about 3 cm deep and 6 cm wide against a long side of the aluminum pan.

2. Add water to a depth of 2 cm in the pan. Stir one spoonful of sand and one drop of blue food coloring into the water.

3. Have one member of your group blow on the water through a straw from one corner of the tray opposite the beach to create little waves.

4. Observe the movement of water along the shore as these waves strike the shoreline. Draw a diagram of your model beach. Use arrows to show the direction of water movement along the shoreline.

5. About one third of the way down the beach, push a spoon into the sand at right angles to the beach. Push it in just far enough so that the handle makes a jetty. Repeat steps 3–5.

CONCLUDE AND APPLY

2. **PREDICT** If you blow waves against the beach for a long time, what will happen to the beach?

2. What happened to the shape of the beach up-current from the spoon handle? Down-current?

GOING FURTHER: Problem Solving

3. What would happen if you had a series of jetties out into the water all along the beach?

123

Design Your Own Experiments, do **Quick Labs**, use **Internet Connections**, and try **Writing in Your Journal**. Use the **Handbook** for help.

Reading Graphs, Diagrams, Maps, and **Charts** help you learn by using what you see.

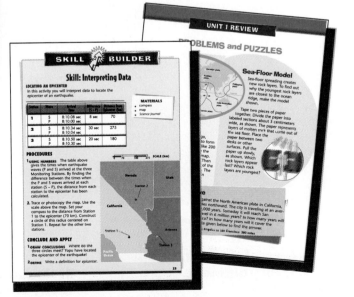

Build your skills with **Skill Builders** and **Problems and Puzzles**.

xi

NATIONAL GEOGRAPHIC

INVITATION TO SCIENCE

Fossil specimens have to be carefully prepared for shipment.

Novacek and his team have found many dinosaur and mammal fossils.

Michael Novacek

As a boy Michael Novacek was fascinated by a book about the discovery of dinosaur bones in the Gobi, a desert in central Asia. In 1993, as a paleontologist "with a passion for exploring," he made his own discoveries in the Gobi. "We found . . . dinosaur skeletons scattered right on the surface," he says.

As a paleontologist Novacek has traveled all over the world. Every expedition requires long-range planning—started a year in advance—and careful goal-setting. Patience is another requirement. "The hardest thing in the field is when . . . you aren't finding anything," Novacek says. "I often spend nine or ten hours straight just walking around alone, looking for stuff."

Over the years Novacek and his team have discovered a lot of fascinating "stuff," such as a dinosaur embryo in the egg and a parent oviraptor sitting on a nest of eggs. These finds are on display at the Museum of Natural History in New York City, where Novacek works.

In addition to field studies, Novacek spends hours in his research lab. There he enjoys "exploring the links between extinct and living species." One link he has discovered is birds, which he calls "examples of living dinosaurs."

Binoculars and sharp eyes are necessary for fossil hunting.

Relaxing in the field is important, too!

BE A SCIENTIST

Have you ever tried the high jump in track? Tried to slam-dunk a basketball? If so, you know how difficult it is to lift yourself very far off the ground. When you jump you are pushing against the powerful pull of Earth. This pull that causes objects to move toward each other is called gravity. Scientists have discovered how gravity works on Earth and in outer space. The information has already helped scientists send space probes to many of the planets in our solar system!

EXPLORE

How does the weight of an object affect the rate at which it falls? Why don't upside-down passengers on a roller coaster fall to the ground?

Investigate How Gravity Works

Will a heavy item fall to Earth faster than a lighter item? Can you make items that would normally fall stay in the air without holding them?

Think of a hypothesis about gravity that you can test. A hypothesis is a statement in answer to a question. You must be able to test the statement.

MATERIALS

- large binder clip
- small binder clip
- thin rubber band
- small yogurt container with 2 holes cut opposite each other near the rim
- string
- *Science Journal*

PROCEDURES

SAFETY Always wear goggles when working with rubber bands or when dropping or twirling objects.

1. Attach the small and large binder clips to opposite sides of the rubber band.

2. Hold the smaller binder clip between your fingers, and let the other one hang down. What happens to the rubber band? Why? Write down your ideas in your *Science Journal*.

3. Drop the binder clips and observe them fall. Write down your observations in your *Science Journal*.

4. Repeat the operation several times. Try changing one variable each time you try it again.

5. Now place the binder clips in the yogurt container, and attach the string through the holes on the sides.

6. Move to a place with lots of room around you. Twirl the yogurt container in a big circle so that the yogurt container travels upside down at the top of its arc. Record what happens to the binder clips as they twirl.

CONCLUDE AND APPLY

1. What happened to the rubber band as the clips fell? Why?

2. What happened when you twirled the clips in the container? Did they fall to the ground?

S5

How Does Gravity Work?

The experiments in the Explore Activity are simple to conduct. The difficulty comes in thinking clearly about the results and drawing the right conclusions. Those simple experiments tell us a lot about how gravity works.

When you hold a small binder clip as in the Explore Activity and let the larger one dangle down, you see the rubber band stretch, especially if you add more than one clip. Why? You can think of the rubber band as a kind of spring scale weighing the lower binder clip before you drop it. The heavier the binder clip hanging on the bottom of your spring scale, the farther it will stretch and the lower it will hang.

When the rubber-band scale is dropped, the top clip snaps down and hits the bottom clip. Why? When you let go of the top clip, both the top and bottom clips fall together. This is because, if we ignore air resistance, all objects fall with the same acceleration. If you fell along with the clips, then the clips would seem to float. It is as if there were no gravity. We say that the system is weightless. From the "point of view" of the clips, there is no longer any gravity to oppose the force in the stretched rubber band. This force causes the smaller clip to snap toward the bigger clip.

Before this skydiver's parachute opens, he is in free fall and weightless!

How can something heavy become weightless? To understand this we need to know more about gravity.

Scientists have shown that gravity is a **force** that can be measured. A force is a push or pull exerted by one object on another.

It causes a change in motion. As far as we know, the force of gravity exists among all objects in the universe. That means that any two objects in space, no matter how distant, will attract each other.

Every object has a gravitational pull toward every other object. The force depends on two variables—**mass** (mas) and distance. Mass is the amount of matter in an object. The greater the mass of objects, the stronger their gravitational pull. The closer objects are to one another, the stronger their gravitational pull.

Mass and weight are related but different. An object's mass stays the same. An object's weight can change because it is the force of gravity on it. Astronauts showed how gravity affects weight on the Moon. A 180-pound astronaut weighs only 30 pounds on the Moon! The astronaut can jump six times higher on the Moon, and it takes six times longer to return to the ground!

If we went far enough out into space, far away from other matter, then the force of gravity on us would be weak. We would weigh less, but our mass would stay the same. We would still be made up of the same amount of matter.

WEIGHT ON DIFFERENT PLANETS

WEIGHT IN POUNDS

	0	50	100	150	200	250	300	350	400	450	500
MERCURY											
VENUS											
EARTH											
MARS											
JUPITER											
SATURN											
URANUS											
NEPTUNE											
PLUTO											

What Have Scientists Learned About Gravity?

Aristotle was a famous philosopher and scientist who lived more than 2,000 years ago. He said that heavy things fall faster than light things. It seemed like a true statement. Rocks fall to the ground faster than leaves, for instance. He also said that the heavier something is, the faster it will fall. According to his explanation, an object that weighs 10 pounds would fall ten times faster than an object weighing 1 pound.

Aristotle's idea sounded convincing to most people of the day. At that time people were just beginning to question the events around them. They did not have the background that people have today.

Aristotle was wrong. This was shown to be wrong in the Explore Activity. Aristotle could have tried a similar experiment himself, but he didn't.

Not all scientists made the mistake of believing Aristotle. The first to prove Aristotle's theory of weight and gravity wrong was Galileo. In 1589 Galileo conducted his own experiment to see if heavier objects fell faster than lighter ones. Galileo was a science professor at the University of Pisa.

Aristotle's theory on weight and gravity was wrong.

The story is told that one day he climbed to the top of the Leaning Tower of Pisa and dropped a 10-pound weight and a 1-pound weight at the same time. They hit the ground at the same time. A very simple experiment had disproved something that had been believed for centuries.

Other scientists learned from Galileo's discovery. More than 300 years ago, so the story is told, Isaac Newton saw an apple fall from a tree to the ground and thought about it in a whole new way. He thought there might be a connection between the way an apple dropped to the ground and the way the Moon circled Earth instead of flying off into space. Newton was the first to explain and try to measure gravity. His discovery changed our understanding of the universe.

How Do Scientists Get Their Ideas?

Dr. Neil Tyson is an **astrophysicist**. An astrophysicist is a scientist who studies space. *Astro* means "space." A *physicist* studies the properties of matter and energy.

Being a scientist begins with looking around and being curious about the things you see in the world. Dr. Tyson says his whole life changed when he was in sixth grade. One night when he was at a ballgame, a friend passed him a pair of binoculars. He looked at the Moon with them. It was a crescent Moon, and the shadows made it look three-dimensional. He could see the craters and the mountains on the surface.

Dr. Neil Tyson is an astrophysicist.

At that moment he became very curious about the Moon and outer space. He wondered what he could see through a telescope if he could see that much through binoculars!

Being a scientist also means not accepting everything you are told. Even when they are told something, scientists still like to learn about it for themselves. They wonder whether the explanations are as accurate as they could be.

After Dr. Tyson became interested in the Moon, he took a course at the Hayden Planetarium in New York City. A *planetarium* (plan′i târ′ē əm) is a theater with special equipment to show the movements of the Sun, Moon, planets, and stars. The movements are shown by projecting lights on the inside of a dome. Dr. Tyson grew up in a big city where the bright lights prevented him from seeing the stars very well. When he saw the planetarium show, he thought it was fake. He didn't believe all those stars could be out there!

Dr. Tyson decided he would have to find out for himself if the night sky could really look that way. When he grew up, he became a scientist. He has observed space through many of the world's most powerful telescopes. In fact he is now the director of the Hayden Planetarium!

How Do Scientists Work?

Being a scientist means comparing things and trying to find explanations for how things work. It often means making small models that can explain big things or making models on Earth that can explain things in outer space.

This was shown in the Explore Activity. When the string was pulled, the container and the clips in it started to move. All objects tend to oppose changes in their motion. This is known as **inertia** (i nûr′shə). To change the motion, a force is needed. The greater the mass of an object, the greater the force needed. The inertia of the container and clips would have kept them moving in a straight line. However, the string pulled inward on the container, keeping it on a circular path. The container, in turn, pulled inward on the clips, keeping them on a circular path. An inward force toward the center of a circle is called a **centripetal** (sen trip′i təl) **force**.

When the container was at the top of its path, there were two forces acting down on the clips. These forces were gravity and the force of the container pushing down on the clips. Why, then, didn't the clips fall out of the container? The reason is that the clips were moving sideways at a very fast speed. This made them both fall and move sideways at the same time. The result was the circular path you observed.

The Explore Activity can help you understand how the Moon orbits around Earth. The Moon is moving very fast. Its inertia would send it flying off into space if not for the pull of gravity. The combination of the Moon's inertia and the pull of gravity between Earth and the Moon keeps the Moon circling Earth. In the same way, you kept the yogurt container and clips moving in a circle.

This combination of inertia and gravity is also what keeps a **satellite** (sat′ə līt′) orbiting Earth. A satellite is any object that revolves around another object. The Moon is a satellite of Earth. However, satellites like the space shuttle need to travel very fast to maintain the balance. The shuttle needs to travel at 28,000 kilometers per hour (18,000 miles per hour) to stay in orbit around Earth.

Scientists are curious about the world around them. This curiosity causes them to ask questions about things they don't understand. Sometimes they question the explanations accepted by others. As recently as 100 years ago, scientists believed that the idea of galaxies outside our own was untrue. Strong telescopes have shown scientists evidence of millions of more galaxies!

Dr. Tyson studies how galaxies form and change. He is especially interested in our own Milky Way galaxy. The problem with studying it is we cannot easily see its structure because we are inside of it. That is why Dr. Tyson studies distant galaxies. He uses them as models of our own galaxy to search for clues they might offer to explain our own galaxy.

Milky Way galaxy

An astronaut in space

How Can I Be Like a Scientist?

Science starts with questions about the things around us. Why doesn't the Moon fly off into space? How can people travel upside down on a roller coaster and not fall to the ground? Do things have weight when they are falling? Why do I feel strange going down fast in an elevator? You may have observed things around you that made you wonder about questions like these. Being a scientist means trying to find answers to questions like these. It means not believing the wrong or incomplete explanations of others.

Scientists conduct experiments to test their ideas. To understand things that are too far away to measure, they think of ways to compare them with things we know more about. For example, to understand things about outer space, they often try to study the way things work here on Earth.

Now let's go back and look at how ideas about gravity, weight, and mass were tested in the Explore Activity.

You Asked Yourself Questions

To start an experiment, you asked some questions. Will a heavy item fall to Earth faster than a lighter item? Can I make items that would normally fall stay in the air without holding them? How can I test my ideas to learn more about how gravity works?

You Set Up an Investigation

The sentence you wrote at the beginning of the Explore Activity was a **hypothesis**. Remember, a hypothesis is a statement that can be tested by observation. You planned an experiment to test your hypothesis. You weighed the objects on the scale and observed what happened when you dropped them. You recorded and organized the information to help you understand it.

An important part of an experiment is changing one part of it to affect the outcome. The factor changed in an experiment to affect the outcome is a **variable**. In the Explore Activity, one variable that could be changed was the height from which the binder clips were dropped.

You Used the Results of Your Investigation to Answer Questions

To be a scientist, you need to observe the process of your experiment closely. You also need to analyze the results and draw conclusions. You thought about the measurements you made and what they meant. You analyzed the information you gathered from the evidence and formed answers to your questions. Because of your experiment, you can explain how gravity and weight are related. You can explain the balance between the forces of gravity and centripetal force.

You write your conclusions in your *Science Journal*. Your findings help you determine if your hypothesis is strong or weak. What is learned about gravity and centripetal force in the experiment also applies to the behavior of the Moon, distant planets, and even satellites orbiting Earth.

Scientists share the findings of their experiments. During the Explore Activity, students should share their analysis of the data with others. Sometimes putting the data in the form of a table or graph helps make it easier to understand. Would a table or graph have helped you understand your data? To be more certain of their findings, scientists often repeat their experiments.

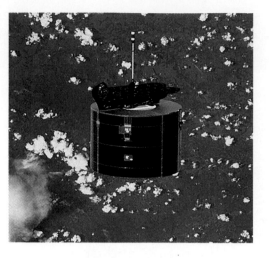

For scientists a successful experiment often raises more questions than it answers. Does the experiment raise any more questions for you about gravity, weight, or mass? Can you think of ways to test these questions to learn more about them?

You might have noticed that the kind of thinking required in the Explore Activity is much like the kind of thinking Dr. Tyson has done throughout his career as a scientist. That's because when you ask questions and look for evidence, you are thinking like a scientist. When you plan an investigation and change one variable at a time, you are experimenting like a scientist.

As you learn about science in this book, you will be asked to think like a scientist. The different steps in the Explore Activities use what's called the scientific method. Answers are important. In science it's also important to know how you found the answers.

Think of how a scientist works each time you do a step in an experiment. See if you can label each step with what a scientist does.

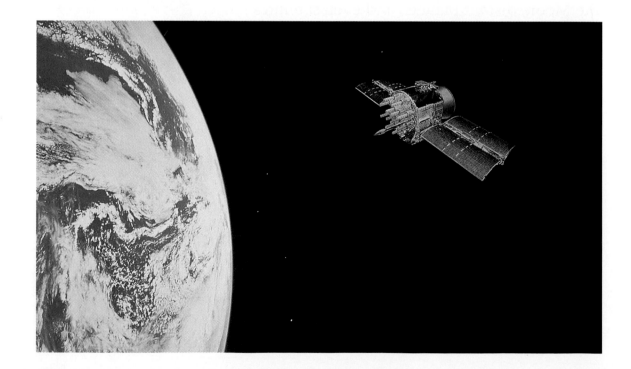

What scientists like Dr. Tyson have discovered about gravity and space is very important. It is one of the most important parts of understanding how the universe works. For instance, it has helped scientists and engineers build satellites that orbit Earth.

Satellites are one of the most important technologies we have ever developed. Satellites send telephone signals thousands of miles, allowing us to have conversations with friends. They send TV signals, allowing us to instantaneously see pictures of events happening on the other side of the globe.

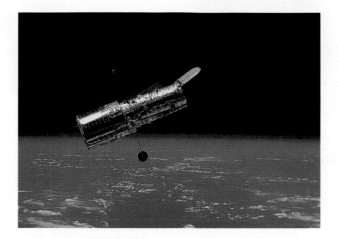

The Hubble Space Telescope orbits 610 kilometers (380 miles) above Earth.

The Hubble Space Telescope is a satellite. It helps scientists see far more distant parts of the universe than they could from a telescope on Earth. Navigation satellites emit radio signals to help ships, aircraft, and even cars know their exact position on Earth. This technology, called the Global Positioning System, makes it much less likely that there will be aircraft and ship collisions. It has already saved many lives!

REVIEW

1. How do scientists study gravity?

2. What does an apple falling to the ground have to do with the orbit of the Moon?

3. How do astrophysicists like Dr. Tyson study our own Milky Way galaxy?

4. What are the forces satellites like the Moon or the space shuttle use to stay in orbit around Earth?

BE A SCIENTIST Glossary

These are words you can use as a scientist as you use this book and in your life.

analyze separate anything into its parts to find out what it is made of and how it is put together

classify place materials that share properties together in groups

collect data put together all useful information

communicate share information

define put together a description that is based on observations and experience

draw conclusions put together the facts you have learned

evaluate find out the value or amount of something

evidence clues used to solve a problem

experiment a test that is used to discover or prove something

identify patterns find a group of facts that repeat or do not change

infer form an idea from facts or observations

interpret data use the information that has been gathered to answer questions or solve a problem

make decisions make up your mind from many choices

measure find the size, volume, area, mass, weight, or temperature of an object or how long an event occurs

model something that represents an object or event

observe use one or more of the senses to identify or learn about an object or event

plan think out ahead of time how something is to be done or made

predict state possible results of an event or experiment

test the examination of a substance or event to see what it is or why it happens

theory an explanation based on observation and reasoning

use numbers ordering, counting, adding, subtracting, multiplying, and dividing to explain data

These are words that you will use as a thinker whenever you read or study.

cause and effect something (cause) that brings about a change in something else (effect)

compare and contrast find out how things are the same (compare) and how they are different (contrast)

identify name or recognize

reproduce results repeat an experiment to verify the findings

revise examine and improve

sequence a series of things that are related in some way

These are new Science Words that you learned in Be a Scientist.

astrophysicist a scientist who studies space

centripetal force a force toward the center of curved motion

force a push or pull exerted by one object on another, causing a change in motion

gravity a force of attraction between any objects with mass

hypothesis a statement that can be tested by observations

inertia the tendency of an object to oppose a change in motion

mass the amount of matter in an object

satellite any object that revolves around another object

variable something in an experiment that can be changed

METHODS OF SCIENCE

Here is a chart that shows the steps to follow when solving a problem in science.

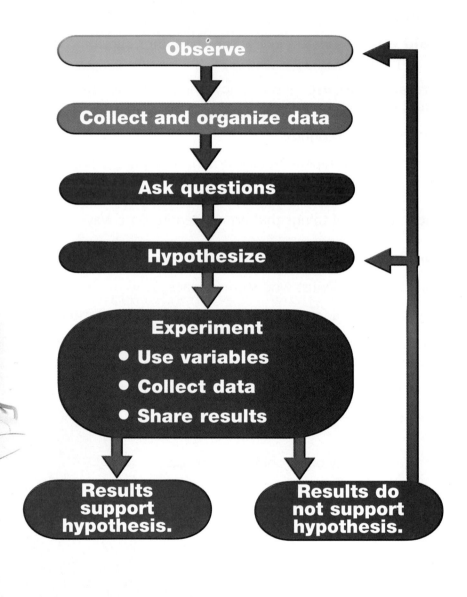

Observe

Collect and organize data

Ask questions

Hypothesize

Experiment
- Use variables
- Collect data
- Share results

Results support hypothesis.

Results do not support hypothesis.

READING N CHARTS

WRITE How would you solve a problem in science? Write a paragraph based on the chart.

PLATE TECTONICS AND EARTH STRUCTURE

CHAPTER 1

IT'S EARTH-SHAKING!

We think of earthquakes as destructive. Cracks open in the ground, and buildings shake until they crumble. Yet earthquakes also create new landscapes. In California, they have built great mountain ranges. How do earthquakes happen? Where does all that energy come from?

In Chapter 1 you will be reading about many examples of cause and effect. One event—a cause—makes something else happen—the effect.

Topic
EARTH SCIENCE
1

WHY IT MATTERS

Earth's crust has many valuable resources.

SCIENCE WORDS

crust Earth's solid, rocky surface containing the continents and ocean floor

original horizontality the idea that many kinds of rocks form in flat, horizontal layers

continental drift the idea that a supercontinent split apart into pieces, the continents, which drifted in time to their present locations

sea-floor spreading the idea that new crust is forming at ridges in the sea floor, spreading apart the crust on either side of the ridges

magma hot, molten rock below Earth's surface

plate tectonics the idea that Earth's surface is broken into plates that move

mantle Earth's layer beneath the crust

subduction where plates collide, the sliding of a denser ocean plate under another plate

Moving Plates

Have you ever put together a jigsaw puzzle? If so, how can you find pieces that fit together? One way is to look for edges that meet and have opposite outlines.

What does a jigsaw puzzle have to do with a map of the world? Think of the continents as huge pieces of a jigsaw puzzle. If the continents were huge, movable puzzle pieces, would any of the pieces fit together?

GEOGRAPHY LINK

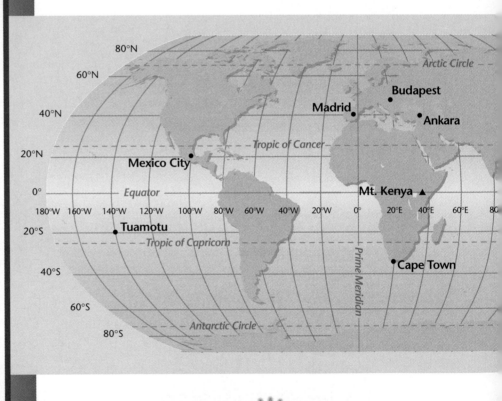

HYPOTHESIZE Find any two coastlines that seem to match, as puzzle pieces match if they fit together. Do all the continents fit together? Write a hypothesis in your *Science Journal*. How would you test your ideas?

Investigate If Continents Are Moving

Use a model of the continents to test if pieces of the model fit next to each other.

MATERIALS
- map of the world
- tracing paper
- pencil
- scissors
- *Science Journal*

PROCEDURES

SAFETY Be careful using scissors.

1. Place tracing paper over a world map. Trace the coastlines of North America, South America, Europe and Asia, Africa, and Australia.

2. Cut out the continents along their coastlines and label them.

3. **COMPARE** Look at the coastlines of the continents for places they might fit together.

4. **EXPERIMENT** Using the continent cutouts like pieces of a jigsaw puzzle, find ways the continents fit together. In your *Science Journal*, draw a sketch showing each way you can fit them together.

CONCLUDE AND APPLY

1. **COMPARE AND CONTRAST** Which continents have coastlines that fit together most closely?

2. **EVALUATE** Which of your sketches shows the greatest number of continents fitting together? Do all of the coastlines in the sketch fit together equally well?

GOING FURTHER: Problem Solving

3. **EXPERIMENT** The map distorts the shape of Antarctica. Find a way to include Antarctica in your finished "puzzle."

4. **INFER** What if the pieces from your finished puzzle moved apart to the positions they are in today? If they keep moving, how might they be arranged in the distant future?

Are Continents Moving?

How do you know whether a clock is working? Easy—if the second hand is moving, the clock is working. What if the clock has only minute and hour hands? These hands move too gradually for you to actually see their motion. How can you tell if the clock is working?

Geologists (jē ol'ə jists), scientists who study Earth, face a similar problem. How can they tell if Earth's solid surface, the **crust**, is moving? During a sudden motion of the crust, such as an earthquake or volcanic eruption, people can actually see and feel the crust move. Can the crust also be moving so slowly that you don't feel it?

Just as the changing position of a clock's hour hand is evidence that it is gradually moving, changes in position of surface features and rock formations are evidence that the crust is gradually moving.

For example, many kinds of rocks tend to form in flat, horizontal layers. This is called **original horizontality** (hôr'ə zon'ta'lə tē). You can see that many layers have been twisted or tilted. This is a sign that the crust is moving gradually.

These layers of sedimentary rock were once horizontal. Then crustal movement folded and tilted them.

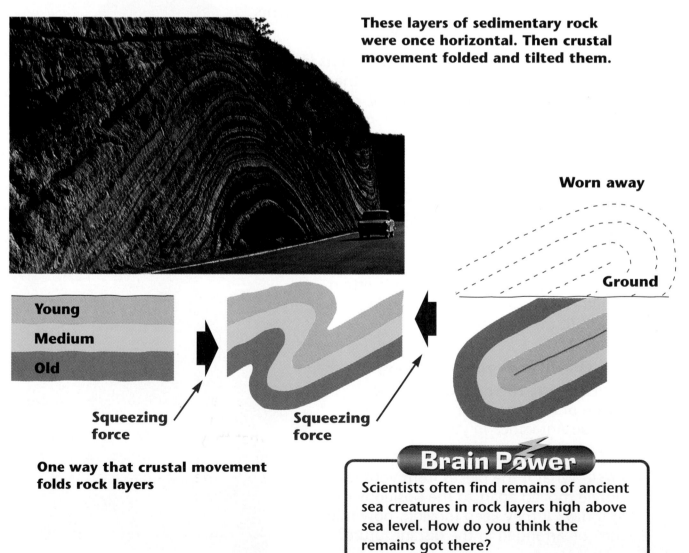

Young

Medium

Old

Squeezing force

Squeezing force

Worn away

Ground

One way that crustal movement folds rock layers

Brain Power

Scientists often find remains of ancient sea creatures in rock layers high above sea level. How do you think the remains got there?

How Can We Tell Earth's Surface Is Moving?

In 1912 a German scientist, Alfred Wegener (vā′gə nər), wrote a book—*The Origins of Continents and Oceans*. In it he listed evidence that Earth's continents had once fit together like pieces of a jigsaw puzzle, forming a huge supercontinent. That is why today the shapes of the continents match—as was shown in the Explore Activity. Wegener claimed that the coastlines also match in other ways besides shape. Coastlines have:

- matching rock types and structures, such as deposits from glaciers
- matching remains of ancient life and living organisms
- matching past climates

Wegener called this huge supercontinent *Pangaea* (pan jē ə) meaning "all lands." He reasoned that about 200 million years ago, Pangaea split into pieces that are today's continents. Then the continents "drifted apart" over the years to their present locations. His ideas became known as **continental drift**.

Wegener did not explain how or why the "drifting" took place. After all, the continents are not "floating" on water. They are part of Earth's solid crust. The crust is a solid layer, including the continents and the ocean floor. Maybe studying the ocean floor would reveal some clues.

MOTION OF CONTINENTS

200 million years ago

135 million years ago

65 million years ago

Today

50 million years later

READING MAPS

1. **REPRESENT** Make a table. List Africa and South America in one column and evidence suggesting that they were joined in another.
2. **REPRESENT** Continue your table with other possible matching coastlines.

What Clues Are at the Sea Floor?

In 1947 the research ship *Atlantis* set out to map the floor of the Atlantic Ocean. Using depth sounders the researchers discovered a series of mountains separated by huge valleys and canyons. They had discovered the Mid-Atlantic Ridge. They dredged up rock samples from the mountains. The rocks seemed to have been formed from volcanic activity.

By 1960 scientists found other oceans had mid-ocean ridges! Together these ridges form a chain of mountains winding through Earth's sea floors. Huge cracks split the tops of the ridges. Elsewhere, parts of the sea floor plunge downward in deep valleys, or *trenches*.

In the early 1960s, scientists suggested a model to explain these features. This model, called sea-floor spreading, states that new crustal material is forming at the ridges. As it forms it spreads apart the old sea floor on both sides of the ridges.

How does it work? The mid-ocean ridges are pushed up by hot rock material from deep beneath the crust. The rock material is softened enough to ooze upward. The rising material pushes up and turns sideways beneath the sea floor, spreading it apart.

The crust cracks where the sea floor is spreading apart. Just below the ridges of the sea floor there is hot, melted rock called magma. Magma flows up through the cracks, cools, and hardens into new solid rock along the ridges. This process keeps making new rock material along the ridges and pushing older rock material farther away along the sea floor.

SEA-FLOOR SPREADING

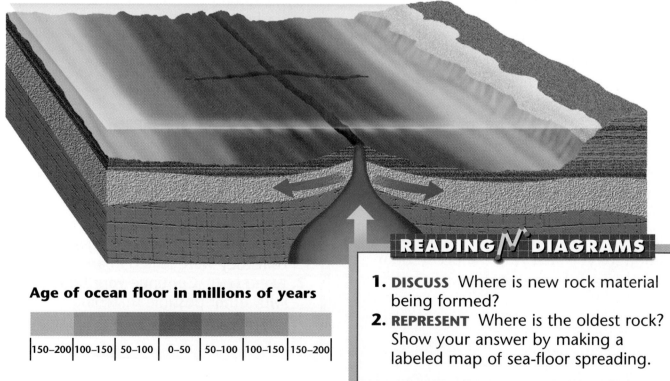

Age of ocean floor in millions of years

|150–200|100–150| 50–100 | 0–50 | 50–100 |100–150|150–200|

READING /\/ DIAGRAMS

1. **DISCUSS** Where is new rock material being formed?
2. **REPRESENT** Where is the oldest rock? Show your answer by making a labeled map of sea-floor spreading.

What Evidence Supports Sea-Floor Spreading?

Later in the 1960s, as scientists focused on the ocean floor, evidence came pouring in. Much of it was based on determining the age of rocks. The scientists found that

- rocks that make up the continents are much older than rocks of the ocean floor
- most ocean floor rocks are volcanic—that is, formed from cooling and hardening of magma
- the youngest ocean floor rocks are found at the mid-ocean ridges
- on either side of the mid-ocean ridge, the ocean floor rocks get older toward the continents

Some of the strongest evidence comes from the studies of Earth's magnetism. Earth has a magnetic field around it. A compass aligns with this field. The arrow points to the north pole of Earth's magnetic field.

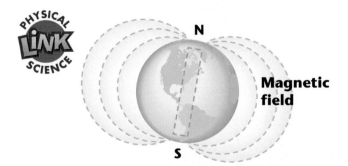

Magnetic field

In the past, however, Earth's magnetic field has reversed itself several times. The north and south poles switched back and forth. The rocks of the sea floor reveal a record of this reversal.

Magma contains magnetic particles, such as particles bearing iron. As the magma flows, the magnetic particles line up with Earth's magnetic field. As the magma cools and hardens, the magnetic particles are locked in place.

Scientists used magnetic detectors to study rocks along the sea floor. They found that the magnetism in the rocks alternates from one direction to the other. It is arranged in a simple pattern of narrow strips. And the pattern matches on either side of the mid-ocean ridges.

The simplest explanation is that rocks hardened along the ridge and then spread apart over time. Each time the rocks hardened in one of the strips, the Earth's magnetic field was in a given direction. When the next strip formed, the magnetic field switched.

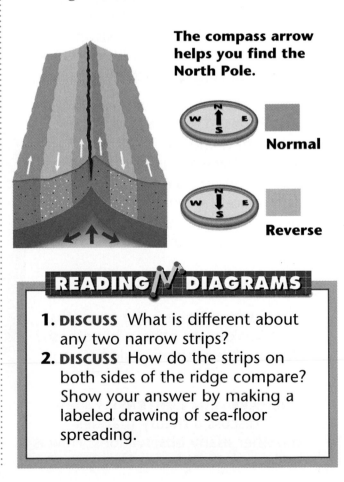

The compass arrow helps you find the North Pole.

Normal

Reverse

READING 🖊 DIAGRAMS

1. **DISCUSS** What is different about any two narrow strips?
2. **DISCUSS** How do the strips on both sides of the ridge compare? Show your answer by making a labeled drawing of sea-floor spreading.

Skill: Forming a Hypothesis

WHAT MAKES THE CRUST MOVE?

Continental drift and sea-floor spreading explain observations. An explanation is called a hypothesis or a theory. Theories are more certain than hypotheses. As more and more evidence is gathered, an explanation may become more and more certain. Scientists are fairly certain that the theories of continental drift and sea-floor spreading are correct.

MATERIALS
- world map
- research books/Internet (optional)
- art materials (optional)
- *Science Journal*

PROCEDURES

1. **COMMUNICATE** In your *Science Journal,* list all the observations you have made involving movements of Earth's crust.

2. **EVALUATE** Make a two-column table, with "Continental Drift" and "Sea-Floor Spreading" as the column heads. In each column list observations that support each hypothesis.

3. **HYPOTHESIZE** Think of your own hypothesis to explain both continental drift *and* sea-floor spreading. To start, trace all the trenches and mid-ocean ridges on a world map. Then trace the world's mountain ranges. (Use a research book if you need to.) Look for patterns.

CONCLUDE AND APPLY

1. **EVALUATE** What are the strengths and weaknesses of your hypothesis? Which observations could you not explain?

2. **COMPARE AND CONTRAST** Pages 9–12 discuss a theory that ties together many observations. How is it like yours? Different from yours?

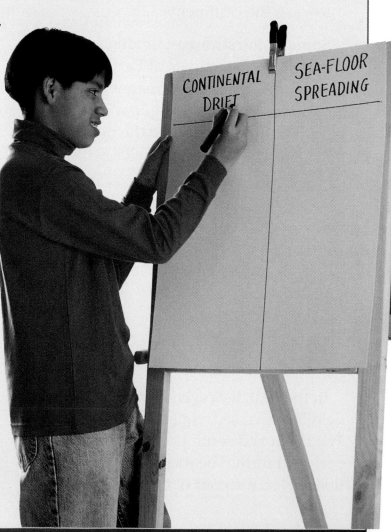

How Can We Explain It All?

In the late 1960s, scientists built a new model to explain how continents and the sea floor move. This new model is **plate tectonics** (tek ton'iks). It describes Earth's crust as broken into pieces, or plates. Along with the crust, each plate contains material from a layer below the crust, the **mantle**. Plates move around on the lower portion of the mantle.

The movement of the plates can explain movements of Earth's crust. At their boundaries, or edges, the plates move away from each other, collide, or slide past each other.

For example, the Mid-Atlantic Ridge is located along a boundary where plates are moving away from each other. This explains sea-floor spreading. Each continent is a part of a plate. It moves with the plate. This movement explains continental drift. What causes the plates to move?

Hot softened rock from deep in the mantle rises upward. As it reaches the plates, the rock cools without becoming harder and turns sideways. It pushes along the bottom of the plates, causing them to move. The rock continues to cool without hardening and sinks. This rising of warm matter and sinking of cooled matter is called a *convection current*.

EARTH'S PLATE BOUNDARIES

A plate is a piece of Earth's crust and upper mantle.

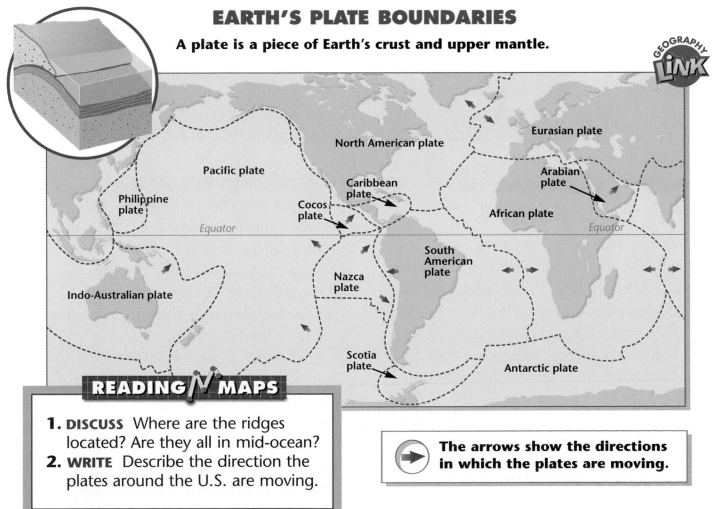

GEOGRAPHY LINK

North American plate

Eurasian plate

Pacific plate

Arabian plate

Philippine plate

Caribbean plate

Cocos plate

African plate

Equator

Equator

Indo-Australian plate

Nazca plate

South American plate

Scotia plate

Antarctic plate

READING MAPS

1. **DISCUSS** Where are the ridges located? Are they all in mid-ocean?
2. **WRITE** Describe the direction the plates around the U.S. are moving.

The arrows show the directions in which the plates are moving.

TYPES OF PLATE BOUNDARIES

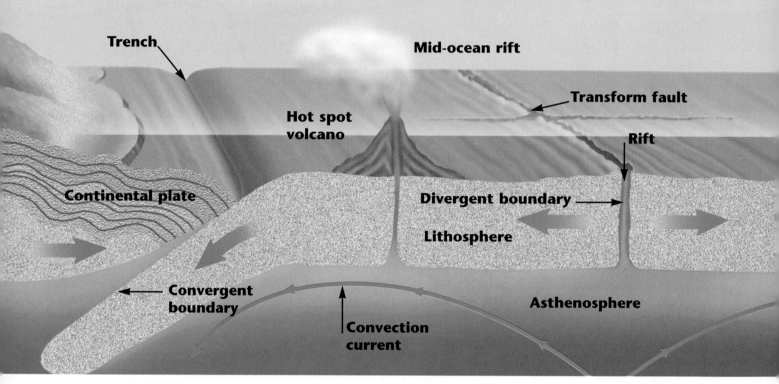

What Happens at the Boundaries?

Places where plates move apart are called *divergent* (di vûr′jənt) *boundaries*. The Mid-Atlantic Ridge is located at a divergent boundary. This is where sea-floor spreading takes place. New rock material is formed when hot rock rises through cracks in the crust and hardens. The Great Rift Valley of Africa is at a divergent boundary. It is located at a place where a divergent boundary splits a part of a continent, rather than the sea floor.

Places where plates are colliding are called *convergent* (kən vûr′jənt) *boundaries*. When there is a continent on both of the colliding plates, the collision can cause rocks to crumple. This crumpling can build up mountains along the edge of a continent. For example, the Himalaya Mountains formed along a convergent boundary. This boundary is located where India meets the rest of Asia.

Some plates are carrying parts of the ocean floor. An "ocean" plate may collide with a plate carrying a continent. The ocean plate has the denser

READING 𝒩 DIAGRAMS

REPRESENT Make a table. List the kinds of boundaries in one column. In another describe what happens at each boundary.

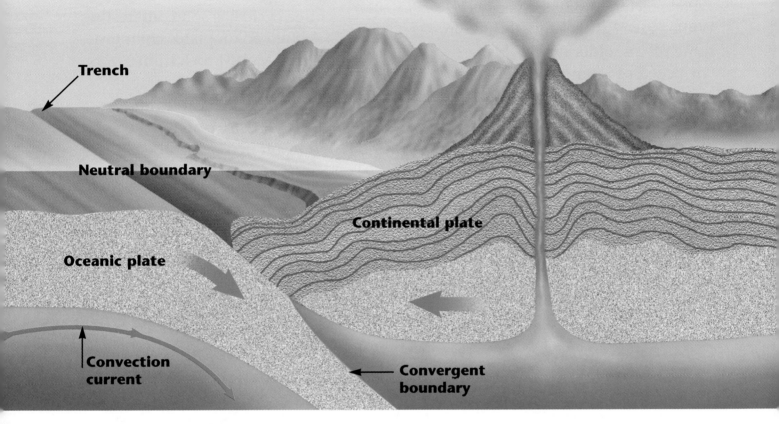

Trench

Neutral boundary

Continental plate

Oceanic plate

Convection current

Convergent boundary

rock material of the two and slides beneath the continental plate. For example, off the coast of Chile, an ocean plate is sliding beneath the plate carrying South America.

Volcanoes are found at these boundaries. As one plate slides under another, hot rock material in the upper mantle is able to melt and become magma. It flows toward the surface, where it can erupt through cracks, producing volcanic mountains.

Two ocean plates may collide. The denser of the two slides beneath the other. The result can be undersea volcanoes. Trenches, deep undersea valleys, also form along these boundaries.

Sometimes plates just slide past each other. Boundaries where plates slide past each other are called *transform faults*. As the plates smash and grind past each other, there are many earthquakes. The rock along these margins gets broken and shattered. As the plates slide along, this shattered rock piles up in long, narrow ridges and valleys. The San Andreas Fault in California is along such a boundary.

Where Does It All Go?

Sea-floor spreading helped explain how continents move apart. It also posed a problem. New sea floor keeps being produced along the mid-ocean ridges. Why isn't Earth getting larger?

Plate tectonics offers an answer. While new crust is being formed in some places, older crust is being "disposed of" somewhere else.

Recall that when two plates collide, a denser ocean plate may slide under another plate. This is a process called **subduction** (səb dək'shən). The process continues as the plate sinks down into the mantle. The plate is carrying a part of the crust from the sea floor. This rock becomes part of the hot, softened rock of the mantle.

Subduction is part of a cycle. It is a huge convection current. Older rock is destroyed by subduction in the trenches. New rock is forming in the mid-ocean ridges.

This huge cycle has some interesting effects. As two ocean plates collide, a trench forms. Melted rock from beneath the sea floor can rise up to produce a string of volcanic mountains. They can rise up above the sea floor and result in a string of islands called an *island arc*. The islands of Japan are a volcanic island arc.

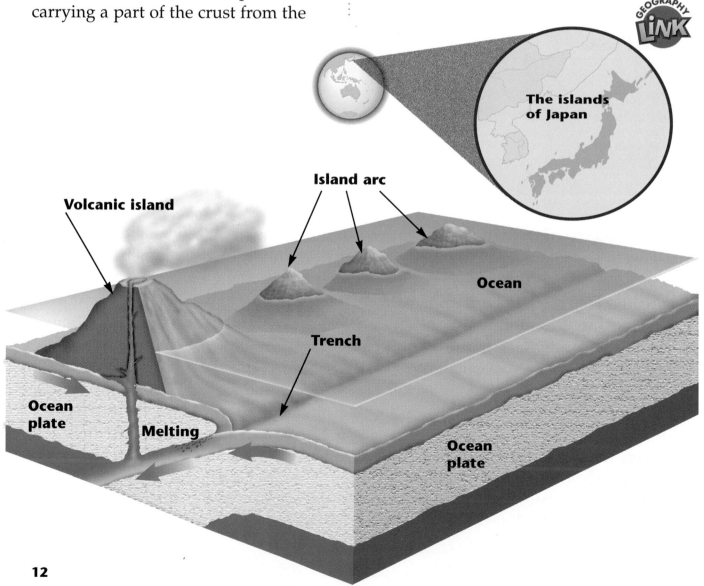

The islands of Japan

Volcanic island

Island arc

Ocean

Trench

Ocean plate

Melting

Ocean plate

Where Is Pangaea Today?

How does this huge convection current affect the continents? Recall what Wegener proposed. About 200 million years ago, all of Earth's land was joined together in a single continent, Pangaea. The rest of Earth's crust was a huge ocean floor covered by ocean.

What happened? Perhaps the crust broke into plates—or was already made up of plates. The forces of plate tectonics pulled the continental plates apart.

It is a gradual process. Sea floors spread only centimeters a year. The process is still going on. You'll find out more of the effects being felt today as you continue this chapter.

REVIEW

1. How can two coastlines be separated by an ocean and have matching shapes?

2. What are mid-ocean ridges? What is happening to the crust at these places?

3. How can the continents and the sea floor move?

4. **HYPOTHESIZE** What do you think causes earthquakes? Make a hypothesis based on plate tectonics. What kinds of evidence would you need to support your hypothesis?

5. **CRITICAL THINKING** *Analyze* Was Wegener's idea of continental drift wrong? Explain your answer.

WHY IT MATTERS THINK ABOUT IT
How do you depend on Earth's crust? Think of items around you at home, at school, or at play that come from the crust.

WHY IT MATTERS WRITE ABOUT IT
How do you think Earth's crust may change in years to come—the near future or the distant future? Base your answer on plate tectonics.

READING SKILL
Write about any examples of cause and effect you learned about in this topic.

ANCIENT CLIMATES

Scientists working in the sub-zero cold of Antarctica have discovered fossils of tropical trees and shrubs. How did the fossils get there? Antarctic rocks also show traces of ancient coral reefs like those in today's tropic zones. How could coral have flourished in a landscape that is now buried in ice? Today we know that the answer to this riddle is plate tectonics. These fossils did not mysteriously come to Antarctica from somewhere else. It was the continent itself that moved!

It seems hard to believe that whole continents can travel from the warm tropics to the icy poles. But given enough time, they can. Plate tectonics can move a continent as much as 5 cm (2 inches) per year. At that rate, in a million years a continent can move 50 km (30 miles). In 100 million years, it can move 5,000 km (3,000 miles)! That is far enough to move through several climate zones.

What is now Antarctica was once part of a larger continent. It was located closer to the tropics, and there were coral reefs along its shores. Then the larger continent broke apart, and Antarctica began moving toward the South Pole. Today, many millions of years later, it is covered by ice sheets.

Fossils indicate that Antarctica was once surrounded by tropical coral reefs. Today, most of the continent is covered by ice.

Geography Link

This same story has been repeated in other parts of the world. What is now North America once straddled the Equator. The fossil record shows dinosaurs, giant tree ferns, and other heat-loving creatures living on a landmass that now includes Canada. The landmass that is today India has also traveled a long distance. Today it lies just north of the Equator and has a mostly tropical climate. Two hundred million years ago, it was located closer to the South Pole and was covered by glaciers. Plate tectonics is the force that has produced these amazing climate changes.

DISCUSSION STARTER

1. Will continued movement of the continents lead to more climate change?

2. What kinds of evidence would indicate that the climate of North America was warmer 200 million years ago?

To learn more about Earth's continents and how they change, visit *www.mhschool.com/science* and enter the keyword CONTINENTS.

*inter*NET
CONNECTION

WHY IT MATTERS

Earthquakes can shake you up.

SCIENCE WORDS

fault a huge crack in the crust, at or below the surface, the sides of which may show evidence of motion

focus the point where an earthquake starts, where rocks begin to slide past each other

seismic wave a vibration that spreads out away from a focus when an earthquake happens

epicenter the point on Earth's surface directly above the focus

aftershock the shaking of the crust after the initial shaking of an earthquake

seismograph a sensitive device that detects the shaking of the crust

magnitude the amount of energy released by an earthquake

Earthquakes

Can earthquakes happen anywhere? Do they tend to happen in just certain places? 1868, 1906, 1957, 1989! These years have a special meaning for the city of San Francisco. In each year the city was struck by an earthquake. That makes four times in just over 100 years.

Other parts of the world also have histories of repeated earthquakes. Japan, China, Mexico, Turkey, and Italy are just a few of these places. Why are certain areas struck by earthquakes over and over again? How might earthquakes result from plate tectonics?

EXPLORE

HYPOTHESIZE Is there a pattern to locations where earthquakes happen? Do earthquakes happen in places that are near each other? Write a hypothesis in your *Science Journal*. How would you test your ideas?

Investigate Where Earthquakes Happen

Plot on a map places where earthquakes happened so that you can identify patterns.

MATERIALS

- world map (or an outline map)
- bits of clay (optional)
- reference books (optional)
- *Science Journal*

PROCEDURES

1. The data table gives you the location of 16 different earthquakes. You may look up more in reference books.

2. COMMUNICATE On a world map, locate each earthquake by its latitude and longitude. Put a dab of clay on the map (or plot a point on a small outline map).

3. To locate by latitude, move north or south of the equator. For longitude move east or west of the prime meridian.

4. INTERPRET DATA On an outline map, shade in areas where earthquakes are relatively near each other.

CONCLUDE AND APPLY

1. INTERPRET DATA Were you able to identify a pattern to where earthquakes happen? Find a way to show frequency of earthquakes in the areas you marked. You might calculate the percent of earthquakes from the data table on the right.

2. INFER Why do you think earthquakes happen in the places you plotted on the map? Do your results support your hypothesis?

GOING FURTHER: Problem Solving

3. PREDICT Do any of Earth's landforms occur near earthquakes—for example, mountain ranges? How can you find out? Explain your results.

1	1993	10°N	145°E
2	1989	37°N	123°W
3	1988	40°N	45°E
4	1987	34°N	118°W
5	1985	19°N	99°W
6	1982	49°N	129°W
7	1982	41°N	30°W
8	1982	37°N	72°E
9	1982	40°N	24°E
10	1981	33°S	73°W
11	1981	44°N	147°E
12	1981	49°S	164°E
13	1976	39°N	118°E
14	1964	61°N	148°W
15	1960	37°S	75°W
16	1923	36°N	140°E

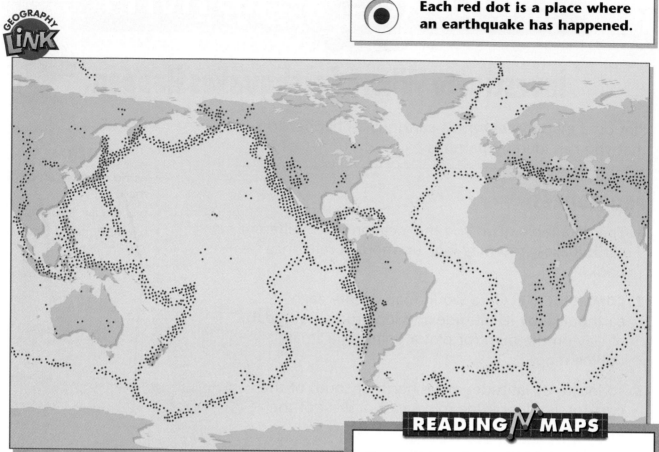

Each red dot is a place where an earthquake has happened.

1. **DISCUSS** Along which ocean coastline are the dots most crowded?
2. **DISCUSS** Where are dots crowded on land?
3. **WRITE** Give a summary of any patterns you see.

Where Do Earthquakes Happen?

An earthquake is a sudden trembling of the ground. It is caused by something happening in the crust. The Explore Activity showed a pattern in where earthquakes happen. Let's explore this pattern further. The dots show some of the places where earthquakes have happened. Compare this map with the map of Earth's plates from Topic 1, on page 9.

Most dots on this map are at the boundaries of Earth's plates. Most earthquakes happen at the edges of plates, where plates meet. About 80 percent of all earthquakes happen along the edges of the Pacific plate.

Along their edges, plates may collide. They may slide past each other. They may pull apart. These motions can cause the rocks to bend and stretch until they break.

Earthquakes are less likely to happen at the centers of plates, far from the edges. There they are shielded by thousands of miles of rock. Plate centers are places of relative quiet.

THREE KINDS OF FAULTS

FAULT	WHERE PRODUCED	HOW PRODUCED	HOW ROCKS MOVE	EXAMPLE
Normal fault	Divergent boundaries	Plates pull apart.	Rocks above the fault surface move down.	Sierra Nevada in California
Reverse fault	Convergent boundaries	Plates push together.	Rocks above the fault move upward.	Himalayas in India
Strike-slip	Transform boundaries	Plates slide past each other without moving up or down.	Rocks slide past each other in different directions.	San Andreas Fault in California

READING N DIAGRAMS

1. **REPRESENT** Make a list of the ways the sides of a fault can move.
2. **WRITE** Describe the faults in a way that explains their differences.

What Causes an Earthquake to Start?

When plates move, great forces are exerted on the rocks of the crust. At first the forces can make the rocks bend and stretch. Every material has a limit to how far it will bend before breaking. When the rocks in the crust reach their limit, they break. As a result **faults** form in the crust. Faults are huge cracks in the crust. They form at the surface and below.

Recall that there are three kinds of plate boundaries. At divergent boundaries plates pull apart. At convergent boundaries plates push together. Along transform boundaries plates move past each other. These different motions produce different faults.

The broken sides of a fault may scrape past each other. They can move gradually, centimeters a year. Sometimes they move all of a sudden. The energy released by this sudden action shakes the crust. It sets an earthquake in motion.

How Do Earthquakes Make Waves?

An earthquake starts the moment rocks begin to scrape past each other along a fault. It may be a new fault that forms just that moment or an old fault that has already formed.

The point where the earthquake starts, where the rocks begin to slide past each other, is the **focus**. It is usually below the surface. The sudden motion causes vibrations to spread out from the focus. These vibrations travel through the crust in the form of waves—**seismic waves**. They soon reach Earth's surface at a point directly above the focus. This point is the **epicenter**. It is at the epicenter that people can first feel the ground shaking.

This shaking is what causes most earthquake damage. Damage is usually greatest at the epicenter because it is so close to the focus. As the waves travel away from the focus, they get weaker. People far from the epicenter may not feel the ground shaking at all.

After the first shaking, there may be relative quiet, followed by **aftershocks**. Aftershocks continue the damage of an earthquake. People have not recovered from the first shaking, and then there is additional shaking and destruction.

HOW A TSUNAMI FORMS

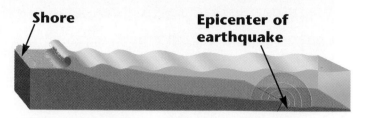

Shore

Epicenter of earthquake

If the focus of the earthquake is beneath the sea floor, the seismic waves can travel through the ocean. They can produce huge ocean waves called tsunamis (tsü nä′mēz). When tsunamis reach a shoreline, they can rise to heights of more than 15 meters (50 feet). They can destroy everything in their path.

FUNtastic Facts

Tsunamis can race across the oceans at speeds up to 900 kilometers per hour (560 mph)—as fast as some jet planes! Produced by an earthquake, a tsunami about 46 meters (150 ft) high occurred off the coast of Chile in April 1971. It reached Japan in 24 hours, a distance of 15,600 km (9,700 mi). What was its average speed?

Brain Power

A vibrating guitar string can make sound waves that travel to your ear. How does that compare with what happens during an earthquake?

Earthquake Waves

How can seismic waves move through Earth's crust? A seismic wave, remember, starts with shaking caused by rocks scraping against each other. The shaking results in several kinds of seismic waves, which travel differently and at different speeds.

In one kind of shaking, rock material squeezes together and spreads apart repeatedly. This motion produces seismic waves that move in the same direction that the rock is shaking. They are the fastest seismic waves—the first to reach faraway locations. They are *primary waves*, or *P waves*.

Another kind of shaking is like a ruler held off the edge of a desk and twanged. This kind of motion in rocks produces seismic waves that move in a different direction from the vibration. These waves travel slower than primary waves. They are the second to arrive at any given faraway location. They are called *secondary waves*, or *S waves*.

A third kind of shaking causes Earth's surface to heave up and down like an ocean wave, or sway from side to side. The motion of these *surface waves* tears apart structures built on the surface.

The 1994 Northridge earthquake destroyed this freeway overpass near Los Angeles.

Fault
Focus
Secondary wave
Primary wave

How Can We Locate an Epicenter?

You are at a seismograph station in California. Suddenly P waves appear on your seismograph. Three minutes later you see S waves. The time difference, or lag, between the arrival of the two waves is important. If you are very near an epicenter, the time lag will be short—just seconds. The farther you are from the epicenter, the greater the time lag.

By knowing the time lag, you can tell how far away you are from the epicenter—but not in what direction. It can be anywhere along a circle around your station. The radius of that circle is the distance to the epicenter.

You call two other seismograph stations, in Arizona and Nevada. You learn the time lag noted at each station. Based on that information, you can tell how far the epicenter is from each

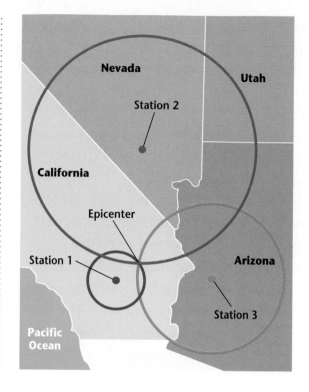

place, but not the direction. You draw a circle around each place. All three circles come together at one point. That point is the location of the epicenter.

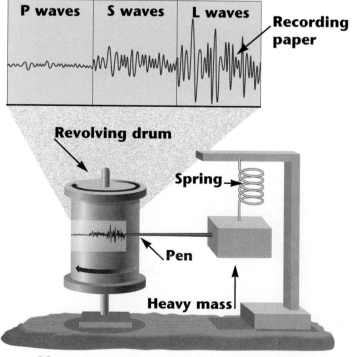

A seismograph shows patterns in the waves that arrive. By carefully studying the waves, a scientist can identify the P waves and the S waves. Long waves, L waves or surface waves, cause the most damage.

Brain Power

Waves from an earthquake in Turkey are detected by seismographs around the world. What difference might you see in a printout from seismographs in northern Africa and in North America? Explain.

Skill: Interpreting Data

LOCATING AN EPICENTER

In this activity you will interpret data to locate the epicenter of an earthquake.

MATERIALS

- compass
- map
- *Science Journal*

Station	Wave	Arrival Time	Difference (S - P)	Distance from Epicenter (km)
1	S	8:10.08 sec	8 sec	70
	P	8:10.00 sec		
2	S	8:10.34 sec	30 sec	275
	P	8:10.04 sec		
3	S	8:10.50 sec	20 sec	180
	P	8:10.30 sec		

PROCEDURES

1. USING NUMBERS The table above gives the times when earthquake waves (P and S) arrived at the three Monitoring Stations. By finding the difference between the times when the P and S waves arrived at each station (S – P), the distance from each station to the epicenter has been calculated.

2. Trace or photocopy the map. Use the scale above the map. Set your compass to the distance from Station 1 to the epicenter (70 km). Construct a circle of this radius centered on Station 1. Repeat for the other two stations.

CONCLUDE AND APPLY

1. DRAW CONCLUSIONS Where do the three circles meet? Yopu have located the epicenter of the earthquake!

2. DEFINE Write a definition for *epicenter*.

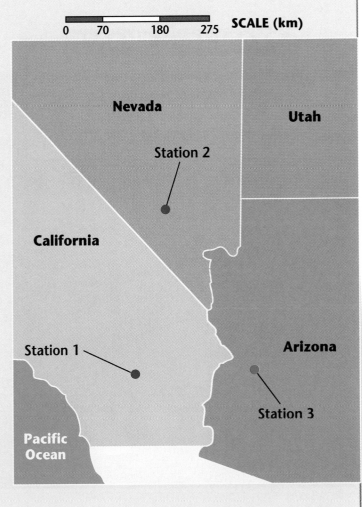

SCALE (km)
0   70   180   275

Nevada

Utah

Station 2

California

Arizona

Station 1

Station 3

Pacific Ocean

How Powerful Is an Earthquake?

The height of a wave on a seismograph is a measure of the magnitude of an earthquake. **Magnitude** is the amount of energy released by an earthquake. The more energy an earthquake releases, the more violent the shaking recorded.

In 1935, Professor Charles Richter of the California Institute of Technology devised a scale for comparing the energy of earthquakes. His scale is now called the Richter scale. It was originally based on measurements of earthquakes in southern California. Now the scale is used by geologists all over the world.

The Richter scale rates earthquakes from 1 to 10 according to magnitude. Each increase of 1 on the scale means an increase of about 30 times the energy released. In other words, each increase of 1 on the scale indicates an earthquake that is tremendously more powerful. An earthquake of magnitude 8.0 releases 900 times more energy than an earthquake of magnitude 6.0!

The Northridge earthquake in Los Angeles in 1994 measured 6.4 on the Richter scale. The Loma Prieta earthquake that struck San Francisco in 1989 measured 7.1 on the Richter scale. By contrast, the great San Francisco earthquake of 1906 measured 8.3 on the scale. Earthquakes of that magnitude strike somewhere on Earth on average once every five to ten years.

READING CHARTS

WRITE What does the chart tell you about the frequency of very powerful earthquakes? Write your answer in the form of a paragraph.

SUMMARY OF THE RICHTER SCALE

Magnitude	Estimated Number per Year	Effects at Epicenter
Less than 2.5	900,000	Not usually felt
2.5–5.4	30,000	Very minor damage
5.5–6.0	500	Some damage
6.1–6.9	100	Much damage; can be destructive in crowded areas
7.0–7.9	20	Severe damage
8.0 or greater	1 every 5 to 10 years	Total destruction

How Destructive Is an Earthquake?

Earthquakes vary not just in magnitude, but also in the amount of destruction they cause. Earthquake damage depends on a number of different factors. One is the intensity of the shaking of the ground. Shaking is normally most intense closest to the epicenter. It becomes less intense as distance from the epicenter increases.

Another factor affecting the amount of damage is the type of soil or rock on which structures are built. Still another factor is the strength of the structures themselves. Damage is lightest where strongly built structures are firmly anchored to bedrock. Where flimsy structures are built on loose soils, even moderate earthquakes can cause severe damage.

The amount of earthquake damage at a given location is measured by the Mercalli (mûr ka′ lē) scale. On this scale, there are twelve different levels of damage. Each level is assigned a Roman numeral from I to XII. After an earthquake, scientists distribute questionnaires to people in the area. The questionnaires ask what people felt and how much damage was done. Based on people's answers, the earthquake is rated on the Mercalli scale.

The Mercalli and Richter scales are very different. The Richter scale measures energy. The rating on that scale is the same no matter where it is measured. The Mercalli scale measures effects. The farther away from an epicenter a place is, the lower the rating will be. The effects of an earthquake are felt less at greater distances from the epicenter.

READING N CHARTS

WRITE How is the Mercalli scale organized differently from the Richter scale? Why is it organized differently? Write an answer in the form of a paragraph.

SUMMARY OF THE MERCALLI SCALE

Mercalli Rating	Effects at Location Where Rating Is Taken
II	May be felt by a few persons at rest.
IV	Felt indoors by many, outdoors by few. Walls creak. Dishes shake. Parked cars rock.
VI	Felt by all. Heavy furniture moves. Books are knocked off shelves. Pictures fall. Chimneys may crack or crumble.
VIII	Monuments and walls may fall. Buildings may partially collapse, unless they were built to withstand damage.
X	Wooden and brick structures collapse. The ground cracks badly. Landslides may happen on steep slopes.
XII	Total or nearly total destruction. Objects are tossed upward. Waves are seen on the ground surface.

Where Is the Worst Earthquake Damage?

The worst damage from an earthquake isn't always at the epicenter. Other factors are also involved. One of the most important is the type of ground on which buildings are built.

Which types of ground can be most dangerous in an earthquake? Away from the epicenter, solid rock will shake during an earthquake, but it will usually stay solid. Buildings that are constructed on bedrock generally experience less damage in earthquakes.

By contrast, sand, clay, and other loose soils can liquefy, or become like liquid, in an earthquake. The liquid state will last only moments, but that is long enough for buildings in the area to collapse. Buildings and roads built on loose soil can be heavily damaged even though they are located far from the epicenter.

An example is the Loma Prieta earthquake that struck San Francisco in 1989. The epicenter of the earthquake was approximately 80 km (50 miles) from the city. When the shock waves reached the city, skyscrapers built on bedrock swayed but remained standing. But one neighborhood of the city was built on loose landfill that had been dumped into San Francisco Bay. In that area, the ground liquefied, and houses and apartment buildings came crashing down.

These San Francisco skyscrapers are anchored in bedrock. They were not damaged when an earthquake struck the city in 1989.

There is no truth to the idea that California might "fall into the sea" in an earthquake. Most coastal areas are rising, not sinking.

What Will *Not* Happen in an Earthquake?

Many people who have not experienced earthquakes have mistaken ideas about them. They develop fears about things are do not actually happen in earthquakes.

Have you ever heard people say, "In an earthquake, California might fall into the ocean"? Luckily, that is not true. There is absolutely no danger that the state is going to fall into the Pacific Ocean. Such an idea could be held only by people who do not understand earthquakes.

You have learned that earthquakes in California are caused by moving plates in the Earth's crust. Under California, one plate is moving past another. During an earthquake, portions of the ground may move sideways. But no part of the state is going to "fall" into the sea. In fact, many coastal areas in California are rising, not sinking. Landslides may tumble down hills during an earthquake, but the ground is generally moving up, not down.

Another common earthquake fear is that cracks will open in the ground and swallow people and houses. Earthquakes may open small cracks in the ground. But the greatest danger in an earthquake comes from collapsing buildings, not from openings in the ground.

If you understand what really happens in earthquakes, you will know how to react.. Knowing the facts can help you stay safe if an earthquake happens.

How Can We Prepare for Earthquakes?

In 1962, a massive earthquake struck Alaska. The city of Anchorage suffered terrible damage. Valdez, on the other hand, suffered relatively little damage. Was Anchorage closer to the epicenter? No, Valdez was closer. Why did Valdez have less damage?

The answer is beneath each location. Valdez is on top of solid rock—granite. Anchorage was built on top of a massive deposit of sediment.

We cannot change the rock underneath places where earthquakes are common. However, we can design buildings and highways to keep them from collapsing—to be *seismic-safe*.

Many new building designs have huge shock absorbers in their foundations. These absorb much of the wave motion of an earthquake. The building sways without collapsing—up to a magnitude of 8.3.

Highways can be made seismic-safe by special supporting structures. They contain vertical rods wrapped with spiral steel rods. The wrapping helps hold the vertical rods together during an earthquake.

Older buildings were built with rigid materials, such as bricks and masonry, which crumble during an earthquake. Newer, flexible materials have a better chance of bending without breaking. Using newer materials for water pipes and gas pipes will better assure they will survive an earthquake.

SUPPORT FOR A BUILDING

Rubber

Steel

SUPPORT FOR A HIGHWAY

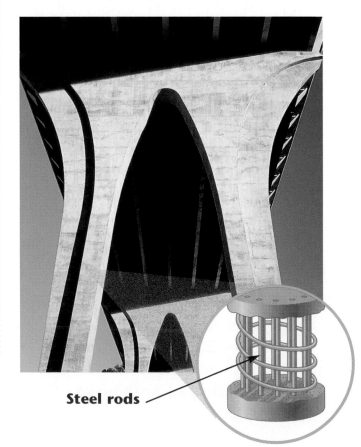

Steel rods

Predicting Earthquakes

Plate tectonics can help us know where earthquakes are more likely to happen. Much earthquake destruction might be prevented if people had warning signs. Scientists use special devices to detect slight motions as warning signs. Tilt meters are used to measure the slight bending of rocks under the force of moving plates. Creepmeters string wires across faults. Laser beams are sent across faults and reflected back. Still, a surefire way to predict earthquakes is yet to come.

Earthquakes are common along the West Coast and in Hawaii. However, they can happen in other parts of the United States as well. In 1811, an earthquake hit New Madrid, Missouri, with a magnitude great enough to level much of St. Louis if it happened today.

HEALTH LINK

Learning what to do if an earthquake happens might save your life. During the shaking keep away from windows or anything that can fall on you. Watch out for sharp objects in rubble and for fallen power lines.

EARTHQUAKE SAFETY

INDOORS
Take cover under a piece of heavy furniture or against an inside wall, and hold on. Stay inside.

OUTDOORS
Move into the open, away from buildings, street lights, and utility wires. Stay there until the shaking stops.

REVIEW

1. Where are earthquakes more likely to happen? Explain.

2. "An earthquake starts at the epicenter." Is this statement true or false? Explain your answer. Include what causes earthquakes.

3. Why is it useful to record seismic waves with a seismograph?

4. **INTERPRET DATA** If an earthquake has a Richter scale reading of 6.6, what damage would you expect?

5. **CRITICAL THINKING** *Analyze* Why might waves from the same earthquake cause more damage in one area than another?

WHY IT MATTERS **THINK ABOUT IT**
A new mayor has been elected in a town where few earthquake precautions have been made. What decisions would the mayor have to make to make the town seismic-safe?

WHY IT MATTERS **WRITE ABOUT IT**
How would you prepare for an earthquake? What kinds of precautions would you take? What steps could you outline to be safe during and after an earthquake?

What's Down Under?

Ever imagine what Earth is like deep down? Writer Jules Verne did in his 1864 novel *A Journey to the Center of the Earth*. In his story Earth's center is a prehistoric world filled with sunlight, water . . . and dinosaurs!

Earth's center is about 6,350 kilometers (3,946 miles) down, so how do we know there aren't dinosaurs there? We can't dig that far! To study inner Earth, scientists track P (primary) and S (secondary) seismic waves during earthquakes. P waves go through solids and liquids. S waves go through solids but not liquids. That difference tells scientists which parts of inner Earth are liquid and which are solid!

As P and S waves move through Earth, they go faster as the density increases. They also bend when they reach material of a different density, just as light rays bend in water to make a pencil seem to bend where it enters the water.

Physical Science Link

Continental crust and oceanic crust

Crust: 5–60 km (3.1–37 mi)

Upper mantle: 670 km (416 mi)

Lower mantle: 2,885 km (1,792 mi)

Outer core: 2,270 km (1,410 mi)

Inner core: 1,260 km (783 mi) to center

By comparing P and S waves traveling through Earth, scientists have made models of Earth's insides. In 1906 P waves located the boundary between Earth's core and mantle. Three years later P and S waves determined the boundary between Earth's crust and mantle.

Scientists also tracked seismic waves to learn about Earth's outer and inner cores.

In 1926 a scientist discovered that S waves didn't go through Earth's core. Conclusion? The outer core is liquid. In 1936 another scientist tracked P waves that reached Earth's core. Conclusion? The inner core must be solid!

DISCUSSION STARTER

1. How can P and S waves determine boundaries of inner Earth?

2. Do you think scientists will ever have actual evidence of what's in Earth's core? Why or why not?

S waves can't move through liquid.

P waves can move through liquid.

Bending of waves

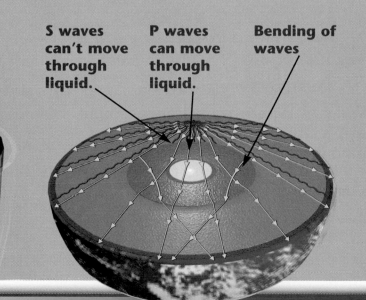

WHY IT MATTERS

While volcanoes can be dangerous, they provide energy and resources.

SCIENCE WORDS

hot spot a very hot part of the mantle, where magma can melt through a plate moving above it

vent a central opening in a volcanic area through which magma may escape

lava magma that reaches Earth's surface and flows out of a vent

crater a cuplike hollow that forms at the top of a volcano around the vent

cinder-cone volcano a steep-sided cone that forms from explosive eruptions of hot rocks, ranging from particles to boulders

shield volcano a wide, gently sloped cone that forms from flows of lava

composite volcano a cone formed from explosive eruptions of hot rocks followed by a flow of lava, over and over

geothermal energy heat from below Earth's surface

Volcanoes

Where are volcanoes located? Can any volcano erupt at any time? Are some more likely to erupt than others?

Mount Etna, in Italy, has the longest record of eruptions in history. Since the first recorded eruption in 1500 B.C., Mount Etna has erupted 190 times! The most recent string of eruptions stretches back over decades. Recent eruptions have included fire fountains in early 1996. However, Mount Etna is not alone. All told, Italy has 13 active volcanoes!

EXPLORE

HYPOTHESIZE Where are volcanoes found on Earth's crust? Are volcanoes more common in certain places than others? Write a hypothesis in your *Science Journal.* How can you test your ideas?

Investigate Where Volcanoes Are Located

Plot on a map places where volcanoes have erupted so that you can identify patterns.

PROCEDURES

1. Using bits of modeling compound or stick-on dots, plot the locations of active volcanoes on a world map. Use the data printed in the table.

2. On a small outline map, shade in the areas where volcanoes are found.

3. **INTERPRET DATA** In your *Science Journal*, compare your finished map with other maps in this chapter, such as in Topic 1 and Topic 2.

CONCLUDE AND APPLY

1. **COMPARE AND CONTRAST** Are most volcanoes located near the edges or near the centers of continents?

2. **INTERPRET DATA** Is there a pattern in the arrangement of volcanoes around the Pacific Ocean? Explain your answer.

3. **DRAW CONCLUSIONS** Are Earth's active volcanoes grouped in certain areas? Explain your answer.

GOING FURTHER: Problem Solving

4. **HYPOTHESIZE** What is the relationship between the locations of active volcanoes and the locations of earthquakes? What data do you need to support your answer? How can you get it?

MATERIALS

- large world map
- modeling compound or small stick-on dots
- small outline map (Explore Data Sheet 5-3)
- colored pencils
- *Science Journal*

Volcano	Latitude	Longitude
1	39°N	44°E
2	38°N	30°W
3	16°N	24°W
4	0.4°S	78°W
5	35°N	52°W
6	4°S	103°E
7	37°N	15°E
8	0.3°S	90°W
9	64°N	19°W
10	58°N	155°W
11	6°S	105°E
12	40°N	121°W
13	19°N	155°W
14	16°S	71°W
15	46°N	122°W
16	42°N	140°E
17	40°S	73°W
18	19°N	102°W
19	15°N	61°W
20	40°N	14°E

Pacific Ring of Fire

●	Hot spots
▲	Active volcanoes
‑‑‑‑	Plate boundaries

Active volcanoes are located around the edges of plates.

Where Are Volcanoes Located?

The Explore Activity showed where many volcanoes are located. Volcanoes occur in belts, or long lines. One circles the Pacific Ocean. It is the Pacific Ring of Fire. Another runs along the Mediterranean Sea through Iran. After a gap it continues through Indonesia to the Pacific.

Over 80 percent of all land volcanoes are found in these two belts. Even more of Earth's volcanoes are at the ocean floor. They line the mid-ocean ridges.

Compare the location of volcanoes with the plate boundaries. Do you see a pattern? Most volcanoes occur along plate boundaries.

Where plates are moving apart, volcanoes form along the gaps at the edges of spreading plates. These are called *rift volcanoes*. Some rift volcanoes can be found in Iceland and in Africa's

READING MAPS

DISCUSS From Topic 1 identify which plates are colliding (convergent boundaries). Which are pulling apart (divergent boundaries)? Are volcanoes more common along one boundary than another?

Great Rift Valley. Most rift volcanoes are located deep underwater along mid-ocean ridges.

Volcanoes also form along the edges of slowly colliding plates. One plate plunges beneath another. The downward-moving plate melts. Magma forms. It moves upward through the rocks and forms volcanoes.

The Hawaiian Islands are a chain of volcanoes, but they are in the middle of a plate. They are not at the edge. Geologists believe the plate is moving over a **hot spot**. A hot spot is a very hot part of the mantle. As a plate moves over a hot spot, magma melts up through the crust and forms volcanoes. The Azores and the Galapagos may have also formed from hot spots.

What Are the Parts of a Volcano?

Just what is a volcano? A volcano is a place where molten rock, hot gases, and solid rock erupt through an opening in the crust. It is also the mountain built up by these materials.

Beneath every volcano is a source of magma. Magma, remember, is molten rock. Magma rises to the surface through cracks in the rock above it. In time it reaches the surface and erupts through a central opening, or **vent**. Once the magma comes out of the vent, it is called **lava**.

Erupted material cools and hardens around the vent in a mound. After many eruptions it can pile up into a big hill or even a mountain. This is also called a volcano. At the top of a volcano is a cuplike hollow around the vent, called a **crater**. Sometimes a volcano collapses, forming a very wide crater, called a *caldera*.

THE FORMATION OF A VOLCANO

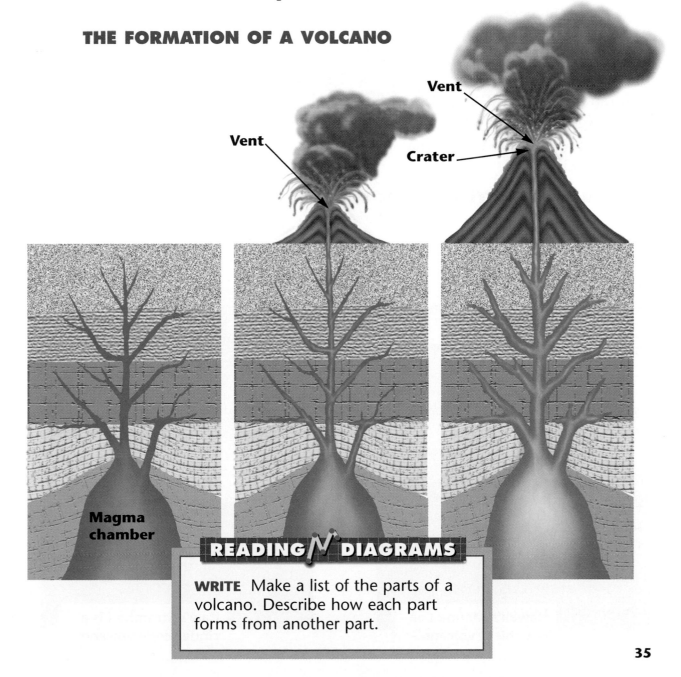

Vent

Vent

Crater

Magma chamber

READING N DIAGRAMS

WRITE Make a list of the parts of a volcano. Describe how each part forms from another part.

35

How Are Volcanoes Different?

Why do volcanoes erupt? Magma is less dense than the rock around it. As a result magma rises up toward Earth's surface. Near the surface there is less rock overhead pressing down on the magma. The pressure decreases. It is like removing the cap of a shaken bottle of soda. Gases that were dissolved in the magma come boiling out. The gases shoot lava or partly hardened chunks of lava out of the vent.

What an eruption is like depends on how much gas is in the magma and how thick the magma is.

Some magma is thick and has a lot of gas in it. Lumps of magma may get stuck as the magma rises to the surface. In time the magma bursts free. Gases explode out of the magma. Lava blasts outward. It hardens.

What falls to the ground is a rain of hot rocks ranging in size from tiny droplets to huge boulders. These build up in a steep-sided cone called a **cinder-cone volcano**.

Some magma is thinner, and gases can leak out of it more easily. This magma doesn't clog up as easily. Instead it squirts out as a fiery lava fountain.

If a lot of the gases have already escaped from the magma, it may just flow out of the vent. The lava spreads out and hardens into a wide, flat mound called a **shield volcano**.

Shishaldin is a **composite volcano** in the Aleutian Islands. Composite

THREE TYPES OF VOLCANOES

Magma

Steep sides

Rock fragment layers

Magma

Hawaii's Mauna Loa is a shield volcano.

Italy's Stromboli is a cinder-cone volcano.

volcanoes may have beautifully symmetrical shapes. That is, the shape on one side of the cone matches the shape on the opposite side.

Sometimes an eruption "takes turns." An eruption may explode. It sends gas and lava high into the air and forms a rain of rocks of different sizes. Then the eruption may switch over to a quiet period. Lava may flow over the rocks from the explosive period. When this switching repeats over and over, it forms a composite volcano.

Brain Power

What properties, if any, do the three kinds of cones have in common? What properties do they not have in common?

Layers of rock fragments and lava

Magma

Shishaldin is a composite volcano.

Cones

MATH LINK

HYPOTHESIZE How are volcanic cones different? Write a hypothesis in your *Science Journal*.

MATERIALS
- modeling compound
- sand, soil, or gravel
- water
- paper towels
- *Science Journal*

PROCEDURES

1. **MAKE A MODEL** Build models of the three kinds of cones. Choose materials that show the differences. (Use water to hold particles together.)

2. Draw diagrams of your finished products in your *Science Journal*.

CONCLUDE AND APPLY

1. **EVALUATE** How well do the models show the differences?

2. How else could you show the differences between cones?

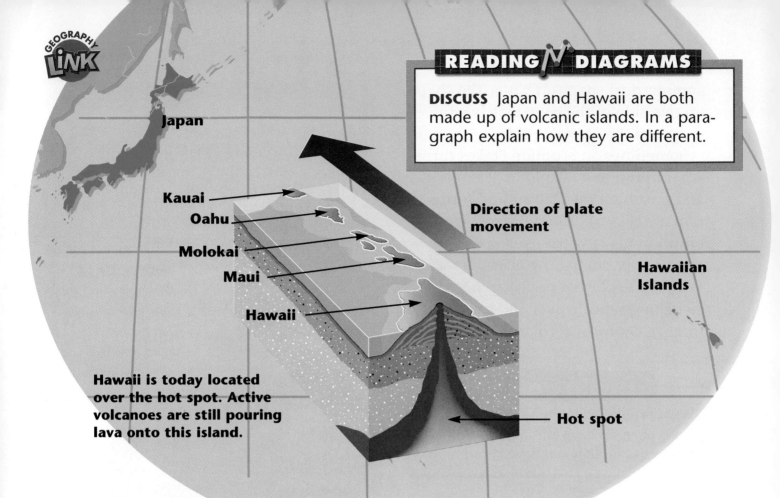

READING DIAGRAMS

DISCUSS Japan and Hawaii are both made up of volcanic islands. In a paragraph explain how they are different.

Japan

Kauai

Oahu

Molokai

Maui

Hawaii

Direction of plate movement

Hawaiian Islands

Hawaii is today located over the hot spot. Active volcanoes are still pouring lava onto this island.

Hot spot

Are All Volcanoes Active?

Thousands of volcanoes are scattered over Earth's surface. However, very few of them are active. That is, very few are erupting now or have erupted recently. Many of Earth's active volcanoes are located in the Pacific Ring of Fire. For example, there are active volcanoes in Japan.

Japan is made up of volcanic islands. These islands were built up from the ocean floor along a convergent boundary. One plate is plunging down under another. Molten rock pushed through to the surface and formed a string, or arc, of volcanoes. The volcanoes grew in size over time, from undersea volcanoes to islands far above sea level.

In time active volcanoes may stop erupting. They may become *dormant*. *Dormant* is from a French word for "sleep." A dormant volcano has not been active for a long period of time but has erupted in recorded history.

Some volcanoes are considered *extinct*. An extinct volcano has not erupted in recorded history.

The Hawaiian Islands are volcanic islands. Many of these volcanoes are no longer active. The Hawaiian Islands, remember, were formed as the Pacific plate moved over a hot spot. The island of Kauai (kou'ī) is the oldest island. It formed when it was located over the hot spot. As the plate moved, Kauai moved away from the hot spot and was no longer active. The plate continued to move, and other islands formed, one at a time.

What Happens Underground?

Sometimes underground magma cools and hardens before it reaches the surface. Magma can harden in many possible shapes and positions.

A *dike* is formed when magma hardens in vertical cracks. Dikes are vertical or nearly vertical structures. A *sill* is formed when magma hardens between horizontal layers of rock. A sill is flat. Dikes and sills vary in size from small to huge. When rocks around a large dike are worn away, the dike is exposed as a long ridge. Exposed sills take the shape of ridges or cliffs.

If the magma pushed into a sill is thick, it may not spread far horizontally. Instead it pushes upward, forming a *laccolith*. A laccolith is shaped like a dome.

When magma pushes upward, it raises overlying rock layers into *dome mountains*. A dome mountain is a broad, circular mountain formed from uplifted rock layers. The Henry Mountains of Utah were formed by laccoliths. Some dome mountains, like the Black Hills of South Dakota, were formed from layers that became folded.

The largest and deepest of all underground formations are *batholiths*. A batholith is huge and irregularly shaped. It reaches deep into the crust. Some batholiths have been uplifted to above sea level. As overlying rocks were worn away, the batholiths became exposed. They look like large, steep hills.

Batholiths have been found in many great mountain ranges. Sierra Nevada in California contains a number of batholiths covering an area of over 40,000 square kilometers (15,444 square miles).

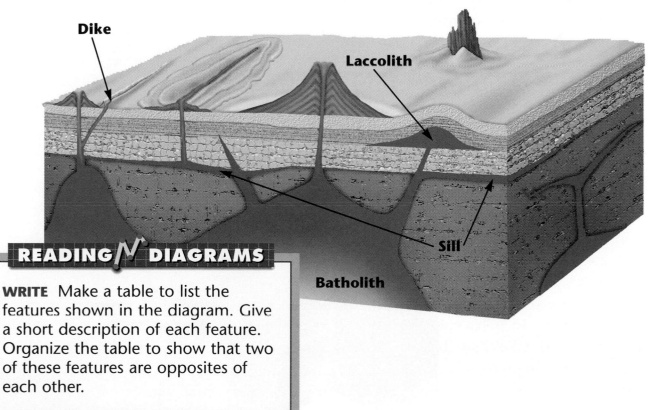

Dike

Laccolith

Sill

Batholith

READING ⁄Ⅴ DIAGRAMS

WRITE Make a table to list the features shown in the diagram. Give a short description of each feature. Organize the table to show that two of these features are opposites of each other.

Can Magma Heat Water?

Perhaps the most spectacular side effect of volcanism is a *geyser*. A geyser is an opening in the ground through which hot water and steam erupt periodically. The main vent of a geyser is filled with water. The water at the bottom of the column is heated and changed to steam. At first the steam is held down by the weight of the water above it. Pressure continues to build up as more water is changed to steam. It is like shaking a bottle of soda with the cap still on.

Finally, some steam pushes high enough to move the column of water. This action relieves some pressure. A jet of hot water and steam soon erupts from the geyser. After the geyser erupts, the vent fills with more water, and the cycle begins again.

Hot springs are also caused by underground heating. A hot spring is an opening in the ground where hot water and gases escape. The water is heated deep underground by magma. The heated water is forced up to an opening in the surface. The water may contain minerals. As the water cools, it may deposit a spectacular mineral load.

Sometimes the water evaporates quickly as it flows out. The remaining water may become thick with broken pieces of rock and minerals. The result is a hot, muddy pool, called a paint pot. The materials mixed in the water may make it look yellow, red, or black.

Can the heat from such hot springs and geysers be used? Today scientists are finding ways to use **geothermal energy**. Geothermal energy is heat from below Earth's surface.

READING 𝒩 DIAGRAMS

WRITE In a paragraph explain what is happening in the diagram. Include a description of what happens before the event shown.

A geyser

In 1965 the first geothermal power plant in the United States was built in Healdsburg, California. Wells were dug to hot rock material below the surface. Steam was produced. It was used to run power plants that produced electricity.

Water is changed to steam by being heated below the surface. The steam can run a power plant.

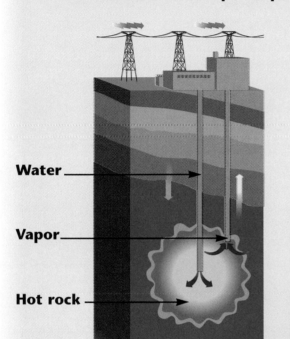

Water

Vapor

Hot rock

Did you know that the United States ranks third (after Indonesia and Japan) in the number of historically active volcanoes? Volcanic eruptions have created many valuable natural resources. For example, volcanic ash falling on the land around a volcano increases soil fertility. Forests and farm crops grow better because the ash adds nutrients and acts as a mulch.

Underground magma heats groundwater. The heated water can be used as a source of heat, or geothermal energy. Heated groundwater also concentrates valuable minerals such as copper, tin, gold, and silver. Over many thousands of years, these minerals built up into deposits that are mined.

READING DIAGRAMS

WRITE In a paragraph explain what is shown by the arrows in the diagram.

REVIEW

1. Are volcanoes distributed randomly or in a pattern?

2. List the parts of a volcano.

3. Why are there different kinds of volcanoes?

4. **COMPARE AND CONTRAST** Describe the different kinds of underground features caused by volcanoes.

5. **CRITICAL THINKING** *Synthesize* How do volcanoes support the theory of plate tectonics?

WHY IT MATTERS **THINK ABOUT IT**
Do you live near a volcano? If so, what is it like? If not, how far are you from one? What would it be like to visit one?

WHY IT MATTERS **WRITE ABOUT IT**
How are volcanoes dangerous? How can they be helpful? Write a composition comparing the effects.

Disaster Alerts

Scientists can predict weather disasters, like tornadoes and hurricanes, thanks to modern technology. Can they also tell when there'll be a volcanic eruption or earthquake, and alert people to the danger?

Predicting Eruptions

In the past when a volcano erupted, there was no escape. Today almost all eruptions can be predicted early enough to warn people.

How do scientists know there might be an eruption? Magma moving inside a volcano causes patterns of small earthquakes that create a steady roar. Nearby seismographs record that magma is on the move. Scientists warn people to leave the area. That's how

30,000 people were saved in 1994 when a giant volcano erupted in New Guinea.

Sometimes a volcano explodes through the side of its cone. Before it blows, a buildup of gases bulges the side. Lasers record ground swells around volcanoes to the nearest millimeter. Satellite radar detects even the tiniest ground motion. These clues predict which side of the cone will blow.

The Dante 2 robot goes into a volcano's crater to measure gases. The composition of gases may predict an eruption.

In 1980 scientists predicted that Mount Saint Helens would erupt, but not exactly when.

Science, Technology, and Society

Predicting Earthquakes

Earthquake prediction is still difficult, but one prediction was a big success. In 1975 the Chinese noted changing water levels in their wells, odd behavior of domestic animals, and a series of small earthquakes. All this evidence predicted a great earthquake would hit Lianong Province. People were warned to get outside of buildings. When the earthquake came, only 300 people were killed. The following year 750,000 Chinese were killed in an unpredicted earthquake in Tangshan.

The map on page 18, Topic 2, showed where earthquake zones are located. There, minor earthquakes are common. California's an exception. It's been hit with destructive earthquakes every 15 years or so for the last century!

DISCUSSION STARTER

1. A volcano covers a small area, while an earthquake zone may be hundreds of kilometers long. How does this affect the amount of destruction each can cause?

2. Do you think it's easier to predict floods, hurricanes, and tornadoes than volcanic eruptions or earthquakes? Why?

In the United States, earthquakes have occurred from the Atlantic to the Pacific.

To learn more about predicting disasters, visit *www.mhschool.com/science* and select the keyword DISASTER.

interNET CONNECTION

SCIENCE WORDS

crust p.4

epicenter p.20

fault p.19

hot spot p.34

lava p.35

magma p.6

magnitude p.24

mantle p.9

plate

tectonics p.9

seismograph p.22

subduction p.12

USING SCIENCE WORDS

Number a paper from 1 to 10. Fill in 1 to 5 with words from the list above.

1. The modern idea of crustal motion is ___?___.

2. Magma that reaches the surface becomes ___?___.

3. The plunging of one plate under another is ___?___.

4. The Hawaiian Islands formed over a(n) ___?___.

5. The point where an earthquake begins is the ___?___.

6–10. Pick five words from the list above that were not used in 1 to 5, and use each in a sentence.

UNDERSTANDING SCIENCE IDEAS

11. Which waves from an earthquake arrive first?

12. What is the surface of Earth called?

13. How do earthquakes affect the oceans?

14. Name three kinds of volcanic cones.

15. What are the two upper-most layers of Earth?

USING IDEAS AND SKILLS

16. **READING SKILL: CAUSE AND EFFECT** How is new rock being formed at the sea floor?

17. How do waves from an earthquake give information about the earth-quake? Tell what kind of information it gives.

18. Why do volcanoes erupt? How do they erupt in different ways?

19. **HYPOTHESIZE** Copy the table. Describe a hypothesis that ties together all the ideas in the table. In each column tell how the hypothesis explains the idea at the top. Add columns to the table as needed. Give the table a name.

	Earthquakes	Volcanoes
Continent		
Coastlines		

20. **THINKING LIKE A SCIENTIST** How do scientists make predictions about plate tectonics in the future? What kind of data do they need to collect to make predictions?

PROBLEMS and PUZZLES

Rock Rumble Volcanism on Earth is an ongoing process. In contrast, most of the volcanism on the Moon occurred between three and four billion years ago. How would scientists know this? What differences do you think there are between volcanic activity on Earth and on the Moon?

R.I.P

CHAPTER 2

THE SHAPE OF THE LAND

From the majestic headlands of the Golden Gate to the mighty Sierra Nevada, and from the fertile Central Valley to the arid Mojave Desert, California has some of the most spectacular landscapes on Earth. What forces built these great mountains and valleys? Are those same forces still at work today? What can maps tell us about the landforms we see around us?

In Chapter 2 you will compare and contrast many things. *Compare* means "to tell how things are alike." *Contrast* means "to tell how things are different."

Topic
EARTH SCIENCE
4

WHY IT MATTERS

The landscape of California affects the lives of people who live there.

SCIENCE WORDS

active fault a crack in Earth's crust where earthquakes take place

blind fault a crack in Earth's crust that is not visible on the surface

rain shadow the effect created when mountains block moist air from reaching areas beyond them

dune a mound of sand created by blowing winds

The Features of California

In what part of California do you live? From where you live can you see hills or mountains? Can you see valleys? Can you see a river or a bay? Can you see a desert? The California landscape has all of these features and more. What are these geological features like? How did they come to be? What forces gave them the shape they have today?

HYPOTHESIZE Millions of people live in California. Is there a pattern to where they live? Write a hypothesis in your *Science Journal.* How would you test your ideas?

Investigate Population Patterns

Compare maps to find relationships between California's physical features and the places where most Californians live.

PROCEDURES

1. OBSERVE Examine the map on this page. It shows where people live in California. The dark red areas are crowded with cities and towns. The orange and dark yellow areas are less crowded. The light yellow areas are thinly populated.

3. OBSERVE Examine the maps in this topic that show the locations of California's natural features. Notice where mountains, volcanoes, deserts, and the San Andreas Fault are located.

MATERIALS

• population density map
• maps from this topic:
  northern California mountains
  southern California mountains
  San Andreas Fault
  California volcanoes
  California deserts
• *Science Journal*

CONCLUDE AND APPLY

1. COMPARE How do the areas where most people live compare to the locations of the various natural features? In what ways are they the same? In what ways are they different?

2. INFER Based on the maps, do earthquakes on the San Andreas Fault put many Californians at risk? Are volcanoes a threat to a large number of Californians?

3. DRAW CONCLUSIONS Do many Californians choose to live in the mountains and deserts? Can you explain their choice? Write your answer in your *Science Journal.*

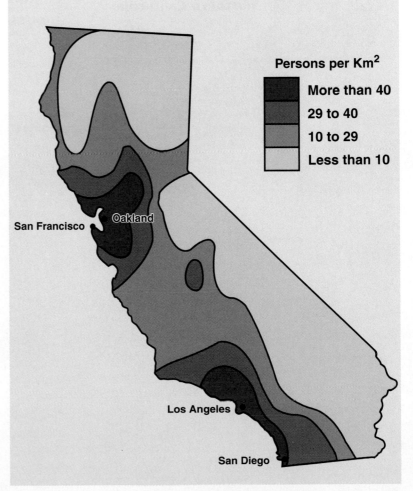

Persons per Km²

More than 40

29 to 40

10 to 29

Less than 10

San Francisco
Oakland
Los Angeles
San Diego

What Are the Major Mountain Ranges in Northern California?

At the center of northern California is the long, flat Central Valley. But all around the Valley are mountains. On the west, running from north to south along the Pacific Ocean, are the Coast Ranges. These mountains are not very high, but they can be rugged. Some rise steeply, directly up from the Pacific shoreline. The Golden Gate at San Francisco is one of the few gaps in the Coast Ranges.

North of the Central Valley, two other mountainous areas extend to the northern border of the state. The first is the Klamath Mountains. These mountains are heavily forested. Between the mountains are deep, steep-sided canyons. Lying inland from the Klamath Mountains is the Cascade Range. These mountains are actually the southern end of a range that extends far to the north of California. The Cascades are steep, high mountains that can be seen from far away.

East of the Central Valley are California's tallest mountains, the Sierra Nevada. This vast range extends north to south like a high wall for 600 km (370 miles). Covered with deep snow in the winter, the Sierra Nevada contains some of the most spectacular mountain scenery in the world.

The Klamath Mountains are a high, rugged range in northern California.

GEOGRAPHY LINK

How Were Northern California's Mountains Formed?

Northern California's mountains have all been formed by plate tectonics, the motion of Earth's crustal plates. Starting in very ancient times—even before the age of the dinosaurs—the floor of the Pacific Ocean slowly collided with the North American plate where California is now located. As the ocean plate slid under North America, the edge of the continent scraped off pieces of the plate itself. These pieces of crust piled up against the continent's edge, one after another. That is why mountain rocks inland are older than those at the coast.

Throughout the age of the dinosaurs, the collision of plates continued. Rock sliding under North America melted and rose through the crust. Some of it erupted at the surface, forming a chain of volcanoes.

The rest cooled underground and formed a gigantic mass of granite under what is now eastern California.

Much more recently—starting about 28 million years ago—a new ocean plate collided with North America. Instead of sliding under the North American plate, this new plate moved slantwise against it. This movement created tremendous pressure on the rocks of the crust. About 5 million years ago, the huge granite mass under eastern California rose upward like a gigantic bubble. The rising granite lifted and stretched the crust above it, causing the crust to break into great tilted blocks. These form the Sierra Nevada. A plateau area farther north also rose, and rivers carving through it formed the Klamath Mountains you see today. Finally, about 3 million years ago, more pressure from the ocean plate squeezed the crust to form the present-day Coast Ranges.

What Are the Major Mountain Ranges in Southern California?

If you live in southern California or have visited there, you've seen some of the area's mountain ranges. Hot and dry much of the year, many of these mountains are high enough to be snow-covered in winter.

GEOGRAPHY
LINK

The major ranges of southern California run from east to west. This feature distinguishes them from most northern California ranges, which run from north to south. The southern California mountains are called the Transverse Ranges. They include the Santa Monica Mountains and the San Gabriel Mountains, which you can see from Los Angeles. The Transverse Ranges run well inland from the coast, and some extend offshore, forming the Channel Islands off Santa Barbara.

Between the mountains of the Transverse Ranges lie a series of flat basins. In these basins you'll find the major cities where most southern Californians live.

Farther south, inland from San Diego, are more mountain ranges. These are called the Peninsular Ranges. Like the northern California mountains, they run generally from north to south. The Peninsular Ranges extend south of the border into Mexico.

Transverse Ranges
Santa Monica Mountains
Los Angeles
San Gabriel Mountains
Channel Islands
Peninsular Ranges
San Diego

HOLLYWOOD

The Santa Monica Mountains are part of the Transverse Ranges of southern California.

The Peninsular Ranges near San Diego were shaped by tectonic forces.

How Were Southern California's Mountains Formed?

The mountains of southern California have also all been formed by plate tectonics. Starting about 28 million years ago, an ocean plate began sliding slantwise against the North American plate. This process created tremendous pressure on the crust in southern California.

In most places, the boundary between the ocean plate and the North American plate runs generally north to south. But in southern California, the boundary bends slightly, running east to west. There the ocean plate pushing northward squeezed against the North American plate. Along this east-to-west plate boundary the crust was pushed together. It crumpled, forming folds running east to west. Some 5 million years ago, the folds had pushed up to form the Transverse Ranges. At the same time, the land between the ranges was pushed down to form basins. Today Los Angeles and other cities have been built in those basins.

Farther south, the Peninsular Ranges were formed in much the same way as the Sierra Nevada in northern California. They were created from rock that melted when an ocean plate slid beneath North America. Much later, tectonic forces pushed up the rock mass to form the mountains you see today.

51

Why Does California Have Earthquakes?

Have you ever felt an earthquake? If you have, that would not be unusual. Every year, there are thousands of small earthquakes in California.

San Francisco

San Andreas Fault

GEOGRAPHY LINK

Los Angeles

San Diego

Earthquakes occur in California because of the motion of plates in Earth's crust. The Pacific plate is moving north and slantwise against the North American plate. Where the two meet, a huge system of transform faults, or cracks in the crust, has developed. The best-known fault in the system is the San Andreas Fault. It comes on shore from the Pacific Ocean north of San Francisco. From San Francisco it runs south just inland from the Coast Ranges. North of Los Angeles it bends to the southeast along the Transverse Ranges. Then it turns south again toward Mexico.

The San Andreas Fault is only one of many in the transform fault system. Many others run parallel to it. The faults are of all sizes. Many of them are the sites of earthquakes. These are called **active faults**. Others are not active.

When an earthquake occurs, the ground on one side of the fault slips past the ground on the other side. Sometimes the slipping happens on only part of the fault. Other parts of the fault may not move, although they may move at another time in another earthquake. At some faults, the slipping happens deep inside the Earth. These are called **blind faults** because there may be no sign on Earth's surface that they exist.

A typical fault cuts through layers of rock on a California hillside.

Where Have Major Earthquakes Happened?

Most California earthquakes have occurred at faults in the San Andreas system. In northern California, one of the largest earthquakes ever recorded was the San Francisco earthquake of 1906. Its epicenter was on the San Andreas Fault just west of the city. The entire 430-km (270-mile) northern part of the fault ruptured at once. The Loma Prieta earthquake of 1989 also took place along the San Andreas Fault. This time, a 40-km (25-mile) segment ruptured in the Santa Cruz Mountains.

In central California, small earthquakes happen frequently on the San Andreas system. Scientists believe that these small earthquakes release pressure, making large earthquakes less likely in this area.

In southern California, major earthquakes have occurred along the San Andreas Fault and also along many parallel faults. A huge earthquake occurred in 1857 along the San Andreas at Fort Tejon, north of Los Angeles. A fault segment 360 km (220 miles) long ruptured. Since that time, this portion of the fault has remained "locked." Scientists fear that the lack of movement is causing pressure to build up. The pressure could cause another great earthquake.

In the Los Angeles area, major earthquakes have occurred at Long Beach (1933), San Fernando (1971), and Northridge (1994). The last two earthquakes occurred on blind faults buried deep beneath the Los Angeles basin.

The 1989 Loma Prieta earthquake destroyed a section of the San Francisco-Oakland Bay Bridge.

Does California Have Volcanoes?

Have you ever seen a volcano in California? There are several, but you may not have spotted them because they are located far away from where most people live.

The Cascade Range is a chain of volcanic mountains that extends through the far northern part of California and continues on farther to the north. In the California Cascades there are two active volcanoes. One is Mt. Shasta, a huge volcano that has erupted at least 13 times during the last 10,000 years. An eruption was last observed in 1786.

Lassen Peak, also in the Cascades, last erupted in the years 1914–1921. The eruption scorched trees in a wide area. Scientists think that earlier eruptions were much more destructive.

Northeast of Mt. Shasta is Medicine Lake volcano, a huge shield volcano that was last active just a few hundred years ago. It is surrounded by a large area of cinder cones and barren lava beds.

Aside from the Cascades there is one other area of volcanic activity in California. This is the Long Valley area east of the central Sierra Nevada. A tremendous eruption took place there 760,000 years ago. Ash from the eruption fell as far east as Missouri. Scientists believe that there is still hot magma under Long Valley. Movements of this magma continue to cause small earthquakes in the area.

Medicine Lake volcano

Mt. Shasta

Lassen Peak

Long Valley

GEOGRAPHY LiNK

Mt. Shasta in the Cascade Range has erupted 13 times in the last 10,000 years.

What Is Causing Volcanic Activity?

Why is there volcanic activity in only a few places in northern California? You have learned that along most of the length of California, the Pacific plate is moving slantwise against the North American plate. At the border between the two plates is a system of transform faults, including the San Andreas Fault. As the plates grind past each other, there are many earthquakes. But this kind of plate motion does not form volcanoes.

At the north end of California, the situation is different. Here the process called subduction is taking place. Another ocean plate that geologists call the Gorda plate is sliding beneath the North American plate. Rock material from the Gorda plate is descending toward the mantle. There it is melting and becoming magma. The hot magma is less dense than the surrounding rocks, so it rises toward the surface. There it erupts through cracks in the crust.

Over time, these eruptions have created a line of volcanoes in the North American plate. This line of volcanoes is the Cascade Range. It runs in a north-south direction just inland from the plate subduction zone. The line continues into the states north of California. There it includes Mount Saint Helens, which erupted violently in 1980. Because the subduction process continues today, Lassen Peak and other Cascade volcanoes are still active.

Brain Power

Someday the Gorda plate will finish sliding under North America. What do you think will happen to the Cascade volcanoes then?

Lava that flowed long ago from vents in the ground covered this northern California area with barren rock.

Why Are There Hills in San Francisco?

In San Francisco people use cable cars to travel around the city. People like riding them because the city is built on a series of steep hills. How did the hills get there?

San Francisco is located on the coast, at a gap in the Coast Ranges. When geologists began exploring the hilly landscape, they found an astonishing mix of rocks. For a long time, they were puzzled. How did all those different rocks get there?

Today we know that the answer is plate tectonics. As you have learned, beginning before the age of the dinosaurs, an ocean plate slid slowly beneath North America where California is now. As the plate moved, it carried pieces of crust with it. These crust pieces were jammed against the continent where San Francisco is today.

Some of the ancient crust was formed on the ocean floor. Based on fossil finds, it was probably formed far away, near the Equator. Other crust pieces are the remains of ancient islands.

Where the crust pieces were jammed together, the harder rocks resisted weathering better than the softer ones. The softer ones eroded or fell away in landslides. The harder rocks remained to form the hills of San Francisco and nearby areas. The landscape has a lumpy look. Geologists call it a "melted ice cream" landscape.

San Francisco's steep hills are made of rocks formed as far away as the Equator.

What Lies Beneath Los Angeles?

Much of Los Angeles lies on the floor of a huge basin. To the north are two mountain chains in the Transverse Ranges. They are the Santa Monica Mountains and the San Gabriel Mountains. Across the Santa Monica Mountains is the San Fernando Valley, another huge basin.

The basins were formed about 5 million years ago by the force of plate tectonics. An ocean plate pressing northward against the North American plate pushed up the Transverse Ranges. The land between the ranges was pushed down. In some places the land was pushed below sea level and was covered by the ocean. Ocean sedi-ments collected on the bottom. In time, so much sediment collected that some basins rose back above sea level.

Today the flat Los Angeles basin is like a deep bowl filled with sediment. The sediment is thousands of meters deep. It is so deep that geologists do not know what kind of rock is at the bottom. Heat and pressure acting on the remains of ancient sea creatures in the sediment created pools of petroleum beneath the surface. Drillers removed much of this petroleum in the early 1900s.

Because of tectonic pressures, the basin is also crisscrossed with faults. Many are blind faults, which show no trace at the surface. Scientists believe that one of these blind faults lies beneath downtown Los Angeles.

Precipitation Patterns

HYPOTHESIZE How do California's natural features affect precipitation? Write a hypothesis in your *Science Journal.*

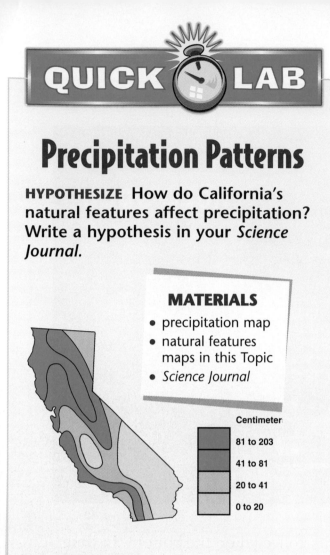

MATERIALS
- precipitation map
- natural features maps in this Topic
- *Science Journal*

Centimeter
	81 to 203
	41 to 81
	20 to 41
	0 to 20

PROCEDURES

1. **OBSERVE** Examine the California precipitation map shown here. Precipitation is heaviest in the dark green areas. In the yellow areas, it rains only rarely.

2. **OBSERVE** Examine the maps in this Topic that show the locations of California's mountains and deserts.

CONCLUDE AND APPLY

DRAW CONCLUSIONS Where are the areas of heaviest precipitation in relation to California's mountains? Where are the areas of lightest precipitation? Write an explanation for this pattern in your *Science Journal.*

Where Are California's Deserts?

Some desert areas in California are less than 200 km (120 miles) from the Pacific Ocean. Why are they so dry?

The answer is that high mountains block almost all ocean moisture from reaching the desert. When moist air from the ocean reaches California's mountains, it is forced upward. It cools, and the moisture falls as precipitation on the western mountain slopes. The result is a **rain shadow** in the deserts to the east. Areas in a rain shadow receive very little moisture. In some years, parts of California's deserts receive no rain at all.

California's deserts cover more land than the state of Ohio. There are desert areas east of the southern Sierra Nevada. The Mojave Desert lies east of Los Angeles, across the San Gabriel Mountains. The Colorado Desert lies east of San Diego and the Imperial Valley, beyond the Peninsular Ranges.

GEOGRAPHY LINK

In the deserts east of the southern Sierra Nevada is Death Valley. In this area, tectonic forces are stretching Earth's crust from side to side. As a result, the floor of the Valley has sunk very low. It is 86 meters (282 ft) below sea level.

In some desert areas there are fields of dunes. **Dunes** are mounds of sand created by blowing winds. Some of these dunes are as high as 183 meters (600 ft).

The hottest temperature ever recorded in the Western Hemisphere was at Death Valley in the California desert.

WHY IT MATTERS

California is where you live. Every day, you walk or ride through some part of the California landscape. You may see one of the great mountain ranges. You may see the desert. You may see a city built on hills or spread out across a vast basin. Wherever you are, you are in a landscape that has been shaped by plate tectonics. That force is still active. It will shape the California you live in tomorrow.

REVIEW

1. What geologic process created the Sierra Nevada and the Coast Ranges?

2. Where in California do most earthquakes occur?

3. **COMPARE AND CONTRAST** How do the Sierra Nevada and Coast Ranges differ from the Transverse Ranges of southern California?

4. What process is producing volcanoes in the far north of California?

5. **CRITICAL THINKING** *Analyze* Why might it be less dangerous to live along a part of the San Andreas Fault where there are many small earthquakes?

WHY IT MATTERS THINK ABOUT IT Is it a good idea to know where geologic faults are located? Why or why not?

WHY IT MATTERS WRITE ABOUT IT What if you were moving into a new house near an active fault. What questions would you ask a geologist about the fault?

READING SKILL
Write a paragraph to explain the sequence of events in the formation of San Francisco's famous hills.

THE WORLD'S MOST FAMOUS FAULT!

Which is the world's most famous geologic fault? It is most likely the San Andreas fault, right here in California! How would you like to take a trip along the entire 1,350-km (850-mile) length of this great crack in Earth's crust?

Your trip would start in northern California near Cape Mendocino, over 320 km (200 miles) north of San Francisco. Here the San Andreas is mostly offshore, running alongside the coast. Quakes in this area have been known to lift the shoreline more than 1 meter (3 ft) at a time, leaving clams and mussels high and dry.

Farther south, the San Andreas passes the epicenter of the great 1906 earthquake, offshore just west of San Francisco. Then it comes on shore and goes right through the Bay area, home to 6 million people.

Here it is visible in a series of straight-line valleys. In the Santa Cruz Mountains south of the Bay it passes the epicenter of the 1989 Loma Prieta earthquake.

In central California the San Andreas runs south across an empty, grassy plain. Here the break in Earth's crust is so easy to see that you can spot it from an airplane! This is the region where many small quakes are thought to be easing pressure on the fault. The little town of Parkfield has been shaken by quakes every 22 years on average since 1881. As the San Andreas approaches southern California, it curves away to the southeast. At Fort Tejon, northwest of Los Angeles, it passes the

In central California, the San Andreas is visible from airplanes.

Geography Link

center of the great 1857 quake. That quake caused the ground to move as much as 9 meters (29 ft)! Beyond Fort Tejon the San Andreas is part of a whole fault system running through the various Transverse Ranges. The San Andreas passes approximately 55 km (40 miles) northeast of Los Angeles, then turns southward again. Geologists have learned that this segment of the San Andreas experiences a major quake on average every 132 years. That is less time than has passed since the Fort Tejon quake!

The San Andreas fault begins near Cape Mendocino in northern California.

Southeast of Los Angeles the San Andreas passes under the Imperial Valley. This is another area of frequent earthquakes. Your trip along the San Andreas would finally end when the fault passes into Mexico and under the Gulf of California.

DISCUSSION STARTER

1. Why do geologists find Parkfield a good place to study the San Andreas fault?

2. Is there a reason to expect a major quake on the southern San Andreas? Why or why not?

To learn more about faults, visit *www.mhschool.com/science* and enter the keyword ANDREAS.

*inter*NET
CONNECTION

WHY IT MATTERS

Maps show features of the surface you live on.

SCIENCE WORDS

shaded relief map a map that shows elevatio`s of Earth's surface by shadows and colors

topographic map a map that shows features of Earth's surface as a pattern of lines

contour line a line on a topographic map that connects points with the same elevation

contour interval the difference in elevation between side-by- side contour lines on a topographic map

map legend table of symbols used on a map

map scale compares a distance on the map with the distance on Earth's surface

geologic map a map that shows the types and positions of rocks at and below Earth's surface

Mapping the Land

Did you ever gaze down into a deep canyon or look up at a mountain top? Canyons and mountains show that Earth's surface can change dramatically from one place to another. Looking at a vast plain shows you something else. At some places, Earth's surface is relatively flat.

Photographs show some features of Earth's surface. Maps do, too. What features of Earth's surface would you show on a map?

HYPOTHESIZE Make a list of the features you would show on a map of Earth's surface. How would you show these features? How would you show differences between them? Write a hypothesis in your *Science Journal.* Test your idea.

Investigate Features of Earth's Surface

Use a road map to see how natural features affect human-made ones.

PROCEDURES

1. CLASSIFY Find at least five different kinds of natural features, like rivers, on your map. List them in your *Science Journal*, under the title "Natural Features." Then do the same for at least five human-made features like roads.

2. Many mountain roads have sharp curves and zigzags. Find an example on your map. Write down the road's name or highway number, and its location, in your *Science Journal*.

3. INFER What might the curvy road tell you about Earth's surface there?

4. INFER Find a straight road. Write down its name or number. What does the straightness of this road tell you about Earth's surface there?

5. Some rivers have roads running alongside them. Find an example on your map. Record the names of the river and the road, and their location, in your *Science Journal*. Why do you think road builders locate roads alongside rivers?

CONCLUDE AND APPLY

1. DRAW CONCLUSIONS What are some ways in which natural features of Earth's surface affect the construction of human-made ones?

GOING FURTHER: Problem Solving

2. Imagine riding along the road near the river. Describe what you would see. Which side would the river be on? Would you be going uphill or down?

MATERIALS
- road map
- pencil
- *Science Journal*

What Maps Show Surface Features of Earth?

Mountains, valleys, and plains are surface features of Earth. One characteristic that all surface features have is elevation. *Elevation* is the height of a location above sea level. A mountain peak has a high elevation.

The elevation farther down the mountain is less. The elevations along a mountain range quickly change from peak to peak. Valleys are found between mountains. They are land areas at low elevations. Plains are large areas of flat land at where changes in elevation are small.

Two types of maps show the shape of surface features of Earth's by their elevation. One type of map is a shaded relief map. The other type of map that shows surface features is a topographic (top'ə graf'ik) map.

Maps can be drawn to show the elevation of surface features such as these plains and mountains.

What Does a Shaded Relief Map of California Look Like?

A **shaded relief map** is a map that shows elevations of Earth's surface features by shading and color. Shading shows changes in elevations. Individual colors show locations that have the same elevation.

California has high mountain ranges in the north, south, east, and west. It has valleys and deserts. Its rugged western coastline faces the Pacific Ocean.

A relief map must show these features, as well as others. Here is a shaded relief map of California. The map shows several different kinds of information about the land features of California. Notice that brown is used to represent higher elevations. What do the more darkly shaded areas of brown represent?

SHADED RELIEF MAP OF CALIFORNIA

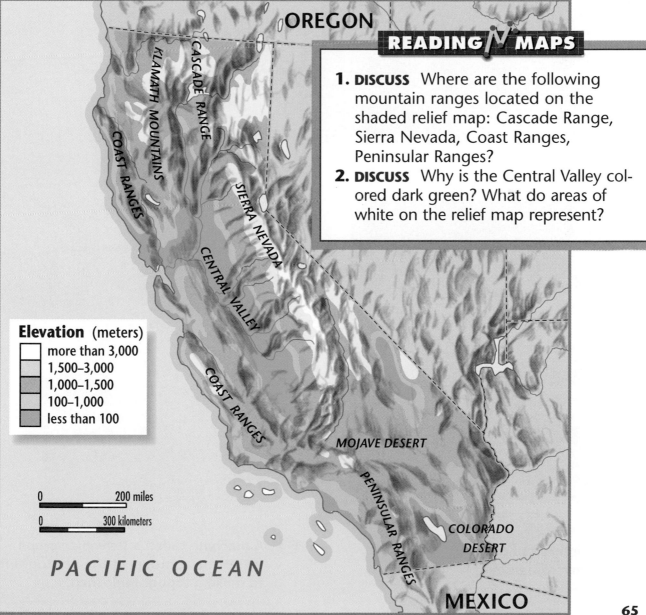

READING MAPS

1. **DISCUSS** Where are the following mountain ranges located on the shaded relief map: Cascade Range, Sierra Nevada, Coast Ranges, Peninsular Ranges?
2. **DISCUSS** Why is the Central Valley colored dark green? What do areas of white on the relief map represent?

OREGON

KLAMATH MOUNTAINS

CASCADE RANGE

COAST RANGES

SIERRA NEVADA

CENTRAL VALLEY

Elevation (meters)

more than 3,000
1,500–3,000
1,000–1,500
100–1,000
less than 100

COAST RANGES

MOJAVE DESERT

PENINSULAR RANGES

COLORADO DESERT

0   200 miles

0   300 kilometers

PACIFIC OCEAN

MEXICO

How Does a Topographic Map Show Elevation?

To show the elevation of different parts of the land, geologists use a special kind of map called a **topographic map**. A topographic map shows elevations of surface features as a pattern of lines. The diagrams on this page show how a topographic map is made.

Each of the lines that make up the pattern is called a **contour line**. Each contour line connects points on the surface with the same elevation. Each brown line on a topographic map is a contour line.

BUILDING A TOPOGRAPHIC MAP

1 The area to be mapped is Point Reyes, California.

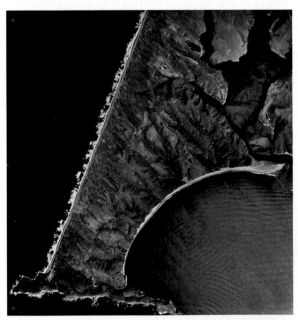

Source: USGS

2 An infared photo is taken from above.

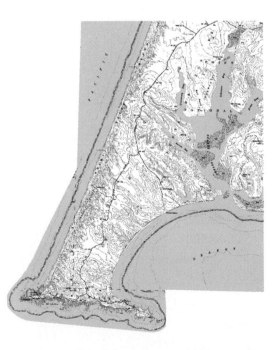

3 A machine called a *stereoplanigraph* traces the contours of the photograph to make a topographic map.

Look at the topographic map below. The contour lines are labeled 5, 10, 15, and 20 meters. The change in elevation between side-by-side contour lines on the map is 5 meters (16 feet). On the island, you would have to climb up 5 meters to go from A to B. You would have to climb down 5 meters to go from A to C.

The change in elevation between side-by-side contour lines is called the **contour interval**. On maps of mountains, the contour interval might be 50 meters (160 feet). On maps of plains and valleys, the contour interval may be as small as 10 meters (33 ft).

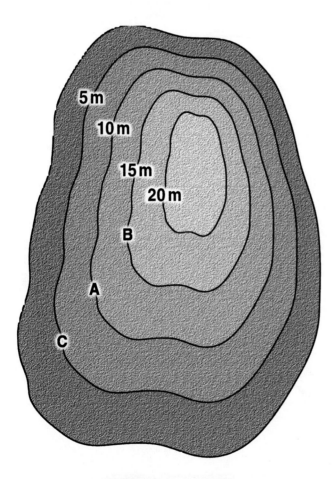

This map shows a contour interval of 5 meters.

Models of Earth's Surface

HYPOTHESIZE How can you use topographic maps to build models of Earth's surface? Write a hypothesis in your *Science Journal.*

MATERIALS
- tracing paper
- pencil
- cardboard
- scissors
- *Science Journal*

PROCEDURES

SAFETY Be careful using scissors.

1. Trace each numbered contour line in the map on this page left onto a separate part of the tracing paper.

2. Cut out each shape. Trace each shape onto the cardboard and cut it out.

3. **MAKE A MODEL** Stack the cardboard pieces in order from largest to smallest on the topographic map.

CONCLUDE AND APPLY

1. **INFER** What does the thickness of the cardboard represent?

2. **COMPARE AND CONTRAST** Compare the slope of the island at different places. Compare the closeness of the contour lines on the map at each place. In your *Science Journal*, write what you observe.

3. Do the steep slopes and flat areas in your model match your hypothesis?

What Do Contour Lines Show?

Contour lines show the elevation of a part of a surface feature. These lines also reveal the shape of the feature at that particular elevation. When contour lines are seen together, they give you a kind of "flat picture" of the feature. In the Quick Lab, you worked backward from the map to construct the shape of the island as it would appear in 3-dimensional space.

Contour lines follow these rules:
- A contour line always makes a closed shape.
- Any contour line that is open on one map continues onto the next map.
- Any contour line inside a closed contour line has a higher elevation.
- Contour lines do not cross.
- The contour interval on a map never changes.
- The elevation of a single location, such as a peak, may be given.

TOPOGRAPHIC MAP

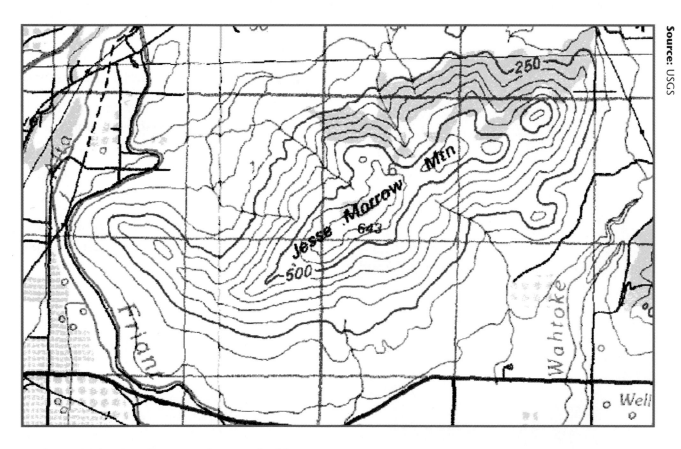

Source: USGS

Scale: 1:100 000 Contour Interval: 50 meters

Brain Power
Look at the map. What is the elevation of the top of Jesse Morrow Mountain?

How Are Index Contour Lines Used?

The elevations of many of the contour lines are not shown. Only *index contour lines* are marked with elevations. You can use the index contour lines to find the elevation of the other contour lines. Use these steps:

1. Find the elevation of the nearest index contour line that wraps around the line.

2. Count the number of contour intervals it is away from the index contour line.

3. Multiply the contour interval by the number of contour intervals.

4. Add the distance from step 3 to the elevation from step 1.

Locate the index contour line marked "250". This line wraps around other contour lines. What is the elevation of the third contour line inside this index contour line? Calculate following the steps as given. Here is what you should get as each step of the process.

1. 250 meters

2. 3 contour intervals

3. 50 meters (contour interval)
   $\times\ 3$
   150 meters

4. 250 meters
   $+\ 150$ meters
   400 meters

Symbols on Topographic Maps

Topographic maps use symbols to show both natural and constructed features. The symbols used in a map are given in a table called a **map legend.** Most topographic maps use the same set of symbols.

Primary highway	
Secondary highway	
Light duty road, principal street	
Other road or street; trail	
Route marker; Interstate; U.S.; State	
Railroad; standard gage narrow gage	
Bridge; overpass; underpass	
Tunnel; road; railroad	
Built up area; locality; elevation	·155
Airport; landing field; landing strip	
National boundary	
State boundary	
County boundary	
National or State reservation boundary	
Land grant boundary	
U.S. public lands survey; range, township; section	
Range, township; section line; protracted	
Power transmission line; pipeline	
Dam; dam with lock	
Cemetery; building	
Windmill; water well; spring	
Mine shaft; adit or cave; mine, quarry; gravel pit	
Campground; picnic area; U.S. location monument	
Ruins; cliff dwelling	
Distorted surface: strip mine, lava; sand	
Contours: index; intermediate; supplementary	
Stream, lake	
Rapids, large and small; falls, large and small	
Marsh, swamp	
Land subject to controlled inundation; woodland	

Source: USGS

Topographic maps use symbols such as these to show natural and constructed features.

How Does a Topographic Map Show Distance?

A topographic map shows distance with a map scale. A **map scale** compares a distance on the map with the actual distance on Earth's surface.

On many topographic maps the scale is written as follows: 1:100 000. These numbers mean that 1 distance unit on the map represents 100,000 of the same distance units on Earth's surface. For example, one centimeter on the map represents 100,000 centimeters on Earth's surface. A distance of 100,000 centimeters is one kilometer. Using this map scale, *one centimeter on the map represents 1 kilometer on the ground.*

TOPOGRAPHIC MAP, SONOMA, CALIFORNIA (1:100 000)

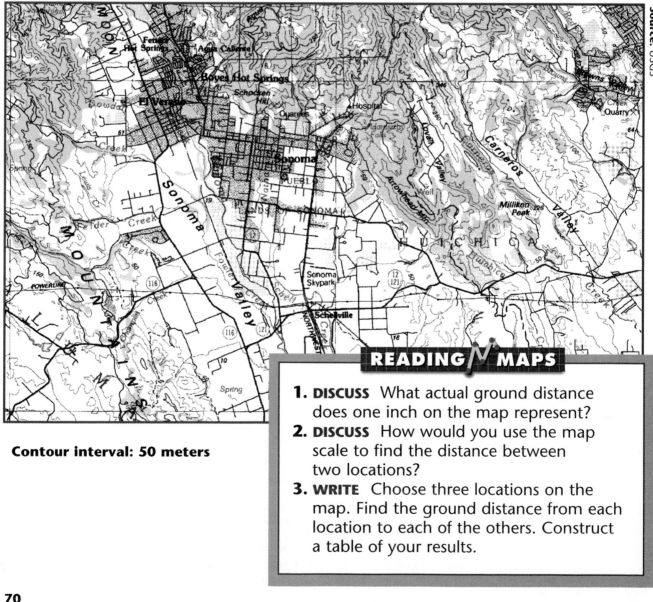

Source: USGS

Contour interval: 50 meters

READING MAPS

1. **DISCUSS** What actual ground distance does one inch on the map represent?
2. **DISCUSS** How would you use the map scale to find the distance between two locations?
3. **WRITE** Choose three locations on the map. Find the ground distance from each location to each of the others. Construct a table of your results.

How Do Maps with Different Map Scales Compare?

The map on page 70 and the map on this page both show Sonoma, California, and the land surrounding it. Yet the two maps appear different. The reason is that they are drawn to different map scales. The map on page 70 has a scale of 1:100 000. The map on this page has a scale of 1:24 000. A distance of 1 km on Earth is shown as a little more than 4 cm on this map. This map scale is larger than the one on page 700. A map with a *large map scale* will show many details in a small area.

Some maps have a map scale of 1: 500 000. On this kind of map, one kilometer on the ground is shown as 0.2 centimeter. This scale is a small map scale. A map with a *small map scale* will show fewer details in a large area.

TOPOGRAPHIC MAP, SONOMA, CALIFORNIA (1:24 000)

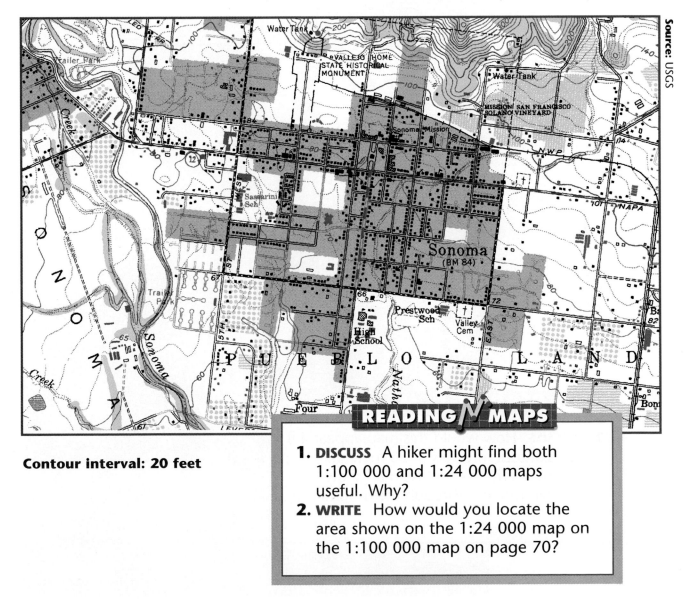

Source: USGS

Contour interval: 20 feet

READING MAPS

1. **DISCUSS** A hiker might find both 1:100 000 and 1:24 000 maps useful. Why?
2. **WRITE** How would you locate the area shown on the 1:24 000 map on the 1:100 000 map on page 70?

How Do Mountains Appear on Topographic Maps?

The pattern of contour lines on this map tells you a great deal about the surface features it maps. The contour lines are closely spaced. This kind of spacing indicates that the land is steeply sloped.

The grouping of the contour lines shows individual mountain peaks. The mountains shown here are part of the Trinity Alps, in the Klamath Mountains.

The map shows streams running through the mountains. Contour lines that pass across a stream are drawn with a small V-shaped arrowhead. The tip of the arrowhead points upstream.

TOPOGRAPHIC MAP, TRINITY ALPS

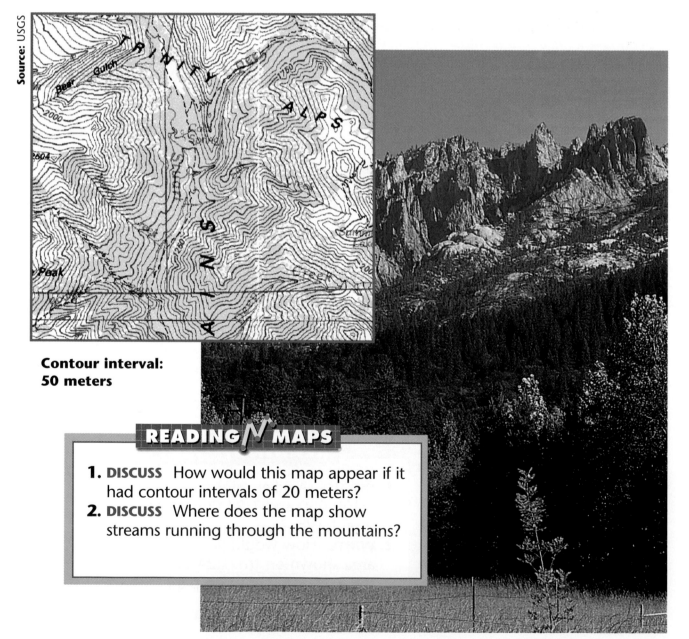

Source: USGS

Contour interval: 50 meters

READING N MAPS

1. **DISCUSS** How would this map appear if it had contour intervals of 20 meters?
2. **DISCUSS** Where does the map show streams running through the mountains?

How Do Valleys Appear on Topographic Maps?

Study the topographic map shown below. What do the contour intervals tell you about the land that is mapped?

The first thing to notice is that the contour lines are widely spaced. Also, the contour interval is much smaller than on the map at the bottom of page 72. From the distance between the lines and the small contour interval, you can conclude that the land is gently sloped.

This map shows an area of land that is gently sloped. The map is, in fact, a topographic map of part of California's Central Valley.

TOPOGRAPHIC MAP, CENTRAL VALLEY

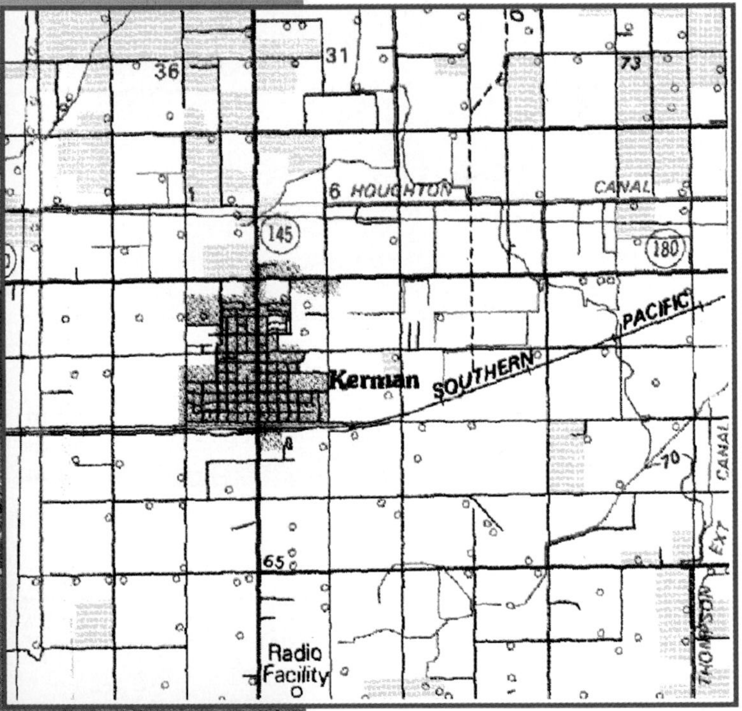

Contour interval: 10 meters

READING N MAPS

1. **DISCUSS** How would this map appear if the contour interval was greater?
2. **WRITE** What do the circles on the map represent? What clue does that give you about how this land is being used?

What Map Shows Features Beneath Earth's Surface?

Can maps show what Earth is like below the surface? You have learned that the twists and turns of layers of rock give scientists evidence that Earth's crust is moving. The nature of other rock formations gives geologists clues about past earthquakes and volcanic activity.

A map that shows rock formations is called a **geologic map.** Geologic maps show the types and positions of rocks at and below Earth's surface. Here are two examples of geologic maps.

GEOLOGIC MAPS

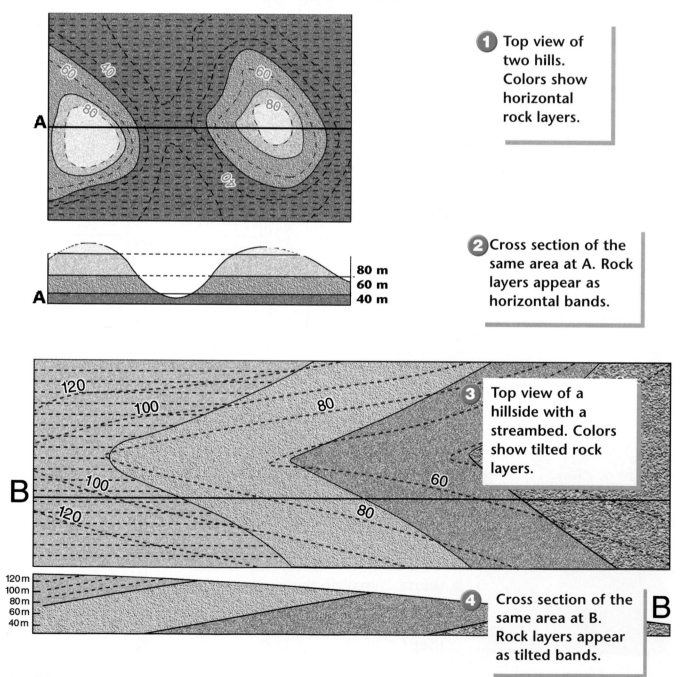

1 Top view of two hills. Colors show horizontal rock layers.

2 Cross section of the same area at A. Rock layers appear as horizontal bands.

80 m
60 m
40 m

3 Top view of a hillside with a streambed. Colors show tilted rock layers.

4 Cross section of the same area at B. Rock layers appear as tilted bands.

120m
100m
80m
60m
40m

A geologic cross section is a view of a vertical slice through Earth's surface. The cross section gives a picture of the rock layers that lie underground.

Geologic maps and cross sections show the position of these layers. The maps also have a special legend to identify the type and age of rocks, using colors. Lighter colors indicate younger rocks. The darker the color, the older the rock.

Maps are models of Earth's surface. They help you picture your surroundings. You can use them to help plan a long car ride or a short hiking trip.

Maps show the arrangement of things on the Earth's surface. They show where cities and towns, mountains and valleys, streams and rock formations are.

Private companies and government agencies use topographic maps to plan and build communities, highway projects, and nature preserves. Geologists use geologic maps to find new sources of minerals and fuels.

REVIEW

1. How does a shaded relief map differ from a topographic map?

2. What does a contour line show about a surface feature?

3. What is a geologic map?

4. USE NUMBERS Map A has a map scale on 1:18 000. Map B has a map scale of 1:40 000. On which map will a ground distance of one kilometer appear larger? Explain.

5. CRITICAL THINKING *Analyze* Why isn't a contour line on a topographic map drawn for every elevation?

WHY IT MATTERS THINK ABOUT IT In what outdoor recreations might you use a topographic map?

WHY IT MATTERS WRITE ABOUT IT Write a plan for making a topographic map of your neighborhood. The plan should include the map scale and why you chose it. Explain why you chose particular contour intervals. Describe what you would include in the map legend and why.

READING SKILL *Compare and Contrast* Compare two maps shown in this topic.

SCIENCE MAGAZINE

WATERY CANYON

A topographic map of surfaces covered by sea water is called a *bathymetric* (bath'ə met'rik) map.

California has a canyon that is deeper in places than the Grand Canyon. But you can't look over its rim, because the canyon is under water.

The Monterey Canyon starts a kilometer off the California coast near Monterey. At places its depth is 3,650 meters (11,970 ft). The canyon is home to many types of sea life.

The Monterey Canyon is a submerged gorge—deep and winding.

Santa Cruz

N

−500

−1000

−1500

−2000

Monterey

km

0   10

contour interval 50 m

DISCUSSION STARTER

1. What do the negative numbers mean on the index contour lines on the map?

2. Who would use bathymetric maps? Why?

To learn more about Monterey Canyon, visit *www.mhschool.com/science* and enter the keyword MAP.

*inter*NET
CONNECTION

SCIENCE WORDS

active fault p. 52

blind fault p. 52

contour line p. 66

dune p. 59

geologic map p. 74

map legend p. 69

map scale p. 70

rain shadow p. 58

shaded relief map p. 65

topographic map p. 66

USING SCIENCE WORDS

Number a paper from 1 to 10. Fill in 1 to 5 with words from the list above.

1. A(n) ___?___ shows features of Earth's surface as a pattern of lines.

2. Symbols used on a map are listed in a(n) ___?___.

3. A mound of sand created by blowing winds is called a(n) ___?___.

4. The effect created when mountains block the passage of moist air is called a(n) ___?___.

5. The types and positions of rocks at and below Earth's surface are shown on a(n) ___?___.

6–10. Pick five words from the list above that were not used in 1 to 5, and use each in a sentence.

UNDERSTANDING SCIENCE IDEAS

11. What is the meaning of a map scale that reads "1 : 100 000"?

12. Which of the following map scales would show more details: 1 : 24 000 or 1 : 500 000?

13. Explain how plate tectonics created the Transverse Ranges of southern California.

14. Describe the geologic process that has created the San Andreas fault.

15. Explain why California's deserts are so dry.

USING IDEAS AND SKILLS

16. Why could a blind fault be very dangerous to people living nearby?

17. Why are there active volcanoes today in northern California but not in southern California?

18. **INFER** On a topographic map, contour lines make a V-shaped arrowhead pointing to the west. What is most likely being shown?

19. **READING SKILL: COMPARE AND CONTRAST** How would a topographic map and a geologic map of the same area be the same? How would they be different?

20. **THINKING LIKE A SCIENTIST** Geologists make careful records of earthquakes along the San Andreas fault system. Why are these records important?

PROBLEMS and PUZZLES

Mapping to Scale Imagine a room that measures 20 feet (6.1 meters) wide by 30 feet (9.2 meters) long. How can you draw an accurate scale outline map of the room? What scale will let you fit your map on a standard size sheet of paper? Determine your scale. Then, using a ruler, draw your map. Be sure to include your scale on your map!

UNIT 1 REVIEW

SCIENCE WORDS

active fault p. 52	**epicenter** p. 20
aftershock p. 20	**lava** p. 35
blind fault p. 52	**magma** p. 6
contour line p. 66	**mantle** p. 9
crust p. 4	**map scale** p. 70

USING SCIENCE WORDS

Number a paper from 1 to 10. Beside each number write the word or words that best complete the sentence.

1. The solid part of Earth's surface is called the __?__.

2. __?__ is hot, melted rock below Earth's crust.

3. The place where an earthquake originates is its __?__.

4. Small quakes or jolts that follow an earthquake are called __?__.

5. Magma is called __?__ once it erupts from a volcano.

6. A crack in Earth's surface where earthquakes take place is a(n) __?__.

7. A __?__ compares a distance on a map with the distance on Earth's surface.

8. A crack in Earth's crust that is not visible on Earth's surface is called a(n) __?__.

9. A line on a topographic map that connects points with the same elevation is called a(n) __?__.

10. Earth's layer beneath the crust is called the __?__.

UNDERSTANDING SCIENCE IDEAS

Write 11 to 15. For each number write the letter for the best answer. You may wish to use the hints provided.

11. The matching shapes of continents' edges is evidence of
    a. geothermal energy
    b. rain shadows
    c. continental drift
    d. sea-floor spreading
    (Hint: Read pages 4–9.)

12. The sliding of plates past each other produces
    a. earthquakes
    b. volcanoes
    c. craters
    d. continental drift
    (Hint: Read page 11.)

13. Volcanoes are most likely to occur
    a. along the edges of plates
    b. in the center of plates
    c. in mountain ranges
    d. anywhere at random
    (Hint: Read page 34.)

14. A topographic map of steep mountain slopes shows
    a. widely spaced contour lines
    b. elevations by shadows and colors
    c. closely spaced contour lines
    d. the rocks at and below Earth's surface
    (Hint: Read page 72.)

15. Most major California earthquakes occur
    a. in the Sierra Nevada
    b. in the Los Angeles area
    c. at blind faults
    d. at faults in the San Andreas system
    (Hint: Read page 52.)

USING IDEAS AND SKILLS

16. What causes sea-floor spreading?

17. **HYPOTHESIZE** What evidence did Alfred Wegener claim was support for his hypothesis of the origins of the continents?

18. What are three kinds of seismic waves?

19. What is the relationship between the magnitude of earthquakes and the number of earthquakes at different magnitudes?

20. Draw a diagram of a volcano and label the important features.

21. What is geothermal energy? How is it being used?

22. On a topographic map, how would the contour lines showing the Sierra Nevada differ from those showing the Central Valley?

23. How have fossils from the floor of tropical oceans ended up in hills near San Francisco?

THINKING LIKE A SCIENTIST

24. **USE VARIABLES** Each increase of 1 on the Richter Scale represents an increase of 30 times the earthquake energy released. What does an increase of 2 represent?

25. **USE VARIABLES** Explain why the time lag between the P waves and the S waves generated by an earthquake gets larger the farther away you are from the epicenter.

WRITING IN YOUR JOURNAL

SCIENCE IN YOUR LIFE
Are earthquakes likely in your part of California? Why or why not?

PRODUCT ADS
Describe the kinds of designs and materials that can make a building better able to survive an earthquake. Which are better, rigid materials or flexible ones? Why?

HOW SCIENTISTS WORK
In this unit you learned about how plate tectonics reshapes oceans and continents. Scientists must often use models to study these changes. Why is the use of models necessary?

Design your own Experiment

Determine a way to model earthquakes on a tabletop. Check with your teacher before carrying out the experiment.

interNET CONNECTION

For help in reviewing this unit, visit *www.mhschool.com/science*

PROBLEMS and PUZZLES

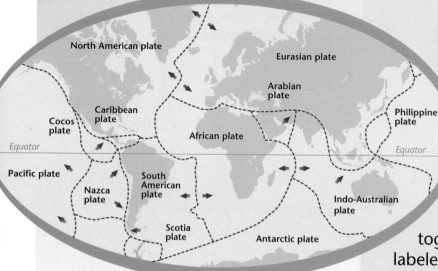

North American plate

Eurasian plate

Arabian plate

Caribbean plate

Cocos plate

Philippine plate

Equator

African plate

Equator

Pacific plate

Nazca plate

South American plate

Indo-Australian plate

Scotia plate

Antarctic plate

Sea-Floor Model

Sea-floor spreading creates new rock layers. To find out why the youngest rock layers are closest to the ocean ridge, make the model shown.

Tape two pieces of paper together. Divide the paper into labeled sections about 3 centimeters wide, as shown. The paper represents layers of molten rock that come out of the sea floor. Place the paper between two desks or other surfaces. Pull the paper up slowly, as shown. Which rock layers appear last? Which rock layers are youngest?

Future Plates

Two hundred million years ago, Earth's continents combined to form Pangea. What will Earth look like 200 million years from now? Trace the continents and plates on this map. Cut out each plate separately. Then make a model of the positions of the continents in 200 million years. The red arrows show the direction in which each plate is moving.

City on the Move

The Pacific plate, sliding against the North American plate in California, is slowly carrying Los Angeles northward. The city is traveling at an average rate of 1 mile every 60,000 years. Someday it will reach San Francisco. How far will it travel in 6 million years? In how many years will it be halfway to San Francisco? In how many years will it cover the whole distance? Use the data given below to find the answer.

Distance from Los Angeles to San Francisco: 380 miles

SHAPING EARTH'S SURFACE

CHAPTER 3

HOW EARTH CHANGES OVER TIME

Mountains give you a pretty good view of Earth, your home. Why are mountains as tall as they are? Will they always be as tall? How do wind, water, and ice affect them?

Mountains and other landscape features change over time. In their form and structure, scientists find clues to events in their history.

In Chapter 3 you will be reading about the order, or sequence, in which these events have happened.

Topic
EARTH SCIENCE
1

WHY IT MATTERS

Soil is needed for things to grow.

SCIENCE WORDS

fold mountain a mountain made mostly of rock layers folded by being squeezed together

fault-block mountain a mountain made by huge tilted blocks of rocks separated from surrounding rocks by faults

weathering the breaking down of rocks into smaller pieces by natural processes

erosion the picking up and removal of rock particles

soil a mixture of weathered rock, decayed plant and animal matter, living things, air, and water

soil horizon any of the layers of soil from the surface to the bedrock below

humus material in soil formed by the breakdown of plant and animal material

groundwater water that soaks into soil and rock by collecting in spaces between rock particles

Building Up and Breaking Down

Have you ever seen mountains in the distance? Up close? From above in a jet? In movies? What shapes do they have? Are the shapes alike or different? Why do you think mountains have the shapes they have?

For example, here are two mountains that look very different from each other. What kinds of processes form mountains such as these? Are there different processes at work forming different kinds of mountains?

EXPLORE

HYPOTHESIZE What kinds of processes could make mountains? Can different processes produce different kinds of mountains? Write a hypothesis in your *Science Journal.* Test your ideas.

Investigate How a Mountain Is Made

Use a model to infer how mountains can be made.

MATERIALS

- waxed paper
- clay
- 2 sturdy wooden rulers
- scissors
- plastic knife (optional)
- *Science Journal*

PROCEDURES

SAFETY Be careful with sharp objects.

1. **MAKE A MODEL** Use the clay to make four thin (0.5-cm thick) square layers. They should be the same size (about 6–8 cm on a side).

2. **COMMUNICATE** Stack the four layers. Pinch them together along opposite sides. Place them on a sheet of waxed paper cut to fit the bottom of the layers. In your *Science Journal*, draw a picture of the clay layers.

3. Place the waxed paper and clay on the table. You need to see the layers. Place the pinched-together sides of the clay against the two rulers.

4. **COMPARE** Slowly move one ruler toward the other. Observe what happens. Draw a picture of the results.

CONCLUDE AND APPLY

1. **OBSERVE** What happened to the clay as you moved the ruler?

2. **DRAW CONCLUSIONS** What does this result tell you about what happens when bendable objects are squeezed from both sides?

3. **INFER** Can rocks bend? How do you know?

GOING FURTHER: Problem Solving

4. **USE VARIABLES** What if a fault (crack) had been cut through the layers before they were squeezed? How might your results differ?

How Is a Mountain Made?

As the crust moves, the rocks of the crust can change. They can change position. They can move up, down, or sideways. Rocks can also change their shape. They can be bent, squeezed, twisted, or broken. These changes can cause different types of features to be made. The Explore Activity showed one example of how this happens.

The most common type of mountain is a **fold mountain**. A fold mountain is a mountain made mostly of rock layers folded by being squeezed together.

A **fault-block mountain** is a mountain made by huge tilted blocks of rocks separated from surrounding rock by faults. A fault is a large crack in rocks along which there is movement.

FAULT-BLOCK MOUNTAINS

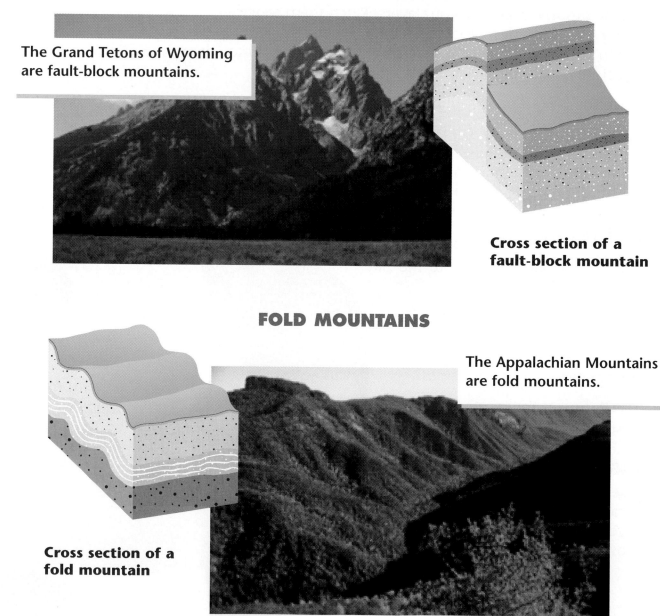

The Grand Tetons of Wyoming are fault-block mountains.

Cross section of a fault-block mountain

FOLD MOUNTAINS

The Appalachian Mountains are fold mountains.

Cross section of a fold mountain

Other Landforms

Another landform created by crustal movement is a *plateau* (pla tō′). A plateau is a large area of flat land at a high elevation.

Plateaus are often found next to mountain ranges. They were probably raised by the same forces that formed the mountains. However, the rock plateaus were not folded and faulted as greatly as the rocks of mountains. Rock layers in a plateau are horizontal. However, the surface of a plateau is often not level. Streams cut deep valleys and canyons into a plateau. The Grand Canyon was formed this way.

A plateau is different from a plain. A plain is a large area of flat land at a low elevation.

At the same time that these forces are building up the crust, other forces are breaking down the crust. The two main forces that are breaking down the crust are **weathering** and **erosion**. Weathering is the breaking down of rocks into smaller pieces by natural processes. Erosion is the picking up and removal of rock fragments and other particles.

These forces work as a kind of balancing act. As land is lifted up, it is being broken down. Land gets higher in elevation when it lifts up faster than it gets broken down.

A PLATEAU AND RELATED STRUCTURES

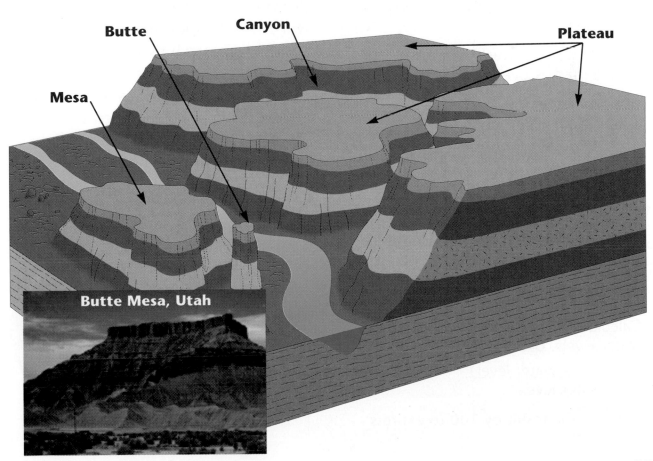

Butte

Canyon

Plateau

Mesa

Butte Mesa, Utah

Freezing

HYPOTHESIZE What happens to water when it freezes? Write a hypothesis in your *Science Journal*.

MATERIALS

- 2 identical plastic jars with screw tops
- marking pencil
- metric ruler
- water
- plastic bags
- twist ties
- *Science Journal*

PROCEDURES

1. Starting with 0 on the bottom, make marks at 1-cm intervals up the side of each jar.

2. Fill each jar with water exactly to the 10-cm mark. Cover each jar.

3. **USE VARIABLES** Put each jar in its own plastic bag. Overnight put one jar in the freezer and the other on the counter.

CONCLUDE AND APPLY

1. **COMPARE AND CONTRAST** Compare the appearance of the water and the water level in each jar. In your *Science Journal*, write what you find.

2. Calculate the percent change in the water levels. Use the formula

$$\frac{(\text{ice level} - \text{water level})}{\text{water level}}$$

Multiply the result by 100 to express as a percent.

What Breaks Down Rocks?

Weathering is not one process, but many. Rocks are broken down by physical and chemical changes. *Mechanical weathering* is the breaking down of rock by physical changes. Frost action, abrasion in moving water, and the actions of plants and animals are some examples.

Frost action, or the repeated freezing and thawing of water, breaks rock apart. When water seeps into cracks in rock and then freezes, it expands. The expanding ice forces apart the cracks. Then the ice melts, and the water seeps in deeper. The next freeze widens the cracks even more.

The growth of plant roots in cracks in rock also breaks the rock apart. Burrowing animals such as ants, earthworms, and moles turn over the soil. This exposes fresh rock to weathering processes. Moving water transports pieces of broken rock. As the water churns through rapids or crashes against shores, pieces of rock collide and crumble into smaller pieces.

Tree roots can break apart rock.

What Is Chemical Weathering?

Chemical weathering breaks down rocks by changing their composition. Oxidation and the action of acids are important chemical weathering processes.

Air contains oxygen. Rocks that are exposed to air can react with the oxygen in it. Many rocks contain iron. When oxygen combines with the iron in a rock, rust can form. This weakens the rock's structure, making it easier to break apart.

The air also contains water and carbon dioxide. When carbon dioxide combines with water, carbonic acid is formed. Carbonic acid reacts with some minerals. It can completely dissolve the mineral calcite, found in limestone, marble, and other rocks. Water with carbonic acid that seeped into the ground dissolved limestone, forming this large cavern. Water and carbon dioxide also dissolve the rock to create holes beneath a stream.

CAVERN FORMATION

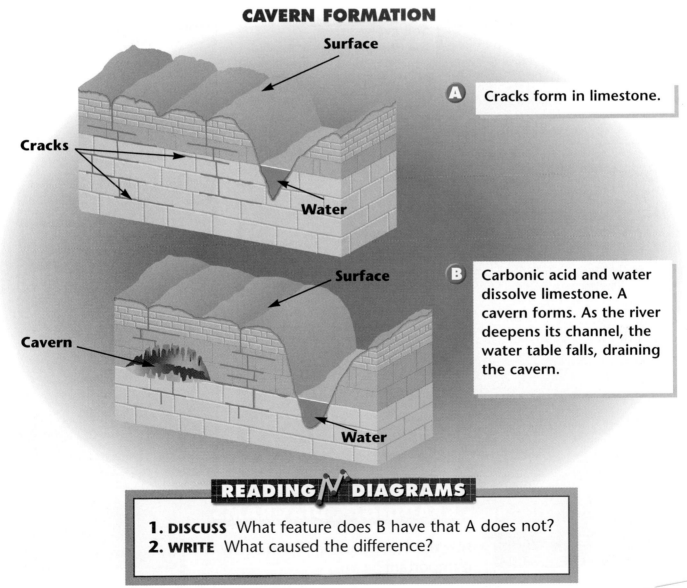

Surface

A Cracks form in limestone.

Cracks

Water

Surface

Cavern

B Carbonic acid and water dissolve limestone. A cavern forms. As the river deepens its channel, the water table falls, draining the cavern.

Water

READING /N/ DIAGRAMS

1. **DISCUSS** What feature does B have that A does not?
2. **WRITE** What caused the difference?

What Is Soil?

The end result of weathering is soil. **Soil** is loose, weathered rock that can support the growth of rooted plants. Soil is a mixture of weathered rock, humus, air, water, and living things. **Humus**, decayed plant and animal remains, is the main source of nutrients for plant growth.

Soil takes thousands of years to form. The first step is the weathering of rock. The rock that a soil forms from is called its parent material. Then plants and animals grow in and on the soil. When they die their remains enrich the soil. Over time the rock in soil breaks down into smaller and smaller pieces. Rainfall after rainfall seeps down through the soil.

Soil is a mixture of weathered rock and organic matter.

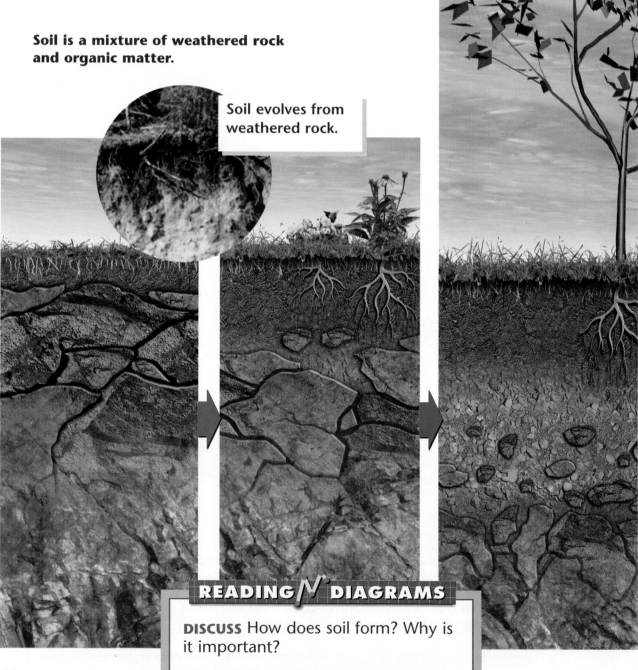

Soil evolves from weathered rock.

READING DIAGRAMS

DISCUSS How does soil form? Why is it important?

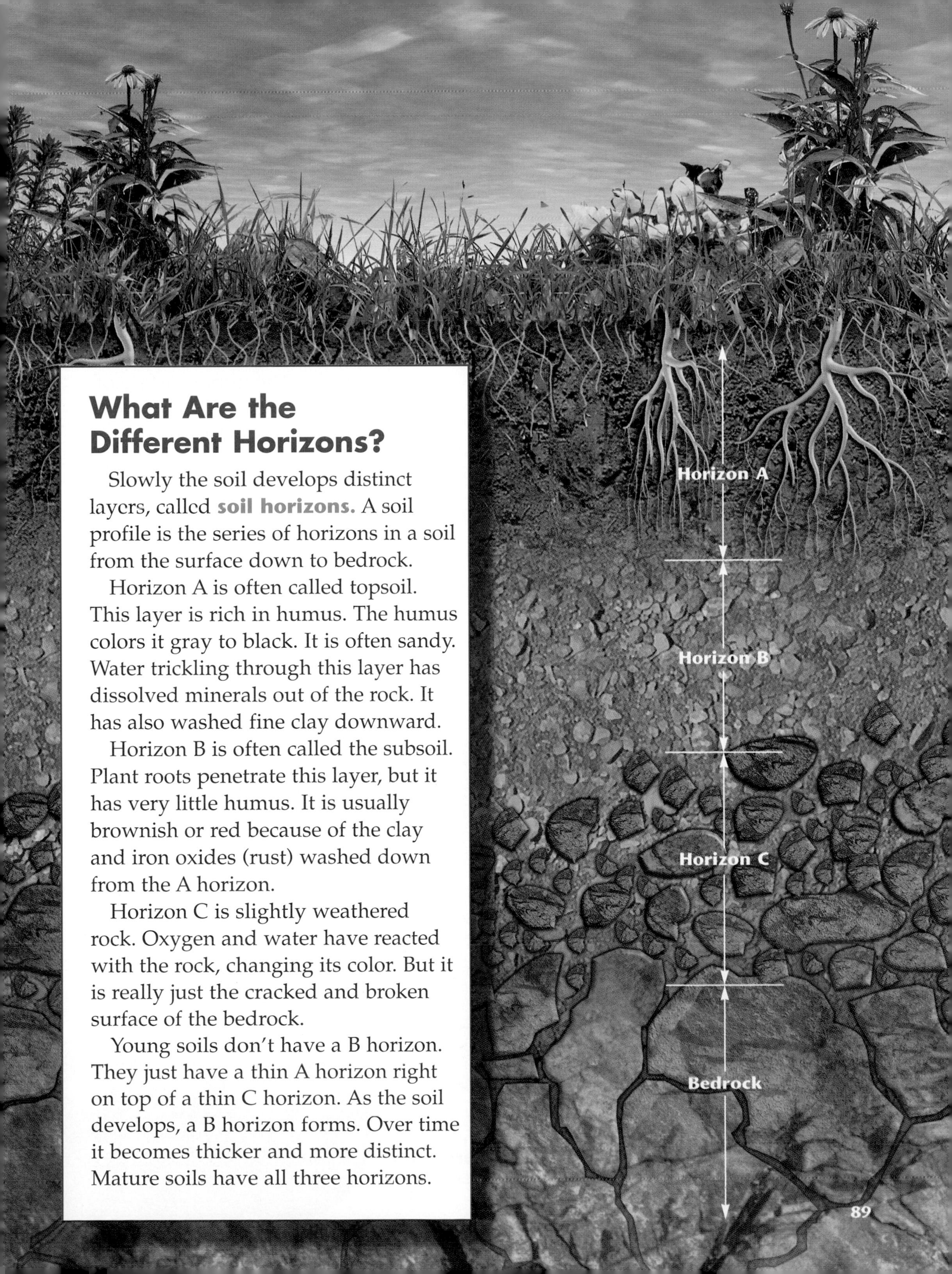

What Are the Different Horizons?

Slowly the soil develops distinct layers, called **soil horizons.** A soil profile is the series of horizons in a soil from the surface down to bedrock.

Horizon A is often called topsoil. This layer is rich in humus. The humus colors it gray to black. It is often sandy. Water trickling through this layer has dissolved minerals out of the rock. It has also washed fine clay downward.

Horizon B is often called the subsoil. Plant roots penetrate this layer, but it has very little humus. It is usually brownish or red because of the clay and iron oxides (rust) washed down from the A horizon.

Horizon C is slightly weathered rock. Oxygen and water have reacted with the rock, changing its color. But it is really just the cracked and broken surface of the bedrock.

Young soils don't have a B horizon. They just have a thin A horizon right on top of a thin C horizon. As the soil develops, a B horizon forms. Over time it becomes thicker and more distinct. Mature soils have all three horizons.

Horizon A

Horizon B

Horizon C

Bedrock

89

How Is Soil Related to Groundwater?

You know that soil is made up of many rock pieces. Below the soil is weathered rock and solid rock layers. Soil and the layers below can act like a sponge when rain falls on the surface. Water soaks into the spaces between rock fragments—the pores. It becomes part of what is called **groundwater**.

A groundwater system is something like a river system. In a river system, many channels connect the water into a main river. If soil and rock are *permeable*, the pores connect, and water can pass through easily. Sandstone is an example of a permeable rock.

Some soil or rock has few pores or none that interconnect. Fine particles of clay are an example. These are *impermeable*. Instead of passing through, water builds up on top of impermeable rocks.

How deep can water soak down into the ground? Groundwater goes down until it reaches an impermeable layer. The layers above it fill up with water. A rock layer that contains water and allows water to move though it is called an aquifer. The upper surface of the soil and rocks that are filled with water is called the *water table*. Where the water table rises above the surface, you will find a lake, a river, or some other form of surface water.

Brain Power

If the water table sinks during a drought, what might happen to a river or pond?

Meadow

Water table

The surface of a river or stream is the same level as the water table.

Pore

Rock fragment

Permeable material

Impermeable material

Woodland

How Can Soil Be Conserved?

It is important that soil be conserved. Soil can easily lose valuable minerals or be blown away by the wind.

Poor soil can be improved by adding fertilizers. It can also be improved by adding humus. Humus is material produced by breaking down plant and animal remains. These methods replace minerals lost through use. Humus also helps soil absorb and retain water. This further aids the growth of plants.

Sometimes different crops are planted in an area each year. This way the soil will not lose the same mineral year after year. This yearly changing of crops is called crop rotation. Planting trees can also stop soil from being blown away by the wind. There are many other ways of protecting soil, which you may wish to learn more about.

Did you know that soil made your supper possible? Everything you eat can be traced back to the soil. Mashed potatoes? Carrots? Green beans? All came from plants grown in soil. Ice cream for dessert? It came from milk from cows that ate plants that grew in soil. Soil is an important part of your life.

Farmers plow soil to get it in condition for planting.

REVIEW

1. How are mountains formed?

2. What types of forces make and shape landforms?

3. **COMPARE AND CONTRAST** Describe the different kinds of weathering.

4. How is soil produced?

5. **CRITICAL THINKING** *Evaluate* Why is soil conservation important?

WHY IT MATTERS THINK ABOUT IT
What did you eat today? Did it grow in the soil? Was it made from something that grew in the soil?

WHY IT MATTERS WRITE ABOUT IT
Write down the foods you ate today. For each food, trace back the process from soil to the food.

READING SKILL
Write a paragraph explaining the sequence of events involved as soil forms from rocks.

The Secret World in Soil

California's Napa Valley has warm, soft soil that is perfect for growing grapes. If you go there, you can see sunshine beaming down on fields of green grapevines. Down in the soil, there is another, secret world you don't see.

Every cup of Napa Valley soil contains millions of tiny life forms. These include bacteria, fungi, and very small worms called nematodes. Larger animals like earthworms, mites, and insects also call the soil home.

The earthworms are like tiny underground plows. They turn dead roots and old plants into rich, deep soils. Tunnels left by burrowing earthworms fill with air, water, and dissolved minerals. Grape roots grow down into these tunnels. The end result is more sweet grapes and raisins. No wonder grape growers call earthworms their friends.

Some soil animals cause damage by feeding on grape roots. Tiny root-knot nematodes turn grape roots into a tangle of knots. Good soil fungi kill root-knot nematodes. Some good fungi are sticky like adhesive tape. Nematodes passing by stick tight. Some fungi have rings like a cowboy's lasso to trap nematodes. Grape growers have a tough job. They must manage soil plants and animals they cannot see!

A tiny insect called the phylloxera (fil äk' sûr'ə) also attacks grape roots. There are no natural enemies in the soil to stop phylloxera. This insect almost destroyed grape growing around the world 100 years ago. The solution was to find a type of grapevine that could survive phylloxera attacks. But even these vines are sometimes still destroyed by phylloxera. When soil life goes bad, it is expensive for grape growers.

Life Science Link

Water and minerals

Earthworm

Phylloxera

Fungi

Root-knot nematodes

DISCUSSION STARTER

1. How do earthworms improve soil and plant growth?

2. Do you think the roots in the soil or the tops of grape plants in the air are more important? Why?

To learn more about soil, visit *www.mhschool.com/science* and enter the keyword SOIL.

*inter*NET CONNECTION

Topic 2
EARTH SCIENCE

WHY IT MATTERS

Wind, water, and ice reshape the world.

SCIENCE WORDS

mass wasting the downhill movement of Earth material caused by gravity

deposition the dropping off of sediment

glacier a huge sheet of ice and snow that moves slowly over the land

till a jumble of many sizes of sediment deposited by a glacier

moraine a deposit of many sizes of sediment in front of or along the sides of a glacier

Lift, Carry, and Drop

What happened here? Why did it happen on a particular day? Why didn't it happen a day earlier or a day later? This is a stretch of the Pacific Coast Highway in California. Do you think this kind of change might have happened here before?

Many processes are at work changing the shape of Earth's surface. These forces act like a sculptor's tools. Even while forces are building mountains in the crust, processes are at work chiseling into them and wearing them down.

EXPLORE

HYPOTHESIZE What can affect whether Earth material will move downhill? Write a hypothesis in your *Science Journal.* Test your ideas.

STREET CLOSED

Design Your Own Experiment

HOW DOES GRAVITY AFFECT EARTH'S MATERIAL?

PROCEDURES

1. MAKE A MODEL Plan an experiment that studies how a change in one condition, a variable, can affect the results. You may use some of these ideas. Mix the sand, gravel, and soil in the pan. Make a flat layer of sediment.

2. USE VARIABLES How would you test for the effect of how steep a hill is? You might try raising one edge of the pan in very small amounts, one amount at a time. What tools might you use? In your *Science Journal*, design a data table to record results. Observe the particle sizes most affected.

3. USE VARIABLES How would you test the effect of wetness? Keep all the other conditions the same as you test the effect of adding moisture gradually to a sloped hillside. Observe the particle sizes most affected.

MATERIALS

- long pan
- fine sand
- coarse gravel
- soil
- water in a spray bottle
- protractor
- paper towels
- *Science Journal*

CONCLUDE AND APPLY

1. DRAW CONCLUSIONS Why do you think the mixture started to slide when you tilted it at a certain angle but not at a smaller angle?

2. DRAW CONCLUSIONS Why do you think water had an effect on when the mixture started to slide?

GOING FURTHER: Problem Solving

3. EXPERIMENT What other factors could affect when the mixture starts to slide? How could you test your idea in an experiment?

QUICK LAB

Soil Motion

HYPOTHESIZE What determines how fast soil moves downhill? Write a hypothesis in your *Science Journal*.

MATERIALS
- dry soil
- water
- toothpicks
- baking pan
- *Science Journal*

PROCEDURES

1. Dump soil into the center of the baking pan, forming a steep pile. Tap the side of the pan firmly. Observe the results. Record them in your *Science Journal*.

2. EXPERIMENT Start again with a steep pile. This time, stick toothpicks into the pile vertical with the level ground. Record what happens when you tap the pan.

3. USE VARIABLES Set up step 2 again. Pour water slowly, drops at a time, onto the top of the pile. Record what happens.

CONCLUDE AND APPLY

1. What did you observe?

2. How are your observations similar to mass wasting?

Soil slump

How Does Gravity Affect Earth's Material?

Along mountaintops and hillsides, weathering is breaking down rock into *sediment*. The sediment can be fine bits of clay. It can be larger particles, such as sand or gravel. As sediment forms, it is moved from place to place by erosion.

For example, most of Earth's surface is not perfectly flat. Some places are higher, and some places are lower. Gravity is always pulling things from high places down to low places, as was shown in the Explore Activity. This downhill movement of Earth material caused by gravity is called **mass wasting.**

Mass wasting depends largely on how steep a slope is. It can happen slowly, particle by particle, over years. It can happen suddenly when a buildup of loosened particles can no longer be supported by material beneath. It can happen after a heavy rain or an earthquake, or anytime.

The sediment is dropped off at the bottom of the hill or at places where the hill becomes less steep. The dropping off of sediment is called **deposition** (dep′ə zish′ən).

The slope of sand dunes is gentler on one side and steeper on the other. The gentler side is where wind is picking up particles. The steeper side is where the particles are dropped off.

These features were shaped by windblown sediment.

How Does Wind Work?

Erosion and deposition work together. Sediment is picked up from one place. Then it is dropped off somewhere else. As this happens the shape of the land changes. Mountains wear down from steep pinnacles to low hills. Valleys widen, fill up with rock and soil, and become plains.

You've seen how gravity works. Wind is another way for erosion and deposition to work. You can see wind working on a beach, a desert, or a plowed field. Wind easily picks up fine sediments, like clay and sand. The faster the wind is, the larger the size of the particles it can carry. As the wind slows down, it drops the particles off—in order. The biggest, densest particles are dropped first.

Wind can blow sediment against rocks. The windblown particles act like tiny sandblasters. They can dig into hillsides. They can polish stones.

As windblown sand is dropped off, the sand can build up into a dune. Wind blows sand particles over the tops of dunes. The dunes change shape and appear to drift forward in the wind direction.

DID YOU KNOW?

There are many sand dunes found in the coastal areas of the United States. During storms these dunes help defend the inland. How might this be so?

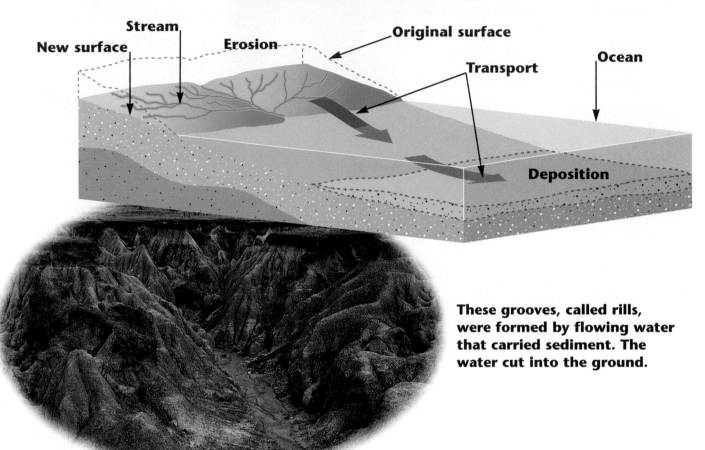

These grooves, called rills, were formed by flowing water that carried sediment. The water cut into the ground.

How Does Flowing Water Work?

Flowing water makes a powerful force that changes the shape of Earth's surface. It can toss loose particles of rock around and carry them along as it flows downhill. The faster the water is moving, the bigger and denser are the particles it carries. In most streams large particles are carried along by rolling, sliding, or bouncing along the bottom. Smaller particles swirl along in the water or are even dissolved in the water.

The bits and pieces carried by moving water act like tiny drills. They slam into rocks and chip away at them. They chip away at the sides of a river,

the banks. They "cut" down into the bottom of the river, the riverbed.

Whenever the water slows down, some of the particles are dropped off. What can cause a stream to slow down? An obstacle could block the flow of water. A steep river could flow onto a flat plain. The water could flow into a big standing body of water, like a lake or an ocean. In each case sediments are deposited when the water slows down. They form a mound or layer.

Brain Power

If Earth's gravity was stronger than it is, what do you think the effect would be on the water of rivers and streams?

How Do Streams Change?

A river or stream carries sediment downhill and deposits it elsewhere. As a result the river or stream changes. Deep, fast streams become slower and shallower.

Curves develop. Water flows faster along the outside of a curve and eats away at it. On the inside of a curve, the water slows down and drops off sediment.

A river may have all these stages along its path. Some rivers are entirely one or two stages.

Flatter, slower-moving stage

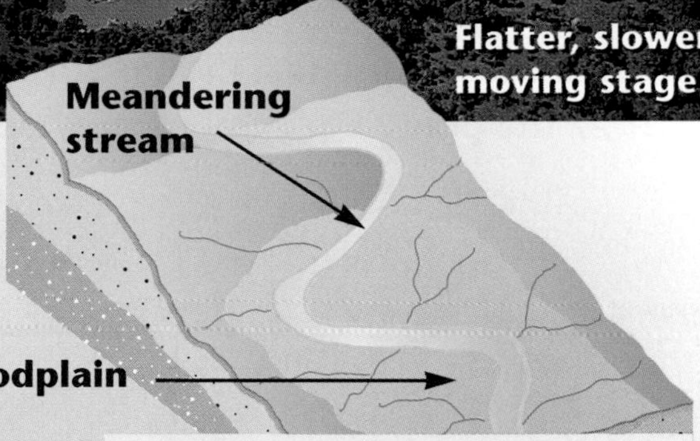

Meandering stream

Floodplain

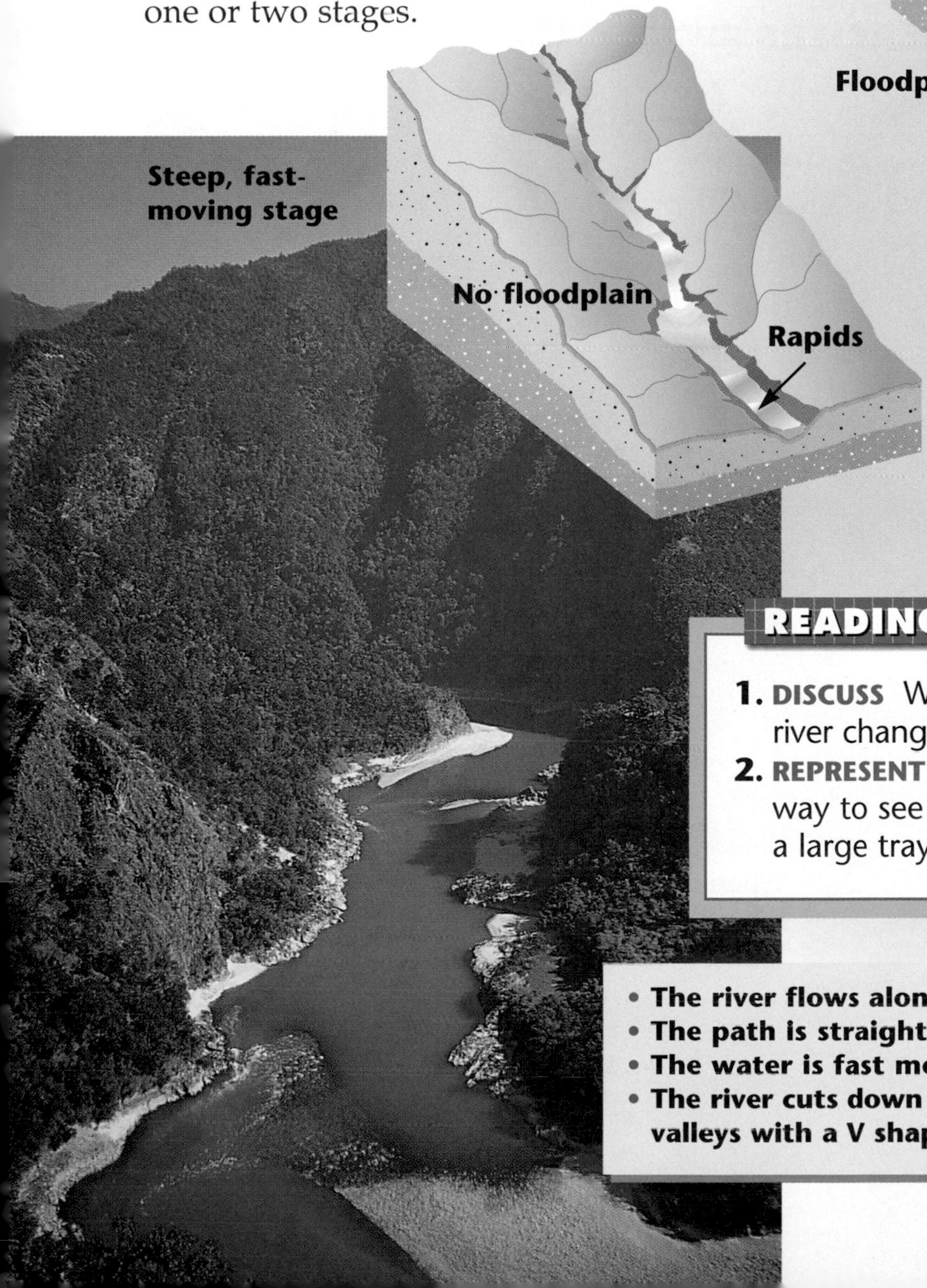

Steep, fast-moving stage

No floodplain

Rapids

- The path is flatter because the river has worn down the land.
- Curves (called *meanders*) develop.
- The river is slower and deposits much sediment.
- The river is shallower and wider.
- Flat plains develop on the sides of the river.

READING N DIAGRAMS

1. **DISCUSS** What are the main ways a river changes from stage to stage?
2. **REPRESENT** Draw a diagram of a way to see all these changes using a large tray of moistened soil.

- The river flows along a steep path.
- The path is straight.
- The water is fast moving and carries much sediment.
- The river cuts down into the bottom. It forms steep valleys with a V shape.

How Does Moving Ice Shape the Land?

The huge sheets of ice you see here are like giant bulldozers. They are moving and can move rocks and sediment. These huge moving sheets of ice are **glaciers**. To know how glaciers can move, you have to understand how they form.

Some glaciers form in valleys high up in the mountains. Others form near the poles. Glaciers form when more snow falls in the winter than melts in the summer. Over time the snow gets deeper and deeper.

Newly fallen snow is fluffy because it has air trapped inside. As snow piles up though, the weight of the snow on top squeezes the snow at the bottom into a solid mass of ice. When the ice gets to be about 100 meters (328 feet) thick, it can move. The weight above makes the ice at the bottom like a superthick syrup. The whole sheet of ice then moves downhill.

SOME FACTS ABOUT GLACIERS

Valley glaciers form in high mountain valleys, where it is cold because of the elevation.

Continental glaciers form near the poles, where it is cold because of the latitude.

When a glacier reaches the edge of a continent, it breaks off into icebergs.

Rocks in a Glacier

Glaciers move like huge, slow bulldozers. They can push loose rocks and soil out of their path. They drag sediment underneath. Loose rocks and soil get pushed up in piles along the front and sides of the glacier.

When a glacier moves over the ground, pieces of rock may freeze into the ice. If a rock freezes into the glacier, it can be "plucked" out of the ground as the glacier moves along. In this way huge chunks of rock may be picked up and carried great distances.

The rocks along the bottom and sides of a glacier can scrape against the land. They are like the blades of a huge plow. Any layers that a glacier passes over may be deeply scratched. Some exposed rock in a valley floor may become polished smooth.

As a glacier moves through a valley, it digs deep into the walls and floor. A once-narrow valley that had a V shape becomes wider. As a glacier moves through, the valley becomes U shaped.

Narrower glaciers dragged soil along. As they merged into one glacier, the soil became trapped in the middle, like a stream of soil.

What clues can tell that a glacier once moved through this valley?

What Happens when Glaciers Melt?

Glaciers eventually reach places where it is warm, and they melt. When the ice melts, the rocks that were frozen into it fall to the ground in a jumble. It is a jumble of many sizes of sediment, known as **till**.

A deposit of many sizes of sediment from a glacier that collects in front of or along the sides of the glacier is called a **moraine** (mə rān′). As the glacier melts away, the moraine is left behind as mounds or long ridges.

As a glacier melts, meltwater flows out from the edges of the glacier. This water carries sediment from the glacier. The water may carry the sediment for some distance before dropping it off. The result may be a wide, flat plain in front of a glacier covered with layers of sediment.

Sometimes chunks of ice get buried in till. When ice chunks finally melt, the till above them collapses, forming a bowl-like hole in the ground. These holes may fill up with water, forming ponds or lakes.

Glaciers also form lakes in other ways. Sometimes they scrape huge holes in the ground. The holes fill up with meltwater when the glacier melts. Also moraines act as dams. They trap flowing meltwater into lakes.

Some piles of till get smoothed out if a glacier flows over them. These teardrop-shaped piles of till are called drumlins.

HOW GLACIERS CHANGE THE LAND

Drumlins have a steeper side and gentler side. The glacier was moving over the drumlin in the direction from the gentle side to the steep side. How is this shape like a sand dune?

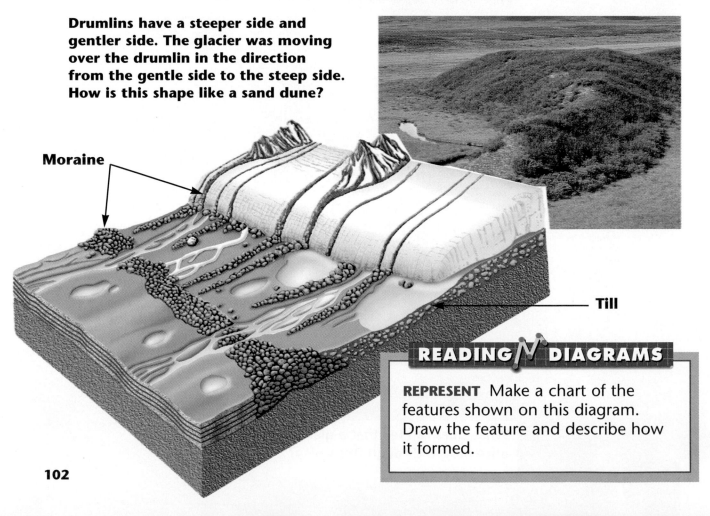

Moraine

Till

READING 〰 DIAGRAMS

REPRESENT Make a chart of the features shown on this diagram. Draw the feature and describe how it formed.

What Have Glaciers Left Behind?

For long times during Earth's history, glaciers covered much of the land. These periods of time are called ice ages. Glaciers from the last ice age began to melt back, or retreat, about 20,000 years ago.

These glaciers left behind a lot of sand, gravel, and clay. These are valuable natural resources. Clay deposited in glacial lakes can be used to make bricks, pottery, and concrete. Sand and gravel are used to make concrete for buildings and roads.

Glacial lake

Erosion and deposition are a part of your world. If you live near a river, that river is a product of these forces. Glaciers may have carried valuable soil to your area in the past.

Do you live in California's Central Valley? If you do, the land you live on is made of sediment deposited by rivers over thousands of years. You can thank California's rivers for making your home possible!

☐ **Ocean**

☐ **Continental glacier**

☐ **Nonglaciated land**

Glaciers covered much of North America 20,000 years ago.

REVIEW

1. How can wind and gravity change Earth's surface?

2. How can flowing water cause erosion?

3. What can happen as a glacier moves through an area?

4. **CAUSE AND EFFECT** Why do glaciers form only in certain areas?

5. **CRITICAL THINKING** *Analyze* How can a slow-moving river become fast-moving? Explain your answer.

WHY IT MATTERS THINK ABOUT IT
What if there was a heavy rainstorm or strong wind in your area? How could it cause erosion and deposition?

WHY IT MATTERS WRITE ABOUT IT
How are rivers important in the economics of a country? How can strong winds affect the economics of a country?

READING THE ROCKS

Rock layers are like story books if you know how to read them. Until the 1950s, scientists lacked the tools to determine the actual age of rocks. They understood, however, that in undisturbed layers, the bottom rocks were deposited first and are oldest. Rocks on top are youngest because they were deposited last. This idea is called the principle of superposition.

In many places, however, the rocks are not so neatly layered and the story is harder to read. Superposition is not a foolproof guide because the rock layers have moved around. Sediments that were laid down horizontally may later have been folded, tilted, and moved by faults. New rocks may intrude into older rock layers. Then glacial action, rivers, and erosion may have further transformed the ancient landscape into something new.

A fascinating example of these forces at work is in the Providence Mountains in the Mojave Desert in eastern California. Near ground level is 250- to 300-million-year-old gray limestone known as the Bird Spring Formation. The limestone contains shell fossils because it was once at the bottom of an ancient sea. Originally the limestone was deposited on the seabed in thick horizontal layers. Today, however, those layers are tilted upward. How did they get that way?

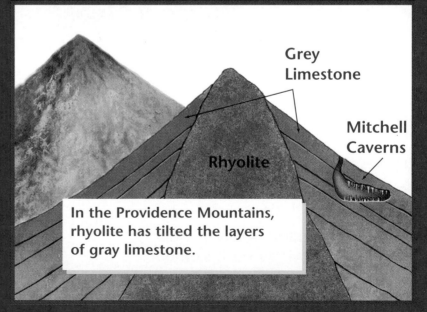

Grey Limestone

Mitchell Caverns

Rhyolite

In the Providence Mountains, rhyolite has tilted the layers of gray limestone.

Geology Link

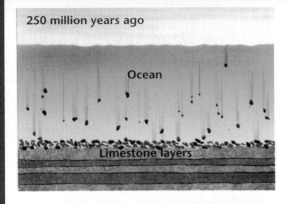

250 million years ago

Ocean

Limestone layers

160 million years ago

Mountains formed by intruding rhyolite layers

Limestone

20,000 years ago,

Lakes

Today

Landform and climate have changed over time in what is today the Mojave Desert.

The answer is that approximately 160 million years ago they were pushed up by hot rock intruding from below. This rock, called rhyolite, is visible today in the high peaks of the Providence Mountains. Its reddish-brown color contrasts sharply with the grey limestone.

Still later, at a time of wet climate, there was a chain of lakes in the area that is now the Mojave desert. Water dripping from the lakes cut caves in the limestone and left behind mineral deposits known as dripstone. This new rock formed within the limestone caves at the rate of one inch every twenty years. Today this limestone cave formation is known as Mitchell Caverns.

DISCUSSION STARTER

1. Why is superposition not a foolproof guide to the age of rock layers?

2. How is new rock formed within ancient rock?

To learn more about rock layers, visit **www.mhschool.com/science** and enter key word ROCKS.

*inter*NET
CONNECTION

CHAPTER 3 REVIEW

SCIENCE WORDS

deposition p. 96

erosion p. 85

fault-block
mountain p. 84

glacier p. 100

groundwater p. 90

mass wasting p. 96

moraine p. 102

soil p. 88

soil horizon p. 89

till p. 102

USING SCIENCE WORDS

Number a paper from 1 to 10. Fill in 1 to 5 with words from the list above.

1. ___?___ is a mixture of weathered rock, decayed plant and animal matter, living things, air, and water.

2. A deposit found at the sides and end of a glacier is a(n) ___?___.

3. ___?___ is the picking up and removal of rock particles.

4. Any of the layers of the soil down to bedrock is a ___?___.

5. ___?___ soaks into soil and rock and collects in spaces between rock particles.

6–10. **Pick five words from the list above that were not used in 1 to 5, and use each in a sentence.**

UNDERSTANDING SCIENCE IDEAS

11. Explain how lakes and rivers relate to the water table.

12. Describe how erosion and deposition work together to change Earth's surface.

13. What is the difference between weathering and erosion?

14. What are two landforms created by forces that lift the crust?

15. What is chemical weathering?

USING IDEAS AND SKILLS

16. **READING SKILL: SEQUENCE OF EVENTS** What is soil? How does it form differently in different places?

17. How do glaciers and running water change Earth's surface?

18. Describe the rock layers in a fault-block mountain. What happens at the fault?

19. **INFER** When a river carves out a deeper channel, what happens to the surrounding water table?

20. **THINKING LIKE A SCIENTIST** You are trying to find out what Earth processes have taken place where you live. What kinds of clues would you look for? Where would you look?

PROBLEMS and PUZZLES

Weathering Model There are two types of weathering. Does physical weathering affect chemical weathering? Find out by filling two cups with water. Put a ground-up sugar cube in one cup and a whole cube in the other. Which type of sugar dissolves more quickly? Can you explain why?

Ground-up sugar cube

Whole sugar cube

CHAPTER 4

SUDDEN CHANGES, SLOW CHANGES

A crystal-clear stream tumbles down a mountainside. Each day it carries rocks and pebbles down the slope. How long do you think it will take for the stream to carve a deep canyon?

The landscape is always changing. Sometimes the change happens one pebble at a time. Other times, a sudden landslide or earthquake may change a whole landscape in a few minutes. Can you think of other ways in which a landscape can change?

In Chapter 4 you will have many opportunities to locate details that support a main idea.

WHY IT MATTERS

Rivers and streams help shape the landscape you live in.

SCIENCE WORDS

relief the three-dimensional shape of the land

delta a fan-shaped area of sediment deposited at the mouth of a river

levee a wall or ridge made of soil or concrete to keep a river from overflowing

arroyo a deep canyon carved by water in a desert mountainside

The Work of Rivers and Streams

Does a stream or river flow through your community? If so, does it flow all year round? Or do you live in a dry area where streams flow only during rainy seasons?

Streams and rivers flow down from California's great mountains, through its valleys, and on to the Pacific Ocean. What determines the paths they take? What effect do they have on the landscape?

EXPLORE

HYPOTHESIZE California's rivers flow in every direction: north, south, east, and west. Why is that so? Write a hypothesis in your *Science Journal*. How might you test your ideas?

Investigate How Rivers Form

Make a model of a river system.

MATERIALS

- sand
- rectangular aluminum baking pan
- water spray bottle
- *Science Journal*

PROCEDURES

1. Fill the pan about half full of sand. Then shape some of the sand into a ridge at one end.

2. Use a book to prop up the pan's deep (ridge) end about 10 cm. Make sure it is stable.

3. **OBSERVE** Gently spray water along the hill until water begins to run in small streams. Make a map of the rivers that form.

4. Aqueducts carry water from one place to another. Use a pencil to create a V-shaped aqueduct in your landscape. How does this change the flow of water?

5. Try damming a stream. Record what happens in your *Science Journal*.

CONCLUDE AND APPLY

1. **OBSERVE** What happened to the water when you kept spraying on the slope?

2. **ANALYZE** Why did the water gather into streams instead of running down in one wide sheet?

3. **DRAW CONCLUSIONS** How might dams across real rivers change the landscape downriver? Upriver?

GOING FURTHER: Problem Solving

4. **EXPERIMENT** How do you think your experiment would have differed if you had propped up the pan more steeply? Form a hypothesis. Describe how you could test your hypothesis.

109

Where Do California's Major Rivers Flow?

On a relief map, the state of California is shaped like a large, long bowl with a spout on one side. The large Central Valley forms the middle, and San Francisco Bay is the pouring lip. Mountains form the rim of the bowl. Smaller mountains called the Coast Ranges line the coast on the west. Larger mountains, the Cascades in the north and the Sierra Nevada farther south, form the eastern edge.

Flowing south through the Central Valley is the Sacramento River. It is joined by the Feather, American, and other rivers flowing westward down from the Sierra Nevada. Flowing north through the Valley is the San Joaquin River. The San Joaquin also receives rivers flowing down from the Sierra Nevada.

A few of California's rivers also flow eastward into the Valley from the slopes of the Coast Ranges. The rivers flow rapidly as they descend the mountain slopes. Then they slow down when they reach the Valley floor. At the center of the Valley, the Sacramento and San Joaquin rivers join together and pour into San Francisco Bay. San Francisco Bay, in turn, empties into the Pacific Ocean.

A number of shorter coastal rivers flow north, south, and west down the slopes of the Coast Range to the Pacific Ocean.

Southern California also has rivers, but most are dry during much of the year. The Los Angeles River flows down from the mountains and through the center of Los Angeles. The river is often dry. During the rainy season, however, it may sometimes flood. The Colorado River forms the state's southeastern border. Most of its water is drained off for use in cities and towns and on farms.

The Colorado River forms California's southeastern boundary.

MAJOR RIVERS OF CALIFORNIA

Klamath River
Trinity Rive
Mad Rive
Russian River
Sacramento River
Pit River
Feather River
American Rive
San Joaquin Rive
Stanislaus River
Merced Rive
Fresno River
Salmon River

San Francisco

Los Angeles

San Diego

Colorado River

GEOGRAPHY LINK

QUICK LAB

Reading a River Map

HYPOTHESIZE Does a river map contain clues about the shape of the land? In your *Science Journal,* write a hypothesis you can test.

MATERIALS
- pencil
- copies of river map
- *Science Journal*

PROCEDURES

1. Copy the California river map on this page into your *Science Journal* or use a copy your teacher made.

2. Draw small arrows at many spots on your map to show which way is downhill.

CONCLUDE AND APPLY

1. **ANALYZE** Look at your river map. What do the arrows tell you about the shape of the land?

2. **PREDICT** Can you tell where highlands are? Where lowlands are?

3. Use the California relief map on page CA32 to check your predictions. Were you correct?

How Have Streams and Rivers Shaped California's Mountains?

Rainwater, streams, and rivers have formed much of the **relief**, or three-dimensional shape, of California's mountains.

California's main mountain ranges are still growing. The fault-block peaks of the Sierra Nevada continue rising. Tectonic forces are pushing the Coast Ranges upward. But even as the mountains rise, water keeps grinding them down. Rainwater erodes their slopes. Streams and rivers carve deep channels in the mountainsides. The action of water has produced the wrinkled, eroded landscape you see in California's mountain regions.

Rain falling on the mountain slopes runs downhill. Why does it not flow downward in a smooth sheet? No mountainside is exactly flat. Even a tiny slant one way or the other causes water to move in that direction. Eventually it wears a shallow channel or gully. The gully winds down the mountainside, but water also flows inward toward the center of the gully. This causes more wear in the center of the gully, deepening it into a full-fledged stream bed.

With every rain, the stream bed gets deeper. The rushing waters carry sand, pebbles, gravel, and even boulders downhill. Just like sandpaper rubbing on wood, over millions of years sandy water can carve rock. Mountains contain harder spots and softer spots. Water always takes the easy route, carving a path through softer soil or soft rock.

What would happen if an earthquake changed the slope of the mountainside? Once again, the water would dig a new channel downhill through the softer soil and rock. The mountainside would be reshaped once again.

Streams and rivers have carved deep canyons in the Sierra Nevada.

112

Sediment from the Sacramento and other rivers has made the Central Valley one of the world's most fertile farmlands.

How Have Streams and Rivers Shaped California's Valleys?

The streams and rivers flowing down from the Sierra Nevada and the Coast Ranges have cut deep, narrow valleys on the higher slopes. Even now, the rivers are constantly cutting downward into the rock and soil. The valleys widen as the rivers eat away at the banks of their channels, especially where the ground is softer. Huge quantities of sediment are carried downstream, particularly during spring floods.

After leaving the mountains, California's largest rivers flow out across the Central Valley. In this flatter landscape, they slow down and deposit the sediment. Over thousands of years, the rivers have covered the Valley floor with sediment from both the Sierra Nevada and the Coast Ranges. Much of the sediment dates from the Ice Ages. During that time glacial meltwater made the rivers even larger and more powerful than they are now.

Today the sediment lies in a thick layer on the floor of the Central Valley. The surface is a flat floodplain crossed by the Sacramento and San Joaquin rivers. The rivers still deposit sediment, especially when they overflow their banks during spring floods.

The soil of this region of California is extraordinarily fertile. In fact, the Central Valley contains some of the most productive farmland in the world. The farms of the Central Valley produce enormous crops of fruits and vegetables. People all across America buy farm products grown in the Central Valley.

What Happens When the Rivers Reach the Sea?

When a river reaches the sea, it slows down dramatically. Much of the sediment that the river has been carrying settles to the bottom. Over time, the sediment builds up into a large fan-shaped deposit just at the point where the river joins the sea. This sediment deposit is called a **delta**.

As a river flows through its own delta, it can split into many smaller channels. This splitting happens when a channel deposits so much sediment that it clogs itself. The water must still head downhill, so it forks to each side of the new sediment.

Do all rivers form deltas when they reach the sea? In California, many rivers do not. Instead, the sediment is washed away by strong ocean currents. The Eel River, Mad River, and Klamath River in northern California have almost no deltas, even though they carry huge amounts of sediment. The sediment is washed along the coast, where some of it forms beach sand.

The rivers of the Central Valley do not reach the ocean directly. Instead, they join together to flow into San

THE RIVERS REACH THE SEA

American River

C E N T R A L

READING IN DIAGRAMS

1. **DISCUSS** What are some of the ways a river might change its course?
2. **WRITE** Write a paragraph about what happens when a river flows into a lake or ocean.

Francisco Bay. The Bay then empties into the ocean through the Golden Gate. At the point where the Sacramento and San Joaquin rivers reach the Bay, they have formed a very large delta. This delta is very unusual because it is inland instead of at the coast. It is very large, stretching nearly 50 km (30 miles) from north to south.

The Sacramento-San Joaquin delta is crisscrossed by winding channels and dotted with marshes. Low, grassy islands alternate with stretches of open water. These wetlands provide a nursery for fish and a home to many thousands of birds and other wildlife.

The Sacramento River is deep enough for ocean-going ships.

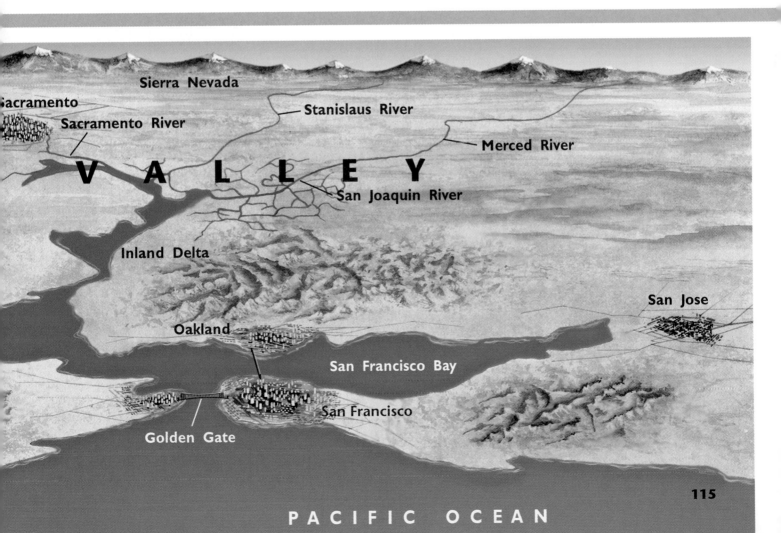

Sierra Nevada

Sacramento

Sacramento River

Stanislaus River

Merced River

V A L L E Y

San Joaquin River

Inland Delta

San Jose

Oakland

San Francisco Bay

San Francisco

Golden Gate

PACIFIC OCEAN

How Much Water Do California's Rivers Carry?

Late in 1994, heavy rains flooded parts of northern California. During the flood, the United States Geological Survey measured the flow of the Eel River. Scientists calculated that the river was carrying 752,000 cubic feet of water per second. That is the highest river flow ever recorded in California.

Certainly, 752,000 cubic feet of water per second is a very large amount. Can you picture how much water that really is? A cubic foot of water weighs about 63 pounds. So 752,000 cubic feet would weigh more than 47 million pounds. Can you imagine that much water rushing past one spot in the river every second?

Here is another way to picture this huge amount of river water. A geology professor calculated the flow in terms of the weight of cars. He chose a large station wagon as a unit. How many of these cars would have to pass by a spot in the river to equal the weight of the water? According to the professor's calculations, 15,000 station wagons would have to pass by every second. To fit that many cars into the river channel, they would have to be packed 100 cars across and 150 cars high!

Now imagine the force of all that weight gouging out the riverbed and eroding the river's banks. That is how a flooding river can cut through soil and rocks and even carry boulders downstream. That is why flooding rivers can sometimes be extraordinarily destructive.

The force of flowing water in California's rivers can cut through soil and rock and even carry boulders downstream.

Brain Power

How large is a cubic foot? How many cubic feet of water would it take to fill your classroom? How could you find out?

Engineers have built dams on more than 1,400 California rivers.

How Have People Changed the Way the Rivers Flow?

People have made great changes in how California's rivers flow. Some changes were made in order to capture and store the water so that people could use it. Some changes were made in order to carry the water away to California's cities and towns. Other changes were made to control flooding.

Engineers have built dams on more than 1,400 California rivers. The dams have created reservoirs that store water supplies for California's cities. Many of these dams have been built on mountain streams in the Sierra Nevada. Others have been built in the southern California mountains in order to catch the runoff from the winter rains. The dams ensure regular water supplies, but they interrupt the normal flow of rivers and streams.

California's system of aqueducts diverts large amounts of water to farms and city water systems. So much water is diverted from the Colorado River that in some years the river fails to reach the sea.

To control flooding, engineers have built many miles of high ridges, called levees, along the banks of rivers. Many levees are in the delta where the Sacramento and San Joaquin rivers join to flow into San Francisco Bay.

In southern California, rivers that are dry for much of the year can suddenly flood after a heavy winter rain. To control this flooding, concrete riverbeds have been built in some rivers. These concrete riverbeds act like huge drainpipes that carry the floodwaters quickly and directly to the ocean.

117

How Has Water Shaped California's Deserts?

You probably do not think of water when you think of California's deserts. After all, the Mojave Desert and the Colorado Desert each receive less than 10 inches of rainfall per year on average. But water plays an important role in shaping the desert landscape.

Rain may not fall often in the desert, but there can be strong storms, especially in the summer. Several inches of rain may fall in a matter of hours.

Because there is so little vegetation, the water does not soak into the ground. Instead, it washes in torrents down the steep mountainsides, carrying rocks and soil with it. Over time, flash floods carve deep canyons, called arroyos, in the mountainsides.

At the base of the mountains, the water flows out of the arroyos and onto the level ground. There it slows down and drops the sediment it has brought down from the mountains. The result is often a huge, fan-shaped deposit spreading out from the mouth of an arroyo. These fan-shaped formations are common in California's deserts.

After a major flash flood in the desert, the rainwater usually collects in low-lying basins. If enough water collects, a temporary lake will form. In time, the water evaporates, leaving a

Flash floods form this kind of fan-shaped deposit in California's desert basins. [Inset] Irrigation has turned the desert into cropland in California's Imperial Valley.

layer of dry, powdery, light-colored minerals. Very little of the rainwater that falls in the desert ever flows out to reach the sea.

One desert area in California has been changed by water in another way. The Imperial Valley, at the southeast end of the state, was once part of the Colorado Desert. Today, it is irrigated with water from the Colorado River. The water has turned the arid desert into productive cropland.

The Sacramento delta provides a home for thousands of waterbirds.

Streams and rivers have shaped much of the landscape that you see around you. They have carved the valleys in California's great mountains. They have shaped the surface of California's deserts. They have created the Central Valley farmlands that supply your vegetables and fruits. Controlling their flow is a big job that occupies many Californians today.

REVIEW

1. Where does river water originally come from?

2. In what direction does river water always flow?

3. **CAUSE AND EFFECT** What causes river water to flow in a particular direction?

4. How do rivers shape the land?

5. **CRITICAL THINKING** *Analyze* Explain why people sometimes change the way rivers flow.

WHY IT MATTERS **THINK ABOUT IT**
Think about a river system near where you live. Where does the river's water come from? Where does the river end? Have people changed this river's flow?

WHY IT MATTERS **WRITE ABOUT IT**
Write a paragraph explaining the results of changes in the flow of California's rivers.

The Plague of the Dead Lakes!

In the early 1960s, people in Sweden noticed something very wrong. There were no more trout in lakes that were once full of them! In fact there were no living organisms in the water at all! The lakes were "dead."

By the 1970s the dead-lake problem spread to mountain lakes and ponds of southeastern Canada. Even waters of the Adirondacks in the United States became abiotic, or without life.

Why did this happen? Scientists tested the water. It was very acid, sometimes as acid as vinegar! Small organisms couldn't live in it. Fish couldn't reproduce in it! Scientists concluded that the acid dropped from the sky, so they measured rainwater, snow, fog, and even windblown dust. Each showed high levels of sulfuric and nitric acids. All airborne acid was labeled "acid rain."

To learn how the acid got into the rain, scientists checked earlier studies. They found that in 1872 a Scottish researcher proved that lake water became acid because of coal smoke. Further research proved that smoke from modern coal-burning electric power plants contained sulfur dioxide. If it mixes with mist in the air, it produces sulfuric acid!

Not all acid rain was caused by burning coal. Truck and auto exhausts contain nitrogen oxide that, when mixed with moisture, creates nitric acid!

Acid rain kills trees by changing soil chemistry and reducing trees' resistance to cold weather.

Many stones dissolve in acid rain. Iron and paint wear away faster in acid conditions.

Science, Technology, and Society

In 1990 the United States Congress passed Clean Air laws to gradually reduce acid rain. The goal was to cut sulfur dioxide production by 10 million tons and nitrogen oxides by 2 million tons. The Clean Air Act encouraged plants to reduce sulfur in smoke and required cars to use antipollution devices to control harmful gases in emissions.

From 1995 to 2000, over 400 coal-burning plants developed ways to reduce sulfur in their smoke.

Forest fires, including those set to clear land, also put nitric acid in the air to mix with rain.

DISCUSSION STARTER

1. Make a list of steps you would follow from discovering an acid rain problem to finding ways to solve it.

2. How does acid rain affect your life?

"Scrubbers" in smokestacks remove particles before they get into the air. Retrieved particles can be "mined" for valuable by-products.

To learn more about acid rain, visit *www.mhschool.com/science* and select the keyword CLEANAIR.

*inter*NET CONNECTION

Topic 4
EARTH SCIENCE

WHY IT MATTERS

The ocean shapes the shoreline where people live and play.

SCIENCE WORDS

beach drift the motion of sand carried along the beach by the ocean

marine terrace a steplike formation above a coast that was once an ancient shoreline

estuary an arm of the sea at the mouth of a river

The Work of the Ocean

Picture yourself at the beach on a sunny summer day. Feel the sand between your toes. Did you ever wonder where the sand comes from? Have you ever returned to the beach in winter to find a lot of the sand washed away? Where did it go?

Many people like to live near the beach. Many more like to visit it when they can. Yet the beach and the shoreline are always changing. What causes that change? What does it mean for people who live near the shore?

EXPLORE

HYPOTHESIZE How do the ocean's waves shape the beach? Write a hypothesis in your *Science Journal*. How would you test your ideas?

Investigate "Current" Events

Find out what happens to beach sand when waves strike the shore at an angle.

MATERIALS

- drinking straw
- blue food coloring
- plastic cup
- rectangular aluminum baking pan
- wet sand
- several plastic spoons
- *Science Journal*

PROCEDURES

1. Obtain 2–3 cups of wet sand from your teacher. Use the plastic spoons to form it into a beach about 3 cm deep and 6 cm wide against a long side of the alumium pan.

2. Add water to a depth of 2 cm in the pan. Stir one spoonful of sand and one drop of blue food coloring into the water.

3. Have one member of your group blow on the water through a straw from one corner of the tray opposite the beach to create little waves.

4. Observe the movement of water along the shore as these waves strike the shoreline. Draw a diagram of your model beach. Use arrows to show the direction of water movement along the shoreline.

5. About one third of the way down the beach, push a spoon into the sand at right angles to the beach. Push it in just far enough so that the handle makes a jetty. Repeat steps 3–5.

CONCLUDE AND APPLY

2. PREDICT If you blow waves against the beach for a long time, what will happen to the beach?

2. What happened to the shape of the beach up-current from the spoon handle? Down-current?

GOING FURTHER: Problem Solving

3. What would happen if you had a series of jetties out into the water all along the beach?

Sandy beaches protect the shoreline from the ocean's waves.

What Is the Structure of a Beach?

Along many shorelines, a sandy beach separates the ocean's waves from the land. Some beaches are wide and straight. Some extend for many miles along the shore. Others are short and confined to narrow coves. In California, many beaches are backed by high, rocky cliffs. Elsewhere in the world, sand dunes, lagoons, and bays lie behind many beaches.

The ocean keeps the sand on the beach and underwater in almost constant motion. Waves carry the underwater sand landward and pile it up on the beach. Ocean currents then pull the beach sand out to sea where it forms underwater sandbars. Sandbars may extend out to where the water is more than 10 meters (30 feet) deep. This process goes on all the time.

Beaches are valuable because they protect the shoreline. When waves crash against a beach, the sand absorbs the wave energy. The land behind the beach is protected from the surf. But if the beach sand washes away, the waves can reach the land and cut into the cliffs or soil. When this happens, the ocean can reshape the shoreline.

Where Does Beach Sand Come From?

Most of the sand on the beach starts as sediment that is carried down to the shore by rivers. In California, some of the beach sand may also come from the shoreline cliffs. The sediment is ground up by wave action to become common beach sand.

Because rivers are the main source of sand, damming a river may cause problems. The dam may interrupt the flow of sand. Without fresh sand, a whole beach may disappear. In time there may be nothing left but rocks.

The sand is carried from the river mouth along the beach by the ocean.

This motion results from the direction of the waves. Most of the time, the waves hit the beach at an angle. As each wave breaks, it pushes sand at an angle up the beach slope. As the water washes back, it pulls the sand straight back. The result is that huge amounts of sand are carried along the beach in the direction of the waves. Geologists use the term **beach drift** to describe the motion of sand along the beach.

In California, waves tend to head in a southeasterly direction. As a result, sand is carried along the beaches to from northwest to southeast. As the sand on a beach flows away, its place is taken by other sand from beaches farther north.

BEACH DRIFT

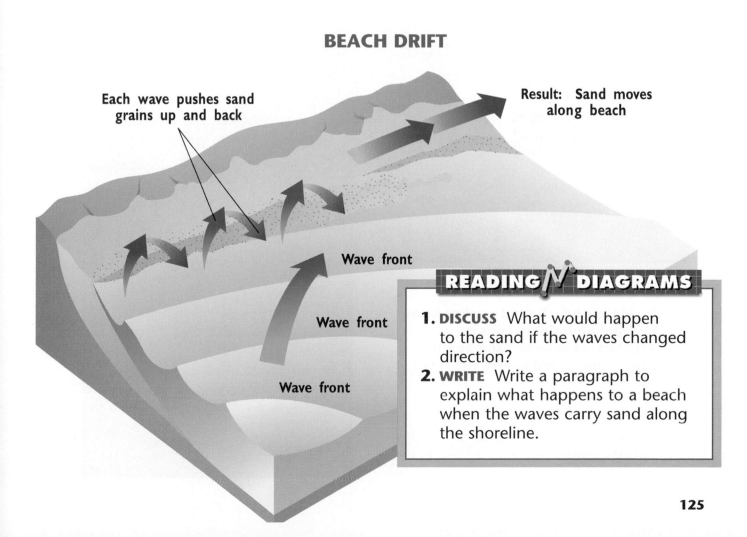

Each wave pushes sand grains up and back

Result: Sand moves along beach

Wave front

Wave front

Wave front

READING IN DIAGRAMS

1. **DISCUSS** What would happen to the sand if the waves changed direction?
2. **WRITE** Write a paragraph to explain what happens to a beach when the waves carry sand along the shoreline.

How Does the Beach Change from Season to Season?

Have you ever been to a California beach in the winter? If so, what you saw looks very different from the beach in summer. In winter much of the beach sand is gone. The underlying rock is exposed to the air. The ocean waves crash directly against the base of the sea cliffs. How do these changes happen?

Winter can be a stormy time in California. Strong storms from the ocean come on shore. Very large waves attack the beach. They wash away the sand and carry it out to sea. Much of the sand ends up offshore. It is deposited in the underwater sandbars that run parallel to the coast. Where there was once a beach, there is now just rock. The ocean waters come straight to the foot of the sea cliffs because there is no beach to hold them back.

When summer comes again, however, the beach returns. The gentle summer waves pick up sand from the offshore sandbars. They pile it up on the beach. Once again there is a wide stretch of sand at the foot of the sea cliffs, and the underlying rock is buried under deep layers of sand. The beach has regained its familiar summer appearance.

In winter, beach sand washes away and the underlying rock is exposed. In summer, the beach sand returns and covers the rocks.

Where Does the Beach Sand Go?

Winter storms carry the beach sand out to offshore sandbars. Beach drift carries it along the coast. Where does it all end up?

In most areas, the movement of beach sand follows a pattern. The sand follows a well-worn "track" that may extend for many miles along the shore. The motion is unbroken until the sand hits a particular undersea formation—the mouth of an undersea canyon. Such canyons may start near shore and extend outward for many miles. Sand traveling along the shore may flow into the canyon and be carried far out to sea.

One undersea canyon off La Jolla extends into the Pacific Ocean. It has steep sides and is very deep. Twenty-seven miles out to sea, it empties into the even deeper San Diego Trough, 1,100 meters (3,600 feet) below the surface. Much of the sand that flows along the beaches north of San Diego ends up in the La Jolla Canyon. Sliding downward through the canyon, it eventually reaches the ocean floor.

On the southern California coast, there are four beach sand "tracks," each as long as 160 km (100 miles). All of them end in underwater canyons much like the La Jolla Canyon.

Just off this beach at La Jolla in southern California, beach sand flows down an undersea canyon and out to sea.

How Do Waves Change the Shoreline Over Time?

Waves beating against the coast year after year are a powerful force. Especially in winter, when much of the protective beach sand is absent, powerful waves can carve through rock. They can undercut the beach cliffs and cause landslides. Over time they can change the shape of the shoreline.

When waves enter a cove or bay, their energy weakens. But when they hit a projecting headland, they strike with full force. Over time, rocky points tend to wear away. Slowly the projecting headland becomes rounded, then gradually straightens. Beaches develop along the shoreline where once there were only rocks.

As the shoreline straightens, beach drift begins. Sand piles up in wide beaches in the bays and coves between headlands. Sometimes sandbars form where beach drift has carried the sand past the headlands.

Over many years, projecting headlands erode back. Bays and coves fill with sand. The shoreline straightens out. The force of waves has reshaped the coast.

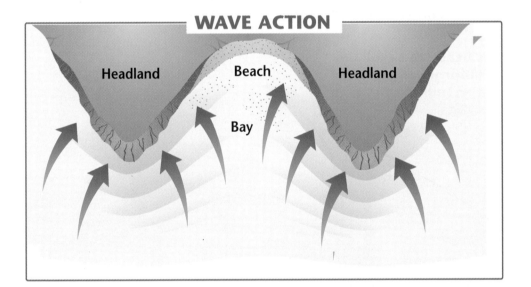

WAVE ACTION

Headland   Beach   Headland

Bay

READING N DIAGRAMS

1. **DISCUSS** What happens over time to headlands that project into the ocean?
2. **WRITE** Write a paragraph to explain how the shape of an older coast differs from a younger one.

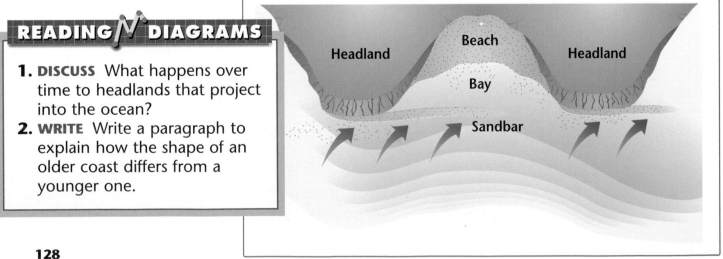

EFFECTS OF WAVE ACTION OVER TIME

Headland   Beach   Headland

Bay

Sandbar

Coastal erosion can undercut sea cliffs and cause houses to fall into the sea.

What Is Coastal Erosion?

The ocean does more than cut away headlands. Everywhere along the coast, winter storms drive powerful waves against the shore. The waves pick up rocks and gravel, hurling them against sea cliffs, sea walls, or whatever else stands in the way. The waves also undercut the base of the sea cliffs. Soon large blocks of rock fall into the ocean. Over time, the ocean advances and the coastline erodes.

The rate at which this process occurs depends on several factors. One is the shape of the coast. Curves in the coastline can deflect the force of the waves in some areas. Another factor is the hardness or softness of the coastal rock. Soft rock will wear away faster than harder rock. Another factor is the strength of the winter storms. Still another is the presence or absence of beach sand. Sometimes a pier or other structure may interrupt beach drift. An area can be "starved" of its normal beach sand. Erosion is more likely in these areas.

Erosion can sometimes occur very rapidly. Scientists have studied the way waves can cut caves in the sea cliffs of southern California. It was once thought that the ocean took centuries to create new caves. Now scientists know that new caves can be created in just a few days. That is how strong the ocean can be!

129

A rising coast is marked by steep cliffs and sea stacks.

What Happens When Coastal Land Rises?

You have learned that parts of California are rising. The pressure from moving tectonic plates is pushing mountains upward. It is also forcing parts of the coast to rise, sometimes very suddenly. What effect do you think that has on the coastline?

Where the coast is rising, new shorelines have been created, one after another. Each time the land has risen, the existing beach has risen with it. The beach would move up and away from the water. Then a new beach would form below it at the point where the ocean now meets the land.

Over time, the land near the coast has come to resemble a series of step-like terraces. Each of these "shelves" is what remains of an ancient shoreline. This formation is called a **marine terrace**. Each terrace is a place where the land and ocean once met. As the coast was pushed up, the ancient shoreline was left high and dry. Fossils of sea creatures are often found in these rock formations high above the waterline.

When you and your family travel on the roads that run close to the ocean, you are traveling on top of these ancient shorelines.

How fast is the coastline rising? Scientists think that some parts of the California coast are rising at the rate of 13 meters (40 ft) every thousand years. In other words, at least every thousand years there is a new beach and a new shoreline.

What Does a Rising Coast Look Like?

How do you know when you are looking at a rising coastline? There are clues that you can use to spot one. A rising coastline has a telltale form.

Where the land is rising, the shoreline curves and winds. The sea cliffs are relatively young. They have not yet been straightened out or eroded back by the force of the waves. The cliffs are steep. Rockslides are common, and huge boulders lie in the surf where they have fallen.

On a young, rising coastline there are still many rocky headlands. They project out into the ocean, where they are hit by the full force of the waves. Tucked between them are many small beaches on little coves or bays. In some places where the rock is softer, the ocean has cut caves and tunnels into the cliffs. Parts of the cliffs have been eroded. Other parts still stand, looking like pillars rising out of the ocean. These pillarlike rocks are called *sea stacks*. Sometimes they even form natural arches. In time, they too will be worn away.

Much of California's coast matches this description. If you visit the shore and see steep cliffs and sea stacks, you are looking at a rising coast.

Waves sometimes cut away coastal cliffs to create natural arches.

What Happens When Coastal Land Is Submerged?

Sometimes coastal areas sink below sea level. When that happens, the sea flows into river mouths and over low-lying areas. If the water is not very deep, lagoons, marshes, and other wetlands form.

You have learned that most of coastal California is rising, not sinking. But some parts are rising very slowly. Sometimes sea levels have risen faster. When the Ice Age glaciers melted, sea levels rose very rapidly. Many coastal areas, including some that were rising, became submerged. Many remain submerged today. One of the most visible examples is San Francisco Bay. When sea levels were much lower, the floor of the Bay was a valley. Rivers ran through it to empty into the ocean. When sea levels rose, the valley was "drowned." Seawater poured in and covered it. The sea rose until it reached the level you see today. Now the Sacramento and San Joaquin rivers empty into the Bay, far from the ocean.

Coastal areas are sinking in other parts of the world, too. In many areas, moving tectonic plates are the cause. Also, according to scientists, sea levels today are slowly rising. Rising sea levels may cause problems for cities and towns built on low-lying coastal areas.

Beneath San Francisco Bay is a "drowned" river valley. It was submerged when sea levels rose.

What Is an Estuary?

An arm of the sea that extends into the mouth of a river is called an **estuary**. Estuaries can form when coastal lands sink. They can also form when sea levels rise. Either way, seawater invades the river channel. Sometimes it fills up the entire lower part of a river valley.

Estuaries create a very special ecosystem. Marsh grasses often grow in wetlands along the estuary's edge. Seawater pushes up the estuary channel as the tide rises. When the tide *ebbs*, or falls, fresh water flows down the channel. The mix of salt water and fresh water nourishes an extraordinary variety of wildlife.

Estuaries are nurseries for many species of ocean fish. In the estuary marshes, the fish are protected from ocean predators. There are plenty of smaller plants and animals to eat. Only when they mature do the fish venture out into the open sea. Estuaries in California are particularly important to the survival of young salmon.

The fish in turn provide food for many species of seabirds. Large seabird populations often nest and raise young in estuary marshes. Many seabirds also use estuaries as stopping places during long migrations.

Because estuaries are so important to fish and birds, it is important to protect them from pollution. Pollutants dumped into upstream waters can harm estuary wildlife and reduce animal and plant populations.

An estuary is an arm of the sea at the mouth of a river.

RIVER DEPOSITS

HYPOTHESIZE How do changes in the amount of water flowing in a river affect the amount of sand deposited in the ocean?
Write a hypothesis in your *Science Journal*.

MATERIALS
- large rectangular aluminum pan
- wet sand
- plastic dripper bottle of water
- *Science Journal*

PROCEDURES

1. Fill two thirds of the tray with wet sand to a depth of 6 cm to represent the land. Add water to the remaining one third of the tray to represent the ocean.

2. Your teacher will give you a plastic "dripper" bottle of water. Hold the water dripper over the land as shown. Adjust for a slow drip of 2–3 drips/second. What happens?

3. Adjust for 5-6 drips/second. What happens?

CONCLUDE AND APPLY

CONCLUDE How does river flow affect depositing of sand in the ocean?

How Do Beach Dunes Form?

Have you ever seen dunes at the beach? *Dunes* are mounds of sand. Most are low, but some can be quite high. Most beach dunes form in flat, low-lying areas. Dunes are less common along high, rocky coasts.

Dunes are formed by wind. Sand particles blowing along the beach collect in mounds. The sand piles up wherever there is a natural wind barrier such as a rock ledge or a clump of bushes. The wind pushes more sand onto the pile and builds it higher. It also pushes the sand up the side of the dune and over the top. If this process continues, the whole dune will move in the direction the wind is blowing.

Brain Power

You may have heard people describe sand dunes as "fragile." How can a big mound of sand be fragile?

Beach dunes are a valuable part of the natural beach system. During storms, they protect the land behind the dunes from the ocean waves. The sand absorbs the force of the waves and prevents the land from being washed away. For this reason, in many places beach dunes are protected by law.

Certain types of grasses grow on dunes. Their roots hold the sand in place. In many places people also plant grasses or build fences along the beach to help dune formation.

Do you like spending a day at the beach? The shoreline is one of the most popular places for people to live and play. To use the shoreline wisely, it pays to understand the natural forces at work. It is important to see how the ocean shapes the beach, and how the beach protects the shore. It is important to know what form the shoreline had in the past, and what form it is likely to have in the future.

REVIEW

1. Where does beach sand come from?

2. How is the beach different in summer and winter?

3. **COMPARE AND CONTRAST** Describe rising and sinking coastal areas.

4. What happens to the shape of a coastline over time?

5. **CRITICAL THINKING** *Analyze* Why is it important to preserve estuaries?

WHY IT MATTERS **THINK ABOUT IT**
Is it a good idea to build houses very close to the ocean? Why or why not?

WHY IT MATTERS **WRITE ABOUT IT**
What if it were your job to protect beach dunes? Write what you would say on signs telling people to be careful.

READING SKILL
Write a paragraph explaining the sequence of events as sand moves through the natural beach system.

SAVE THE CLIFFS

The sea cliffs of California are a wonderful place to live. Up and down the coast, people have built houses on top of the cliffs so that they can enjoy being near the ocean. But there's a problem: the cliffs are on a naturally eroding coastline.

Parts of the coast are eroding away at a rate of 1.5 meters (5 ft) per year. Landslides along the cliffs are common. Many coastal bluffs are sandstone, so they crumble easily. Others are shale, siltstone, clay, or mudstone. These rocks liquefy or disintegrate when wet, causing landslides after heavy rains. Building practices also contribute to cliff erosion. Drain pipes, septic tanks, and lawn watering may saturate the cliffs with water, causing them to collapse.When the cliffs collapse, houses can fall down, too.

People have worsened the erosion problem in another way. Normally California's sand beaches protect the cliffs by absorbing the force of the ocean's waves. In the natural system, sand carried to the ocean by rivers and streams replaces beach sand that is washed away. But today many of those rivers and streams have been dammed. New sand no longer reaches the beach. Without new sand, ocean waves can undercut the cliffs and cause them to collapse.

So what can people do? One solution has been to truck sand to the beaches. Over the past fifty years, sand from coastal construction projects has been used to widen beaches throughout southern California.

People in one town placed a huge plastic tube filled with sand on the beach. The tubing was supposed to keep the sand in place. But instead it burst, and the sand washed away.

People have also constructed elaborate sea walls on the cliffs to keep them from eroding.

In some places they have covered the cliffs with concrete. They have also built jetties and breakwaters to deflect the ocean's waves.

These defenses may stop the ocean for now. But the fact remains that the shoreline is naturally eroding. Who knows how long today's sea cliffs will last?

Geography Link

To learn more about changes at the seashore, visit *www.mhschool.com/science* and enter the keyword COAST.

*inter*NET
CONNECTION

In some California coastal areas, huge rocks are piled along the shore to hold back the sea.

DISCUSSION STARTER

1. Why are coastal cliffs likely to erode?

2. Why are some beaches losing sand and shrinking?

3. How have tried to combat beach erosion?

137

WHY IT MATTERS

Learning about natural hazards helps you protect yourself.

SCIENCE WORDS

floodplain the flat area above a river bank formed by flooding

scarp a steep, sharp break in the earth at the top of some landslides

debris flow a wet mix of rocks, soil, and water that moves quickly

colonization the process that brings new plants and animals into an area

brushfire a wildfire in an area with mixed trees, shrubs, and grasses

El Niño a periodic warming in the tropical Pacific Ocean that affects weather in many parts of the world

Natural Hazards

Have there ever been floods in the area where you live? Have you ever felt an earthquake? Are brushfires a problem in the hot, dry autumn months? Have you seen television pictures of roads blocked by landslides?

California has a lot of natural hazards, and for good reason. The climate of much of the state is dry, but there are heavy rains in some seasons. California has mountains and volcanoes. The land is also at the junction of moving plates in Earth's crust.

Learning about natural hazards is important. If you understand what causes natural hazards and where they occur, you'll be better able to protect yourself and others.

EXPLORE

HYPOTHESIZE Why might floods today in California do more damage to property than floods 50 or 100 years ago? Write a hypothesis in your *Science Journal.* What data would you need to test your ideas?

Investigate Data About California Floods

Use data to discover patterns in flooding in California.

MAJOR CALIFORNIA FLOODS

Dates	Area flooded	Dollar cost
March 1938	Southern coast, Mojave	$79 million
December 1955	Northern part of state	$166 million
December 1964	Northern part of state	$239 million
January–February 1969	Southern, central coast, Mojave	$400 million
January–February 1980	Central, southern coast	$350 million
January 1982	San Francisco	$75 million
February 1986	Northern half of state	$379 million
January, March 1995	Northern (January), central (March)	$3 billion
December 1996–January 1997	Sierra Nevada, Great Valley	$1.6 billion

PROCEDURES

1. Study the data table about floods in California.

2. Draw a bar graph to show the flooding pattern for each month. Write the months of the year along the horizontal scale. Divide the vertical scale into even intervals from 1 to 7. Count the number of floods that occurred during each month given in the table and draw a bar to match that number.

3. Draw a line graph of the dollar cost of each period of flooding. Write dates from 1938 to 2000 along the horizontal scale. Write dollar intervals along the vertical scale using intervals of $300 million.

MATERIALS

- graph paper
- pencil
- *Science Journal*

CONCLUDE AND APPLY

1. **INTERPRET DATA** Which months had no floods? Which months had the most flooding? Why is this?

2. **ANALYZE** What is the trend in costs from 1938 to 1997? What could explain the trend?

How Do Floods Happen?

A flood happens when a river cannot carry all the water that drains into it. In California the cause is often too much runoff water from rain and melting snow. When a river receives more water than it can carry, the water over-flows its banks.

Most floods in California happen in winter and early spring when rains and melting snow add the most water to rivers. In 1862, huge floods covered the entire Central Valley. Water covered the tops of telegraph poles!

Nothing can change the amount of rain or melting snow. However, people do some things that increase runoff water and make floods more likely. Paving roads and building cities both prevent water from entering the soil. That makes more runoff.

Vegetation can help reduce the amount of water that runs off into a river. Roots help water soak into the ground. Roots also absorb water from the ground and return it to the air. People can make floods less likely by planting vegetation. Another step is to keep unpaved areas where water can enter the ground.

SACRAMENTO RIVER FLOW RATES

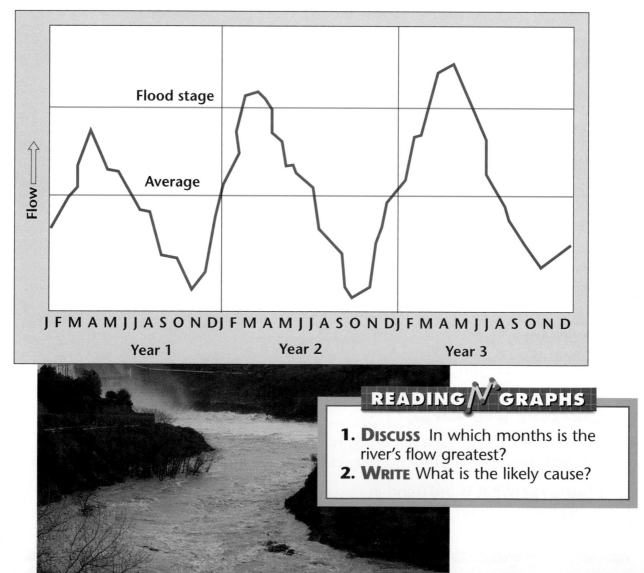

Flood stage

Average

Flow

J F M A M J J A S O N D J F M A M J J A S O N D J F M A M J J A S O N D

Year 1   Year 2   Year 3

READING GRAPHS

1. **Discuss** In which months is the river's flow greatest?
2. **Write** What is the likely cause?

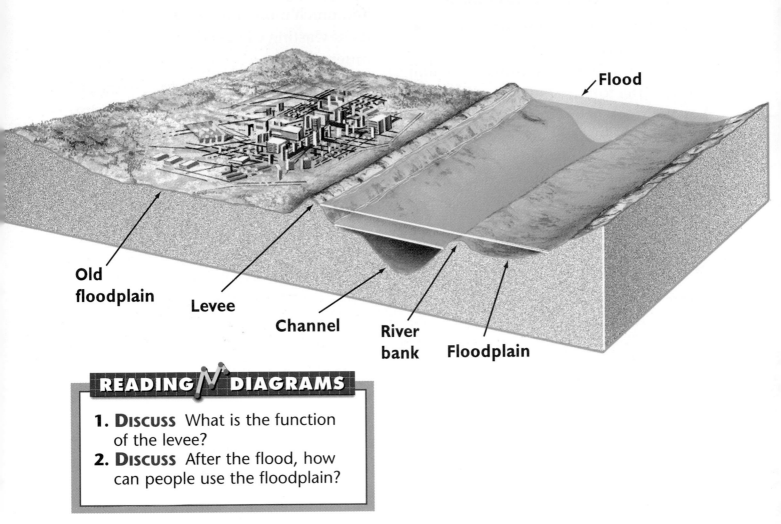

Flood

Old
floodplain

Levee

Channel

River
bank

Floodplain

READING IN DIAGRAMS

1. **DISCUSS** What is the function of the levee?
2. **DISCUSS** After the flood, how can people use the floodplain?

How Does Flooding Change Landscapes?

Floods are natural events that create floodplains. **Floodplains** are flat, higher areas next to rivers where there is water during floods. How are floodplains formed? Rivers carry a flow of fine soil, or sediment. When a river rises above its banks, the overflowing water slows down. As it slows, the sediment sinks to the ground. It becomes part of the the floodplain.

Sediment makes floodplains fertile, so they are good for farming. Because floodplains are flat, they are also an easy place to build cities. However, because these cities are built on floodplains, where rivers overflow their banks, the cities sometimes get flooded. Some cities build walls, called *levees*, to keep water in the river channel. Also, engineers may deepen riverbeds so that they can carry more water. These actions may prevent flooding in one place, but they may make it worse in other areas.

A river bounded by levees may back up and flood upstream areas. A deeper channel may increase the river's flow and cause flooding downstream.

What Is a Landslide?

You have learned how air and water can move rocks and soil by erosion. Rocks and soil can also move downhill without the forces of water and air. Soil and rock begin moving when the ground below can no longer support their weight. People usually call this movement a landslide. As you learned in Chapter 3, geologists call it *mass wasting*.

When slow mass wasting occurs, it can be hard to see.

• Soil can creep downhill just one centimeter (0.4 in.) each year.

• A part of a hillside can slip downhill over a period of a few hours.

Rapid mass wasting is easier to see—and much more dangerous! Rapid mass wasting can occur in several different ways.

• A large body of soil and rocks may suddenly slump downhill. At the top of this slump you may see a scarp. A **scarp** is a steep cut that shows where the slump started.

• A rockfall may occur when rocks fall from a cliff.

• A **debris flow** is a wet mix of soil, rock, and water that moves very quickly. Debris flows are most common during or after heavy rains, especially where there is not much vegetation to hold the soil in place.

MASS WASTING

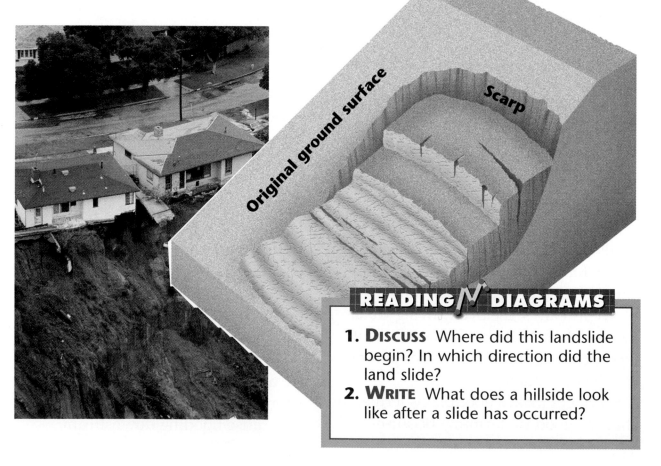

Original ground surface

Scarp

READING N DIAGRAMS

1. **DISCUSS** Where did this landslide begin? In which direction did the land slide?
2. **WRITE** What does a hillside look like after a slide has occurred?

Can You Tell Where Landslides Have Happened?

A landslide happens when the land below cannot support the land above. When landslides occur, they can change the landscape. These changes can be large or small. Geologists are trained to recognize the results of mass wasting. You can spot these results, too, if you know what to look for.

Some signs of mass wasting are easy to spot. When a road is cut through a hill, you may see fallen rocks. At the top of a slump, you may see the steep cut of a scarp. A hillside that moves may cause trees to become tilted or crooked. You may see a *deposit*, a pile of rocks and soil at the bottom of a hill. A deposit is a sure sign of mass wasting.

If you can spot places where mass wasting has occurred, you'll be better able to recognize places where it may happen in the future. These mass wasting hazard areas include steep slopes of river valleys, mountainsides in rainy areas along the coast, and places where roads cut through hills. Building structures in these places can be dangerous. The weight of heavy structures can even make mass wasting more likely to occur.

MASS WASTING HAZARD AREAS

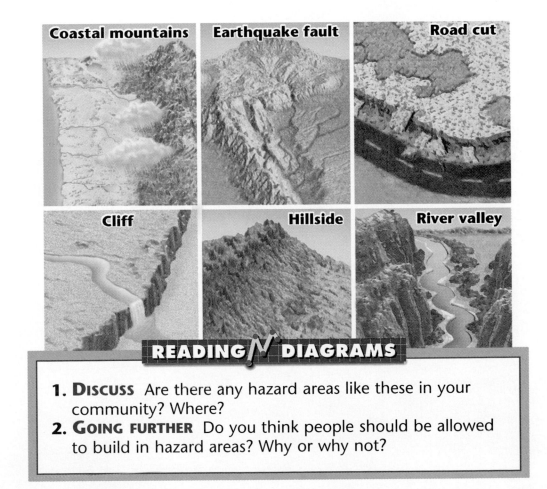

Coastal mountains   Earthquake fault   Road cut

Cliff   Hillside   River valley

READING 📐 DIAGRAMS

1. **DISCUSS** Are there any hazard areas like these in your community? Where?
2. **GOING FURTHER** Do you think people should be allowed to build in hazard areas? Why or why not?

What Are the Dangers from Landslides?

Mass wasting is a serious problem in California. Heavy winter rains along the coast make the soil water-logged and unstable. When earthquakes jolt the soil, they can trigger landslides. There are large areas of steep land where rocks and soil tend to move downhill. Rocks and soil from the San Gabriel Mountains above the Los Angeles area often slide down, striking houses in the hills below.

Major landslides can destroy homes and other structures as well. They can also block roads and make driving hazardous. They can even change the course of streams. In areas of steep mountains, such as Yosemite Valley, rocks can fall from the high peaks and endanger campers and hikers. Fallen rocks often break into pieces. The broken rocks left on the ground after a rockfall are called *talus*. Talus can often block roads completely.

Slow mass wasting can also cause problems in cities. For more than 40 years, a neighborhood on the coast near Los Angeles has been sliding toward the ocean. Although the houses are on a gentle slope, the slide harms their foundations, as well as roads nearby.

Landslides can be a serious hazard in some California coastal communities. Seasonal rains can make the ground unstable, and coastal cliffs sometimes crumble.

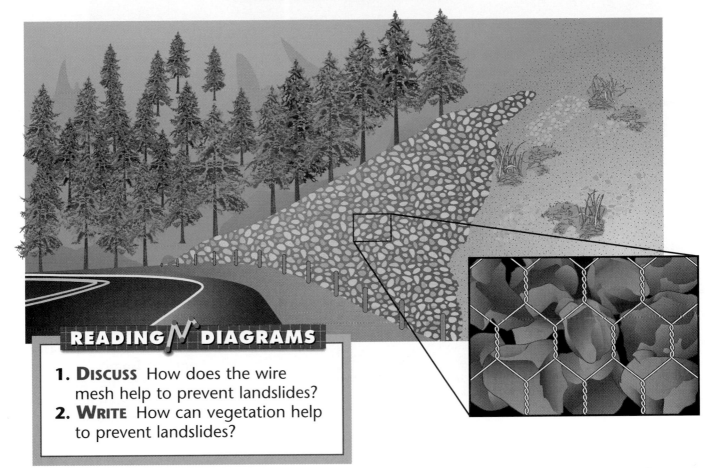

READING ⁄ DIAGRAMS

1. **DISCUSS** How does the wire mesh help to prevent landslides?
2. **WRITE** How can vegetation help to prevent landslides?

How Can People Prevent Landslides?

There are steps people can take to prevent landslides. One is to plant hillsides with vegetation, especially trees with deep roots. These roots help hold soil together. They also remove water from the soil, helping to dry it and making it less likely to slide. If there is already vegetation on a hillside, keeping the trees and bushes there helps to avoid landslides.

Building roads wisely can prevent landslides. Some roads cut through hills in such a way that land on the uphill side becomes unstable. Engineers can design retaining walls to prevent land slides in these areas. These walls may include rough-shaped rocks. Engineers use these rocks because the rough shape keeps them from sliding. Some walls are wrapped in metal mesh to hold them together. Some have drains to let water escape. Water-logged soil is a major cause of slides.

In some areas there is always a risk of landslides. In these places, the best way to prevent damage is to avoid building there.

145

**Mount Saint Helens in Washington State erupted with more destructive force than a nuclear bomb.
[inset] Mount Saint Helens looked like this before the eruption.**

What Are the Dangers from Volcanoes?

Volcanoes are another natural hazard in a few areas of California. You've learned that different kinds of volcanoes erupt in different ways. A few erupt quietly and produce lava that flows quickly. Others make thick, sticky lava and can explode violently.

Each type of volcano has different effects on the land.

- Volcanoes that make quick-flowing lava coat the land below them with lava. They do not explode or send out huge clouds of ash.

- Volcanoes that make thick lavas are much more dangerous. They can explode if melted rock gets stuck

inside them. When enough pressure builds up under the melted rock, it forces the lava out. This is what blew apart Mount Saint Helens in Washington State in 1980. Explosive volcanoes can spread ash, mud, and lava over huge areas.

Big volcanic explosions are very rare but can be very destructive. More than 750,000 years ago, a volcano in the Long Valley area of California erupted with tremendous force. It spread thick ash over much of the western United States. Living Californians have never seen anything like this. The most recent eruption occurred at Mt. Lassen, in Northern California. This series of eruptions went on for seven years, from 1914 to 1921. Yet no one was killed.

How Do Volcanoes Affect Plants and Wildlife?

The lava and ash from a large eruption can kill all forms of life around a volcano. After some years, plants begin growing on the lava and ash. Finally, soil is formed and life continues.

In 1883, the volcano Krakatau (krak' ə tä'ü) erupted on an island in the Indian Ocean. This eruption was one of the largest ever recorded. It buried everything on the island under tons of hot ash.

After the eruption, Krakatau was a dead island. Yet, in time, plants and animals began to reappear on the island. Scientists call this process **colonization**. Colonization is carried out by plants and animals that move easily and can live in harsh conditions. These *pioneer species* have much in common with the pioneers from the East who crossed the continent to settle in California!

Pioneer plants and animals arrive at new homes in different ways. Birds and insects fly. Light seeds travel on the wind. Some animals swim, and some seeds and animals float on logs. Some seeds and small animals are carried in by flying animals. Some animals arrive by walking.

Brain Power

Why is it so difficult to prepare for major volcanic eruptions?

COLONIZATION AFTER A VOLCANIC ERUPTION

READING DIAGRAMS

1. **DISCUSS** How are plants and animals colonizing this area?
2. **CLASSIFY** Which animals are arriving by air?

What Are the Dangers from Earthquakes?

Imagine this: the ground starts shaking. Tall buildings sway. Bridges and parking ramps collapse. Underground natural gas pipes burst and fires break out. Water mains break and the tap runs dry. The shaking destroys hundreds of homes and damages thousands of others. The shaking sets off landslides and the city shuts down.

Californians living along the coast, from San Francisco to the south, know how the ground shakes during an earthquake. Some have seen serious destruction. The 1994 Northridge quake, centered near Los Angeles, was one of the worst natural disasters in U.S. history. The cost was estimated to be from $25 to $40 billion dollars.

The Northridge earthquake was less intense than three other recent California quakes, but it showed that relatively small quakes can cause a lot of damage.

Earthquakes cause damage in two ways:

- The crack in the Earth right above a fault destroys buildings and pipelines. This effect is strong but affects only places directly on the fault.

- Waves moving out from the earthquake's focus affect a much wider area. These waves cause much more damage.

Although earthquakes cannot be prevented, good building techniques can make them less dangerous. Because of the earthquake danger, California has strict building standards.

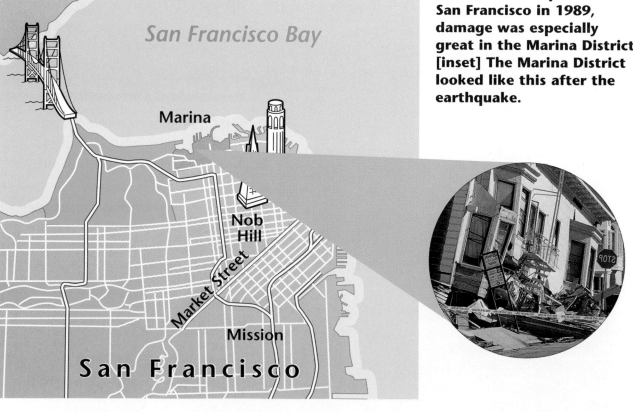

When an earthquake struck San Francisco in 1989, damage was especially great in the Marina District. [inset] The Marina District looked like this after the earthquake.

How Do Earthquakes Affect Wildlife ?

Earthquakes may be more dangerous to people than to wildlife. Animals that live underground can be hurt if their burrows collapse, but most animals survive earthquakes fairly well.

Did you know that some people think animals can predict earthquakes? It's not true, but there is a reason for the belief. Remember that earthquakes make P waves and S waves. P waves move faster, so they reach most places first. An animal with good hearing can hear P waves that we cannot. A dog may jump after hearing a P wave, but well before you feel the S wave. You might then believe that the dog "knew" that the earthquake was coming!

Some animals can hear the fast-moving P waves at the beginning of an earthquake. People may not sense the earthquake until the slower S waves arrive.

Seismographs

HYPOTHESIZE How can you detect an earthquake? Write a hypothesis in your *Science Journal.*

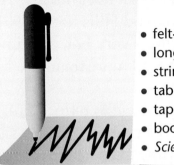

MATERIALS
- felt-tip pen or marker
- long sheet of paper
- string
- table
- tape
- books to use as weights
- *Science Journal*

PROCEDURES

1. Place a sheet of paper on a table. Hold a felt-tip pen right over the paper to make a mark.

2. Hold the pen securely so that it does not move. Have your partner pull the paper underneath the pen. Notice that your pen makes a line as the paper moves.

3. Tap the table continuously for five seconds as your partner pulls the paper. The line zigzags. This is how a seismograph works.

4. **MAKE A MODEL** Design a way to position the pen over the paper so you don't have to hold it and so it records a zigzag line when the table shakes. Describe it in your *Science Journal.*

CONCLUDE AND APPLY

INFER How do you think your model would work if the ground trembled?

What Are the Dangers from Wildfires?

Have you ever seen a **brushfire** — a fire in grass, shrubs, and trees? If you have, you know how quickly hot, dry vegetation can burn. Along California's central and southern coast, autumn is brushfire season. If the trees and brush catch fire, they burn hot and fast. The disastrous Oakland Hills fire in 1991 occurred during a very hot, dry time. The fire destroyed more than 3,000 houses.

What can be done to reduce fire danger? Where brushfires are possible, people can prune trees near their houses. People can remove fast-burning trees like eucalyptus. They can also build houses using fire-resistant materials.

Fire: Nature's Recycler

In many places where lightning starts fires, plants have evolved to survive fires. In fact, seeds of some plants in the dry shrubland called chaparral need fire to begin growing.

Some plants grow back because their roots live through fires. Other plants return by colonizing, as they do after a volcanic eruption. Once the plants return, animals return, too.

Fires are one way nature recycles. When a plant burns, some of its chemicals enter the soil. These chemicals, called *nutrients*, feed other plants. A plant is mostly carbon. Fire changes this carbon into carbon dioxide gas. Living plants take in this carbon dioxide and get the carbon they need from it.

In 1991, brushfires destroyed thousands of homes in Oakland, California.
[Above] After a wildfire, new plant growth quickly covers the burnt area.

FIRE: NATURE'S RECYCLER

Carbon dioxide

Soil

Nutrients

Natural hazards are part of living on Earth. It is important for us to understand them. We know ways to predict fires and floods, but not earthquakes or volcanic eruptions. Many hazards we call "natural" are affected by what people do. If people build in areas with natural hazards, they put themselves at risk.

READING N DIAGRAMS

DISCUSS What are two ways that plant nutrients are recycled after a fire?

REVIEW

1. Describe what happens in a landslide.

2. Explain why many brushfires occur in autumn in southern California.

3. Explain why the danger of flooding is usually greatest in winter and early spring.

4. **CAUSE AND EFFECT** What actions can people take to reduce the danger from brushfires? From floods?

5. **GOING FURTHER** *Analyze* Hot, dry winds can increase the danger of which natural hazard?

WHY IT MATTERS THINK ABOUT IT
Suppose you were deciding where a developer might build homes. What kinds of places do you think are too much at risk from natural hazards?

WHY IT MATTERS WRITE ABOUT IT
Write a paragraph about why it is important to be aware of any natural hazards in your area.

READING SKILL LOCATE SUPPORTING DETAILS Write about different ways that rapid mass wasting can occur.

STORMY WEATHER

The year 1998 was a nasty one for storms in California. Thirty-foot waves slammed the coastline. A combination of floods and landslides destroyed hundreds of houses. Mud and water blocked roads and rail lines. The storms seemed to come one right after the other. Some brought winds close to 75 miles per hour—almost hurricane speed!

The weird weather of 1998 was blamed on an unusual warming in the Pacific Ocean called El Niño. Every few years, El Niño changes the location of giant rain clouds. That affects weather in many parts of the world. Places that usually get lots of rain are very dry. And places that are usually dry get lots of rain.

El Niños last for a year or two, and then disappear. Once an El Niño appears, we can predict the changes for many parts of the world. This pattern makes it easier to forecast weather.

DISCUSSION STARTER

1. What is one advantage of knowing more about El Niño?

2. How long does an El Niño last?

To learn more about unusual storms, visit *www.mhschool.com/science* and enter the keyword WEATHER.

interNET CONNECTION

SCIENCE WORDS

arroyo p. 118	**estuary** p. 133
beach drift p. 125	**floodplain** p. 141
brushfire p. 150	**marine**
debris flow p. 142	**terrace** p. 130
delta p. 114	**scarp** p. 142
El Niño p. 152	

USING SCIENCE WORDS

Number a paper from 1 to 10. Fill in 1 to 5 with words from the list above.

1. A periodic warming in the tropical Pacific Ocean is called a(n) __?__.

2. A(n) __?__ is an arm of the sea at the mouth of a river.

3. Water running down a desert mountainside can carve a deep canyon called a(n) __?__.

4. Ocean waves carry sand along the beach in a process called __?__.

5. A fan-shaped area of sediment at the mouth of a river is called a(n) __?__.

6–10. Pick five words from the list above that were not used in 1 to 5, and use each in a sentence.

UNDERSTANDING SCIENCE IDEAS

11. What causes arroyos to form in the desert?

12. Explain how beaches protect the shoreline.

13. How can vegetation reduce the danger of landslides?

14. What can people do to reduce danger from wildfires?

15. Explain what happens to beach sand in the winter.

USING IDEAS AND SKILLS

16. Will marine terraces form where a coastline is sinking? Why or why not?

17. Why are floodplains good places for farming?

18. **INTERPRET DATA/INFER** Based on the table below, what time of year are floods likeliest in San Diego County?

San Diego County Floods

Year	Flood Date	Year	Flood Date
1960	March 6	1978	January 31
1969	February 25	1984	January 15
1970	December 28	1993	November 6

19. **READING SKILL: LOCATING SUPPORTING DETAILS** What details support the idea that beach sand is in almost constant motion?

20. **THINKING LIKE A SCIENTIST** A jetty 1,000 meters (3,250 ft) long is built out into the ocean. On one side, beach sand disappears. Why?

PROBLEMS and PUZZLES

Flowing Back and Forth In a typical estuary, an arm of the sea at the mouth of a river, the water reverses direction several times a day. Can you explain why this happens?

UNIT 2 REVIEW

SCIENCE WORDS

arroyo p. 118
debris flow p. 142
deposition p. 96
fold mountain p. 84
glacier p. 100

levee p. 117
mass wasting p. 96
moraine p. 102
till p. 102
weathering p. 85

USING SCIENCE WORDS

Number a paper from 1 to 10. Beside each number write the word or words that best complete the sentence.

1. A(n) __?__ is a deposit of sediment in front of a glacier.

2. If you push two halves of a sheet of paper together, you are modeling the formation of a(n) __?__.

3. A(n) __?__ is a huge sheet of ice and snow that moves slowly over the land.

4. __?__ is the downhill movement of Earth material caused by gravity.

5. A wall or ridge built to keep a river from overflowing is called a(n) __?__.

6. A broken-up mix of rocks and soil left by a landslide is a __?__.

7. __?__ is a jumble of many sizes of sediment deposited by a glacier.

8. A(n) __?__ is a deep canyon carved by water in a desert mountainside.

9. The breaking down of rocks by natural processes is called __?__.

10. __?__ is the process by which sand and soil are dropped off at a new location.

UNDERSTANDING SCIENCE IDEAS

Write 11 to 15. For each number write the letter of the best answer. You may wish to use the hints provided.

11. Plateaus are different from mountains because plateaus
    a. are at low elevations
    b. are not as folded or faulted
    c. are caused by weather
    d. have vertical rock layers
    (Hint: Read page 85.)

12. Huge masses of rock that are tilted upward form
    a. moraines
    b. meanders
    c. till
    d. fault-block mountains
    (Hint: Read page 84.)

13. When rivers reach the sea, they often form a
    a. moraine
    b. floodplain
    c. levee
    d. delta
    (Hint: Read page 114.)

14. In the desert, flash floods carve deep canyons called
    a. estuaries
    b. arroyos
    c. moraines
    d. depositions
    (Hint: Read page 118.)

15. Landslides can occur when hillsides are made unstable by
    a. heavy rains
    b. brushfires
    c. weathering
    d. deposition
    (Hint: Read page 142.)

USING IDEAS AND SKILLS

16. Explain how paving over the ground may increase flood hazards.

17. Is a coastal headland a wise place to build a home? Why or why not?

18. Where does groundwater come from?

19. What role do the roots of trees play in weathering?

20. Why is coastal erosion often a problem during winter?

21. What good do brushfires do for living things?

22. How are fault-block mountains formed?

23. Why do people build cities on flood-plains?

THINKING LIKE A SCIENTIST

24.  **HYPOTHESIZE** One spring during alternating warm and cold spells, potholes appear in nearby streets. What natural process do you think is causing them?

25. What makes plateaus a good place to study rock layers?

*inter*NET CONNECTION

For help in reviewing this unit, visit **www.mhschool.com/science**

WRITING IN YOUR JOURNAL

SCIENCE IN YOUR LIFE
Are natural hazards a threat where you live? Why or why not? What steps have people taken or might they take to protect against them?

PRODUCT ADS
Car advertisements sometimes show vehicles being driven along the beach. What are those advertisements trying to demonstrate? In your opinion, is driving on the beach a good idea?

HOW SCIENTISTS WORK
In this unit you learned about how glaciers reshape the land. Scientists study till and moraines to trace ancient glaciers. What do they find in these deposits? How can their findings tell us about an ancient glacier's path?

Design your own Experiment

Compare a river that flows down steep slopes with one that crosses flat plains. Form a hypothesis about which one erodes the landscape more quickly. Design an experiment to test your hypothesis. Review your experiment with your teacher before you attempt it.

PROBLEMS and PUZZLES

California Beach House

Your best friend owns a house on a cliff overlooking a beautiful California beach. The sandy beach is great in summer, but in winter much of the sand washes away and waves erode the cliff. Your friend wants to protect the house by building a breakwater, a long line of heavy rocks extending out into the ocean. Do you think a breakwater would help? What do you think it would do to the beach? Explain your answers.

The Catfish Pond

The Calaveras Catfish Company needs a new fishpond to raise catfish. The owner asks you where to build it. You suggest getting the water from a nearby river, which flows across areas of clay soil and sandy soil. Should the pond be dug in the soft sand or the hard clay? Explain your answer.

Home Site Hazards

Two houses are for sale in southern California. Both are near an active earthquake fault. One is high on a dry, brush-covered hillside made of soft, crumbly rock. The other is in a flat, vegetation-free, open area near a riverbed that fills with water after it rains. Use the following chart to rate the natural hazard risk for each house. Write "L" if the risk is low or "H" if the risk is high. Explain your ratings.

	Hillside Home	Flatland Home
Flood		
Landslide		
Earthquake		
Brushfire		

ENERGY

CHAPTER 5

HEAT

Every 65 minutes Old Faithful erupts. It's just water — but what a sight! It is caused by a complicated series of events, but it all "boils" down to heat. The rocks beneath Old Faithful are very hot. They heat water in the ground. Think of what can happen to water heated in a pot on the stove. Water boils!

Heat is a form of energy. In a geyser, the energy of the hot rocks is transferred into the water. How does energy transfer work? You'll read all about it in Chapter 5.

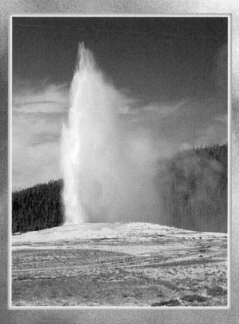

 In Chapter 5 you will get many chances to read for the main idea and look for supporting details.

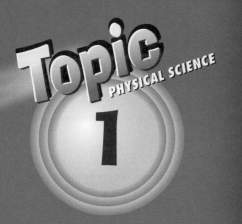

WHY IT MATTERS

You hear sounds and see objects because energy is traveling as sound and light.

SCIENCE WORDS

wave a motion that carries energy

vibration a back-and-forth movement

sound wave a vibration that spreads away from a vibrating object

matter anything that has mass and takes up space

vacuum a space where there is no matter

electromagnetism the production of magnetism by electricity and the production of electricity by magnets

light wave an electromagnetic wave that can travel without matter or through matter

electromagnetic spectrum all the wavelengths of visible and invisible light in order from short to long

Energy Moving from Place to Place

How long does it take for a ripple to cross the surface of a pond? How long does it take to see light when you turn on a lamp in a darkened room? How long does it take for the sound of a car horn to reach you from across the street?

Sound, light, and even the pond ripple are examples of energy in motion. In all three, the energy is moving in waves. How are water waves like light waves and sound waves? How are they different?

EXPLORE

HYPOTHESIZE How can you make waves move faster or slower? Write a hypothesis in your *Science Journal.* Test your ideas.

Investigate How Waves Move

Build a wave maker to explore what makes waves move faster or slower.

MATERIALS

- two 1-m strips of tape
- 20 straws
- meterstick
- 20 paper clips
- stopwatch or digital watch
- *Science Journal*

PROCEDURES

1. Work in groups of four. Starting 10 cm from one end, press 20 straws onto the sticky surface of a strip of tape. Be sure the straws are 4 cm apart, centered, and parallel. Secure them with the second strip.

2. OBSERVE Have two members of your group each take one end of the model, so it spreads out lengthwise. Have a third person tap a straw at one end. Have the fourth person time how long the wave takes to travel across from one end of the model to the other. In your *Science Journal*, record the time it takes.

3. EXPERIMENT Repeat step 2 several times, sometimes with the model tightly stretched, other times with it loosely stretched. Record your results.

CONCLUDE AND APPLY

1. OBSERVE In what direction does the wave move? In what direction do the straws move?

2. DRAW CONCLUSIONS How does holding it tighter or looser change how the wave moves?

GOING FURTHER: Problem Solving

3. EXPERIMENT Place paper clips at the ends of the first ten straws. Repeat steps 2 and 3 of the procedure. What happens?

What Is a Wave?

In a pond ripple, the sound of a car horn, or a beam of light from a flashlight, energy is traveling in waves. A **wave** is a motion that carries energy. You can set a ripple in motion by tossing a pebble into the pond. Your action transmits energy to the water in the pond. The wave motion carries the energy across the surface of the pond in the form of a ripple.

Sound energy also travels in waves. So does light energy. The wave motion carries the energy from its source to your ears and eyes. That is how you can hear a car horn or see a flashlight beam.

In the Explore Activity, you investigated how waves move. The model you made showed wave motion. The motion carried energy from one end of the model to the other.

Different forms of energy travel in different kinds of waves. In the pond ripple, energy is traveling as waves through water. In the sound of the car horn, energy is traveling as waves through the gases in the air. The waves in a beam of light move in a way that is like the motion of water waves.

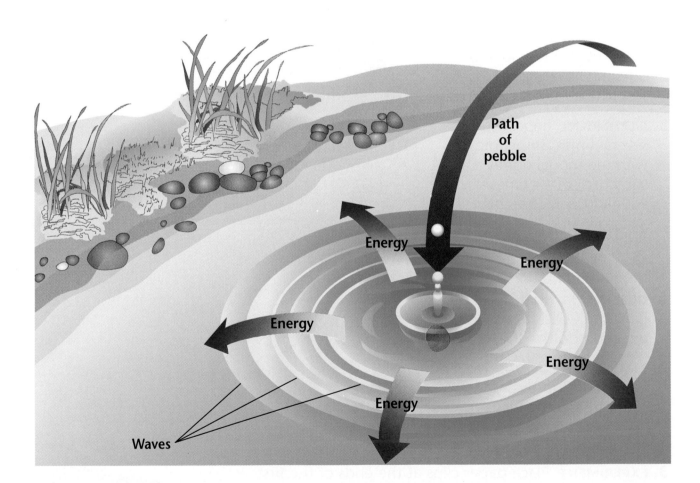

When you toss a pebble into a pond, water waves carry energy outward from the spot where the pebble landed.

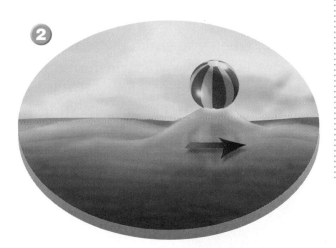

How Do Water Waves Travel?

When a wave travels across the surface of a pond, energy is traveling through the water particles, called *molecules*. Without these molecules, the energy cannot travel.

A ball floating on the surface will show you how the water molecules move. The diagram on this page gives a picture of what happens. As the wave moves from left to right, the water and the floating ball go up and down. In other words, as the energy travels in one direction, the water molecules move in a different *direction*.

After the wave has passed by, the water molecules and the floating ball stop moving up and down.

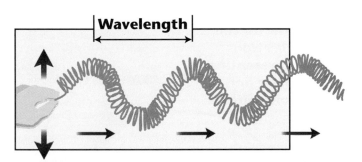

By vibrating one end of a spring toy up and down, you can see waves travel much as waves do on a watery surface.

As the wave moves from left to right, in what direction do the water and the ball move?

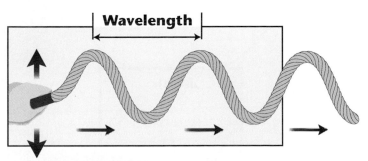

How do the waves made by a jump rope behave?

What Is Sound?

How does energy in motion produce the sounds you hear? How does that energy reach your ear? Are sound waves like water waves?

Vibration

Sound is created when something moves back and forth to produce waves of energy. That back-and-forth motion is called **vibration**. Unless something vibrates, there can be no sound.

How do you know that vibrations make sound? An air hammer drills through the pavement with a deafening "putt-putt." Often you can see the vibration that causes the sound. You can see an air hammer rattle up and down. If you are near the air hammer, you can feel the sidewalk shake.

Many vibrations are too fast for you to see. When a baseball is hit by a bat, you may not see the bat vibrating as the ball hits it, but the batter can still feel it. You hear the "crack" of the bat.

Energy Transfer

If you pluck a violin string, you can see it moving back and forth. You provide the energy necessary for this vibration when you strike the string. This energy is transferred to the string and causes it to vibrate. The vibration produces sound.

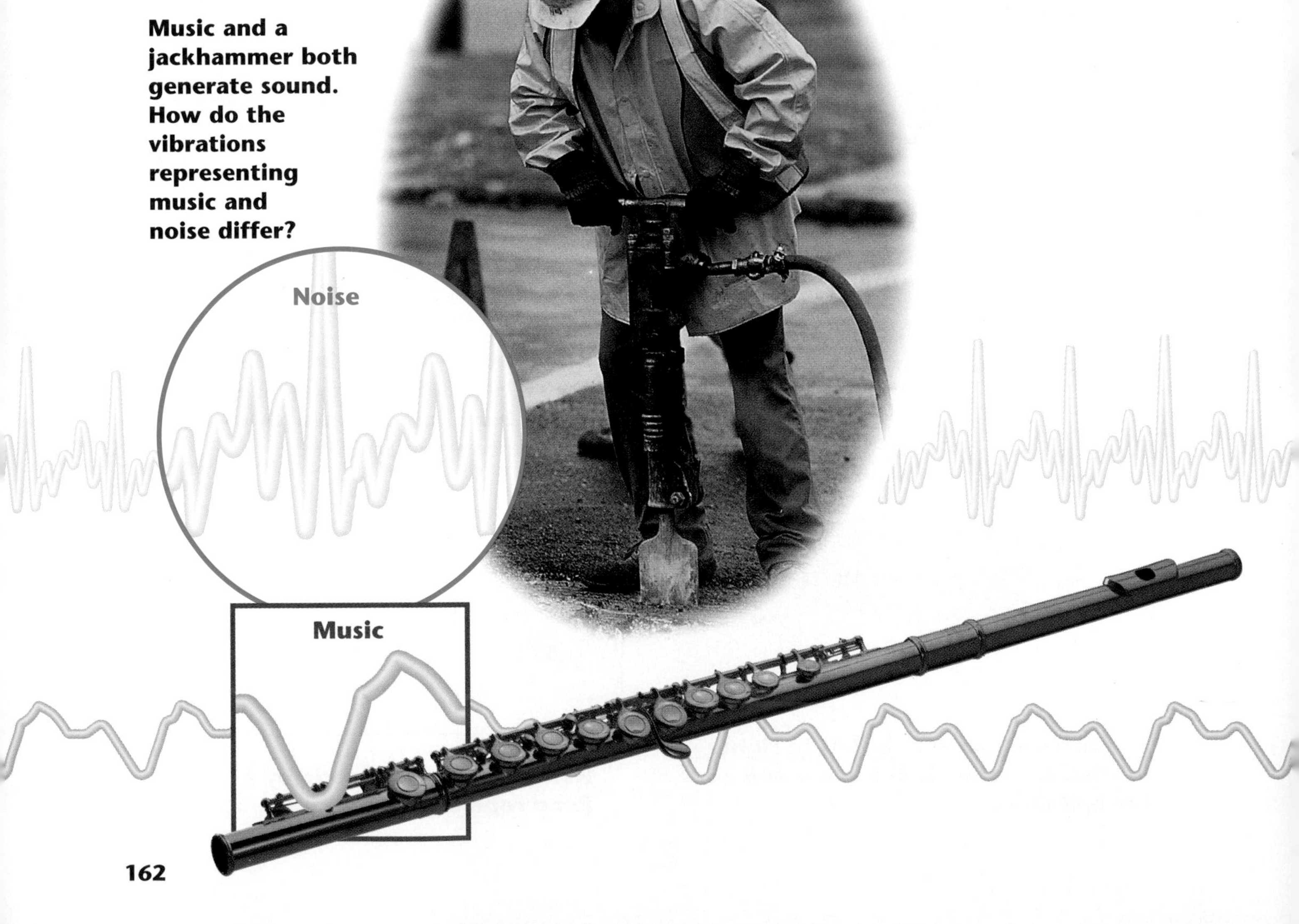

Music and a jackhammer both generate sound. How do the vibrations representing music and noise differ?

Noise

Music

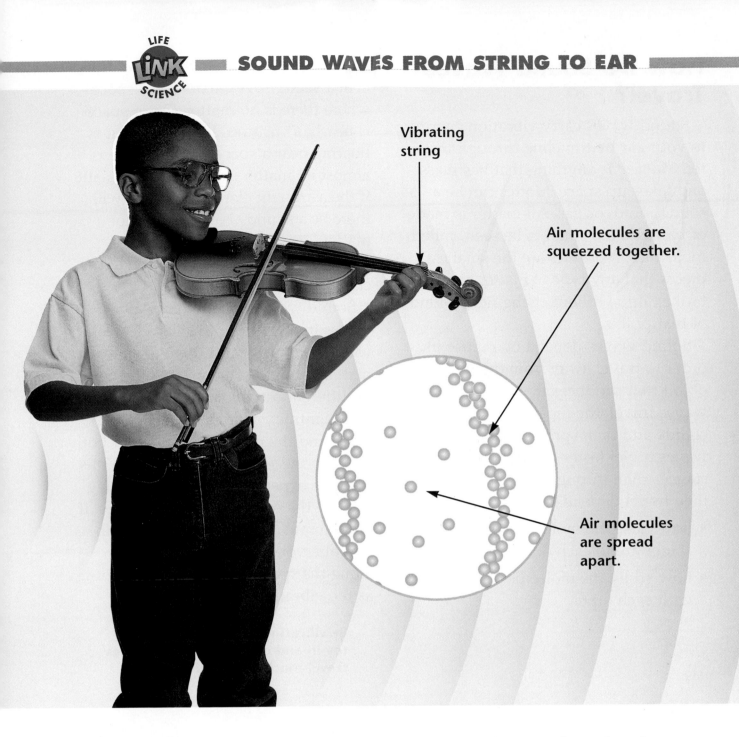

Vibrating string

Air molecules are squeezed together.

Air molecules are spread apart.

What Are Sound Waves?

When a violin string or other object begins vibrating, it produces sound waves. How does that happen?

When a string vibrates, it makes molecules of gases in the air next to it vibrate. The molecules squeeze together, then spread apart. The vibrating molecules near the string then make the molecules next to them start to vibrate.

The vibration continues to spread. A vibration that spreads away from a vibrating object is a **sound wave**. Sound vibrations carry the energy from the vibrating object outward in all directions. Once they reach your ear, you hear the vibrations as sound.

How Do Sound Waves Travel?

Sound waves carry vibration energy to your ear by traveling through matter. **Matter** is anything that has mass and takes up space. Matter can be a solid, liquid, or gas. All matter is made of particles too small to be seen, called molecules. *Molecules* are the smallest pieces that any type of matter can be broken into without changing the kind of matter it is.

Sound waves depend on matter in order to travel away from the vibrating object that produces them. As the waves travel, the molecules of matter collide and then spread apart. Sound waves travel faster through some substances than through others. How fast they travel depends on two things:

- how close the molecules of the substance are to each other;

- how easily the molecules can collide with each other.

One place sound waves cannot travel is in a vacuum. A **vacuum** is a space where there is no matter. Outer space is nearly a vacuum. If an astronaut is floating near a space vehicle, there is almost no matter around the astronaut. If the astronaut claps her hands, will there be a sound? No. There is no matter—no atmospheric gases, for example—to carry the vibration of the clap anywhere.

Sound waves differ from water waves in one important way. In water waves, the wave and the molecules of matter through which it travels move in different directions.

By contrast, in sound waves the wave and the molecules of matter both move in the *same* direction. To see this, imagine experimenting with a spring toy like the one shown on this page. If you vibrate one end of the spring in and out, you will see waves travel along the spring in the same direction as the vibration.

By vibrating one end of a spring toy in and out, you can see waves travel much as sound waves do.

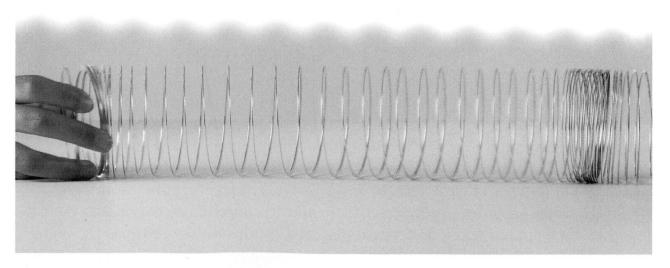

What Can Sound Waves Travel Through?

Sound waves can travel through all forms of matter. When you hear sounds, what is usually around you? Air! Sound waves coming through the air make parts inside your ear vibrate. Because air is a mixture of gases, you may conclude that sound can travel through gases.

Sound waves can also travel through both solids and liquids. You can tell that sound travels through solids just by putting your ear against a tabletop. If someone taps the table at the other end, the sound will be louder than the sound you will hear if you lift your head away from the table. What other examples can you think of? Have you ever heard loud sounds through the glass of a closed window?

If you do any underwater swimming, you probably know that you can hear sounds underwater. You can hear someone calling you from above the surface. You can also hear sounds in the water around you.

Brain Power

What if you put a ticking clock inside a box and pumped all the air out of the box? The clock is hanging on a thin string attached to the inside top of the box. The clock is not touching the walls of the box. Would you hear the clock tick?

QUICK LAB

Sound Carriers

HYPOTHESIZE Can sound travel through solids? Liquids? Write a hypothesis in your *Science Journal*.

MATERIALS
- sealable pint-sized plastic food bag filled with water
- wind-up clock
- wooden table or desk
- *Science Journal*

PROCEDURES

1. **OBSERVE** Put the clock on the wooden table. Put your ear against the table. Listen to the ticking. Lift your head. How well can you hear the ticking now? Record your observation in your *Science Journal*.

2. **USE VARIABLES** Hold the water-filled bag against your ear. Hold the clock against the bag. How well can you hear the ticking? Move your ear away from the bag. How well can you hear the ticking?

CONCLUDE AND APPLY

1. **DRAW CONCLUSIONS** Rate wood, air, and water in order from best sound carrier to worst.

2. **EXPERIMENT** How would you test other materials, like sand?

What Is Light?

Another form of energy that travels by wave motion is light. What is light?

Have you ever picked up a paper clip with a magnet? This is an example of magnetism. A Danish scientist, Hans Christian Oersted, discovered the relationship between electricity and magnetism known as **electromagnetism** (i lek′ trō mag′ ni tiz′ əm). Electromagnetism refers to forces that come from electricity and magnetism. Magnets can set up a flow of electricity, and electricity can produce a kind of magnet.

In the 1850s, James Clerk Maxwell concluded from his work that light is electromagnetic energy. Electrical and magnetic energy can travel through space as a moving wave.

Light waves are electromagnetic waves that can travel through empty space or through matter. Light waves vibrate back and forth across (*perpendicular to*) the direction in which the light travels. In this way, they resemble water waves. In fact, water waves are usually used as models for light waves. The length of a wave, or wavelength, is measured as the distance from crest to crest. Yet light is not just one wavelength. Light has many wavelengths. Different colors of light each have a different wavelength. A prism *refracts*, or bends, light into different wavelengths.

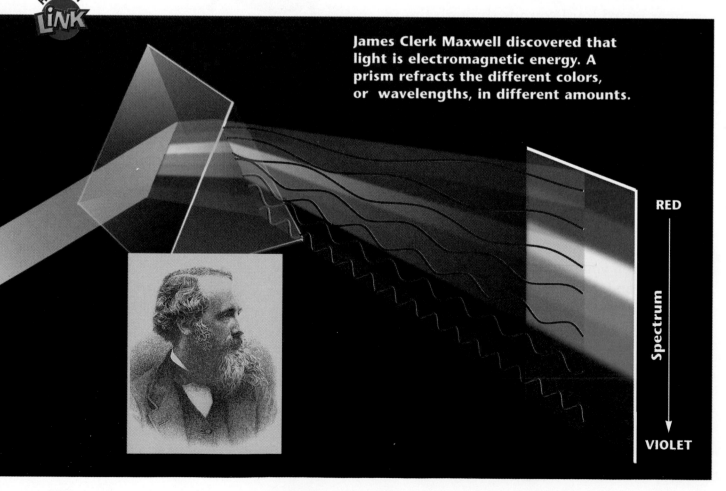

HISTORY LINK

James Clerk Maxwell discovered that light is electromagnetic energy. A prism refracts the different colors, or wavelengths, in different amounts.

RED

Spectrum

VIOLET

ELECTROMAGNETIC SPECTRUM

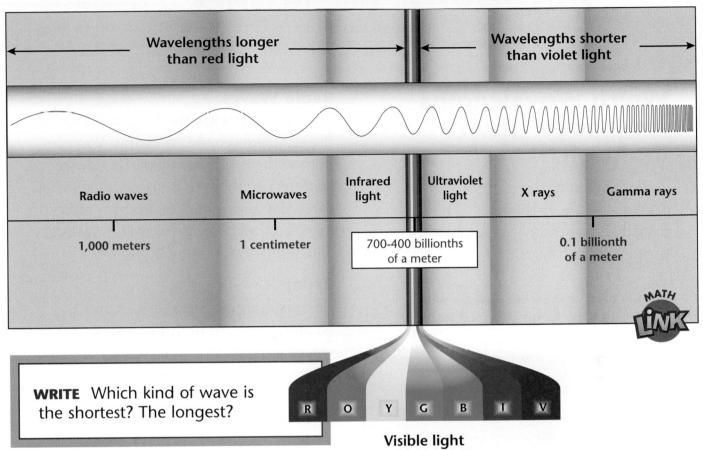

Wavelengths longer than red light

Wavelengths shorter than violet light

| Radio waves | Microwaves | Infrared light | Ultraviolet light | X rays | Gamma rays |

| 1,000 meters | 1 centimeter | 700-400 billionths of a meter | | 0.1 billionth of a meter | |

R O Y G B I V

Visible light

WRITE Which kind of wave is the shortest? The longest?

How Do Light Waves Travel?

All the wavelengths of light travel through empty space at the same speed—more than 300 million meters (186,000 miles) per second. Light slows down when it travels through matter. Yet it always travels much, much faster than sound. That's why you see a lightning flash before you hear the thunder.

Since Maxwell's work, scientists have formed another idea of how light travels. Rather than as a smooth vibrating wave, perhaps light travels as tiny bundles of energy. Scientists call these bundles *photons*.

Waves or photons? The answer is, both. Light sometimes acts as waves and sometimes acts as photons.

The Electromagnetic Spectrum

Can we see all wavelengths of light? Based on the work of Heinrich Hertz from the 1880s, we know that there are wavelengths of light that we do not see.

When light passes through a prism, we see colors from red to violet. However, there are wavelengths longer than the color red. We cannot see them. There are also wavelengths shorter than violet. We cannot see these wavelengths, either. Together, all these wavelengths of light, the ones we see and the ones we cannot see, make up the **electromagnetic spectrum**.

It is true that we cannot see wavelengths longer than red or shorter than violet. Yet we have other ways to detect them and have discovered ways to use them.

167

Which Wavelengths Are Longer Than Red Light?

The wavelengths of light shown above are longer than red. They are invisible, but they have important properties and uses.

This photograph was taken with film that picks up infrared light.

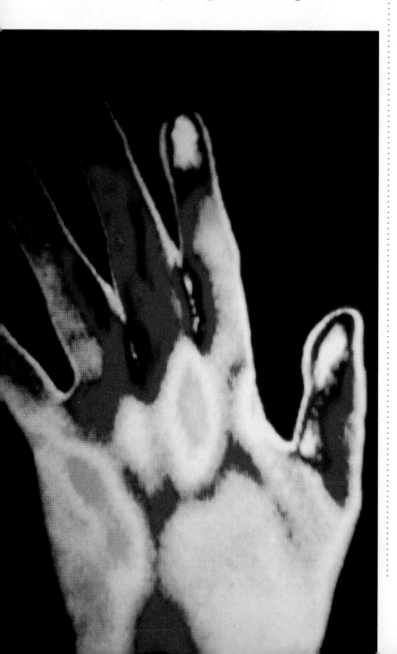

Radio Waves

Radio waves are the longest waves of the electromagnetic spectrum. You cannot see them or hear them. Broadcast stations use them to carry signals. When these signals are picked up by a radio or television set, they produce the sounds and sights that you hear and see.

Radar

Some animals, such as bats and whales, send out high-pitched sound waves. The echo of the waves helps the animals locate things. Radar works in a similar way. Radar stands for "**ra**dio **d**etecting **a**nd **r**anging." Radar devices send out radio waves that reflect off many objects. The waves, reflected from drops of water, help weather forecasters detect rain and thick fog.

Microwaves

A microwave oven uses electromagnetic waves, too. Microwaves are shortwave radio waves. Water in foods absorbs microwaves very readily. The energy from the absorbed microwaves speeds up the water molecules inside the food. As the water molecules move faster, the food gets hot very quickly.

Infrared Light

Infrared means "just below red." Infrared waves are next to visible red waves in the spectrum. When you stand in sunlight, it is the Sun's infrared waves that warm you. Special photographic film and electronic sensors can be used to detect infrared light.

Which Are Shorter Than Violet Light?

The wavelengths of light shown above are shorter than violet. They are invisible but have important properties and uses.

Ultraviolet Light

Ultraviolet (UV) light is made up of waves just shorter than visible violet light on the spectrum. UV light causes chemical changes. It can produce vitamin D in your body, which you need for healthy bones and teeth. Ultraviolet light produces vitamin D in milk.

Hospitals use ultraviolet light to kill harmful bacteria in equipment used in operating rooms. However, UV light can cause harm. UV light from the Sun causes a sunburn. Scientists have found that UV light can also cause some forms of cancer on the skin. Cancer is a disease in which cells multiply rapidly with harmful effects.

X Rays and Gamma Rays

The shortest wavelengths of the spectrum—X rays and gamma rays—have great penetrating power. X rays can pass right through most objects. Thicker or denser objects tend to absorb X rays. This means that X rays can produce a picture when they pass through an arm, leg, or jaw. The denser objects, such as bones and teeth, show up very clearly on the finished picture.

Ultraviolet light from the Sun can cause skin damage. Wearing sunscreen lotions that block both long and short ultraviolet rays—UVA and UVB—can help protect you.

169

How Do Moving Objects Carry Energy?

Think of the energy you use to make your bicycle move. A moving bike, a falling rock, and a baseball whizzing through the air are all objects in motion. The energy of a moving object is called *kinetic energy*.

If you push a rock up a hill and put it on the edge of the cliff, the rock has *potential energy*. Potential energy is a measure of work that has already been done. It is also called stored energy.

When the rock topples over the cliff, the potential energy becomes kinetic (moving) energy.

Energy Transformation

What happens when the rock hits the ground? Energy from the movement of the rock is transferred into the ground or back into the rock as different forms of energy. The thump you hear is caused by kinetic energy that is transformed into sound waves. The ground beneath may get warm as kinetic energy is transformed into heat. The ground may even shake as kinetic energy from the rock is transferred into kinetic energy in the

This hydroelectric plant is using the kinetic energy of moving water to generate electricity. Kinetic energy is transformed into electric energy.

ground. Energy is constantly being changed from one form to another.

Energy Transfer

Energy can be carried from one place to another by heat flow, by water waves, by sound and light, or by moving objects.

- Heat transfers energy through solids, liquids, gases, and even through empty space.

- Water waves, sound, and light transfer energy through matter. Like heat, light also transfers energy through empty space.

- Moving objects transfer energy in the form of kinetic energy, which can be transformed into other kinds of energy.

WHY IT MATTERS

Energy in motion is all around you. Sound waves bring you information as you listen to and speak with others. They also bring you the music you enjoy hearing. Sometimes they even protect you from danger. Think about how important it is to hear fire alarms or car horns.

Visible light waves enable you to see the world around you. Invisible light waves are also extremely useful. Radar waves help forecasters tell us what the weather will be. X rays help dentists and doctors check for cavities and broken bones. Every time you turn on a radio or TV, you are picking up invisible light waves.

REVIEW

1. What is needed to make a sound?

2. What can sounds travel through?

3. How does light travel? Does it travel the same way sound does?

4. **USE NUMBERS** If a spacecraft were 900 million meters from Earth, how long would it take to send a radio signal from Earth to the spacecraft?

5. **CRITICAL THINKING** *Analyze* Does sound travel faster through air or though a solid? Explain your answer.

WHY IT MATTERS THINK ABOUT IT

Double-pane windows have a dead-air space between the panes. How could this help to muffle outside noises?

WHY IT MATTERS WRITE ABOUT IT

Write a paragraph about how energy waves affect you. Which ones are most important to you? Why?

READING SKILL

Write a paragraph to describe a cause and effect relationship you read about in this topic.

BULBS: The Bright Idea!

Whose bright idea was the light bulb? No one person can take all the credit because you need electricity to light the bulb!

It began in 1800, when Alessandro Volta produced the first steady electric current. In 1820 an inventor put a current through a metal wire, saw a glow, and put it in a closed glass container, creating the first light bulb.

In 1841 someone built the first light with glowing carbon. Other inventors used other kinds of filaments—thin

For more than 60 years, the typical light bulb has had a tightly coiled tungsten filament inside a glass bulb, which is filled with an inert gas.

Filament

Glass →

Alessandro Volta

Thomas Edison

materials that glow when electrified.

The first popular light bulb in the United States was a carbon-filament bulb invented by Thomas Edison in 1879. Two years later Lewis Howard Latimer patented an improved bulb with a carbon filament he invented. Latimer was later hired by Edison.

By 1902 metal-filament light bulbs were for sale, but they were very expensive. The General Electric Corporation set up a laboratory to create new bulbs. By 1910 lab workers discovered how to make inexpensive, bright bulbs with tungsten filaments. Sadly, black material coated the inside of the bulbs, dimming the light.

Lab scientist Irving Langmuir found that by filling the bulbs with a special gas, they didn't turn black. By 1934 he'd learned that coiling the filament made the light brighter. Our modern

In the 1980s small fluorescent bulbs that screw into ordinary sockets were introduced. These use much less electricity than ordinary light bulbs.

light bulb had arrived!

Fluorescent light bulbs were also produced in the 1930s. They use light from a glowing gas to make a coating inside the bulbs glow. Fluorescent lights use less electricity and are cooler than ordinary bulbs.

DISCUSSION STARTER

1. What's the difference between a light bulb and a fluorescent light?

2. How has the invention of the light bulb affected the space shuttle? The camera? The automobile?

Lewis Howard Latimer

Irving Langmuir

To learn more about electricity, visit *www.mhschool.com/science* and enter the keyword BRIGHT.

*inter*NET
CONNECTION

WHY IT MATTERS

Microwave ovens heat foods with a special kind of radiation.

SCIENCE WORDS

kinetic energy the energy of a moving object

potential energy energy stored in an object or material

temperature the average kinetic energy of the molecules in a material

heat energy that flows between objects that have different temperatures

radiation the transfer of energy by electromagnetic waves

conduction the transfer of energy by the direct contact of molecules

convection the transfer of energy by the flow of a liquid or gas

insulation prevents heat from flowing in or out of a material

Temperature and Heat

What kinds of things can you feel with your skin? Your skin is filled with nerve endings. They are sensitive to touch, to pressure, to pain, and to hot and cold.

How good is your skin at telling hot from cold? Usually it is good enough to trigger you to pull your hand away from extreme heat or cold—even before you get a chance to think about it. Why is that important?

EXPLORE

HYPOTHESIZE Is your skin a good tool for measuring warm and cool? Can anything affect the way your skin senses warmth? Write a hypothesis in your *Science Journal.* How might you test it safely?

Investigate How You Can Tell Warm from Cold

Test how reliable your sense of touch is in telling temperature.

MATERIALS

- 3 cups or glasses
- *Science Journal*

PROCEDURES

1. Fill glass 1 with warm water, not hot water. Caution: Hot water can burn the skin.

2. Fill glass 2 with room-temperature water.

3. Fill glass 3 with cold water from a refrigerator.

4. OBSERVE Hold the three middle fingers of your left hand in the warm water. Hold the three middle fingers of your right hand in the cold water. Record in your *Science Journal* the difference in what you feel.

5. EXPERIMENT Hold your fingers in the same glasses again, as in step 4. Then quickly put both the left- and right-hand fingers in room-temperature water. What do you feel in each set of fingers?

CONCLUDE AND APPLY

1. HYPOTHESIZE When you put both hands in the room-temperature water, did they feel the same? Explain why you felt what you did.

2. EVALUATE Based on your observations, do you think your skin is a reliable way to tell how hot or cold something is?

GOING FURTHER: Problem Solving

3. EXPERIMENT Try other ways to repeat this activity to investigate your ideas. For example, you might replace the room-temperature water with warm water—or cool water. Safety is important—use warm, never hot, water.

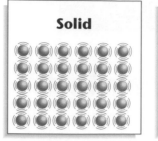 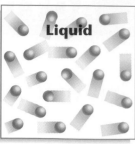 

Motion of molecules in solids, liquids, and gases

How Can You Tell Warm from Cold?

The Explore Activity showed that skin is not the best way to tell warm from cool. Why? To explore this further, you should first understand why objects feel warm or cold in the first place. What makes something feel warm?

The words *hot, warm, cool,* and *cold* are words used to describe the *temperature* of something. For example, the heating coils of a toaster oven are red hot. They have an extremely high temperature. You must not touch them because you would severely burn yourself. Why do they have a high temperature? The answer to this important question has to do with the movement of molecules or atoms.

Although we can easily see the motion of large objects—trees swaying in the wind, cars speeding down the highway, or rocks tumbling down a mountainside—we cannot see the tiny molecules that make up all of these things. What kind of motion do the molecules themselves have?

Through many experiments scientists have learned about molecular motion. For example, molecules in solids vibrate back and forth. Molecules in gases move in straight lines between collisions. Molecules in liquids show a mix of these types of motion.

Any moving object—from a molecule to a car—has energy due to its motion. This energy is not a fluid that can flow from the moving object, nor is it any kind of matter we could pluck from the moving object. Energy is more like an ability than a material "thing"—it is the ability to move other matter around. A swung bat, for example, shows that it has energy by knocking a baseball into the outfield.

The heating coils in a toaster oven are extremely hot. Some of the coils' energy warms and toasts the bread.

What Are Two Main Kinds of Energy?

The energy of any moving object is called **kinetic** (ki net′ik) **energy**. A speeding roller coaster has a great deal of kinetic energy as it reaches the bottom of the first hill. What happens to this energy when the roller coaster slows as it climbs the next hill?

Since about 1840, scientists have known that energy cannot be destroyed or created. It can only be changed from one form to another. The kinetic energy of the roller coaster cannot disappear. In fact the kinetic energy turns into a new form, called **potential** (pə ten′shəl) **energy**, as the roller coaster climbs a hill.

Potential energy is energy stored in an object or material. Moving an object upward against gravity is one way to give it potential energy. Chemical bonds can also be a source of potential energy.

Regardless of the type or source of energy, we measure it with the same units. The amount of kinetic energy gained by a 1-kilogram object falling from a height of 10.2 centimeters is known as a *joule* (jül). A joule is also equal to 0.24 calorie. One calorie is the amount of energy that will raise the temperature of 1 gram of water by 1°C.

	Form of Energy	Source
Kinds of potential energy	atomic	radioactive materials
	chemical	batteries
	gravitational	any two masses in the universe
Kinds of kinetic energy	heat	the Sun
	mechanical	machines
	sound	vibrations

The energy of a roller coaster changes between kinetic energy (motion) and potential energy (height).

This mass will gain 1 joule of kinetic energy if the student lets it fall to the tabletop.

If these cars were molecules, the temperature would be the average speed of the cars.

A thermometer works because a liquid inside expands as it gets hotter.

So Just What Is Temperature?

Do you know what *temperature* means? It has to do with motion. For example, when you watch cars go by, they are traveling at a number of different speeds. However, if you think of them as a group, you can understand what the average speed of the cars is. Many of the cars will move at speeds near the average speed, while only a few will drive at extra-high or extra-low speeds.

Like the cars the molecules in a material move about at different speeds. Taken together they have an average speed. Most of the molecules have speeds near the average, while only a few molecules travel at speeds far above or below the average.

The average speed of the molecules in a material determines the molecules' average kinetic energy. In turn the average kinetic energy of the molecules determines how hot or cold the material is. Since **temperature** measures "hotness," a temperature reading tells you something about the average kinetic energy of a material's molecules.

Thermometers can be used to measure temperature. They often have a liquid that expands when the thermometer is placed in warmer materials. The expansion pushes the liquid along a scale that has degree marks. The Explore Activity showed that your hands did not work very well as thermometers because your brain can play a trick on you. Scientists prefer to use instruments like thermometers to avoid having to depend directly on human senses for measurements.

Does Energy Flow?

Here is a puzzle for you. Two heat-sealed containers of water are connected by a metal bar. *Heat-sealed* means heat cannot move through the walls—from outside in or from inside out. Metals, you recall, conduct heat. The metal bar is wrapped with thick rubber, which will not let the heat escape. The water in the two thermos bottles is at different temperatures.

What will happen to the temperature readings as time goes by?

The experiment below shows what happens when a hot object is placed in contact with a cooler one—energy always flows from the hotter object to the cooler one, never the reverse. Energy will continue to flow until the two objects reach the same temperature. When the objects are both at the same temperature, their molecules will have the same average kinetic energy, as in the diagram.

When energy flows between two objects because they have different temperatures, we call the energy **heat**. Heat is a form of energy, so we measure it in energy units—such as joules or calories.

When two objects with different temperatures are placed in contact, heat flows from the hotter one to the cooler one until they reach the same temperature.

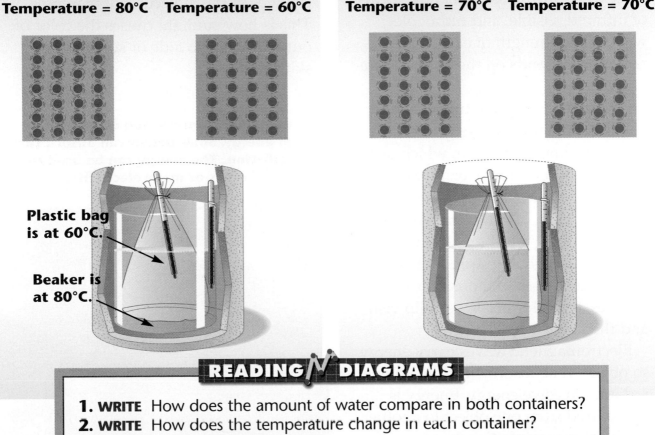

AT START

Temperature = 80°C   **Temperature = 60°C**

Plastic bag is at 60°C.

Beaker is at 80°C.

ONE HOUR LATER

Temperature = 70°C   **Temperature = 70°C**

READING N DIAGRAMS

1. **WRITE** How does the amount of water compare in both containers?
2. **WRITE** How does the temperature change in each container?

When a stove burner is hot enough, its electromagnetic waves are visible as red light.

How Can Heat Move?

Radiation is the transfer of energy by electromagnetic waves. The Sun producing light is one example of radiation. All objects give off a wide range of *electromagnetic waves*. Electromagnetic waves can travel from the Sun to Earth through space. However, it can also be produced by objects on Earth. It comes in the forms of infrared, visible, and ultraviolet waves. The strength of each type of radiation depends on the temperature of the object.

Objects with temperatures near or below room temperature give off mainly infrared radiation, which our eyes cannot see. However, when objects are heated to about 600°C, they begin to give off a lot of visible light. We can see them "glowing" dull red, like the stove burner in the photograph. As the temperature rises to thousands of degrees, the color becomes yellowish and then blue-white.

Electromagnetic waves carry energy, so objects that absorb electromagnetic radiation receive energy. Energy is transferred from one object to another by the electromagnetic waves.

When a material absorbs electromagnetic energy, many things can happen. The material's temperature may rise, as in the solar collectors shown in the photograph.

The material may change from one state of matter to another, such as snow melting in warm sunshine. The energy in the Sun's rays, especially the ultraviolet waves, can even cause chemical changes in the molecules of materials. This is how sunlight causes the color of outdoor paint to fade or sunbathers' skins to burn.

Radiation from the Sun contains a lot of energy. Solar panels can absorb that radiation. The energy can be used to heat homes or make electricity.

180

What Are Other Ways Heat Can Move?

What happens to the sauce in a pan when the heater is on? It gets warmer! Why? The answer has to do with the movement of atoms and molecules in the burner, pan, and sauce.

The burner on a stove is very hot, which means its atoms are moving very, very fast. When these fast-moving atoms hit the pan, the pan's atoms move faster, too. When the pan's atoms hit the molecules in the sauce, the sauce molecules speed up, making the sauce hotter.

The movement of energy through direct contact is called **conduction**. Conduction is the only way heat can travel through solids.

Another type of heat transfer, called **convection**, can occur in liquids and gases. Convection is the transfer of energy by the flow of a liquid or gas. In the atmosphere, for example, warmer air carries heat upward. The warm air rises because of its lower density. Cooler air is more dense and sinks.

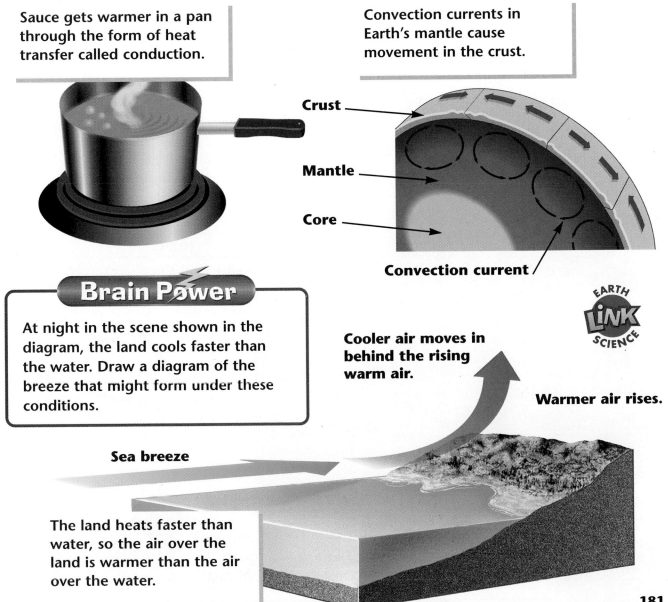

Sauce gets warmer in a pan through the form of heat transfer called conduction.

Convection currents in Earth's mantle cause movement in the crust.

Crust

Mantle

Core

Convection current

Brain Power

At night in the scene shown in the diagram, the land cools faster than the water. Draw a diagram of the breeze that might form under these conditions.

EARTH LINK SCIENCE

Cooler air moves in behind the rising warm air.

Warmer air rises.

Sea breeze

The land heats faster than water, so the air over the land is warmer than the air over the water.

Do Some Materials Warm Faster than Others?

The photo shows an experiment: identical beakers, one containing 1 kilogram of water and the other containing 1 kilogram of copper pellets, are placed on a hot plate. The graph shows how the temperatures of the water and copper change. As you can see, the copper wins the temperature race—it warms up faster than the water.

The copper and the water show us that equal masses of different materials have a different temperature change for the same amount of heat absorbed.

The particular rate at which a material warms up upon absorbing heat is a physical property that can tell one material or substance from another. Examine the table to see how the temperature of 1 gram of various materials will rise for each calorie of heat absorbed.

You can see from the table that 1 gram of liquid water rises less in temperature than 1 gram of many other substances per calorie of heat absorbed. This makes water a good coolant. When cool water is pumped through a hot car engine, for example, the water can absorb a relatively large amount of heat as it warms toward the temperature of the engine.

TEMPERATURE CHANGES

Material	Temperature Rise for 1 Gram Absorbing 1 Calorie of Heat
Water (liquid)	1.0°C
Water (solid)	1.7°C
Aluminum (solid)	4.7°C
Rock (solid)	4.8–5.6°C
Copper (solid)	10.8°C
Mercury (liquid)	30.3°C

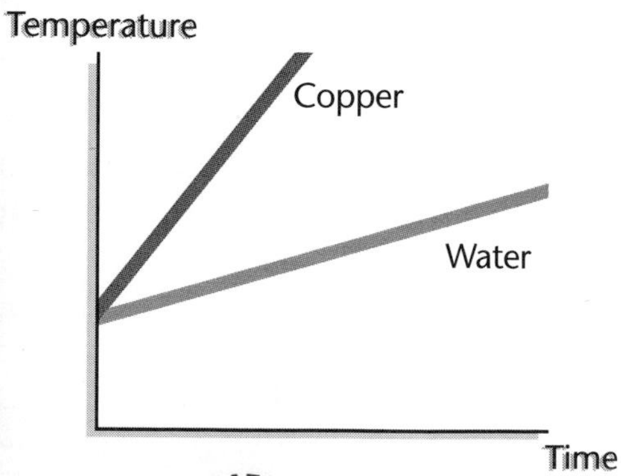

Temperature

Copper

Water

Time

READING N CHARTS

MATH LINK

Which material here wins the temperature race? That is—which shows the biggest change in temperature by absorbing just 1 calorie of heat?

Skill: Separating and Controlling Variables

WHICH WARMS FASTER—WATER OR SAND?

Perhaps you have visited a sandy beach on a sunny day and noticed that the sand is too hot to walk on, while the water feels comfortable. Does sand warm up faster than water for the same amount of heat? Design an experiment to answer this question.

In an experiment a variable is something that can affect the outcome. For example, in testing how rapidly water and sand warm up, the length of time the materials are heated would affect their temperature. To make the test "fair," you would have to heat both materials for the same length of time. Making sure that a variable is the same for all samples being tested is called *controlling the variable*.

> **MATERIALS**
> - desk lamp
> - thermometers
> - sand
> - water
> - 2 containers
> - *Science Journal*

PROCEDURES

1. HYPOTHESIZE Which warms up faster—water or sand? Write a hypothesis in your *Science Journal*.

2. USE VARIABLES Make a list of the variables that could affect how rapidly sand and water would warm up when heated.

3. PLAN Write a procedure to compare how fast water and sand warm up for the same amount of heat. Have your teacher check your plan.

4. If possible carry out your procedure. Write a report that describes your results.

CONCLUDE AND APPLY

1. COMMUNICATE Summarize your results. Use graphs to show temperature changes of the two substances over time.

2. Explain your results.

The Trans-Alaska Pipeline carries hot crude oil about 800 miles (1,287 kilometers) across Alaska. The oil must be kept warm to keep it flowing well. To keep the oil hot, the pipeline is insulated with fiberglass. The insulation also prevents heat from damaging the frozen land where the pipe is buried.

This worker is blowing loose-fill fiberglass insulation into the attic of a home.

How Can We Keep Heat from Going In or Out?

There are many instances in our everyday lives when it is important to keep heat from entering or leaving something. Look at the photographs on these pages to see several important examples of how we can control the flow of heat.

Preventing heat from flowing in or out of a material is called **insulation**.

You *insulate* something by wrapping it securely with a material that is not a good conductor of heat.

In cold months much of the heat lost from a home tends to escape through the roof, so it is important to insulate the attic well. The glass fibers in the insulation are poor conductors of heat. More importantly there is a great deal of air trapped in the fluffy material. Air is a very poor conductor of heat, and the air adds greatly to the insulating ability of the fiberglass.

Foam insulation is a poor conductor of heat and will prevent heat from entering once the lid is in place. This foam is made by stirring air into a type of plastic, producing millions of tiny air bubbles. The air bubbles make it a good insulator and also make it light in weight.

How Do Insulated Bottles Work?

Have you used an insulated bottle to keep a drink cold or soup hot? Study the diagram to see how some insulated bottles keep heat from leaving or entering.

Outer bottle

Vacuum—no material to conduct heat between bottle walls

Inner bottle

Mirrorlike coating—bounces radiant heat

Liquids in the inner bottle of this insulated bottle stay at their original temperature because heat neither enters nor leaves easily.

Does your family cook meals in a microwave oven? If so you may have noticed that the food gets hot, but the dish does not. Microwave ovens take advantage of a transfer of heat by radiation. They produce microwaves, which only water molecules tend to absorb. Anything containing water, such as food, gets hot, but materials without water do not.

However, microwaves can produce electric currents in metal objects. These currents can generate enough heat to cause sparking and start fires!

REVIEW

1. How does energy change as a bicycle rider pushes off from the top of a hill and coasts down?

2. How do molecules in an ice cube at 0°C compare with molecules in liquid water at 20°C?

3. If you stand near a hot toaster, why can you feel the heat?

4. **VARIABLES** To see which warms faster, Ralph heats a liter of water on one stove burner and a liter of oil on another burner. Which variables should he control in this experiment?

5. **CRITICAL THINKING** *Analyze* Will wrapping a warm sandwich in aluminum foil keep it warm longer than a foam box? Make a hypothesis. How would you test it?

WHY IT MATTERS **THINK ABOUT IT**
What are some rules for cooking safely with a microwave oven?

WHY IT MATTERS **WRITE ABOUT IT**
How can heating snacks and meals be dangerous? What must you do to stay safe when you are near heat in a kitchen?

Energy to Heat Your Home

You feel warmer when you enter a heated room on a cold day. Thermometers show warmer temperatures inside the room than outdoors. The indoor air molecules feels warmer because the air molecules have more kinetic energy than the outdoor air molecules. This is because heating fuels have released their potential energy into the room as heat.

At one time in human history, wood was the most common heating fuel. In 1940, about 75 percent of United States households heated with coal or wood. But today natural gas and electricity are the most common heating fuels. In California, 73 percent of homes use natural gas as heating fuel. Most of the rest use electricity for heating. In the New

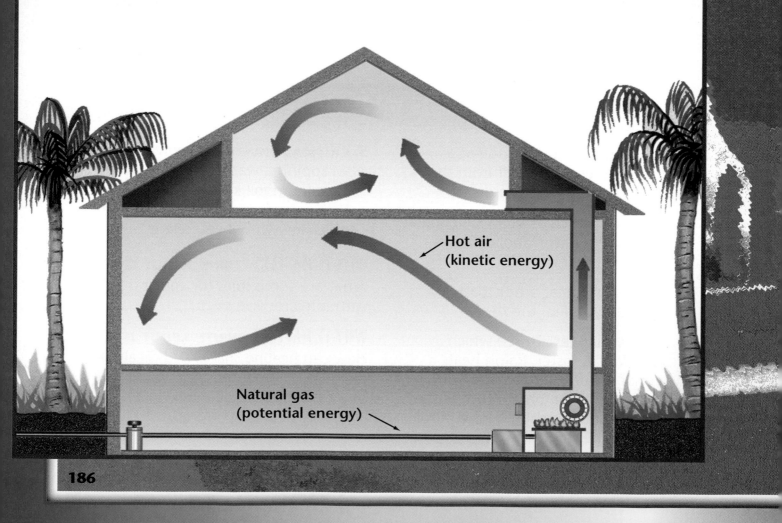

Hot air
(kinetic energy)

Natural gas
(potential energy)

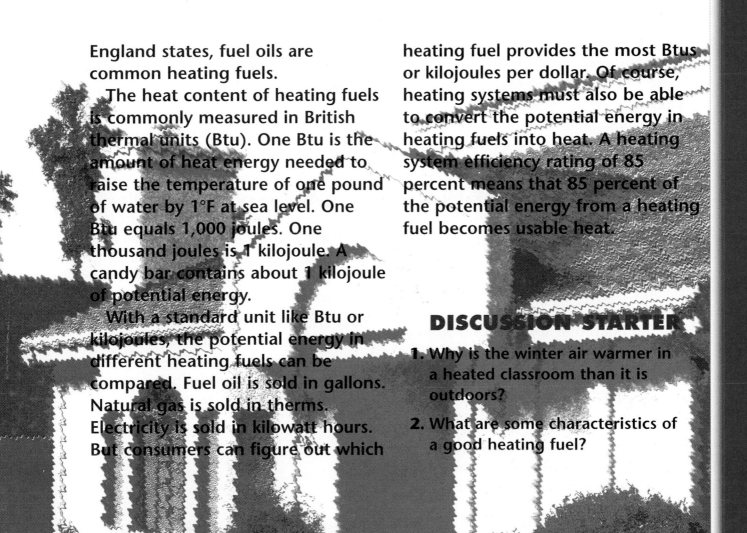

England states, fuel oils are common heating fuels.

The heat content of heating fuels is commonly measured in British thermal units (Btu). One Btu is the amount of heat energy needed to raise the temperature of one pound of water by 1°F at sea level. One Btu equals 1,000 joules. One thousand joules is 1 kilojoule. A candy bar contains about 1 kilojoule of potential energy.

With a standard unit like Btu or kilojoules, the potential energy in different heating fuels can be compared. Fuel oil is sold in gallons. Natural gas is sold in therms. Electricity is sold in kilowatt hours. But consumers can figure out which

heating fuel provides the most Btus or kilojoules per dollar. Of course, heating systems must also be able to convert the potential energy in heating fuels into heat. A heating system efficiency rating of 85 percent means that 85 percent of the potential energy from a heating fuel becomes usable heat.

DISCUSSION STARTER

1. Why is the winter air warmer in a heated classroom than it is outdoors?

2. What are some characteristics of a good heating fuel?

To learn more about meeting energy needs, visit **www.mhschool.com/science** and enter the keyword FUELS.

SCIENCE WORDS

conduction p. 181
convection p. 181
electromagnetic
    spectrum p. 167
insulation p. 184
kinetic
    energy p. 177
light wave p. 166

potential
    energy p. 177
radiation p. 180
sound wave p. 163
temperature p. 178
vacuum p. 164
wave p. 160

USING SCIENCE WORDS

Number a paper from 1 to 10. Fill in 1 to 5 with words from the list above.

1. A(n) __?__ is a motion that carries energy.

2. __?__ is the transfer of energy by electromagnetic waves.

3. A vibration that spreads away from a vibrating object is a(n) __?__.

4. A(n) __?__ is a place where there is no matter.

5. The energy of motion is called __?__.

6–10. **Pick five words from the list above that were not used in 1 to 5, and use each in a sentence.**

UNDERSTANDING SCIENCE IDEAS

11. How does energy change when a roller coaster slides down a track?

12. What are three methods of transferring heat?

13. When waves travel across the surface of a lake, how do the water molecules move?

14. Can energy be created or destroyed?

15. Describe how a thermometer works.

USING IDEAS AND SKILLS

16. What would happen if you put a hot pan on a table? Would you expect heat to travel from the pan to the table, making the pan colder and the table hotter? Why?

17. **READING SKILL: MAIN IDEA** Explain what a sound wave is and how it travels.

18. Can radio waves travel without matter?

19. **USE VARIABLES** Suppose you have samples of six different fabrics. Design an experiment to show which fabric best keeps an object warm. In your experiment, identify the variable you are testing and the variables you are controlling.

20. **THINKING LIKE A SCIENTIST** Do you think louder sounds travel faster than softer ones? State and explain a hypothesis. Describe how you might test your idea.

PROBLEMS and PUZZLES

Noises Off Determine where and what are the loudest, most irritating noises in your school. What can you and your class do to help solve the problem? Make a chart of the noises, causes, and possible solutions. Which solutions can you actually carry out? How can you make the school a quieter place to learn and to have fun?

CHAPTER 6
ENERGY IN EARTH'S SYSTEM

Hot melted rock comes bursting out in a volcanic eruption. What can it tell us about the inside of the Earth? Where does all that heat come from?

Where else does Earth's heat energy come from? How does the Sun's energy warm Earth? How does it affect the atmosphere, the land, and the oceans? You'll learn the answers in Chapter 6.

In Chapter 6 you will read for sequence of events.

Topic 3
EARTH SCIENCE

WHY IT MATTERS

Heat from inside Earth shapes the landscape all around us.

SCIENCE WORDS

density a measure of the amount of mass in a given volume of matter

radioactive decay a process in which some atoms break down into smaller atoms and release energy

friction a force that opposes motion of one object in contact with another

insulator a material that conducts heat poorly

mass the amount of matter in an object

Earth's Fiery Interior

Miners dig deep into Earth, but even the deepest mines barely scratch the planet's surface. In fact, if Earth were the size of an apple, the deepest mine ever dug would not go through the apple's skin! Scientists have no direct evidence of what happens deep below Earth's surface. But they have other ways to study this important part of our planet. How do scientists learn about a place they have never seen? What could it possibly be like thousands of kilometers down inside Earth?

EXPLORE

HYPOTHESIZE Scientists often need to study things they cannot see. The inside of Earth is one example. How would you study something you could not see? Write a hypothesis in your *Science Journal.* How would you test your ideas?

Investigate Learning Without Seeing

Identify objects without seeing them.

PROCEDURES

1. OBSERVE Try to determine what is inside one of the boxes without opening it. You can feel how heavy it is, tilt it, shake it, listen for sounds coming from it, and so on.

2. In your *Science Journal,* write down the box number and all of your observations about its contents.

3. PREDICT Based on your observations, predict what is inside the box. Write down your prediction.

4. Repeat steps 1 and 2 for the other boxes.

CONCLUDE AND APPLY

1. When you have completed your examination of all boxes, your teacher will give you an answer key. Which of your predictions were correct? Which ones were not?

2. What techniques did you use to learn about the objects?

3. Can you think of other ways (besides looking inside) that would have helped you determine the contents of these boxes?

GOING FURTHER: Problem Solving

4. PREDICT Would you have learned much more about the object(s) by looking inside the box? What different kinds of data could you have gained?

5. INFER How does this activity relate to the work of geologists who study Earth's interior?

MATERIALS

- six numbered boxes, each with a different object inside, taped shut
- six different objects
- *Science Journal*

QUICK LAB

Measuring Density

HYPOTHESIZE Do different objects of the same material have the same density? Write a hypothesis in your *Science Journal*.

MATERIALS
- rock
- 50 pennies
- balance
- graduated cylinder
- beaker
- overflow pan
- calculator
- *Science Journal*

PROCEDURES

1. MEASURE Find the mass of the rock in grams. Record the mass in your *Science Journal*.

2. Place the beaker in the pan. Fill the beaker to the top with water. Gently drop the rock into the water. Pour the water spilled from the beaker into the graduated cylinder. The volume of spilled water equals that of the rock.

3. MEASURE Measure and record the volume in cubic centimeters.

5. Repeat steps 1–3 for 25 pennies. Then repeat for all 50 pennies.

6. USE NUMBERS Calculate and record the density of each object. (Density = mass/volume)

CONCLUDE AND APPLY

INTERPRET DATA Was your hypothesis correct or incorrect?

192

How Hot Is Earth's Interior?

The inside of Earth is extremely hot. As a matter of fact, in some places it is almost one half as hot as the surface of the Sun! Near the surface, for every kilometer you go farther down toward the center of Earth, the temperature rises by about 25°C (77°F).

Besides what is known from drilling, other facts also suggest the presence of heat inside Earth. These include the visible action of hot springs and geysers, the action of volcanoes, and the motion of Earth's plates.

The motion of Earth's plates also tells scientists that the rock inside our Earth is so hot that it turns to liquid. When underground rock gets hot enough, it melts into magma. Like all liquids, magma will support objects that are less dense. Earth's plates float on the magma because they are less dense than the magma. **Density** is a measure of how much mass an object has for a given volume.

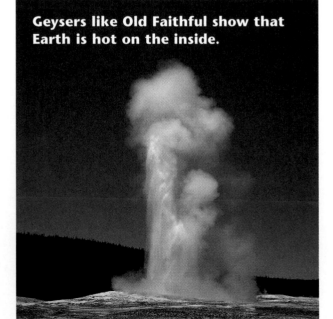

Geysers like Old Faithful show that Earth is hot on the inside.

FORMATION OF EARTH AND OTHER PLANETS

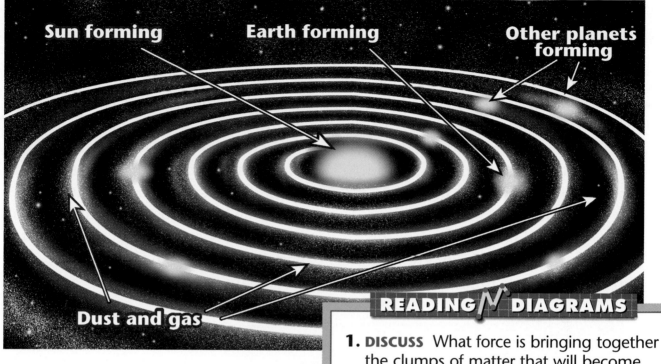

Sun forming   Earth forming   Other planets forming

Dust and gas

READING $\sim$ DIAGRAMS

1. **DISCUSS** What force is bringing together the clumps of matter that will become the Sun and planets?
2. **REPRESENT** Make a labeled drawing of the planets in the solar system.

Where Does the Heat Come From?

Scientists say the heat in Earth's interior comes from several sources:

Formation of Earth

About 4.5 billion years ago, giant clouds of swirling dust and gas came together to form Earth. Gravity caused this material to condense. As the material grew more dense, it heated up. Some of the heat from Earth's formation remains inside.

Radioactive decay

Some substances are unstable. They break down, or decay, and form atoms of completely different materials.

Scientists call this process **radioactive decay**. As this decay occurs, enormous amounts of heat energy are released. Most of the heat inside Earth's core comes from this decay.

Friction

Have you ever rubbed your foot against a carpet? The warm feeling is caused by friction—the "dragging" that happens when one thing slides past another. **Friction** is the force that opposes the motion of one object in contact with another. Friction inside Earth occurs as molten rock circulates in the mantle. This movement produces great heat.

PHYSICAL
LINK
SCIENCE

What Is the Structure of Earth's Interior?

Have you ever knocked the outside cover off a baseball? Then you know it has many layers underneath. Earth also has many layers. The crust is like the baseball's outside cover. Under the crust is a hotter layer called the *mantle*. The mantle is molten, liquid rock. It flows something like thick, soft ice cream.

About 2,900 kilometers below the surface is the *core*. Nobody knows for sure, but scientists think temperatures in the core could be above 5,000°C. The outer core is liquid, but the inner core is solid. Both the inner and outer core contain a lot of iron. They are also very dense. Pressure in the core is intense.

Why is Earth's interior so much hotter than the surface? The answer is that rock is a good insulator. An **insulator** is something that conducts heat poorly. Some heat does reach the crust. When it reaches the crust, the heat is lost to space by radiation. Otherwise, the crust might melt, and we would be in very serious trouble indeed!

INTERIOR OF EARTH

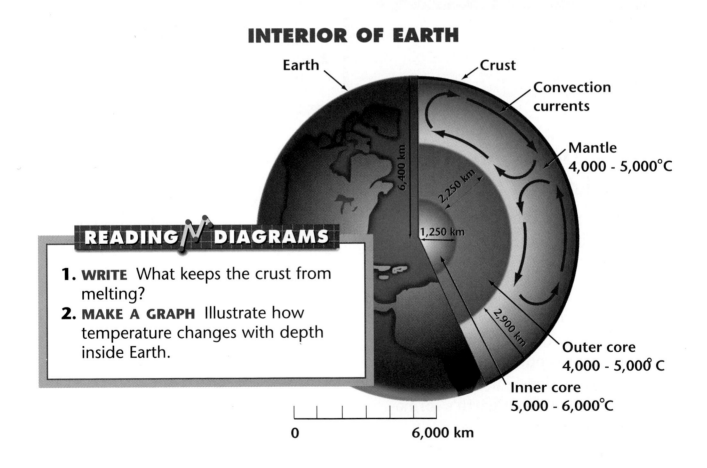

Earth

Crust

Convection currents

Mantle
4,000 - 5,000°C

6,400 km

2,250 km

1,250 km

2,900 km

Outer core
4,000 - 5,000°C

Inner core
5,000 - 6,000°C

0   6,000 km

READING IN DIAGRAMS

1. **WRITE** What keeps the crust from melting?
2. **MAKE A GRAPH** Illustrate how temperature changes with depth inside Earth.

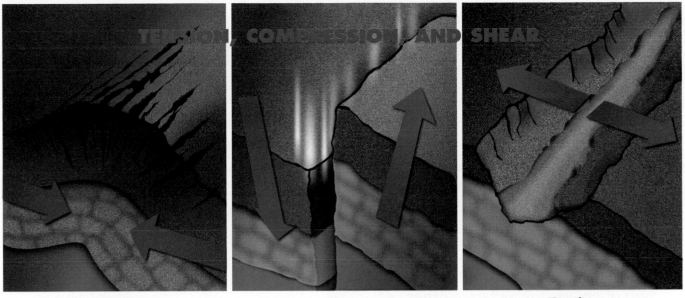

TENSION, COMPRESSION, AND SHEAR

Compression   **Shear**   **Tension**

How Does Heat from the Interior Affect Earth's Crust?

Heat from Earth's interior affects the crust in two major ways. First, it causes the continental plates to move on the mantle. Because the plates are actually lighter than the mantle, they float on the mantle. So, heat energy literally powers plate movement.

Second, the heat warms the crust from below, supplying the layer of magma that fuels volcanoes and hot springs. The magma also powers the spreading that takes place at mid-ocean ridges in the sea floor.

Most of the heat reaches the crust from below through convection currents. Convection can place three kinds of force on the crust:

Compression is a force that presses in, squeezing matter together. A nutcracker crushes a nut by compressing it. Compression on

READING N DIAGRAMS

1. DISCUSS Which force tends to build mountains? Why? Which is most likely to cause earthquakes? Why?

2. DRAW A DIAGRAM How does convection cause these forces to act on the crust?

Earth's crust is still forming the tallest mountains, the Himalayas.

Tension is a force that pulls things apart. When you sit on a swing, the ropes are under tension. The surface of Earth at the Great Rift Valley in Africa is under great tension. It has caused plates there to separate, creating a valley more than 1,600 km (1,000 miles) wide.

Shear happens when two opposing forces actually break something into parts. The two parts slide past each other. Shear is occurring along the San Andreas Fault in California. One side of the fault is moving past the other. When the shear gets too strong, earthquakes occur to relieve the strain.

What Is the Role of Gravity?

Why do falling objects always fall down? Why don't you fly off Earth when you jump? The reason is simple but amazing. You and Earth are attracted to each other by the force of gravity.

Gravity is the force of attraction between all objects with mass. Gravity is a basic force in the universe. It is the pull of objects toward each other. Gravity "holds" planets in their orbits. It keeps millions of stars together in the galaxies. Gravity is the force that caused Earth to form, and it still holds Earth together.

Although gravity is powerful, physicists do not understand it well. They do know how it acts:

- Gravity is stronger between objects with more mass. **Mass** tells us how much matter an object has. At Earth's surface, objects with more mass are heavier and exert more gravitational pull. The gravitational attraction between a locomotive and Earth is stronger than the attraction between you and Earth. That's why the locomotive is heavier than you are!

- Gravity affects both objects equally. Say you are standing on Earth. You "pull" up on Earth just as hard as it pulls down on you! (Earth is so huge that your tiny pull doesn't affect it much.)

- Gravity depends on the distance between the objects. If two objects are 6 feet apart and you cut the distance by one half, to 3 feet, the gravitational attraction becomes four times as great. If you put them twice as far apart, at 12 feet, the attraction will be one fourth as great.

GRAVITY

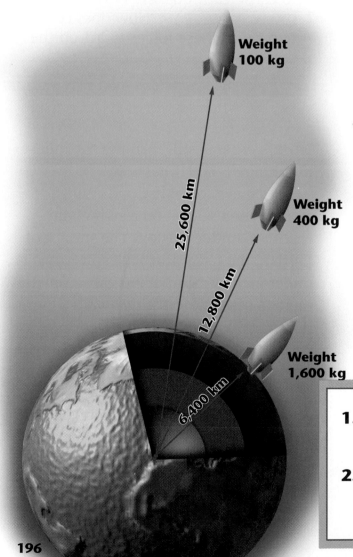

Weight 100 kg

25,600 km

Weight 400 kg

12,800 km

Weight 1,600 kg

6,400 km

READING ∿ DIAGRAMS

1. **DISCUSS** What happens to the weight of the rocket as distance from Earth increases?
2. **REPRESENT** Graph the relationship shown between distance and weight. What is the shape of the curve?

196

How Does Gravity Affect the Shape of Earth?

Over billions of years, the force of gravity pulled much of the densest material to the center of Earth. Because of gravity, the inside of Earth is denser than its outside crust. For a given volume, rocks at Earth's surface are about two and a half times as dense as water. The same volume of material at Earth's core is about 12 times as dense as water.

Because of gravity, upper layers of Earth's crust press down on lower layers. Far down inside Earth, this pressure becomes enormous! Near the Earth's center, gravity causes rocks to press down with a force of 3.6 million kilograms—on each square centimeter. That is the weight of 100 semi-trailers, each weighing 36,000 kg (79,200 lb)!

Earth is affected by its rotational spin as well as by gravity. The rotation causes force directed outward from the center. One result of this rotation is rather surprising. The diameter of Earth, the distance through the center from one side to the other, is not the same everywhere. It is slightly greater at the Equator than it is from the North Pole to the South Pole. At the Equator the diameter is about 12,756 kilometers (7,909 miles). At the poles, it is about 12,714 km (7,883 miles). This provides more evidence that Earth is not completely solid.

Brain Power

If you were able to go deep inside Earth, what would happen to your weight? Explain.

THE SHAPE OF EARTH

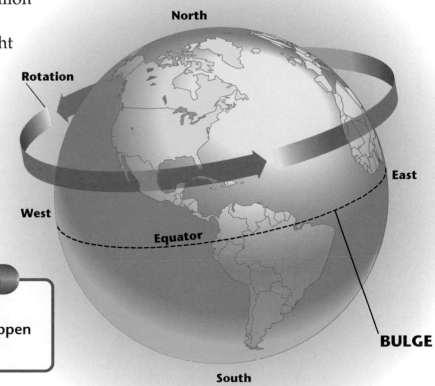

North

Rotation

West

Equator

East

BULGE

South

Earth is not a perfect sphere. The crust bulges slightly at the Equator.

What Is the Magma Like?

As you know, the magma beneath Earth's crust is rock melted by the heat energy from Earth's interior. Magma is glowing hot. It ranges in temperature from 650°C to 1,350°C (1,200–2,460°F). In general, the hotter magma is, the more fluid it is. Magma also contains dissolved gases. Pressure from inside Earth keeps the gases trapped in the magma.

The chemical composition of magma depends on the type of rock from which it was formed. The chemistry of magma also affects how slowly or quickly it flows. Magma in the mantle probably flows very slowly.

Magma that breaks through Earth's surface is called *lava*. The temperature of surface lava is lower than the temperature of magma. Lava can range in temperature from 750°C to more than 1,100°C (1,380–2,000°F). Once at the surface, lava releases many of the dissolved gases it contains. Within a short time, it cools and hardens into solid rock. Although magma cannot be observed directly, lava can be analyzed to find its chemical composition.

When lava cools, it changes from a liquid to a solid.

GEOTHERMAL PLANTS MAKE ELECTRICITY

This geothermal plant makes electricity using Earth's natural heat energy.

Turbine

Cool recharge water

Geothermal reservoir

Hot upwelling water

Hot rock heat source

What Is Geothermal Energy?

Heat energy in Earth's interior is called *geothermal* ("Earth-heat") *energy*. Geothermal energy can be used to produce electricity or to warm houses. For example, on the island of Iceland in the north Atlantic Ocean there are many volcanoes. Icelanders use this available geothermal energy to heat thousands of houses.

California has one of the world's largest geothermal fields, north of Santa Rosa. This field makes enough electricity to supply thousands of houses. The heat comes from magma rising from the zone where the ocean plate is sliding under the continental plate.

Most electric generating plants burn fuel to make electricity. Geothermal electric plants do not burn anything. Because they get their energy directly from Earth, geothermal plants can be a very clean source of electricity and heat.

Why have geothermal plants been built in only a few places? The reason is the high cost of reaching heat sources that are far underground. Geothermal energy is practical only in places where magma is fairly, close to Earth's surface.

READING DIAGRAMS

1. **DISCUSS** Why does California have so much geothermal energy?
2. **DISCUSS** What supplies the energy in a geothermal plant? What is the plant's output?

Deep drilling experiments at sites like this one in northern Europe help scientists learn more about Earth's interior.

How Do We Know About Earth's Interior?

Scientists and engineers have learned a lot about Earth by drilling very deep holes. However, drilling is difficult and expensive. Deep drills are very hard to guide. Hot rock can ooze into a hole and close it. The deepest hole ever drilled was 12 km (about 7 miles). The drill weighed 450,000 kg (990,000 lb)! That hole stopped inside the crust but never reached the mantle at all.

The main way scientists learn about Earth's interior is by studying seismic waves. To do this, scientists use instruments called seismographs.

Seismic waves change in various ways as they pass through Earth.

- They change speed when they pass through different layers of material.

- They change direction when they enter a different material. This bending, called *refraction*, also occurs when a camera lens focuses light.

- Waves bounce back when they meet a different material. This action, called *reflection*, also occurs when light strikes a mirror.

- Some types of waves cannot travel through certain materials.

Scientists track these waves and compare them. This information allows scientists to draw conclusions about the structure of Earth's interior.

How Do Seismic Waves Tell About Earth's Interior?

In 1909, Yugoslav geologist Andrija Mohorovičić (mō hō rō' vi chich') made a great discovery. He noticed that seismic waves changed speed at depths of 30 to 60 km (19–37 miles).

Mohorovičić knew that sound waves travel faster through denser material (like water or steel) than in air. He realized that the seismic waves were passing through the dense region of the liquid mantle. The break between the light rock of the crust and the mantle was named the "Moho" to honor its discoverer.

Seismic waves tell us other things about the inside of Earth. After a big earthquake, waves can be detected in many parts of Earth. There are exceptions, however. On the side of Earth opposite to where an earthquake occurs, there are "shadow zones." In these areas, there are no S waves. Because S waves are stopped by liquids, scientists know that something liquid is in the way. This liquid is the molten rock of the outer core.

The fact is, S and P waves are both absent from shadow zones. The S waves are blocked by the liquid in the outer core. The P waves are bent at the outer core, so they also miss the shadow zones.

SEISMIC WAVES AND EARTH'S INTERIOR

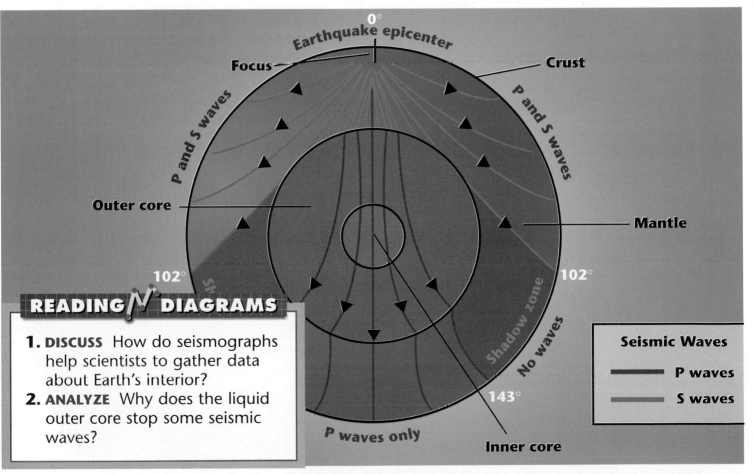

READING DIAGRAMS

1. **DISCUSS** How do seismographs help scientists to gather data about Earth's interior?
2. **ANALYZE** Why does the liquid outer core stop some seismic waves?

What Do Meteorites Tell About Earth?

Most people call meteors "shooting stars." Meteors are rocks from space that move very fast and carry a lot of energy. As they enter our atmosphere, friction with the atmosphere changes some energy to heat, and most meteors burn up, leaving a trail of light. If a meteor does not burn up in the atmosphere, it may hit Earth. Then it is called a *meteorite.*

Meteors come from the asteroid belt, a region between Mars and Jupiter. *Asteroids* are rocky objects that orbit the Sun. They are much smaller than planets but often larger than meteors. Asteroids and meteorites were formed from the same material that formed Earth about 4.5 billion years ago.

Scientists like to study meteorites. These rocks are made of the same materials that formed the planets. Meteorites can tell us what kinds of materials came together to form the Earth.

There are three types of meteorites:

- Some are made of the metals iron and nickel.
- Some are made of iron and stone.
- Some are made of carbon.

Most meteorites contain minerals such as silicates, similar to rocks found in Earth's crust.

Brain Power

Physics is the study of heat, light, and movement. How does physics help us understand Earth's interior?

Meteors and asteroids such as this one are formed from the same materials that formed Earth.

How Have Asteroids Affected Earth?

Many scientists think that a comet or asteroid probably hit Earth about 65 million years ago. (Comets are balls of ice and dust that also orbit the Sun.) The impact may have brought about the death of the dinosaurs.

According to this impact theory, the collision raised huge clouds of dust that prevented sunlight from reaching Earth. This produced a long period of extreme cold. The dinosaurs died off during this cold period. With no dinosaurs around, the number of mammals began to increase, eventually leading to the appearance of humans.

A huge, buried crater exists near the Yucatan Peninsula in Mexico. Some scientists think that it may be due to the asteroid or comet impact that killed off the dinosaurs.

Earth's hot interior plays a big role in shaping the surface. Most of the heat in Earth's core is created by the decay of radioactive substances. Heat is also created by the friction of crustal plates and by magma moving in the mantle.

This heat powers the movement of continents. It powers the formation of mountains. It drives volcanoes and earthquakes. It gives us geothermal energy and geysers. Even though you can't see the inside of Earth, what goes on there plays a vital and necessary part in what happens on Earth's surface.

REVIEW

1. What are some ways to learn about things you cannot see?

2. What does seismology tell us about the structure of Earth?

3. **ANALYZE** The gravitational attraction between two objects varies inversely as the square of the distance between them. Explain, using an example.

4. **INFER** The fact that Earth's diameter is not constant throughout suggests that Earth is not solid. Explain.

5. **CRITICAL THINKING** *Analyze* How does studying meteorites and asteroids help us learn about earth?

WHY IT MATTERS **THINK ABOUT IT**
How does heat from inside Earth affect Californians?

WHY IT MATTERS **WRITE ABOUT IT**
Convection transfers heat within Earth. Where else does convection play a role?

STUDYING VOLCANOES

Volcanoes are sometimes called "sleeping giants." They may go for very long periods without erupting. During that time, people may not recognize the danger of eruptions. They may build towns or even large cities that would be at risk in an eruption. Geologists who study volcanoes are concerned about this risk. They use scientific methods to study the volcanoes and try to predict eruptions.

Right now, geologists in California are carefully watching Mammoth Mountain, a volcano in the Long Valley caldera. A caldera is a ring-shaped set of hills. It forms when a volcano collapses during a huge eruption. The Long Valley caldera formed about 750,000 years ago. Geologists suspect that Mammoth Mountain or one of the other nearby volcanoes could once again become active.

What are the signs that a volcano may become active? How can geologists monitor volcanoes and try to predict eruptions? (*Monitoring* is watching something closely for a long time.)

In an active volcano, magma is rising toward the surface. What would you expect to happen when fiery-hot rock rises inside a mountain? The mountain might move. It might warm up. The magma might release gas.

Volcano experts, called volcanologists, study all three of these possibilities.

- **Movement:** When magma moves inside a volcano, it rises up, often pushing aside rock that blocks its path. That movement can trigger earthquakes. Magma may also push up rock in the crater. You can see this from the crater rim. Scientists can sometimes predict an eruption by studying seismic waves caused by movements of magma.

- **Heat:** Magma brings a lot of heat to the surface. This heat may warm up lakes or hot springs in the crater. It may also warm up *fumaroles*—holes in the ground where hot gas escapes.

- **Gases:** Magma carries a lot of gas. When the magma nears the surface, its pressure drops, releasing the gas. Scientists monitor the soil and air for gases. A big release of carbon dioxide gas at Mammoth Mountain has killed many trees. Some scientists think the gas is a warning of an eruption.

Volcanologists monitor volcanoes to try to predict eruptions.

Science, Technology, and Society

About 1,500 volcanoes around the world could become active. There is no perfect way to predict eruptions. Each volcano is different, and lessons from one place may not apply somewhere else. Because eruptions are so dangerous, scientists are always looking for better prediction methods. Maybe you will be the volcanologist who finds the solution to this problem!

DISCUSSION STARTER

1. Why are there so many ways to tell if an eruption is coming?

2. What is one major reason why volcano predictions are not perfect?

3. Why is volcano forecasting so important?

Long Valley caldera, in southern California, is the remains of an ancient volcano. Scientists believe that it may erupt again.

To learn more about volcanoes, visit *www.mhschool.com/science* and enter keyword VOLCANO.

*inter*NET
CONNECTION

Topic
EARTH SCIENCE
4

WHY IT MATTERS

Sunlight is the driving force for climate, weather, and life on Earth.

SCIENCE WORDS

insolation the sunlight that reaches Earth ("incoming solar radiation")

greenhouse gases chemicals in the atmosphere that act like greenhouse glass, reflecting infrared radiation back toward Earth

greenhouse effect the way greenhouse gases warm Earth

climate the long-term trend in weather conditions

convection cell the system of air circulation in the atmosphere

Spreading the Heat Around

We know Earth would be a cold place without the energy from the Sun. The Sun's radiation powers almost every natural process on our planet: wind, rain, storms, and ocean currents. The Sun also makes plants grow. Plants give us food and life-giving oxygen to breathe. What happens when sunlight reaches Earth's surface? How is its energy distributed? How does the Sun create weather?

EXPLORE

HYPOTHESIZE Sunlight is stronger at noon than in the late afternoon. Sunlight is a lot stronger in summer than in winter. How do angle and color affect solar absorption? Write a hypothesis in your *Science Journal*. How would you test your ideas?

Investigate Absorption of the Sun's Energy

Find how different colors and Sun angles affect absorption of sunlight.

PROCEDURES

1. On each square, draw a circle 3.5 cm (1.4 in.) in radius.

2. Stick a straight pin into the cardboard at the circle's center on each card.

3. Tape a thermometer to the back of each square, with the thermometer bulb near the center.

4. Adjust each straight pin so it sticks straight up 2 cm (0.8 in.) out of the cardboard.

5. Prop up the squares in a sunny place. One square of each color goes at 90° to the Sun. At 90° the Sun shines straight down onto the stickpin. So adjust the position of these three squares so their pins have no shadow.

6. The other three squares go at 30° to the Sun. At 30°, the shadow of a 2-cm tall pin is 3.5 cm long. Adjust the position of these three squares so their pins' shadows just reach the 3.5-cm circles you drew. Make sure you adjust the squares' positions, and not the length of the pins, which should remain at 2 cm.

7. After 15 minutes, record each of the temperatures.

8. Graph the relationship between color and temperature. Graph the relationship between angle and temperature.

MATERIALS

- two 15-cm (6 in.) squares of cardboard for each color: white, gray, black
- drawing compass
- six straight pins
- 6 thermometers
- tape
- ruler
- *Science Journal*

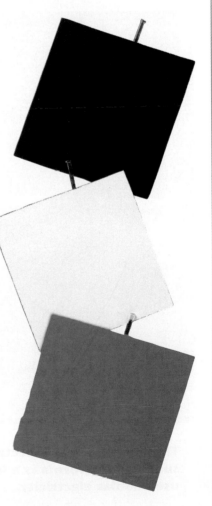

CONCLUDE AND APPLY

1. CONTROL VARIABLES When you measure how color affects absorption of the Sun's energy, which variable must you control? Which variable must you control when you measure how angle affects absorption?

2. INTERPRET DATA Which color absorbed the most energy from the Sun? How can you tell from your data? At which angle was the most energy absorbed? How do your data show that?

How Much Energy Comes from the Sun?

The Sun may be an average star, but it puts out a huge amount of energy. Earth, which is relatively small and far away, receives less than one-billionth of that energy. But even that tiny fraction is enough to make Earth a planet that will support life. It is enough to keep us warm, to grow our crops, and to power just about every process that takes place on Earth.

The sunlight that reaches Earth's surface is called **insolation**. That term stands for "incoming solar radiation." There is a huge quantity of energy in the insolation at the top of the atmosphere. When the Sun is directly overhead, a solar panel one meter square at the outer surface of Earth's layer of atmosphere would collect 1,370 watts of energy each second. This amount is slightly more than the total energy used for all purposes by the average American during an entire year!

If we could somehow harvest all this energy, we would need no other energy sources. Our energy problems would be over. That is not possible, however. The Sun is over any one spot for only a short time each day. Even if we could place solar collectors at the outer edge of the atmosphere, there is as yet no way to get the energy down to Earth.

These panels make electricity from sunlight. California is a leader in the use of solar electricity.

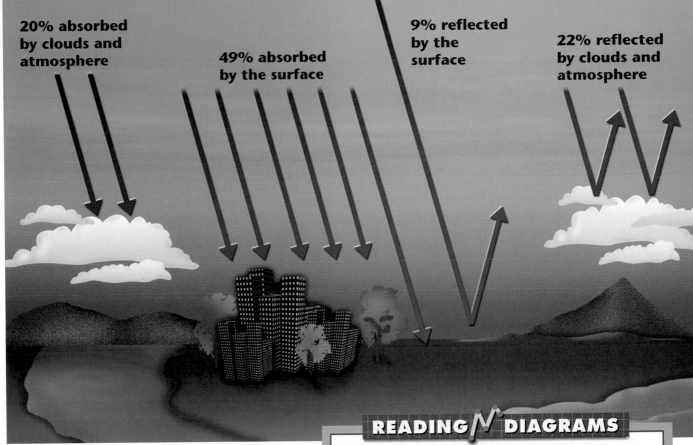

20% absorbed by clouds and atmosphere

49% absorbed by the surface

9% reflected by the surface

22% reflected by clouds and atmosphere

Only about half of the solar energy entering Earth's atmosphere reaches Earth's surface.

READING DIAGRAMS

1. **DISCUSS** The diagram shows average conditions. What factors could change the way energy is distributed?
2. **REPRESENT** Make a circle graph showing what happens to sunlight entering the atmosphere.

What Happens to Solar Energy Entering the Atmosphere?

One way or another, energy from the Sun drives everything in the atmosphere. It creates wind, rain, and snow. It moves energy from the tropics to the poles. It evaporates water from the oceans and makes clouds. The solar energy that creates these effects is absorbed by the atmosphere and Earth.

Not all the Sun's radiant energy makes it to Earth's surface. Here is what happens to solar energy:

- 22 percent is reflected back to space by clouds and gases in Earth's atmosphere.
- 9 percent is reflected back to space from Earth's surface.
- 20 percent is absorbed in Earth's atmosphere.
- 49 percent is absorbed by Earth's surface.

As you can see, more than 30 percent of solar energy is reflected back to space. This portion has little impact on what happens on Earth. We will concentrate on the other 69 percent.

What Happens to Solar Energy That Strikes Water?

Most of the sunlight reaching Earth's surface is absorbed by land or water. How much is absorbed depends on the color of the surface. Dark surfaces absorb more energy than light surfaces.

About 71 percent of Earth's surface is covered by water. When solar energy strikes ocean water the water molecules move more quickly. Molecular motion warms things. So sunlight makes the ocean warmer.

Some of the fastest molecules escape from the water. They become the gas form of water, called *water vapor*. As these molecules escape, they take energy from the water. This energy loss cools the water, but it adds a lot potential energy to the air

Sunlight does three things to ocean water:

- It warms the water.
- It removes water vapor, cooling the water a bit.
- It transfers energy from the water to the air.

The motion of waves and wind moves the heat energy deeper into the ocean. Heat energy spreads through the cold ocean water by conduction. It warms colder water nearby and the warm water stores this thermal energy. As a result, the water temperature does not change dramatically when the Sun sets.

HOW THE SUN'S ENERGY AFFECTS THE OCEANS

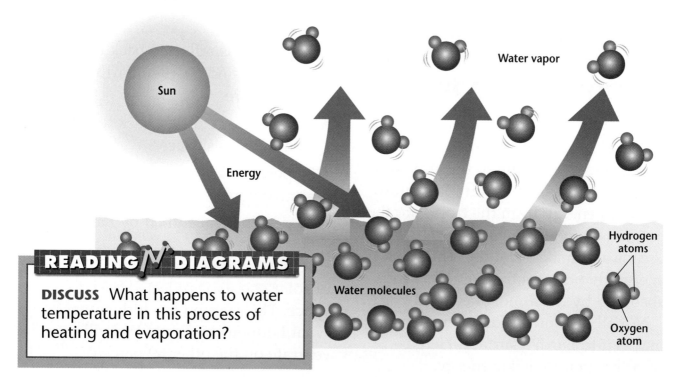

Sun

Energy

Water vapor

Water molecules

Hydrogen atoms

Oxygen atom

READING IN DIAGRAMS

DISCUSS What happens to water temperature in this process of heating and evaporation?

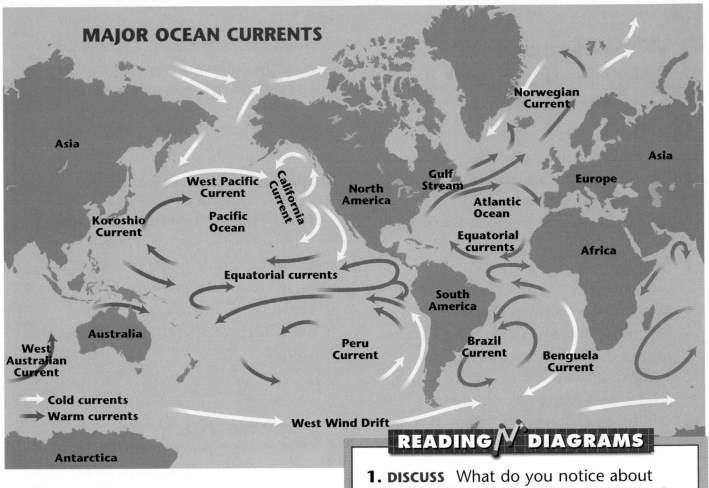

MAJOR OCEAN CURRENTS

Norwegian Current

Asia

Asia

West Pacific Current

California Current

North America

Gulf Stream

Europe

Koroshio Current

Pacific Ocean

Atlantic Ocean

Equatorial currents

Africa

Equatorial currents

South America

Australia

Peru Current

Brazil Current

Benguela Current

West Australian Current

→ Cold currents
→ Warm currents

West Wind Drift

Antarctica

How Do Ocean Currents Occur?

Molecules move faster in warm water than in cold water. Heat gives them energy, and they move away from each other. This causes water to get less dense as it warms.

Density is important in the ocean. You know that objects float on liquids that are denser than they are. Warm water is less dense than cold water, so it floats on cold water. You can also say that cold, dense water sinks below warm water.

In some parts of the ocean, surface water cools and becomes denser than the water below it. This water sinks, pushing aside the water under it. This movement causes the large movements of ocean water called *currents*. In this

READING N DIAGRAMS

1. **DISCUSS** What do you notice about currents in the Northern Hemisphere?
2. **REPRESENT** Graph latitude and ocean temperature. Assume water leaves the equator in a northward current at 30°C (86°F). What happens as the water nears the North Pole?

way, the atmosphere and oceans move major amounts of energy from the Equator toward the poles. If this were not so, the Equator would be much hotter and the poles much colder.

In the Atlantic Ocean, the Gulf Stream moves a large amount of thermal energy northward, warming New England and northern Europe. In the Pacific Ocean, the Japan Current carries thermal energy from the Philippine Sea northward past Japan and across to the west coast of North America.

What Happens to Solar Energy That Strikes Land?

When sunlight strikes the land, once again the amount absorbed depends on color. Dark surfaces, such as forests and black pavements, absorb more energy than light surfaces. Snow and ice reflect most of the light striking them.

More energy is absorbed when the rays of the Sun shine almost directly down, as happens in summer. When the tilt of Earth causes sunlight to strike at an angle, less energy is absorbed. That is what happens in winter. Near the poles, sunlight strikes at an angle all year long.

When a land surface absorbs solar energy, the soil warms quickly during the day. However, soil and rock are poor conductors of heat. They also store little thermal energy. This energy from the soil and rocks radiates back into the atmosphere. As a result, the land surface cools quickly at night.

Because soil temperature changes quickly, inland areas have larger seasonal temperature changes than coastal ones. In coastal areas, thermal energy is stored in the nearby ocean. This helps to keep temperature changes moderate.

Stored energy in the ocean warms City A in the winter and cools it in the summer.

READING DIAGRAMS

1. **CALCULATE** What is the average annual temperature at City A? At City B?
2. **WRITE** How does this graph show that the land stores less heat energy than the ocean?

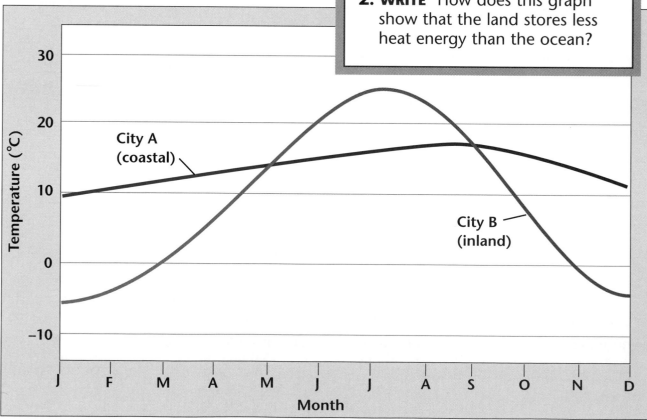

Why Doesn't Earth Get Too Hot?

If Earth absorbs so much solar energy from the Sun, why doesn't it get too hot? The answer is that Earth radiates huge amounts of infrared energy back into space.

You cannot see infrared radiation, but it feels warm to the skin. It is a kind of electromagnetic energy located just beyond visible red light on the electromagnetic spectrum. Infrared radiation regulates Earth's temperature and keeps the planet from overheating.

How does the amount of sunlight Earth receives compare to the amount of infrared energy it radiates? You might be suprised at the answer.

MATH LINK Imagine that energy were money. Suppose you have saved $10, and you earn $5 dollars one week for feeding the neighbor's cat. If you spent $5 that week, you would have the same amount of money ($10) at the end of the week as you did at the beginning of the week.

It is the same with sunlight and infrared radiation. Scientists say infrared radiation "balances the budget" because it takes away as much energy as the Sun supplies. If more energy were radiated away, Earth would grow cooler. If Earth absorbed more energy than was radiated away, Earth would become too hot. Infrared radiation from Earth cools the land and oceans, but it warms the air. Did you know the atmosphere gets more heat from below than it does from above?

QUICK LAB

Sun, Wind, and Temperature

HYPOTHESIZE How does exposure to the wind and Sun affect air temperature? Write a hypothesis in your *Science Journal.*

MATERIALS
- thermometer,
- pen or pencil
- *Science Journal*

PROCEDURES

1. Take a walk outside your school on a sunny, breezy day. Find a shady location that is exposed to the wind.

2. **MEASURE** Measure the air temperature at this location. On one line of your *Science Journal*, write "Shady, exposed to wind", and record the temperature.

3. Repeat steps 1 and 2 in three other locations: (1) shady, out of the wind; (2) sunny, out of the wind; and (3) sunny, exposed to wind. Note: Do not hold the thermometer in direct sunlight in any location. Shade it with a piece of paper.

CONCLUDE AND APPLY

2. **INTERPRET** Where was it warmest? Coolest?

4. **CONCLUDE** Do your data agree with your hypothesis? Explain.

5. **INFER** In winter, ice may form in protected spots along a river bank while water flowing down the main stream remains ice-free. How is this situation similar to the air temperature patterns you measured?

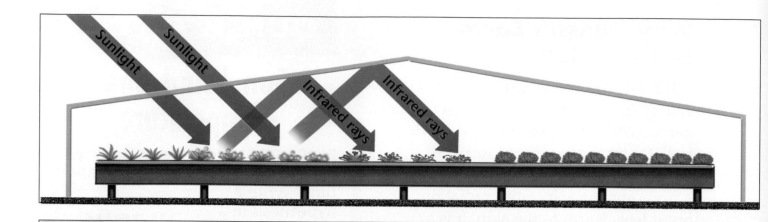

READING N' DIAGRAMS

DISCUSS How do gases in the atmosphere act like greenhouse glass?

Glass warms a greenhouse by keeping infrared rays from escaping. Greenhouse gases in the atmosphere have the same effect.

What Is the Greenhouse Effect?

Have you ever been in a greenhouse on a hot, sunny day? Then you know that glass lets sunlight in but stops infrared radiation from escaping.

Sunlight and infrared (heat) radiation are different kinds of radiation. Visible light waves are short. Infrared waves are long. Glass stops infrared radiation. Visible light passes right through. (Otherwise, you could not see out a glass window.)

The atmosphere acts like the glass of a greenhouse. The atmosphere allows sunlight to enter but prevents infrared radiation from escaping. The major **greenhouse gases** are water vapor and carbon dioxide. They act like greenhouse glass. The warming effect that these gases have on Earth has been called the **greenhouse effect**.

The greenhouse effect makes life on Earth possible. However, as people burn more and more fossil fuels, the effect increases. As Earth warms, ice at the poles may melt, raising sea levels. Increasing temperatures could also affect weather patterns and rainfall.

What Is Climate?

What is the difference between climate and weather? *Weather* refers to the atmospheric conditions over a short period of time—from a day to a week or two. **Climate** refers to average, long-term patterns in weather. If today is sunny and tomorrow rainy, the weather has changed. If the climate of a place includes regular periods of sun and rain, the climate has not changed.

Climates can change over very long periods of time. Sometimes however, changes may have effects that actually speed up the climate changes. Scientists call these effects *feedback*.

One period of feedback occurred 15,000 years ago. During one of many Ice Ages, much of the northern United States was covered by huge sheets of ice. The ice reflected sunlight into space and cooled Earth still further.

Feedback effects can also speed up warming trends in Earth's climate. When temperatures rise and ice melts, trees can grow in places that were formerly too cold for them. Forests grow in places that were once covered by ice. Unlike ice, which reflects sunlight back into space, forest trees absorb solar energy. As a result, the warming speeds up, more ice melts, and still more areas become covered with forests.

Scientists disagree about how quickly changes in climate can occur. However, new measurements of Antarctic ice layers may provide an answer. They indicate that the warming that ended the last Ice Age took place very rapidly.

During the last Ice Age, thick sheets of ice like this one in Greenland covered much of North America.

What Causes Wind?

Have you ever blown up a balloon and then released it? The high-pressure air inside the balloon escapes as "wind" from the opening. Similar pressure differences also cause wind in the atmosphere. Winds are powered by differences in density between air masses.

Winds are generated in much the same way as ocean currents. When air warms, it expands and becomes less dense. Colder, denser air sinks under it. The warm air is forced to rise. The warm air "floats" on top of the dense, cold air. The rising air is called an *updraft*.

The cold, dense air moves into the space left by the updraft. We call this movement *wind*. Meanwhile, high in the atmosphere, the rising air begins spreading out and moving sideways. As it does, it cools off and begins to sink in a *downdraft*. This whole system of air circulation is called a **convection cell**. Convection cells in the atmosphere may be hundreds of kilometers across.

CONVECTION CELL

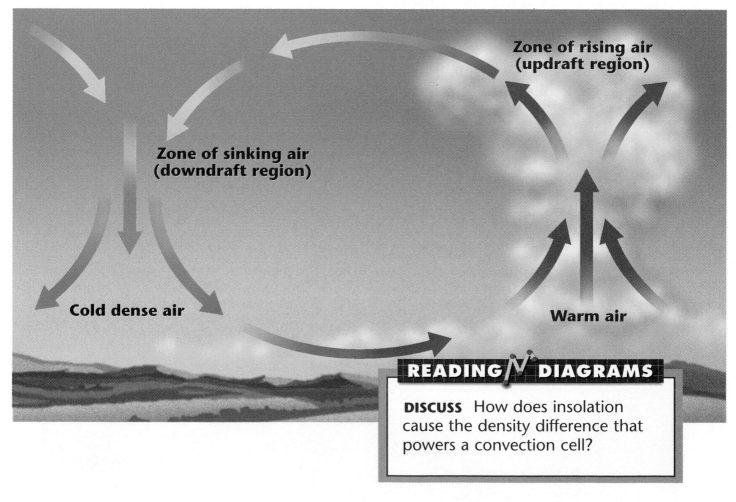

Zone of rising air (updraft region)

Zone of sinking air (downdraft region)

Cold dense air

Warm air

READING *N* DIAGRAMS

DISCUSS How does insolation cause the density difference that powers a convection cell?

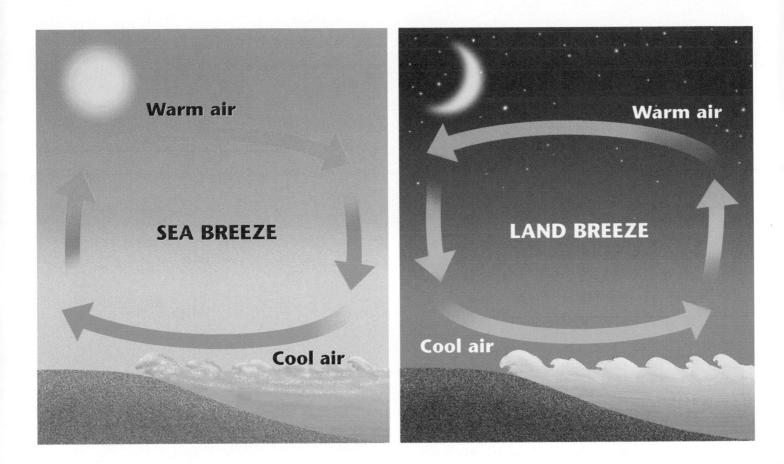

SEA BREEZE

Warm air

Cool air

LAND BREEZE

Warm air

Cool air

What Causes Land and Sea Breezes?

On a sunny day, land near the ocean gets warmer than the ocean. A convection cell forms, with warm air rising above the land. The cooler air over the water sinks and moves landward to replace the rising warm air. This is a *sea breeze*. The wind comes from the sea.

At night the land cools off, and this circulation system runs backwards. Now the ocean is warmer than the land, so an updraft forms above the ocean. As a result, cooler air blows from the land toward the sea. This is a *land breeze*.

This kind of wind pattern can affect very large areas during certain seasons. A *monsoon* is a wind pattern that is controlled by seasonal changes in land temperatures. In winter in California's deserts, a monsoon pattern regularly brings warm, moist air up from the Gulf of Mexico. Thunderstorms and flash floods often result.

Convection currents in the atmosphere bring cool sea breezes on a summer day at the beach.

How Do Plants Respond to Sunlight?

People and animals get their energy from food. Plants get their energy entirely from sunlight. Green plants have a special chemical called *chlorophyll*. The plants use this chemical in a process called *photosynthesis*. During this process, the plants use energy from sunlight to make sugar from carbon dioxide in the atmosphere and water. The plants store the sugar and change it into substances they need for growth.

Without photosynthesis, almost no life could exist on Earth. Plants are at the bottom of almost every food chain. Lions eat antelopes, but antelopes eat plants. So lions depend on plants just as much as antelopes do.

Plants turn the Sun's energy into sugars for their own nourishment. The energy in the sugar passes to animals that eat the plants.

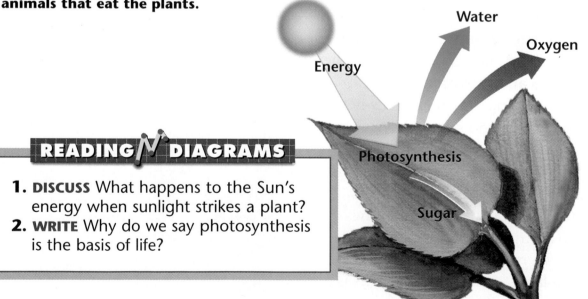

Energy

Water

Oxygen

Photosynthesis

Sugar

READING *N* DIAGRAMS

1. **DISCUSS** What happens to the Sun's energy when sunlight strikes a plant?
2. **WRITE** Why do we say photosynthesis is the basis of life?

Just as important, plants release oxygen during photoshythesis. All animals need oxygen to breathe and survive.

Plants also provide a kind of "natural air-conditioning." You may have noticed that a shady park full of trees is much cooler than a parking lot next to it. Two things are responsible for this cooling:

- Plants use photosynthesis to absorb some of the Sun's energy and convert it into potential energy stored in sugar. Heat is used in the process.

- Plants also put a lot of moisture into the air. This moisture carries potential energy away into the atmosphere because energy is used to convert water into water vapor. This also cools the atmosphere.

WHY IT MATTERS

The Sun seems far away, but it is at the root of most of what happens on Earth. Energy from sunlight causes plants to grow. Without plants, animal life could not exist. Sunlight heats the atmosphere and the oceans. It causes the atmospheric conditions that produce both climate and weather. Plants release atmospheric gases that keep the Sun's heat from escaping. These greenhouse gases help Earth's temperature to stay fairly constant. Solar energy brings life to Earth and sustains it.

Brain Power

Scientists are trying to understand the greenhouse effect. What questions do you have about it? How would you design an experiment to answer them?

REVIEW

1. How does the angle at which sunlight strikes Earth's surface cause the change in seasons?

2. When solar energy strikes land, what happens?

3. **COMPARE AND CONTRAST** Compare the way that land and ocean respond to the Sun's energy.

4. **DISCUSS** "The natural greenhouse effect is a good thing." Give reasons to support this statement.

5. **ANALYZE** The oceans cover most of Earth. What does this mean for planetary climate?

WHY IT MATTERS THINK ABOUT IT
Coastal California has an oceanic climate. Contrast the temperature of a coastal city with the temperature of an inland city. How has the ocean helped California grow?

WHY IT MATTERS WRITE ABOUT IT
Changes in density play a large role in atmospheric and ocean currents. Write a paragraph to describe the cause of changes in density and how they affect the atmosphere or the ocean.

READING SKILL SUMMARIZE
What is the greenhouse effect? What would Earth be like without it?

How Hot Is It?

The average temperature on Earth's surface is 15°C (59°F). The coldest temperature, –89°C (–128.6°F), was recorded in Antarctica in 1983. The highest temperature, 58°C (138°F), was recorded in northern Africa in 1922. In comparison the temperature of Earth's core is 6,650°C (12,000°F)!

Record highs and lows like these are exceptions. Looking at the average temperatures in the five climate zones gives a clearer picture of how hot or cold Earth's air is.

°F   °C   Record high
140   60
120   50
100   40
80   30
60   20
        10
40   0
20   –10
0   –20
–20   –30
–40   –40
–60   –50
–80   –60
–100   –70
–110   –80
        –90

Record low

The Sun warms Earth by radiation, and Earth heats the air above it by convection. The farther air is from Earth's surface, the less heat it gets by convection.

Some scientists believe that a buildup of gases, such as carbon dioxide, nitric oxide, and methane, forms a layer and traps heat that normally would escape from Earth. Called the "greenhouse effect," this raises temperatures and leads to global warming.

ZONE	AVERAGE TEMPERATURES
Polar	below 10°C (50°F) all year
Cold	0–4 months at 10–20°C, other months colder
Temperate	4–12 months at 10–20°C, other times colder
Subtropical	4–11 months above 20°C, "cold" months 10–20°C (50–68°F)
Tropical	normally above 20°C (68°F)

Physical Science Link

Since 1850 the average temperature on Earth has risen 1°C (1.8°F). Some scientists predict it will rise 2°C (3.5°F) more by the year 2100. They believe this will lead to many problems, including the melting of polar ice caps that would cause sea levels to rise and flood coastal areas.

At the troposphere's outer edge, temperatures are –51°C to –79°C (–60°F to –110°F). The ozone layer traps the Sun's radiation, so temperatures rise. In the thermosphere it may be 1,200°C (2,200°F)!

DISCUSSION STARTER

1. What is global warming?

2. How have people contributed to an increase in Earth's temperatures?

Exosphere

Thermosphere

Mesosphere

Stratosphere

Troposphere

To learn more about global warming, visit **www.mhschool.com/science** and select the keyword TEMPS.

*inter*NET
CONNECTION

WHY IT MATTERS

The food crops we eat depend on water circulating between air and Earth's surface.

SCIENCE WORDS

water vapor water in the form of a gas

humidity the amount of water vapor in the air

evaporation the changing of a liquid into a gas

relative humidity a comparison between the actual amount of water vapor in the air and the amount the air can hold at a given temperature

condensation the changing of a gas into a liquid

convection current a circular flow of air that transfers heat energy through the atmosphere.

precipitation any form of water particles that falls from the atmosphere and reaches the ground

water cycle the continuous movement of water between Earth's surface and the air, changing from liquid to gas to liquid

The Water Cycle

What if you were walking on this bridge? What would you see and feel all around you? Here's a hint. Put a cold glass of lemonade outside on a table on a hot, humid day. What do you see and feel on the outside of the glass?

What is a humid day like? You can feel a humid day. The word *humid* may make you think of moisture—fine droplets of water. Where is the moisture on a humid day?

EXPLORE

HYPOTHESIZE The lemonade glass has moisture on the side and a puddle around the bottom. Where does the moisture come from? Is it from inside the glass? Write a hypothesis in your *Science Journal.* How might you design an experiment to test your ideas?

Design Your Own Experiment

WHERE DOES THE PUDDLE COME FROM?

PROCEDURES

1. EXPERIMENT Describe what you would do to test your idea about where the puddle came from. How would your test support or reject your idea?

2. COMMUNICATE Draw a diagram showing how you would use the materials. In your *Science Journal,* keep a record of your observations.

CONCLUDE AND APPLY

1. COMMUNICATE Describe the results of your investigation.

2. COMMUNICATE What evidence did you gather? Explain what happened.

3. INFER How does this evidence support or reject your explanation?

GOING FURTHER: Problem Solving

4. USE VARIABLES Do you get the same results on a cool day as on a warm day? How might you set up an investigation to show the difference?

5. USE VARIABLES Do you get the same results on a humid day as on a dry day? How might you set up an investigation to show the difference?

MATERIALS
- plastic drinking glasses
- ice
- paper towels
- food coloring
- thermometer
- *Science Journal*

223

...e Does the Puddle ... From?

The Explore Activity showed that the water in the puddle on the table did not come from inside the glass. The water came from the air around the glass. When the warm air touched the cold glass, the air cooled. Droplets of water formed, ran down the side of the glass, and formed the puddle.

The water in the air is water vapor. **Water vapor** is water in the form of a gas. Water vapor is invisible, colorless, odorless, and tasteless. The amount of water vapor in the air is called **humidity.** Do not confuse humidity with droplets of liquid water you see in rain, fog, or clouds.

How does water vapor get into the air in the first place? Think about planet Earth. More than two-thirds of this planet is covered with liquid water—in oceans, rivers, and lakes.

Each day the Sun turns trillions of tons of Earth's water into water vapor. The changing of a liquid into a gas is called **evaporation.** This takes lots of energy. The main energy source for Earth is the Sun. When the Sun's energy strikes molecules of liquid water, it gives them a "lift." Some molecules near the surface evaporate into the air as water vapor.

Plants also contain water. They absorb it from the ground through their roots. Then they transport it to their leaves. To get into the air, this liquid water must be changed into water vapor.

Plant leaves give off water in the process called *transpiration.* This is the second-largest source of water vapor in the atmosphere.

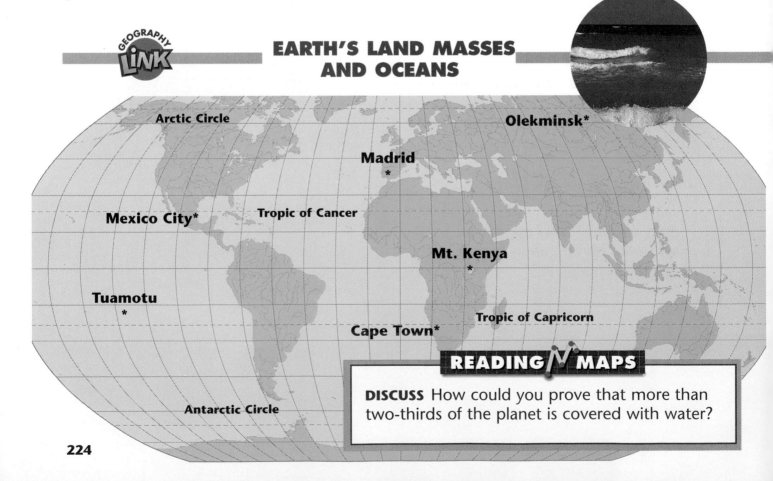

GEOGRAPHY LiNK

EARTH'S LAND MASSES AND OCEANS

Arctic Circle

Olekminsk*

Madrid *

Mexico City*

Tropic of Cancer

Mt. Kenya *

Tuamotu *

Tropic of Capricorn

Cape Town*

Antarctic Circle

READING MAPS

DISCUSS How could you prove that more than two-thirds of the planet is covered with water?

RELATIVE HUMIDITY

READING N GRAPHS

1. DISCUSS How does the amount of water vapor that air can hold compare at 25°C and 40°C?

2. WRITE How does the little van stand for 100% relative humidity?

Cold air   Warm air

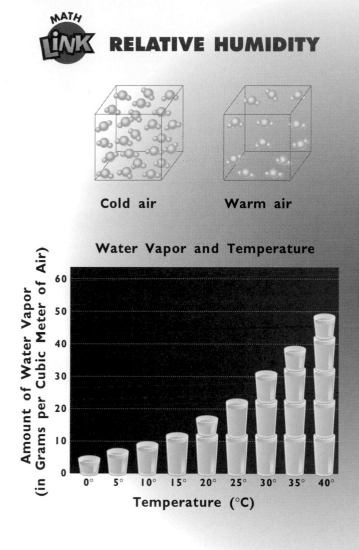

Water Vapor and Temperature

Amount of Water Vapor (in Grams per Cubic Meter of Air)

Temperature (°C)

$\dfrac{6 \text{ people}}{6 \text{ seats}} = 1 = 100\%$ relative humidity

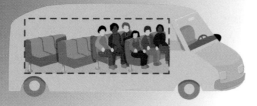

$\dfrac{6 \text{ people}}{12 \text{ seats}} = \dfrac{1}{2} = 50\%$ relative humidity

people = water vapor
little van = cooler air
bigger van = warm air

Can Air Fill Up With Water?

Does water just keep evaporating? For example, a puddle may evaporate in minutes until all the water from the puddle has gone into the air. What about water from a lake, a river, the ocean? Does all water keep evaporating, or is there a limit to how much water the air can "hold"?

A given amount of air can hold only so much water. Eventually, all the spaces between air molecules fill up with water vapor. At that point, just as many water molecules are entering the air as are leaving it. The air is filled.

In warm air, gas molecules are spread out and moving fast. A "box" of warm air can hold more water vapor than cooler air. In cooler air, gas molecules are moving more slowly and are crowded together. Water vapor entering cool air is more likely to drop back into the water.

Relative humidity is a comparison between how much water vapor is in the air and how much the air can hold at a given temperature. Relative humidity is given in percents. "100%" means the air is filled with water vapor at that temperature. "50%" means the air is half-filled. Water can still keep evaporating into the air.

①

②

Why Can Air Feel "Sticky"?

Relative humidity can be used to predict how the air will feel to a person. The higher the relative humidity, the less water can evaporate into the air. The less water, such as sweat, can evaporate from our skin, the wetter and "stickier" the air feels.

Relative humidity can also be used to predict when condensation will occur. **Condensation**, like the drops of water on the lemonade glass, is the changing of a gas into a liquid. In the atmosphere, condensation is usually the result of warm air being cooled.

When warm air cools, it holds less water vapor. The water vapor already there occupies more of the available space. We say the air is becoming more moist. When the air cools enough so

The process that forms droplets of water on the lemonade glass is also the process that forms clouds—condensation.

that it can no longer hold any more water vapor, condensation occurs.

Condensation explains what happened to the glass of lemonade. The cold glass cooled the air that touched it. The cooled air could no longer hold as much water vapor as when it was warm. Water vapor condensed, forming droplets on the glass.

Condensation in the atmosphere forms clouds. The greater the relative humidity, the greater the chance of clouds—and rain.

Brain Power

You may have heard people complain on a hot day, "It's not the heat, it's the humidity!" Why do you think the humidity is so important, especially when the weather is hot? Why doesn't a hot day with 30 percent humidity feel as uncomfortable as a hot day with 70 percent humidity?

Cloud forms

Warm air

Cool air

③

READING ⁄⁄ DIAGRAMS

1. **DISCUSS** What can cause air to rise?
2. **WRITE** What happens to the air temperature as air rises?

What Happens Next?

How can warm, moist air cool off? Warm air rises. As it does, it gets colder. At high altitudes, air pressure is lower, so the air expands. Energy is used up in this process, so the air cools. What can cause air to rise and cool?

- Air rises and cools when it is pushed upward over mountains by winds.

- Heating of air also causes it to rise. When the ground is strongly heated by the Sun, air above the ground gets warmed and rises. It expands as it rises. As the air expands, it cools.

- Air can also be pushed upward when cooler air and warmer air meet. When the two air masses meet, they don't mix. The lighter, warm air is pushed up over the heavier, cold air. The result is that the warm air is pushed up higher into the atmosphere, where it cools.

What happens to the air after it rises and cools? It spreads out and starts to sink. When it nears the ground, it moves in beneath other air that is warming and rising. The cycle is then repeated. This circular movement of the air is called a **convection current**. It is a natural way of transferring heat energy through the atmosphere.

Whatever causes air to rise and cool, the end result is the same. As the air rises and cools, the water vapor in it condenses into tiny water droplets.

In order for water vapor to condense, it must have a surface on which the liquid droplets will form. This surface is provided by the tiny dust particles that are part of the air.

As the droplets increase in number, they begin to form clouds. If the temperature falls below the freezing point of water, the water vapor that condenses will form a cloud of tiny ice crystals.

227

Stratus clouds

Cumulus clouds

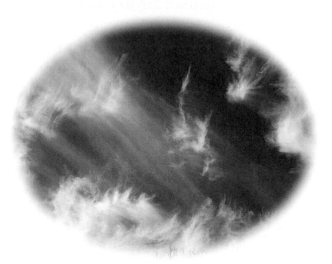

Cirrus clouds

What Kinds of Clouds Are There?

Clouds look different depending on what they are made of. Water-droplet clouds tend to have sharp, well-defined edges. If the cloud is very thick, it may look gray, or even black. That's because sunlight is unable to pass through. Ice-crystal clouds tend to have fuzzy, less distinct edges. They also look whiter.

Clouds are found only in the layer of the atmosphere that is closest to Earth's surface. There are three basic cloud forms. *Stratus clouds* form in blanketlike layers. *Cumulus clouds* are puffy clouds that appear to rise up from a flat bottom. *Cirrus clouds* form at very high altitudes out of ice crystals and have a wispy, featherlike shape. If rain or snow falls from a cloud, the term *nimbo*—for "rain"—is added to the cloud's name.

Clouds are further grouped into families by height and form. There are low clouds, middle clouds, and clouds that develop upward—clouds of vertical development. *Cumulonimbus clouds* develop upward. They can start as low clouds and reach up as high as the highest clouds. These are the clouds that often bring thunderstorms.

If moist air at ground level cools, a cloud can form right there. A cloud at ground level is called *fog*.

TYPES OF CLOUDS

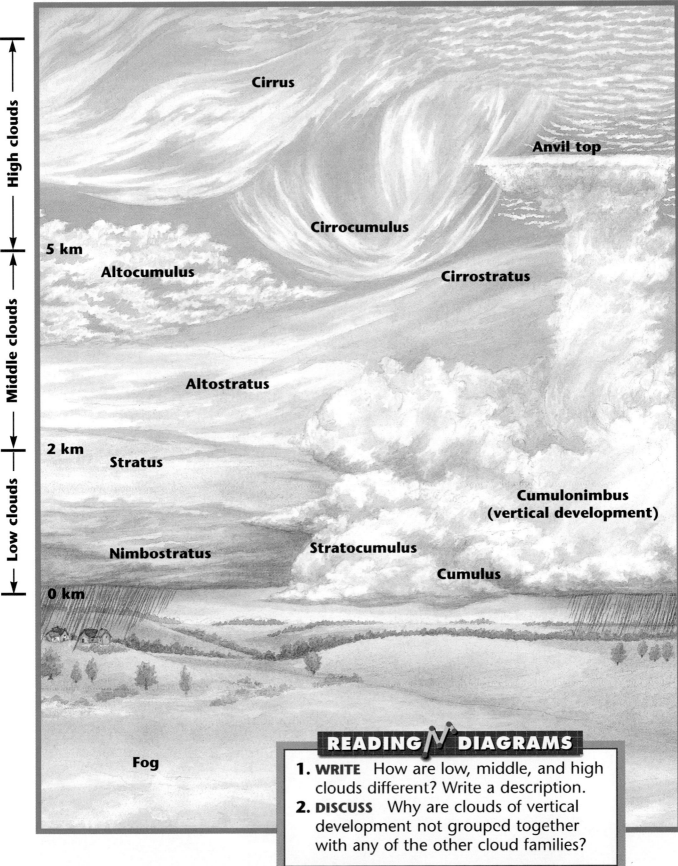

High clouds

Cirrus

Anvil top

5 km

Altocumulus

Cirrocumulus

Cirrostratus

Middle clouds

Altostratus

Clouds of vertical development

2 km

Stratus

Cumulonimbus
(vertical development)

Low clouds

Nimbostratus

Stratocumulus

Cumulus

0 km

Fog

READING DIAGRAMS

1. **WRITE** How are low, middle, and high clouds different? Write a description.
2. **DISCUSS** Why are clouds of vertical development not grouped together with any of the other cloud families?

229

How Do Rain and Snow Happen?

How do rain and snow form and fall? **Precipitation** is any form of water particles that falls from the atmosphere and reaches the ground. Precipitation can be liquid (rain) or solid (such as snow).

Clouds are made up of tiny water droplets or ice crystals. The droplets are only about 1/50 of a millimeter. They are so light that they remain "hanging" in the air. This is why many clouds do not form precipitation.

Precipitation occurs when cloud droplets or ice crystals join together to form very large droplets or crystals. Droplets that do not freeze in the atmosphere fall as rain or sleet. Droplets that form ice crystals in the atmosphere fall as snow or hail.

READING IN CHARTS

1. **DISCUSS** Classify the precipitation types as solids or liquids.
2. **WRITE** Which types of precipitation form in similar ways? Explain.

TYPES OF PRECIPITATION

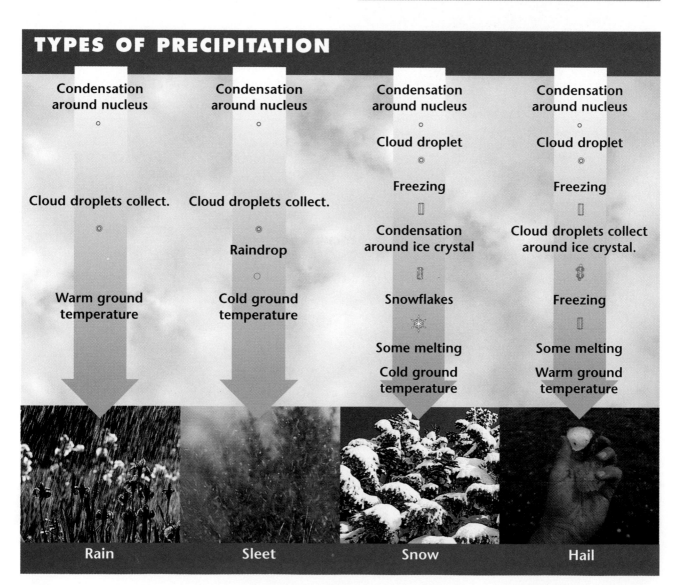

Condensation around nucleus	Condensation around nucleus	Condensation around nucleus	Condensation around nucleus
		Cloud droplet	Cloud droplet
		Freezing	Freezing
Cloud droplets collect.	Cloud droplets collect.	Condensation around ice crystal	Cloud droplets collect around ice crystal.
	Raindrop	Snowflakes	Freezing
Warm ground temperature	Cold ground temperature	Some melting	Some melting
		Cold ground temperature	Warm ground temperature
Rain	**Sleet**	**Snow**	**Hail**

How Are Cloud Type and Precipitation Related?

Do certain kinds of clouds produce certain kinds of precipitation? Yes.

- In tall clouds, there is more chance for droplets to run into one another and combine, making larger raindrops.

- Precipitation from large cumulus clouds often falls as heavy rain or snow showers. However, it usually doesn't last too long.

- Precipitation from stratus clouds is usually long-lasting, with smaller drops of rain or snowflakes.

- Clouds with great vertical development hold a lot of water. These clouds are very *turbulent*, or violent. Their tops often reach heights where the temperature is below freezing. They often produce great downpours. They also sometimes produce hail. *Hail* is pellets made of ice and snow.

Vertical clouds have updrafts— strong winds that move up inside. Hail forms when updrafts in these huge clouds hurl ice crystals upward again and again. As the crystals fall, they become coated with water. As they rise, the water freezes into an icy outer shell. This process usually happens over and over, adding more and more layers of ice to the hailstones. The more violent the updrafts, the larger the hailstone will get before it finally falls to the ground.

Path of Growing Hailstone

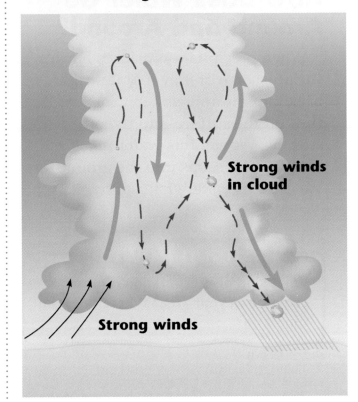

Strong winds in cloud

Strong winds

NATIONAL GEOGRAPHIC

FUNtastic Facts

In March, 1952, the island of Réunion in the Indian Ocean was drenched with 74 inches of rain in just 24 hours! That's more than 6 feet of water! How many inches of precipitation did your state receive this month?

How Does Water Go Around and Around?

When precipitation reaches Earth's surface, some of it evaporates right back into the atmosphere. Some of it runs off the surface into rivers and streams. We call this water *runoff.*

Much of it seeps into the ground. We call this water *groundwater.*

Groundwater collects in tiny holes, or pores, in soil and rocks. Groundwater can often seep down through soil and rocks when the pores are interconnected. It can fill up all the pores in a layer of rock below the surface. Much of this water eventually moves back to the rivers and then to lakes or oceans.

Earth's water moves from place to place through the processes of

Brain Power

What kind of precipitation is most common in your area? Where does the runoff go?

THE WATER CYCLE

Condensation the process in which a gas is changed to a liquid

Transpiration the process by which plant leaves release water into the air

Evaporation the process in which a liquid changes directly to a gas

evaporation, condensation, and precipitation. Condensation and precipitation take water out of Earth's atmosphere. Evaporation puts water back into the atmosphere. This complex web of changes is called the water cycle.

The **water cycle** is the continuous movement of water between Earth's surface and the air, changing from liquid to gas to liquid. The diagram shows the many different paths water can take into and out of the atmosphere in the water cycle.

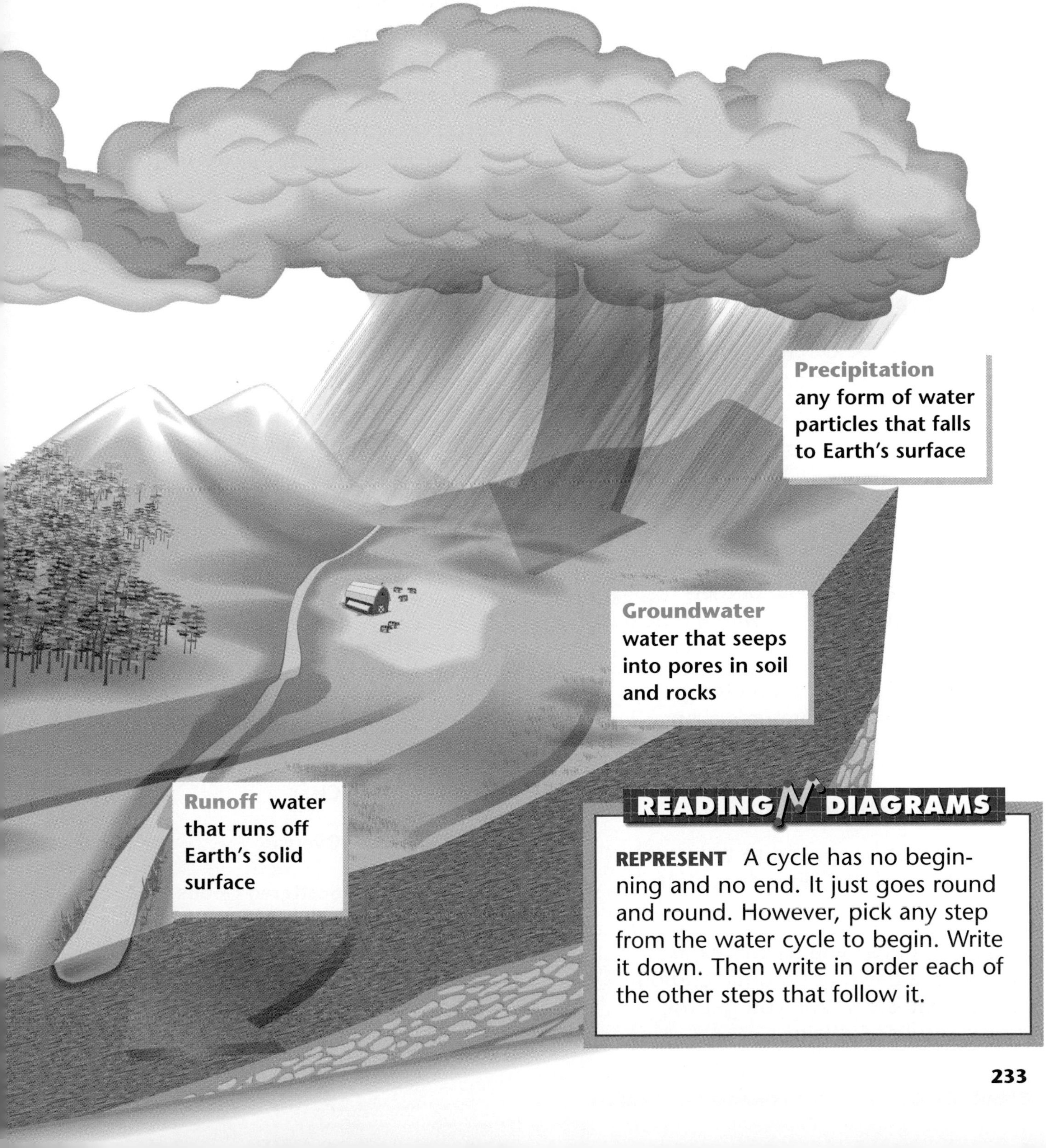

Precipitation
any form of water particles that falls to Earth's surface

Groundwater
water that seeps into pores in soil and rocks

Runoff water that runs off Earth's solid surface

READING 🔍 DIAGRAMS

REPRESENT A cycle has no beginning and no end. It just goes round and round. However, pick any step from the water cycle to begin. Write it down. Then write in order each of the other steps that follow it.

QUICK LAB

Feel the Humidity

HYPOTHESIZE Why do you feel warmer on a high humidity day? Write a hypothesis in your *Science Journal*.

MATERIALS
- 2-in.-square piece of old cotton cloth
- rubber band
- thermometer
- $\frac{1}{2}$ c of cold water
- 1 c of warm water
- *Science Journal*

PROCEDURES

SAFETY Be careful handling warm water.

1. **OBSERVE** Record the air temperature in your *Science Journal*.

2. Put thermometer in cold water. Add warm water slowly until water temperature matches air temperature.

3. Wrap cloth around bulb of thermometer. Gently hold it with a rubber band. Dampen cloth in the water.

4. **OBSERVE** Wave thermometer gently in air. Record temperatures every 30 seconds for three minutes.

CONCLUDE AND APPLY

1. **INFER** What happened to temperature of wet cloth? How does cloth feel? Explain.

2. **INFER** Suppose you try this experiment on a day that is humid and on a day that is dry. Will you get the same results? Explain.

How Do You Record the Amount of Clouds?

Now that you have learned about humidity, clouds, and precipitation, let's find out how scientists record these weather conditions.

Every day, scientists at weather stations record the kinds of clouds in the sky. They indicate the cloud type and cloud family using the terms shown in the charts in this lesson.

They also estimate the cloud cover—that is, the amount of the sky covered by clouds. They use the terms *clear, scattered clouds, partly cloudy, mostly cloudy,* or *overcast* to describe the cloud cover.

Weather scientists use circles as symbols to record the cloud cover. A different circle is used for each day. Portions of the circle are shaded to show different amounts of cloud cover. An empty circle means "clear skies." A fully shaded circle means "completely overcast."

Weather scientists use circle symbols to record cloud cover.

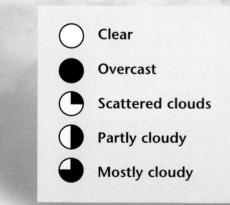

Clear
Overcast
Scattered clouds
Partly cloudy
Mostly cloudy

How Do You Measure Rainfall?

Precipitation is measured with a rain gauge. Weather scientists use gauges that have been carefully designed for very exact measurements.

You can make a simple rain gauge from an empty coffee can. Just place it outside, open end up. Keep it out in the open, away from buildings or trees. When the precipitation stops, measure its depth in the can. You may measure in inches with a standard ruler. If you have a metric ruler, use millimeters (the smallest unit). Record the type of precipitation and how much falls. Keep track of the amount of precipitation by measuring it at frequent intervals.

WHY IT MATTERS

If you ever had a baseball game rained out, you know how rain can ruin your day.

Rain may ruin your plans for a day, but rain is vital for life on Earth. Rain helps crops grow. That means food for you and others! Rain helps build the amount of water in wells and water-collecting areas, such as reservoirs. If you ever had a drought in your area, a time when there was little or no precipitation, you know how scarce water can be.

REVIEW

1. Where does water vapor in the air come from? What produces it?

2. How does water vapor get cooled in the atmosphere?

3. How do clouds form?

4. **CRITICAL THINKING** *Apply* Would you say that the Sun is a cause of clouds? Defend your answer.

5. **SEQUENCE OF EVENTS** What are the main processes that show how liquid water changes in the water cycle? List the parts in order to show the changes.

WHY IT MATTERS **THINK ABOUT IT**
How do the two processes of evaporation and condensation depend on each other? Why can't there be one without the other?

WHY IT MATTERS **WRITE ABOUT IT**
If there were a drought in your area, what could you do to cut back on using water?

Riding the Winds

Prevailing westerlies

Doldrums

Trade winds

Weather forecasters report that good or bad weather is "on the way." How do they know? What's pushing weather their way? Global winds!

Because the Sun's rays hit most directly near the Equator, the warmest air is there. It has a low density above denser cold air moving in from the North and South Poles. Earth's rotation turns air north of the Equator to the right and air south of the Equator to the left. All this movement results in distinct wind patterns that influence our weather.

Between the Equator and 30° latitude north or south are the trade winds. Once these winds blew the sails of giant trade ships from Europe to the New World.

Between the 30° and 60° latitudes, winds blow in the opposite direction from the trade winds. These prevailing westerlies once pushed sailing ships back to Europe.

At higher altitudes narrow belts of strong winds—the jet stream—blow west to east. These winds average 100–185 kilometers per hour (60–111 miles per hour). Pilots often ride the jet stream for the fastest way home!

DISCUSSION STARTER

1. Why are there different types of global winds circling Earth?

2. The doldrums are a windless zone on the Equator where the air seems motionless. Which direction is the air going? Why?

To learn more about global winds, visit *www.mhschool.com/science* and select the keyword GLOBAL.

SCIENCE WORDS

climate p. 215

condensation
  p. 226

convection
  current p. 227

density p. 192

evaporation p. 224

friction p. 192

greenhouse
  effect p. 214

humidity p. 224

mass p. 196

precipitation
  p. 230

USING SCIENCE WORDS

Number a paper from 1 to 10. Fill in 1 to 5 with words from the list above.

1. ___?___ is the amount of matter in an object.

2. A gas changes into a liquid in the process called ___?___.

3. The way in which certain chemicals in the atmosphere warm the Earth is called the ___?___.

4. ___?___ is any form of water that falls from the atmosphere and reaches the ground.

5. ___?___ is the amount of water vapor in the air.

6–10. **Pick five words from the list above that were not used in 1 to 5, and use each in a sentence.**

UNDERSTANDING SCIENCE IDEAS

11. Describe what happens when sunlight strikes Earth's oceans.

12. Explain how a cloud forms.

13. Describe the structure of Earth's interior.

14. What causes ocean currents to form?

15. Why does Earth not overheat from solar energy?

USING IDEAS AND SKILLS

16. Where might you go to find a cool breeze on a hot summer day?

17. If an object at Earth's surface has more mass than you do, is it heavier or lighter than you are?

18. **READING SKILL: SEQUENCE OF EVENTS** Describe how moisture can form on the outside of a glass of cool lemonade.

19. **INTERPRET DATA/INFER** Based on the table below, what is the total percent of incoming solar energy that is *not* reflected back into space?

INCOMING SOLAR ENERGY (INSOLATION)

Percent	Where It Goes
22	Reflected back to space by Earth's atmosphere
9	Reflected back to space by Earth's surface
20	Absorbed by Earth's atmosphere
49	Absorbed by Earth's surface

20. **THINKING LIKE A SCIENTIST** On a very cold day, closed car windows can sometimes mist over on the inside. What process is occuring?

PROBLEMS and PUZZLES

Draft Drift Observe updrafts and downdrafts in your classroom. Make a sketch of the room. Use a compass to determine north, south, east, and west. Drop a feather and watch its drift. Mark the "wind direction" on your map. Repeat in many parts of the room. Explain your results.

UNIT 3 REVIEW

SCIENCE WORDS

climate p. 215
conduction p. 181
convection p. 181
density p. 192
evaporation p. 224
insulator p. 194

light wave p. 166
potential
  energy p. 177
relative
  humidity p. 225
water vapor p. 224

USING SCIENCE WORDS

Number a paper from 1 to 10. Beside each number write the word or words that best complete the sentence.

1. The quantity of matter in a unit of volume is a measure of the ___?___ of the matter.

2. ___?___ is water in the form of a gas.

3. The long-term trend in weather conditions at a particular location is called the ___?___.

4. A(n) ___?___ is a material that conducts heat poorly.

5. ___?___ is the changing of a liquid into a gas.

6. If you mix hot and cold water, all of the water becomes the same temperature due to ___?___.

7. A(n) ___?___ is an electromagnetic wave that can travel without matter or through matter.

8. ___?___ is the movement of energy through direct contact between two substances.

9. Energy stored in an object or material is ___?___.

10. ___?___ is a comparison between the actual amount of water vapor in the air and the amount the air can hold at a given temperature.

UNDERSTANDING SCIENCE IDEAS

Write 11 to 15. For each number write the letter for the best answer. You may wish to use the hints provided.

11. Water drops that collect on a cold glass of lemonade come from
    a. the lemonade
    b. the air
    c. a puddle
    d. the glass itself
    (Hint: Read page 224.)

12. The water cycle describes how water
    a. flows upstream
    b. spins in a circle
    c. changes form
    d. heats up the atmosphere
    (Hint: Read pages 232–233.)

13. Sound waves cannot travel through
    a. solids
    b. gases
    c. a vacuum
    d. liquids
    (Hint: Read page 164.)

14. The transfer of energy by electromagnetic waves is called
    a. radiation
    b. convection
    c. conduction
    d. insulation
    (Hint: Read page 180.)

15. When warm, moist air rises and cools, the water vapor in it
    a. evaporates
    b. expands
    c. sinks
    d. condenses
    (Hint: Read page 227.)

USING IDEAS AND SKILLS

16. A sled pulled up a hillside is gaining what kind of energy?

17. Explain what happens when a mass of warm air in the atmosphere meets a mass of cold air.

18. How does water vapor get into the air?

19. What is fog, and how does it form?

20. If you move two objects twice as close to each other, what happens to the gravitational pull between them?

21. Why is it better to use a thermometer to determine the temperature of things instead of using touch?

22. How do we get heat from the Sun?

23. Explain how molecules of air move as sound waves pass through them.

THINKING LIKE A SCIENTIST

24.  **PREDICT** On a hike in the desert, will you be more comfortable in light-colored clothes or in dark clothes? Explain.

25. What is the climate like where you live? What data do you need to describe climate?

interNET CONNECTION

For help in reviewing this unit, visit **www.mhschool.com/science**

 WRITING IN YOUR JOURNAL

SCIENCE IN YOUR LIFE
How does the weather affect your daily activities? Is there a difference between what you do on rainy days and what you do on clear, sunny days?

PRODUCT ADS
Describe the types of housing insulation used in the area where you live. Is it more important to keep heat in or out? Why is that so? What resources can insulation save?

HOW SCIENTISTS WORK
In this unit you learned how scientists collect information about Earth's interior without actually going there. What method do they use, and what have they discovered?

 **Design your own Experiment**

How much does humidity change over the course of a day? To find out, design an experiment using a glass of cold water, a thermometer, and a timer. Check your experiment with your teacher before you perform it.

PROBLEMS and PUZZLES

Heat Index

When the temperature and the relative humidity are both high, the air temperature may "feel" greater than what the thermometer reads. The temperature that you feel is called the *heat index*.

Find 90° F on the graph. Move your finger across the 90° F line to where it meets the 70% relative humidity line. At that the point where the two lines meet, the heat index is 105° F. As you move your finger rigtht to higher relative humidities, the heat index gets higher.

The greater the heat index, the greater the chance of the heat affecting your health. How can knowing the heat index help you?

A Light Maze

Build a light maze. Use scissors, a flashlight, a box with a lid, heavy tape, strips of cardboard, mirrors, or just aluminum foil taped to cardboard squares. Start by drawing a plan of the maze to show the path of light. Then build the maze. Find what happpens as you add turns into the maze. Have a contest to see who can build a maze with the most turns.

Greenhouse Oceans

How will the greenhouse effect change the world's oceans? Make a model using a pan and a flat-bottomed bowl. Add water to the pan until it is half full. Turn the bowl upside down in the center of the pan and cover it with ice cubes. The ice represents the Earth's ice caps. Mark the water level. Allow the ice to melt, and mark the new water level. How did the level change? How might the level of Earth's oceans change if the greenhouse effect melts the ice caps?

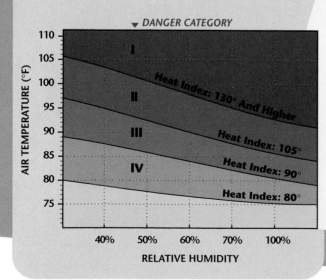

▼ DANGER CATEGORY

AIR TEMPERATURE (°F)

I
II
III
IV

Heat Index: 130° And Higher
Heat Index: 105°
Heat Index: 90°
Heat Index: 80°

110
105
100
95
90
85
80
75

40% 50% 60% 70% 100%

RELATIVE HUMIDITY

UNIT 4

ECOLOGY

CHAPTER 7
ECOSYSTEMS

The water around you, the air above you, the rocks and soil under your feet, and all living things around you make up your ecosystem. Living things in an ecosystem depend on each other and on the nonliving things around them. They need each other to survive.

Earth is home to many different ecosystems. The one you live in has its own climate, soil, plants, and animals. Can you think of any other ecosystems? What plants and animals live in hot, tropical climates or in cold, polar ones? Do California's mountains, deserts, and seashores have different ecosystems?

 In Chapter 7 you will have many opportunities to read diagrams for information.

Living Things and Their Environment

WHY IT MATTERS

Both living and nonliving things in an area interact with each other.

What do you need in order to survive? Your answers could include food, water, the right temperature, and a place to live.

What kinds of things do the animals and plants shown here need to survive? Where do you think they get these things?

SCIENCE WORDS

ecosystem all the living and nonliving things in an area interacting with each other

ecology the study of how living things and their environment interact

abiotic factor a nonliving part of an ecosystem

biotic factor a living part of an ecosystem

population all the organisms of one species that live in an area at the same time

community all the populations living in an area

habitat the area in which an organism lives

niche the role an organism has in its ecosystem

EXPLORE

HYPOTHESIZE How do living things interact with each other and their environment? What do living things need in order to survive? Write a hypothesis in your *Science Journal.* How would you design a special environment to test your ideas?

Design Your Own Experiment

WHAT DO LIVING THINGS NEED TO SURVIVE?

PROCEDURES

1. For a water environment, add 4 cm (1.5 in.) of thoroughly washed sand or gravel to the jar. Fill the jar to about 4 cm (1.5 in.) from the top with water. Add a few floating plants, rooted plants with floating leaves, and submerged plants. Do not crowd the plants. Add two large or eight small water snails.

2. For a land environment, place a 2-cm (0.75-in.) layer of gravel on the bottom of the jar. Cover the gravel layer with a 5- to 7-cm (2- to 2.75-in.) layer of moistened soil. Add plants, and plant grass seeds. Add earthworms, sow bugs, and snails.

3. Place each jar in a lighted area but not in direct sunlight.

4. Cover each jar with its own lid or with a piece of plastic wrap. Record in your *Science Journal* how many and what kinds of living things you used.

5. OBSERVE Examine your jars every other day, and record your observations.

CONCLUDE AND APPLY

1. INFER What are the nonliving parts of your system? What are the living parts of your system?

2. INFER What do the living things need to survive? How do you know?

GOING FURTHER: Problem Solving

3. EXPERIMENT How could you design an environment that contains both land and water areas?

MATERIALS

- wide-mouthed, clear 3.8-L (1-gal) container with lid
- washed gravel
- pond water or aged tap water
- water plants such as *Elodea* or duckweed
- 2 large water snails or 8 small water snails
- soil
- small rocks
- grass seed and small plants
- 2 earthworms, 2 land snails, 4 sow bugs, or other small land animals that eat plants
- *Science Journal*

What Do Living Things Need to Survive?

What or whom do you interact with every day? Make a list. The Explore Activity showed how living things and nonliving things interact in an **ecosystem**. An ecosystem is all the living and nonliving things in an area interacting with each other. **Ecology** is the study of how all these things interact in order to survive.

Most ecosystems are much larger than a jar. Some, like the prairie ecosystem of North America, the deserts of Africa, and the rain forests of Brazil, cover large areas of a country or continent. Freshwater ecosystems cover less space than saltwater ecosystems. Saltwater ecosystems can cover entire oceans. It doesn't matter where they are or what they look like. All ecosystems have the same parts.

The nonliving parts of an ecosystem are the **abiotic** (ā′bī ot′ik) **factors**. Abiotic factors include water, minerals, sunlight, air, climate, and soil.

All organisms need water. Their bodies are 50 to 95 percent water. The processes that keep living things alive—like photosynthesis and respiration—can take place only in the presence of water. Living things need minerals, such as calcium, iron, phosphorus, and nitrogen. Some living things, like plants and algae, need sunlight to make food. Animals and plants need oxygen to produce the energy for their bodies. Plants and algae also need carbon dioxide. The environment must also have the right temperature for organisms to survive.

EARTH **LiNK** SCIENCE

Brain Power

What abiotic factors have recently changed where you live? How did the changes affect living things?

Abiotic factors in an ecosystem include light, water, soil, temperature, air, and minerals.

What Do Living Things Contribute?

The right abiotic factors help make it possible for the *organisms*, or living things, in an ecosystem to survive. The living parts are animals, plants, fungi, protists, and bacteria. Mushrooms and molds are fungi. Protists include one-celled organisms. Microscopic bacteria live everywhere.

These organisms—animals, plants, fungi, protists, and bacteria—make up the **biotic** (bī ot'ik) **factors**, or living parts, of an ecosystem.

Each organism contributes something to the others in the ecosystem.

Plants and algae are called *producers*. They produce oxygen and food that animals need. Animals are *consumers*. Animals consume, or eat, plants or animals that eat plants. Animals also give off carbon dioxide that plants need to make food.

What do the fungi and bacteria contribute? They are a very important part of any ecosystem. Fungi and bacteria are *decomposers*. They *decompose*, or break down, dead plants and animals into useful things like minerals that enrich soil. Plants need these in order to grow.

Each of these kinds of organisms helps the others survive.

Biotic factors in an ecosystem include plants, animals, fungi, protists, and bacteria.

READING IN DIAGRAMS

1. **DISCUSS** How do these two diagrams differ? What does each diagram show?
2. **WRITE** Which of these two diagrams best shows the abiotic factors in the ecosystem? Explain your answer.

245

What Is a Redwood Forest Ecosystem Like?

The tallest trees in the world grow in California. They are redwoods — evergreen, cone-bearing trees that can reach 60 to 90 meters (200 to 300 feet) and may live more than 2,000 years.

Redwoods grow best along the cool, rainy Pacific Coast of north and central California. They thrive on low mountain slopes that receive 250 or more centimeters (100 in.) of rain each year and are often blanketed in thick fog.

Redwood forests once covered much of California's northwest. Native Americans lived in and around the forests for thousands of years but had little impact on them. In the mid-1800s, however, thousands of people flocked to the state in search of cropland, timber, gold, and other resources. In less than 150 years, loggers eliminated most of the original redwood forests.

Fortunately, people can still experience the majesty of a redwood forest in national parks and protected reserves.

A redwood forest is damp, cool, and full of shadows. Arrow-straight trunks, wrapped in thick, reddish-brown bark, rise up on all sides. The tops of many redwoods are so far above the ground they are hard to see, often hidden in swirling mist. Drops of moisture collect on the branches and needles high overhead and fall to earth with a gentle drip, drip, drip.

A spongy carpet of fallen needles and tiny redwood cones covers the forest floor. Ferns, mosses, and small bushy plants crowd around the bases of the tall trees. Colorful wildflowers and berries brighten the deep shade. Many different kinds of small animals live in the redwood forest. But most are shy and secretive, and visitors must wait patiently and quietly to catch a glimpse of them.

Towering redwoods grow on coastal mountain slopes in north and central California. [Inset] A redwood forest is home to many animals, such as this Pacific giant salamander.

What Plants Live in a Redwood Forest?

Towering redwood trees dominate a redwood forest. But they share moist mountain slopes with Douglas fir, grand fir, and western hemlock. In slightly drier parts of the forest, tanoaks, Pacific madrones, and laurels grow among the redwoods. With long, leathery, evergreen leaves, tanoaks are not true oaks, but members of the beech tree family. They produce large quantities of acorns that are food for many forest animals.

Smaller trees, such as wax myrtle and golden chinquapin, grow in the forest, too. Beneath them, huckleberry, dogwood, and salmonberry bushes form a dense layer of head-high greenery.

The forest floor is crowded with the lacy fronds of ferns — sword ferns, lady ferns, wood ferns, and many others. Patches of redwood sorrel, with its clover-like leaves, compete for growing space with wild cucumbers, tiny orchids, columbines, violets, false lily-of-the valley, and velvety soft mosses.

In open or disturbed patches of the forest, young tree seedlings reach for the light. Redwood seedlings grow quickly, more than 30 cm (1 ft) per year, under the right conditions.

Redwood Forests

San Francisco

In the cool shade of redwoods, ferns and wildflowers crowd together on the damp forest floor. [Inset] Patches of redwood sorrel are common sights in the forest.

What Animals Live in a Redwood Forest?

Many species, or different kinds, of animals live in California's redwood forests. The largest are mule deer, black bears, and Roosevelt elk.

Squirrels compete with chipmunks, deer mice, and wood rats for seeds and nuts. Raccoons are common, as are rabbits, shrews, skunks, and porcupines. At night bobcats prowl the forest, hunting for small mammals.

Birds are more easily heard than seen. The tweezling calls of chestnut-backed chickadees are mingled with the sweet songs of wrens and warblers, the scolding cries of jays, and the tap-tapping of woodpeckers. Band-tailed pigeons, hawks, and owls are some of the larger birds in the forest. One of the rarest is the marbled murrelet. This seabird catches fish in the ocean but builds nests in the high branches of redwood trees.

Pacific giant salamanders and red-bellied newts scurry across the forest floor. These animals lay their eggs in the streams that meander through the trees. Silver salmon and steelhead trout dart through the water.

Pillbugs, centipedes, and insects crawl among the rotting logs. Finger-long banana slugs slither slowly along, leaving a trail of slime as they go.

Many animals in the forest depend on the redwoods and other plants for their food. The plant-eaters, in turn, provide food for predators such as bobcats and hawks.

To understand the redwood ecosystem, this genetic biologist is classifying redwood samples.

How Are the Living Things Organized?

The redwood forest, like all ecosystems, is home to many different organisms. Each kind of organism, whether an animal, plant, fungus, protist, or bacterium, is a member of a single species. All the organisms of a species living in an area make up a **population.**

The redwood forests of California have redwood, Douglas fir, and madrone trees. They have populations of Roosevelt deer, Douglas' squirrels, and giant salamanders. They have mushrooms that grow out from the trunks of trees or sprout from rotting logs. There are huge numbers of insects, from beetles and bees to butterflies. In the damp, spongy soil, there are populations of bacteria, algae, and microscopic worms.

Most people are satisfied with identifying the populations of living things around them, knowing what kinds of trees or mammals or insects they see.

Scientists want to know how populations interact. Scientists investigate the activities of animals, plants, fungi, protists, and bacteria in an ecosystem.

Researchers also are interested in how bacteria and fungi make the soil fertile and break down dead organic matter to release the nutrients it contains back into the ecosystem. All these questions need to be answered to understand how a redwood forest, or any other ecosystem, functions and stays healthy.

Scientists have to do more than study individual organisms and individual populations in an ecosystem. They have to study the interactions of all the populations. All the populations living in an area make up a **community.**

Brain Power

What are some populations in the ecosystem where you live? Why is it important to understand your ecosystem?

Where Do They Live? What Do They Do?

The place where a population lives is called its **habitat.** The red-bellied newt's habitat, for example, is the moist forest floor of a redwood forest.

Each species in an ecosystem also has a role or place in the activities of its community. The role of an organism in the community is its **niche.**

A species' niche includes many factors. It includes what a species eats and what eats that species. It includes the kind of environment the species needs to live in. It even includes whether the species is active by day or night.

Scientists study the habitats and niches of organisms in a community. They do this to see if the community is healthy or in trouble. What would happen if streams that run through the redwood forests became polluted? Insects that live in the streams might die. The eggs that frogs and salamanders lay in the water might not hatch, and the adults might be harmed. Salmon and trout, as well as other fish in the streams, could be harmed or killed, too.

The problem wouldn't stop there. Stream insects are food for birds like the dipper. Amphibians and fish are the prey of snakes, raccoons, bobcats, and bears. As populations of stream-dwelling organisms dwindled, the animals that eat them would have less food. Some of them might not survive.

Pollutants in the water might also be absorbed into the soil and harm trees and other plants living nearby. In short, whatever happens to streams and the organisms that live in and around them will eventually affect the lives of many other forest organisms.

If conditions of an organism's niche change, it may have trouble surviving. When a large redwood tree falls over or is cut down, an opening is created in the forest. Shade-loving plants such as mosses and ferns may suddenly get too much sun, dry out, and die. However, tiny redwood seeds might germinate and begin growing into new young trees.

The American Dipper's habitat is mountain streams. Dippers dive into fast-flowing streams and then walk along the bottom looking for insect eggs and larvae.

How Do Organisms Survive Changes?

The world is a place of changes. One day the weather may be dry and cold. The next day it may be wet and warm. Heavy rains may drench the land one spring and summer. The next year's spring and summer may have cloudless skies day after day. A good habitat for a certain organism at one time may be a threatening one at another time. How do populations survive difficult times?

Redwoods' Remarkable Roots

Severe floods periodically occur in redwood forests. Heavy rains sweep sediment into streams. The streams overflow their banks and deposit a thick layer of sediment around the bases of many trees.

Yet redwoods are adapted to handle this sudden environmental change. When the bases of their trunk suddenly are buried under several feet of sediment, new roots sprout from existing ones, and grow straight up through the soil until they reach the surface. New horizontal roots also grow out from the tree trunks just below ground level. In a very short time, the redwood trees have new sets of roots at just the right level in the soil.

Scientists have discovered that such flooding and sedimentation in redwood forests is part of a natural environmental cycle that has been going on for thousands of years. Many old redwood trees have multi-level root systems — proof that floods have buried their bases in sediment time and time again.

Floods, fires, and other environmental changes destroy some redwood trees, but make it possible for redwood seeds to sprout and young trees to begin growing.

Elk Populations

At one point in California's history, hunting and the destruction of habitat reduced the state's elk population to just a few individuals. Thanks to conservation efforts, elk are making a comeback in redwood forests.

Wildlife biologists study elk to understand what elk need in their habitat, and how elk populations change over time. On the next page, you can analyze data to discover how the size and composition of an elk herd changes from year to year.

Skill: Use Numbers

COUNTING ELK FROM THE AIR

Wildlife biologists often use aerial surveys to collect data about elk populations. They fly over an area in a helicopter and count the number of elk—males (bulls), females (cows), and calves—within the area. Their data can be used to show changes in the elk population over time. The chart below gives the total number of elk observed in an area over a 6-year period.

MATERIALS

- pencil and paper
- calculator
- *Science Journal*

Elk Populations

YEAR	TOTAL NUMBER
1988	1,919
1989	2,200
1990	1,700
1991	2,004
1992	2,036
1993	2,035

PROCEDURES

1. COMMUNICATE Make a bar graph of the data, with the year on the horizontal axis and the number of elk on the vertical axis. How did the elk population change during the 6-year period?

2. USE NUMBERS In 1989, researchers found that the elk population was composed of 5% bulls, 55% cows, and 40% calves. In 1990, the composition was 2% bulls, 70% cows, and 28% calves. Calculate the actual number of bulls, cows, and calves in the herd in 1989 and 1990.

CONCLUDE AND APPLY

1. INFER Based on your calculations, what might you infer about the cause of the decrease in the elk population between 1989 and 1990?

2. HYPOTHESIZE What might have caused the number of bulls to decrease from 110 (1989) to 34 (1990)? How might you test your hypothesis?

Can the Redwood Forests Survive?

Redwood trees provide useful, beautiful lumber that resists decay and so lasts a long time. But the value of redwoods as a source of building material is a great threat to their survival.

Less than 5 percent of California's original redwood forests are left. Yet lumber companies are still cutting redwood trees. Should people work to change this situation? What can be done to protect these forests for your generation and the generations that follow?

WHY IT MATTERS

In nature, ecosystems tend to stay in balance. Different kinds of living things contribute to the health and well-being of the community of organisms that live there.

But balance in an ecosystem can be upset by the actions of people. Trees are cut down. Rivers are dammed. The land changes and its natural inhabitants disappear. In the process, people gain certain things but lose others. It is important to make wise decisions when you think of changing an ecosystem.

REVIEW

1. Describe the structure of a typical ecosystem.

2. What is the difference between a population and a community?

3. How does an animal's habitat relate to its niche?

4. **USE NUMBERS** Explain how changes in the size of an organism's population can provide clues to changes in that organism's habitat.

5. **CRITICAL THINKING** *Apply* Identify changes caused by human activity in your ecosystem. Explain what was lost and what was gained. Evaluate the results.

WHY IT MATTERS THINK ABOUT IT
Give an example of how a change in one population can affect two or more other populations. Use real organisms in your example.

WHY IT MATTERS WRITE ABOUT IT
Write a fictional short story in which the theme is a changing ecosystem. Make sure the events in your story involve the lives or activities of people.

What's Wrong with This Picture?

Antarctica is too inhospitable for humans and polar bears!

These people call the Arctic home.

A polar bear is looking for a meal. It spots a plump penguin. What happens next? Well . . . nothing. In real life a polar bear and penguin wouldn't meet in the wild. The penguin lives in Antarctica, and the polar bear lives in the Arctic. Both regions are covered with ice and snow most of the year, but there are big differences between them.

The Arctic, at the top of the world, is water surrounded by land. Antarctica, at the bottom of the world, is land surrounded by water. When it's winter in the Arctic, it's summer in Antarctica. Antarctica is the coldest place on Earth. Its lowest recorded temperature was $-88°C$ ($-126.4°F$). The Arctic's lowest temperature was only $-68°C$ ($-94°F$)!

More than 400 kinds of flowering plants are native to the Arctic. Mosses, lichens, grasses, herbs, and shrubs cover the area in warm months. Fewer plants can survive in Antarctica. Some 350 species live in small areas that are ice free, but only three of them are flowering plants.

The Arctic hosts polar bears, foxes, wolves, walruses, reindeer, and caribou. No land-based animals with backbones live full-time in Antarctica. Its largest animal is a fly called a midge! Other animals, like penguins and seals, visit in warmer months.

People are also more common in the Arctic than in Antarctica. Antarctica has no native peoples. Usually people stay in Antarctica only to study the region. With howling winds, frigid cold, and endless ice, Antarctica isn't most people's idea of a great place to live . . . or even to visit!

Arctic

Antarctica

Discussion
Starter

1 Why wouldn't you find polar bears and penguins in the same picture?

2 Compare and contrast the animals native to Antarctica with those native to the Arctic.

To learn more about the Arctic and Antarctica, visit *www.mhschool.com/science* and enter the keyword **POLES.**

WHY IT MATTERS

Climate and soil conditions affect where different populations live.

SCIENCE WORDS

biome one of Earth's large ecosystems, with its climate, soil, plants, and animals

taiga a cool, forest biome of conifers in the upper Northern Hemisphere

tundra a cold, treeless biome of the far north, marked by spongy topsoil

desert a sandy or rocky biome, with little precipitation and little plant life

deciduous forest a forest biome with many kinds of trees that lose their leaves each autumn

tropical rain forest a hot, humid biome near the equator, with much rainfall and a wide variety of life

Places to Live Around the World

Where are you? In summer the Sun doesn't set here. In winter it never rises. Below the surface the soil is always frozen. Not much snow or rain falls. There are no tall trees.

Six thousand miles away, hot sunlight beats down. The air is dry as dust. The soil is sandy. You rarely see a tree. Where are you now?

Soil varies greatly and is a distinctive factor in each ecosystem. Soil content can determine what plants and animals can live there.

EXPLORE

HYPOTHESIZE Why is the soil in one kind of ecosystem different from the soil in another kind of ecosystem? What determines what the soil is like? Write a hypothesis in your *Science Journal*. Test your ideas.

EXPLORE ACTIVITY

Investigate Why Soil Is Important

Test sand and soil samples to see which have the most nutrients.

PROCEDURES

SAFETY Wear goggles and an apron.

1. Place 1 tsp. of washed sand in a plastic cup.

2. OBSERVE Using the dropper add hydrogen peroxide to the sand, drop by drop. Count each drop. Bubbles will form as the hydrogen peroxide breaks down any decayed matter.

3. COMMUNICATE Record the number of drops you add until the bubbles stop forming in your *Science Journal*.

4. EXPERIMENT Perform steps 1–3 using the compost or soil.

CONCLUDE AND APPLY

1. COMPARE AND CONTRAST Which sample— soil or sand—gave off more bubbles?

2. INFER Why was the sand used?

3. INFER Decayed materials in soil release their nutrients to form humus. The amount of humus in soil depends on the rate of decay and the rate at which plants absorb the nutrients. Which sample had more humus?

GOING FURTHER: Apply

4. EVALUATE In which sample could you grow larger, healthier plants? Why?

MATERIALS

- washed sand
- compost, potting soil, or garden soil
- hydrogen peroxide
- 2 plastic cups
- 2 plastic spoons
- dropper
- goggles
- apron
- *Science Journal*

Why Is Soil Important?

Where would you rather try to grow plants—in sandy soil or in rich potting soil? As the Explore Activity showed, certain kinds of soil are better for growing plants than other kinds of soil are.

The land on Earth is divided into six major kinds of large ecosystems, called **biomes** (bī′ōmz). Each biome has its own kind of climate, soil, plants, and animals. Most biomes can be found in different parts of the world. For example, a desert biome is found in North America. Another is found in Africa. Still another is found in South America. Others are found in Asia and Australia. The map shows where Earth's six biomes are located around our planet.

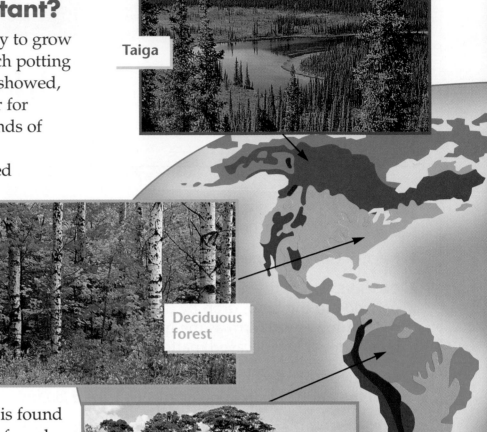

Taiga

Deciduous forest

Tropical rain forest

Desert

Location: Midlatitudes
Climate: Generally very hot days, cool nights; precipitation less than 25 centimeters (10 inches) a year
Soil: Poor in animal and plant decay products but often rich in minerals
Plants: None to cacti, yuccas, scattered bunch grasses
Animals: Rodents, snakes, lizards, tortoises, insects, and some birds. The Sahara in Africa is home to camels, gazelles, antelopes, small foxes, snakes, lizards, gerbils, grasses, shrubs, and some trees.

Tundra

Location: High northern latitudes
Climate: Very cold, harsh, and long winters; short and cool summers; 10–25 centimeters (4–10 inches) of precipitation each year
Soil: Nutrient-poor, permafrost layer a few feet down
Plants: Grasses, wildflowers, mosses, small shrubs
Animals: Musk oxen, migrating caribou, arctic foxes, weasels, snowshoe hares, owls, hawks, various rodents, occasional polar bears

Grassland

Location: Midlatitudes, interiors of continents
Climate: Cool in winter, hot in summer; 25-76 centimeters (10–30 inches) of precipitation a year
Soil: Rich topsoil
Plants: Mostly grasses and small shrubs, some trees near sources of water
Animals: American grasslands include prairie dogs, foxes, small mammals, snakes, insects, various birds. African grasslands include elephants, lions, zebras, giraffes. What animals might live in Australia's grasslands?

Desert

Tundra

Grassland

READING MAPS

1. **WRITE** Which kind of biome is most abundant?
2. **WRITE** Which is least abundant?

Deciduous Forest

Location: Midlatitudes
Climate: Relatively mild summers and cold winters, 76–127 centimeters (30–50 inches) of precipitation a year
Soil: Rich topsoil over clay
Plants: Hardwoods such as oaks, beeches, hickories, maples
Animals: Wolves, deer, bears, and a wide variety of small mammals, birds, amphibians, reptiles, and insects

Taiga

Location: Mid- to high latitudes
Climate: Very cold winters, cool summers; about 50 centimeters (20 inches) of precipitation a year
Soil: Acidic, mineral-poor, decayed pine and spruce needles on surface
Plants: Mostly spruce, fir, and other evergreens
Animals: Rodents, snowshoe hares, lynx, sables, mink, caribou, bears, wolves

Tropical Rain Forest

Location: Near the equator
Climate: Hot all year round, 200–460 centimeters (80–180 inches) of precipitation a year
Soil: Nutrient-poor
Plants: Greatest diversity of any biome; vines, orchids, ferns, and a wide variety of trees
Animals: More species of insects, reptiles, and amphibians than any place else; monkeys, other small and large mammals, including in some places elephants, all sorts of colorful birds

What Has Happened to the Grasslands?

Why have so many grasslands become farmlands? As the name tells you, *grasslands* are biomes where grasses are the main plant life. They are areas where rainfall is irregular and not usually plentiful. Prairies are one kind of grassland.

Called the "bread baskets" of the world, few temperate grasslands look as they did years ago. *Temperate* means "mild." Grasslands such as those in the United States and Ukraine are temperate grasslands. Today many of these grasslands are covered with crops such as wheat, corn, and oats.

However, large parts of the world's tropical grasslands still look much as they have for hundreds of years. Called *savannas* these lands stay warm all year round. Their soil is not as fertile as that of temperate grasslands. However, they get more precipitation—about 86–152 centimeters (34–60 inches) a year.

Lions on the African savanna live in social groups called prides.

The most famous savanna covers the middle third of Africa. Here the dust rises as countless hoofed animals thunder across the land. There are more hoofed animals in the African savannas than anywhere else on Earth. Graceful zebras and giraffes live here. Wildebeests travel in awesome herds of tens of thousands. Antelopes run from sprinting cheetahs. In the heat of the afternoon, lions rest in the shade of a thorny acacia tree. Nearby hyenas prowl through the low grasses in search of dead or weak animals.

If you want to get a glimpse of a savanna while it still looks like this, you'd better do so soon. The land in savannas is being used more and more to graze domestic cattle. It won't be long until they replace the native animals, at least in unprotected parts of the savanna.

Where Are Evergreen Forests Found?

Evidence indicates that about 100,000 years ago, huge fingers of ice, called glaciers, inched down from Earth's arctic regions. The ice was thousands of feet thick. As it moved southward like a giant white bulldozer, it gouged great chunks of land out of northern Europe, Asia, and North America.

Some of the sediment carried by the glaciers dammed up streams, forming ponds and lakes. More lakes formed when the ice began to pull back. Holes dug by the glaciers filled with fresh water. These are the lakes and ponds of a cool, forested biome called the **taiga** (tī′gə).

Taigas are mostly conifer forests. They spread out over 11 percent of Earth's land. They are located in the upper latitudes of the Northern Hemisphere—in Alaska, Canada, Norway, Sweden, Finland, and Russia.

If you visit the taiga in the summer, you may hear the pleasant songs of birds. Many different kinds migrate to the taiga in summer. However, they head for warmer regions in the fall. You might also hear the whining sound of chain saws. That's because the taiga is a major source of lumber and pulpwood. Much of the lumber is used for making houses for the world's growing population. The pulpwood is turned into paper products of all kinds, such as the pages of this book.

Thousands of years ago, moving sheets of ice dug away the land of the taiga. The dug-out land would become some of its lakes and ponds. Today these bodies of water are guarded by great stands of evergreen trees.

Where Is the Land of Frozen Earth?

Where is the ground frozen even in summer? Only 10–25 centimeters (4–10 inches) of precipitation fall here each year. Winters are long and icy cold. Summers are short and cool. Just a few feet below the surface, the ground is frozen all the time.

You can't find any plants taller than about 30 centimeters (12 inches). Yet you may be able to spot weasels, arctic foxes, snowshoe hares, hawks, musk oxen, and caribou. Near the coast you may see a polar bear. When warmer weather comes, mosquitoes by the millions buzz through the air. There are snakes and frogs. Where are you?

You are in the far north. You're between the taiga and the polar ice sheets. It could be northern Alaska or northern Canada. It could be Greenland, or frigid parts of Europe or Asia. No matter which of these places

Among the large animals of the tundra is the caribou, a member of the deer family, and its predator, the 1,600-pound, nine-foot-long polar bear. Other tundra animals include weasels, arctic foxes, and snowshoe hares.

you are in, you are in the same biome. This cold biome of the far north is the **tundra**.

Why is it so cold? Even in summer the Sun's rays strike the tundra only at a low, glancing angle. The Sun melts ice in the top layer of the soil. Yet this water is kept from flowing downward by a layer of *permafrost*, or permanently frozen soil, underneath. The top layer of soil acts like a vast sponge for the melted ice.

Most tundra plants are wildflowers and grasses. The permafrost keeps large plants from developing the deep root systems they need. The growing season is very short—as little as 50 days in some places. The tundra soil is poor in nutrients, so the tundra cannot support large plants.

How Dry Is Dry?

Their names stir up thoughts of adventures in strange, dangerous places—Sahara, Gobi, Atacama. These are among the world's greatest **deserts**. A desert is a sandy or rocky biome, with little precipitation and little plant life.

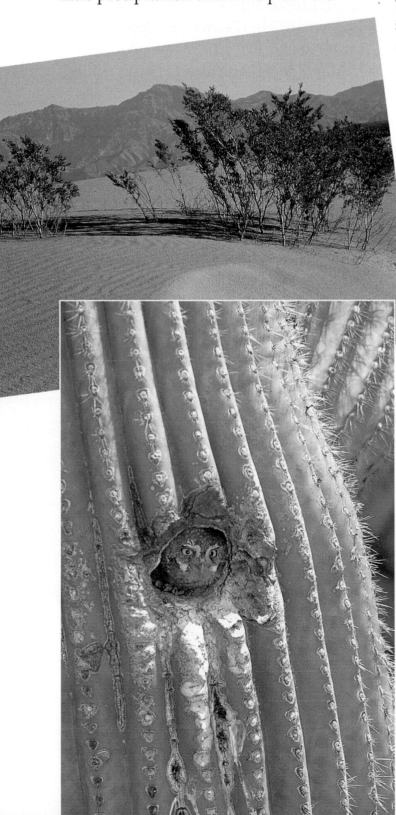

Every continent has at least one desert. Africa has an enormous desert called the Sahara. Its sands dip down to the Atlantic Ocean in the west, the Mediterranean Sea to the north, and the Red Sea to the east. It is the largest desert on Earth, with an area of about 9,000,000 square kilometers (3,500,000 square miles). It is so large that it could cover all of the United States south of Canada. Picture those 48 states covered with sand and you get an idea of the size of the Sahara.

The Gobi Desert in China and Mongolia is the world's third largest desert. It is about 1,300,000 square kilometers (500,000 square miles). That's about twice the size of Texas.

In South America the Atacama Desert runs 968 kilometers (600 miles) from the southern tip of Peru down through Chile. It lies in between the Andes Mountains to the east and the Pacific Ocean in the west. The driest place on Earth is found in Arica, Chile. It averages only about $\frac{8}{100}$ centimeter ($\frac{3}{100}$ inch) of rain a year. That's about the depth of six sheets of paper.

Few animals and plants live in deserts. Those that do are very hardy. They are well adapted to living in the desert.

To reach water the roots of the mesquite plant (above) have been known to grow more than 79 meters (260 feet) deep. That's the height of a 26-story building. Elf owls (left) build nests in cacti.

Where Is the Land of Falling Leaves?

When someone says, "I love the way the leaves change color in the fall," what biome is that person talking about? It's the **deciduous** (di sij'ü əs) **forest** biome. This is a forest biome with many trees that lose their leaves each year.

This is where broad-leaved trees grow. Each autumn the leaves turn yellow, orange, and red, painting the land with glorious colors. Then the leaves fall to the ground—which is what *deciduous* means—and decay. The dead leaves help make the soil rich and fertile.

Deciduous forests once covered most of the United States east of the Mississippi River and almost all of western Europe. Much has been cut down to make room for towns, cities, farms, and factories.

Many animals that once lived in deciduous forests still live on the land that was cleared for suburbs, farms, and towns. Chipmunks dart around bushes. Squirrels leap from branch to branch. Raccoons turn over trash cans. Skunks meander through the underbrush.

In some places deer have become a menace to drivers and gardeners alike. Birds like cardinals, robins, crows, and hawks, and insects such as bees still live in deciduous forests. Turn over a rock and you might discover a salamander or garter snake.

Many deciduous forests in the United States and Europe are now part of national parks or are in places where few people live. As long as they stay that way, people will be able to see the changing seasons.

The trees of a deciduous forest shed their leaves each autumn, painting the land yellow, orange, and red.

Although you'd probably not enjoy an encounter with this family, it's an important part of the deciduous forest biome.

Where Is It Hot and Humid?

In areas along and near Earth's equator are **tropical rain forests**. These biomes are hot and humid, with much rainfall. They support a wide variety of life.

The canopy of a tropical rain forest spreads like a huge umbrella. It is so thick that little sunlight ever reaches the ground. With little light few plants can grow on the ground. Most of the life is up high in the branches, where howler monkeys and purple orchids cling.

There are no tropical rain forests in North America or Europe. They are too far from the tropics. However, Central America, South America, India, Africa, Southeast Asia, Australia, and many Pacific Islands have rain forests. Each has its own kinds of plants and animals.

Millions of species of animals live in the world's tropical rain forests. Many species have yet to be discovered.

In Africa you might see a silverback gorilla or a troop of playful chimpanzees.

On the island of Borneo, you might see a red-haired, long-armed orangutan (ə rang'ủ tan') swinging through the trees.

The world's most colorful birds—such as toucans (tü'kanz) and quetzals (ket sälz')—live in tropical rain forests. Giant snakes like the 9-meter-long (30-foot-long), 136-kilogram (300-pound) South American anaconda also live in tropical rain forests.

The anaconda, which lives in the South American rain forest, is the largest snake on the planet. The anaconda is an excellent swimmer. It often lurks in a river waiting to grab a mammal or bird.

The world's tropical rain forests have been victims of people's needs for lumber, farmland, and minerals. Fortunately, people are now replanting and restoring tropical rain forests. Still, some of their millions of undiscovered plant and animal species may become extinct before they are discovered.

Some of the most colorful birds on Earth, like this toucan, live in tropical rain forests like those of South America.

Freshwater Communities

HYPOTHESIZE Do different organisms live in different locations in aquatic ecosystems? Write a hypothesis in your *Science Journal*. Test it.

MATERIALS

- dropper
- microscope slide
- coverslip
- microscope
- at least 3 samples of pond, lake, or stream water
- 3 or more plastic containers with lids
- *Science Journal*

PROCEDURES

1. Obtain samples of pond, lake, or stream water taken at different locations. CAUTION: Do not go beyond wading depth. Use a different container for each sample. Record the location each sample came from on the container.

2. OBSERVE Place a drop of water on a slide, and carefully place the coverslip over it. Examine the slide under a microscope.

3. COMMUNICATE Record the location of each sample and what you see. Use low and high power.

CONCLUDE AND APPLY

INTERPRET DATA What does this tell you about aquatic ecosystems?

What Are Water Ecosystems Like?

For Earth's watery ecosystems, the main difference is saltiness. Lakes, streams, rivers, ponds, and certain marshes, swamps, and bogs tend to have little salt in them. They're all freshwater ecosystems. Oceans and seas are saltwater ecosystems.

In fresh water or salt water, organisms can be divided into three main categories. *Plankton* (plangk'tən) float on the water. *Nekton* (nek'ton) swim through the water. *Benthos* (ben'thos) live on the bottom.

Freshwater Organisms

Many plants live in the shallow waters of lakes, ponds, and other bodies of fresh water. If you were to wade here, you might get your feet tangled in cattails, bur reeds, wild rice, and arrowheads. You might also spot a frog, a turtle, or maybe a crayfish.

Farther out, where the water gets deeper, are microscopic plankton like algae and protozoa.

Look beneath the surface, and nekton come into view. There might be large trout or other game fish. All the way to the bottom, an aquatic worm might be burrowing into the mud.

Saltwater Organisms

Like the freshwater ecosystem, the marine, or ocean, ecosystem is divided into sections. The shallowest is the *intertidal zone*. There the ocean floor is covered and uncovered as the tide goes in and out. Crabs burrow into the sand. Mussels and barnacles attach to rocks.

The open ocean is divided into two regions. The first region is up to 200 meters deep. In this upper region are many kinds of fish and whales. The world's largest animals—the 150-ton blue whales—live here.

The lower region goes from 200 meters to the ocean bottom— perhaps 10.5 kilometers down. At depths greater than about 330 meters, there is no sunlight. It is completely black!

Photosynthetic organisms, like algae, can only live where there is sunlight. They are found in the intertidal zone and in waters up to about 100 meters deep. Many fantastic creatures live on the dark ocean bottom. Some of these fish "light up" like underwater fireflies. There are even bacteria that live in boiling water where fiery lava seeps out of the sea floor.

WHY IT MATTERS

The world's biomes remain undisturbed as long as their climates and the populations that live there remain basically unchanged. However, human and natural activities can change these factors. Changes in a biome can affect the kinds of plants that can grow there and the kinds of animals that can live there. It can also affect the lifestyles of the people who live there. It is important to know whether, how, and why these factors may be changing.

REVIEW

1. Describe the taiga biome in terms of its climate, soil, and nutrients.

2. **COMPARE AND CONTRAST** How do organisms found in desert and tundra biomes adapt to their environments?

3. Explain why few plants live on the floor of tropical rain forests.

4. Briefly describe the two types of aquatic ecosystems.

5. **CRITICAL THINKING** *Evaluate* Choose one biome, and explain how a change in its climate might affect its populations.

WHY IT MATTERS THINK ABOUT IT
How might a change in the biome you live in affect your way of life?

WHY IT MATTERS WRITE ABOUT IT
Write a paragraph explaining how your lifestyle might change if the biome where you live got warmer. What might happen if it got colder? What might happen if the amount of precipitation increased? What might happen if it decreased?

READING SKILL
Write a paragraph summarizing what this topic was about.

SCIENCE MAGAZINE

Are Rain Forests

Where would you be if you took a trip to the most famous ecosystem on Earth? You'd be in a tropical rain forest!

Rain forests are full of secrets because they're hard to get through and you can't see everything in them. More different kinds of organisms live in 1 square kilometer of a rain forest than in any other ecosystem!

Many plants and animals in the rain forests have never been seen or identified. Many could never survive outside the rain forests.

The greatest of Earth's rain forests is in the Amazon River Basin of South America. Each year about 13,000 square kilometers (5,019 square miles) of this rain forest are destroyed by burning or construction. The Amazon rain forest is at least 8,000 years old, but in 100 years it could be gone!

Worth Saving?

Green plants release oxygen in photosynthesis. Why are people destroying the rain forests? The human population around the Amazon is growing fast, and people need a place to live. Some people want to replace part of the rain forest with farms.

Most minerals in a rain forest are in the plants, not the soil. After trees are cleared for farms, the soil is rich for only a year or so. Then most of the nutrients are washed away by rain.

Parts of the rain forest are also rich in minerals, like gold. Some people want to clear the trees and build mines. Do you think they should?

DISCUSSION STARTER

1. How can there be unidentified animals and plants in the rain forest?

2. Why do some people want to destroy the rain forest?

■ Cleared forest land
■ Frontier forest today

The Amazon rain forest is about three-fourths the size of the United States.

To learn more about rain forests, visit *www.mhschool.com/science* and enter the keyword RAINFOREST.

*inter*NET
CONNECTION

WHY IT MATTERS

The wide variety of ecosystems in California makes the state a fascinating place to live.

SCIENCE WORDS

timberline region on mountain slopes above which trees cannot grow

alpine tundra cold, dry, windy ecosystem found on high mountaintops

tide pools small pools of water that remain at low tide on rocky seashores

holdfast rootlike base of a seaweed that holds it in place

intertidal zone part of a seashore between the lowest and highest tides

Places to Live in California

Why don't redwood trees grow in the Mojave Desert? If you answered "Because it is too dry!" you're right! The amount of precipitation that falls in a place is an important factor in determining what kinds of plants grow there, and what kind of ecosystem it is. Precipitation is water that falls to earth as rain, sleet, snow, or hail. How much rain falls where you live? What kind of ecosystem do you live in?

EXPLORE

HYPOTHESIZE How does rainfall affect ecosystems? How would you measure rainfall? Write a hypothesis in your *Science Journal.* How might you design a device to measure rainfall in an ecosystem?

Investigate How to Make a Rain Gauge

Construct a simple device to measure rainfall in an ecosystem.

MATERIALS

- 2-liter soda bottle with the top cut off (cut bottle should be 20 cm [8 inches] high)
- plastic ruler
- clear tape
- clean aquarium gravel
- water
- *Science Journal*

PROCEDURES

1. Position the ruler vertically on the outside of the bottle, with the zero mark resting on the rim of the bottle's plastic base.

2. Tape the ruler to the bottle. Apply tape near the bottom of the ruler and about halfway up its length. Tape should go all the way around the bottle and overlap in order to hold the ruler securely in place.

3. Put enough gravel in the bottle to fill the plastic base. This will keep the bottle from tipping over.

4. When ready to use the device as a rain gauge, pour water into the bottle until it reaches the zero mark on the ruler.

5. **RECORD DATA** Place the rain gauge outside on a rainy day. When the rain stops, or after a specified period of time, bring the bottle in and record the new water level.

CONCLUDE AND APPLY

1. **CONCLUDE** What is the difference in water levels after the rain gauge has been left out in the rain? What was the total rainfall?

2. **INFER** Why was it important to begin the experiment with the water level at the zero mark on the ruler?

GOING FURTHER: Problem Solving

3. **ANALYZE** How does the amount of rainfall in the area where you live relate to your local ecosystem?

What Are Some California Ecosystems?

California, the third largest state in the United States, covers 412,602 square kilometers (158,693 square miles) of land. Let's take a look at the diversity of California's natural ecosystems.

Mountains

There are a half dozen major mountain ranges in California. The Sierra Nevada is the largest, longest, and tallest. Other major mountain ranges include the Coast Ranges, along the west coast; the Cascade Range and Klamath Mountains in the north; the Transverse Ranges, which run diagonally east of Los Angeles; and the Peninsular Range, which runs east of San Diego.

Mountain ecosystems are complex and change with *elevation*, that is, how far above sea level they are. If you were to climb one of the peaks in the Sierras, for example, you would pass through several distinct ecosystems. In the foothills, you'd find mainly oak trees growing in open woodlands. Next would come a cooler ecosystem where scattered groves of giant sequoia trees grow among Douglas fir and ponderosa pine.

Keep climbing and you'd eventually come to a dense forest of lodgepole pine and red fir. This mountain ecosystem receives the greatest amount of precipitation, which falls mostly as snow. Farther up, the tall trees would give way to an ecosystem of scattered shrubs and low-growing trees. At roughly 3,150 meters (10,500 feet) up, the trees would abruptly end at the **timberline**, the point above which it is too cold and too dry for trees to grow. The mountaintop ecosystem is called **alpine tundra.** The plants here are like those in the Arctic tundra. They hug the ground and thus escape the cold winds.

Map labels: Klamath Mountains, Cascade Range, SIERRA NEVADA, COAST RANGES, Transverse Ranges, Mojave Desert, Peninsular Ranges, Colorado Desert

Alpine tundra is the type of ecosystem you find on high mountaintops in California's Sierra Nevada range.

Forests

You already know quite a bit about the redwood forests found in the Coast Ranges. We'll look more closely at California's other forest ecosystems in the next few pages.

Grasslands

Long ago, an immense grassland covered California's interior. Dry and windy, this land of native grasses supported large herds of pronghorn and elk. Coyotes and foxes pursued rabbits, ground squirrels, and mice through the waving grass, while hawks, golden eagles, and prairie falcons kept watch from the skies. Fires were frequent, burning off the tops of the grasses, but leaving underground root systems undamaged.

Over time, almost all of California's grasslands were plowed and planted and turned into cropland. On protected reserves, visitors may still glimpse now-rare grassland animals such as Tule elk.

Chaparral

In old westerns, cowboys on horseback often galloped through dry scrubland known as *chaparral.* Chaparral is found mostly in the foothills of California's southern mountain ranges. The plants of the chaparral are mostly evergreen shrubs and small trees that can survive heat, drought, and fire. In the fall, the chaparral is tinder dry. Hundreds of acres can burn in a very short time. The fires clear out dead plant matter and add nutrient-rich ashes to the soil.

The evergreen shrubs of chaparral form dense thickets. Left: Tule elk, once hunted almost to extinction, roam on grassland preserves today.

What Are Some Other California Ecosystems?

California also has extensive areas of desert, some of the world's most spectacular coastline, and large areas of farmland that once were grassland.

Deserts

Dry, desolate, but strangely beautiful, deserts cover much of eastern California. The three major deserts of California are the Great Basin, the Mojave, and the Colorado. East of the Sierra Nevada lies the Great Basin, a high-elevation desert of barren plains and rugged mountains covered with sagebrush, pinyon pine, and juniper trees.

In spring, cacti and other plants bloom in the deserts.

Southeast of the Sierra Nevada lies the great Mojave Desert. The Mojave is hot in the summer, but can be quite cold in winter. Creosote bush, yucca, mesquite, and Joshua trees can tolerate these temperature extremes.

The Colorado Desert lies in extreme southeastern California. The landscape is dotted with creosote bush, yucca, ocotillos, smoke trees, and many different kinds of cacti.

Great
Basin

Death
Valley

Mojave
Desert

Colorado
Desert

Heat waves shimmer above the parched ground in Death Valley.

Seashores

Pounded by waves and exposed to changing tides, rocky seashores are home to organisms that can withstand drastic changes in their environment. Barnacles and snails cling tightly to wave-splashed rocks. Brown, green, and red algae, commonly called seaweed, sway in the surf.

At low tide, small pools of trapped water, called **tide pools**, remain along the shore. Tide pools are like natural aquariums where you can see anemones, sea stars, sea urchins, and many other marine animals.

Storm petrels, auklets, puffins, cormorants, murres, and other seabirds build their nests on towering sea cliffs.

From Grassland to Farmland

Before the 1800s, the Central Valley was an untouched grassland. When settlers arrived, ranchers began to graze large herds of cattle in the Valley. Farmers planted crops, replacing the native grasses with wheat, oats, and other grains, along with grape vines and citrus trees.

Irrigation has made it possible to raise crops even in the driest parts of the Central Valley. Today, the native grassland ecosystem has all but disappeared. Only one percent of California's original grasslands remains as protected reserves.

Brain Power

When the native grasses were replaced by crops, what do you think happened to native grassland animals?

Above: Rocky seashores are home to many hardy plants and animals. Right: Modern irrigation systems make it possible to grow crops in the Central Valley where only native grasses once grew.

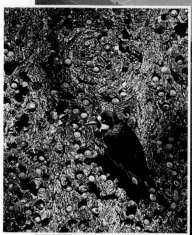

Oaks are the dominant trees in the woodlands. [inset] Acorn woodpeckers store thousands of acorns in trees.

Where Are the Forest Ecosystems?

You can find some of the world's most diverse and beautiful forests in California. Pines, firs, cedars, and other conifers are the dominant trees.

Temperate Rain Forest

In the extreme northwestern corner of California are cool, wet temperate rain forests. In these dark, deeply shaded ecosystems, Douglas fir, red cedar, western hemlock, and Sitka spruce grow hundreds of feet tall. The forest floor is a tangle of ferns, while mosses, lichens, and fungi thickly cover fallen logs and rocks.

One small mammal is unique here— the secretive mountain beaver. About the size of a muskrat, this tailless rodent munches leaves and digs complex networks of burrows.

Sitka spruce seeds sometimes sprout on fallen logs. When the logs rot away, the spruce trees look like they are growing on stilts.

Foothill Oak Woodlands

In the foothills of many mountain ranges in California, you find oak woodlands, where stately oaks stand surrounded by open, grassy areas. Oaks produce acorns, which are eaten by many kinds of small mammals and birds. The acorn specialists, however, are acorn woodpeckers. These large woodpeckers store acorns to eat during the winter by drilling countless holes in dead or dying trees and then stuffing acorns into the small openings.

Mixed Evergreen Forests

Above the oak woodlands on mountain slopes are forests in which many different kinds of evergreen trees grow. Douglas fir trees grow alongside tan oak, California bay, Pacific madrone, and various kinds of oaks. On the western slopes of the Sierra Nevada, groves of giant sequoias are scattered throughout the mixed evergreen forests.

Pine Forests

Several kinds of pine forests occur at different elevations throughout California's mountain ranges. On many drier mountain slopes, forests of ponderosa pine are common. At higher elevations stands of Jeffrey pine cover the mountainsides.

The White Mountains of eastern California are home to bristlecone pines, the oldest known living trees. Some bristlecone pines are more than 4,000 years old.

Groves of giant sequoias grow in mixed evergreen forests. They are among the largest living organisms on Earth. [inset] The arrow-straight trunks of ponderosa pines grow close together.

How Do Plants and Animals Survive in the Deserts?

Many desert plants survive with little rainfall by sending down long roots. The roots of mesquite bushes may grow more than 10 cm (4 inches) a day to reach underground water. Most desert plants have small leaves from which little water evaporates.

Cacti have expandable stems that can store large quantities of water. The thick waxy skins of cactus stems also reduce water loss to the environment.

Left: the barrel cactus at left has a stem full of water. After a long dry spell, the water is used up. Above: Very large ears help the kit fox stay cool.

Most desert animals avoid the heat of the day by lying quietly in the shade or retreating to underground burrows. They are much more active at night, when it is cooler. Kit foxes and desert jackrabbits have large ears that radiate heat and work like natural air conditioning to keep their bodies cool.

How Do Plants and Animals Survive at the Seashore?

The organisms that live at the edge of the sea live in a constantly changing environment. Waves ceaselessly pound the shore. Tides come in and go out. How are living things at the seashore adapted to such conditions?

In order to survive the push and pull of waves, many seashore organisms are firmly attached to rocks and other surfaces. Barnacles glue themselves permanently to rocks to keep from being washed away. Limpets—relatives of snails with little cap-like shells—use a muscular foot to cling to rocks. Sea stars hang on with hundreds of tiny tube feet that have suction-cup tips.

Seaweeds anchor themselves in place with holdfasts. A **holdfast** is a rootlike structure that grips rocks or grows into sediments. Seaweeds you see growing along the shore are also very tough and flexible. They can be tossed and twisted by waves without being damaged.

Seaweeds swirl in the pounding surf of the California coastline. [inset] Using tiny tube feet, sea stars cling tightly to rocks.

A Snail's Escape

HYPOTHESIZE How do pond snails respond to being out of the water? Write a hypothesis in your *Science Journal*.

MATERIALS
- pond snail
- spring water
- clear plastic cup
- plastic forceps
- paper towel
- hand lens
- *Science Journal*

PROCEDURES

1. Fill a plastic cup about one-third full with spring water.

2. Using your forceps, gently transfer a pond snail from a container into your cup.

3. After the snail comes out of its shell, observe how it moves along the bottom and sides of the cup. Identify the snail's foot, head, and the small circular structure near the back of the foot called the operculum (o' pûr' kyə' ləm).

4. Now remove the snail from the cup with your forceps and place it on the paper towel. Observe how the snail responds to being out of the water.

5. **COMMUNICATE** Write a paragraph in your *Science Journal* in which you describe the snail's response.

CONCLUDE AND APPLY

HYPOTHESIZE How does the operculum help keep a pond snail from drying out when it is exposed to air?

What Is the Intertidal Zone?

Twice a day the ocean recedes from the shoreline for several hours. Then the water returns to cover it up again. The part of the shore that is exposed at low tide and submerged at high tide is called the **intertidal zone.** At low tide, organisms in the intertidal zone bake in the sun and risk drying out. Land predators, like birds, can also get at them.

To protect themselves from these dangers, animals like barnacles and mussels retreat inside their hard shells with enough water to last until the water returns. Snails hide in their shells, too, and seal off the entrance with a hard disc that is attached to their muscular foot. Sea anemones pull in their tentacles. Some sea urchins try to hide by covering themselves with pebbles and broken shells.

Organisms that live in the intertidal zone can survive being exposed to air at low tide.

What Organisms Live in Coastal Waters?

California's coastal waters are a good place to look for whales and other marine mammals. Gray whales swim up and down the coast as they migrate between their Arctic feeding grounds and their calving grounds off Baja California. Humpback, blue, and fin whales also cruise the coastal waters, along with orcas and dolphins.

Fur seals, elephant seals, and harbor seals frequent the entire coast. Along with sea lions, these marine mammals form large breeding colonies on the Channel Islands off California's southern coast. Many fish, including great white sharks and albacore tuna, also inhabit coastal waters.

One of California's most valuable resources is the great diversity of plants and animals that live within its borders and coastal waters. It's easy to think those living communities will be there forever. But the disappearance of California's native grasslands is a reminder of how quickly ecosystems can disappear if they are not carefully protected.

As the population of cities and towns increases, the pressure on ecosystems increases, too. Is enough being done to protect California ecosystems?

REVIEW

1. What is the longest mountain range in California?

2. What happened to California's native grasslands?

3. How is elevation related to mountain ecosystems?

4. **COMPARE AND CONTRAST** How is alpine tundra similar to Arctic tundra? How is it different?

5. **CRITICAL THINKING** *Hypothesize* How might the acorn-storing activities of acorn woodpeckers help oak trees?

WHY IT MATTERS THINK ABOUT IT
A builder is proposing to put up a resort in a chaparral ecosystem. Most of the buildings will be made of wood. What advice would you have for the builder?

WHY IT MATTERS WRITE ABOUT IT
What is your favorite California ecosystem? Describe it, and your reasons for liking it, in your *Science Journal*.

THE ABALONE AND

The seas off California's rocky coast are home to a very special mollusk called the abalone. Abalone are snail-like animals with a flattened, somewhat spiral shell. They are also part of a complex food web that includes one of California's most remarkable animals: the sea otter.

Both the abalone and the sea otters live in an ocean ecosystem dominated by a seaweed called giant kelp. The kelp forms huge underwater "forests" that sway to and fro in the ocean currents. The abalone cling to the rocky bottom and eat algae and drifting kelp. Young abalone are eaten by crabs, lobsters, octopuses, and fish. Many larger abalone are eaten by the sea otters.

The numbers of sea otters and abalone have varied dramatically over time. In the 1700s and 1800s, the sea otter was hunted almost to extinction for its fur. More than 200,000 were killed. But the sea otter slaughter freed the abalone from an important predator, and abalone populations exploded. Abalone became common. People harvested them for their meat and for their beautiful shells.

By the early 1900s, the sea otter was thought to be extinct. But in 1938, a small colony of 200 to 300 otters was found hidden near Big Sur. Since that time, helped by laws protecting them, the otters have increased in number to about 2,000. However, this population is still far smaller than it once was.

In the meantime, abalone, once common, have become scarce. They are so few in number that the

Life Science Link

THE SEA OTTER

state has restricted abalone harvesting. What happened?

Some blame the growing population of sea otters for the abalone's decline. They think that to protect the abalone, the otters will have to be controlled. But biologists believe that the otters are responsible for no more than 10 percent of the abalone loss. They think that people are more to blame for what happened to the abalone.

Biologists think that ocean pollution, sewage dumping, and diseases are the real reasons the abalone population has declined. Years of excessive abalone harvesting by people are also to

blame. Even when scientists established new abalone colonies off southern California, poachers soon harvested those colonies to extinction. If the abalone population is ever to recover, it is people who will have to change their ways, not the sea otters.

DISCUSSION STARTERS

1. Why are abalone scarce today?

2. What could help the abalone increase in number?

To learn more about ocean ecosystems, visit *www.mhschool.com/science* and enter the keyword UNDERSEA.

283

SCIENCE WORDS

abiotic factor p.244   ecosystem p. 244
biome p. 258   habitat p. 250
biotic factor p. 245   niche p. 250
community p. 249   population p. 249
desert p. 263   taiga p. 261
ecology p. 244   tundra p. 262

USING SCIENCE WORDS

Number a paper from 1 to 10. Fill in 1 to 5 with words from the list above.

1. Living things make up the ___?___ in an ecosystem.

2. Water is an example of a(n) ___?___.

3. A(n) ___?___ includes all the members of a single species in a certain place.

4. Ferns, squirrels, and red-bellied newts are part of the ___?___ of the redwood forest ecosystem.

5. The study of how living and nonliving things interact in the same place is called ___?___.

6–10. **Pick five words from the list above that were not used in 1 to 5, and use each in a sentence.**

UNDERSTANDING SCIENCE IDEAS

11. What is the difference between biotic and abiotic factors?

12. Why do many seashore plants and animals attach themselves to rocks and other surfaces?

13. Why are fungi and bacteria an important part of every ecosystem?

14. Why do certain parts of California have an ecosystem like that of the Arctic?

15. How would you describe deserts, tropical rain forests, grasslands, and tundras?

USING IDEAS AND SKILLS

16. Compare and contrast freshwater and saltwater ecosystems.

17. A stream in a redwood forest becomes polluted. Describe what might happen to the forest community.

18. **DEFINE** At the beach, you watch the tide go out and expose rocks and shellfish that were submerged at high tide. What do you call the area you are looking at?

19. **READING SKILL: READING DIAGRAMS** Examine the diagram on pages 258-259. What biomes lie between the taiga and tundra in the north and the tropical rain forest at the Equator?

20. **THINKING LIKE A SCIENTIST** Imagine you have moved to another part of California. Your new home is surrounded by huge redwood trees. What does that tell you about the local climate?

PROBLEMS and PUZZLES

Home Sweet Biome Collect data for the abiotic factors in your biome. What kind of organisms can be found in your biome? Where else does your kind of biome exist?

CHAPTER 8
LIVING THINGS INTERACT

Penguins spend a lot of time in the water catching fish, but they lay eggs and raise their young on land. They make nests in the grass or in a hollow dug in the bare ground. They gather together in large groups, or colonies, called rookeries. As many as a million birds can live together in one rookery.

How large can a population of penguins get? Why doesn't the population just grow and grow?

In Chapter 8 summarize as you read. Write what each two pages are about before you move on to the next two.

Topic
LIFE SCIENCE
4

WHY IT MATTERS

Living things depend on each other for energy.

SCIENCE WORDS

food chain the path food follows as one organism eats another

food web overlapping food chains in a community

herbivore an animal that eats plants

carnivore an animal that eats other animals

predator a living thing that hunts other living things for food

prey a living thing that is hunted for food

scavenger an animal that feeds on the remains of dead animals

omnivore an animal that eats both plants and animals

Food Chains and Food Webs

Where does food in a community come from? Every community includes many kinds of organisms, each of which needs food to survive. Organisms get the energy to grow and reproduce from food. But different organisms need different kinds of food.

In California's coastal foothills there are complex communities with many insects and mice. Grasses and other green plants provide food for insects, such as grasshoppers, and for mice. Lizards and birds eat the insects. Gopher snakes eat the mice. A snake, in turn, may become a meal for a sharp-eyed red-tailed hawk. What do you think might happen if some of the grass died because of a lack of rain?

HYPOTHESIZE How can changes in one population lead to changes in other populations in an ecosystem? Write a hypothesis in your *Science Journal*. How might you test your ideas?

Investigate How Populations Interact

Use these cards to see what happens to a model ecosystem when changes occur in a population.

MATERIALS

- tape
- string
- Population Card Resource Master
- *Science Journal*

PROCEDURES

1. Cut out the cards representing the plants and animals in the ecosystem.

2. Label the top of your paper *Sunlight.*

3. Place the plant cards on the paper. Link each to the sunlight with tape and string.

4. Link each plant-eating animal to a plant card. Link each meat-eating animal to its food source. Link only two animals to a single food source. Record the links in your *Science Journal.*

5. Fire destroys half the plants. Remove four plant cards. Rearrange the animals cards. Remove animal cards if more than two animals link to any one food source. Record the changes.

CONCLUDE AND APPLY

1. OBSERVE What has happened to the plant eaters as a result of the fire? To the animal eaters?

2. ANALYZE Half of the plants that were lost in the fire grow back again. What happens to the animal populations?

3. EXPERIMENT Try adding or removing plant or animal cards. What happens?

GOING FURTHER: Apply

4. DRAW CONCLUSIONS If plants or prey become scarce, their predators may move to new areas. What will happen to the ecosystem the predators move into?

Grasshopper
Food: plant leaves and stems

Rufus-sided Towhee
Food: crickets, grasshoppers

Deer Mouse
Food: seeds, insects, insect grubs

Gopher Snake
Food: burrowing rodents, lizards, birds, eggs

Red-Tailed Hawk
Food: rats, mice, rabbits, snakes, lizards, small birds

Grasses and bushes
Food: made from water, carbon dioxide, and sunlight

Coyote
Food: insects, rodents, a wide variety of fruits

Ground Squirrel
Food: green plants, seeds, nuts, mushrooms, fruits, berries, birds' eggs, insects

How Does Energy Move in a Community?

Every organism needs energy in order to survive. A mouse may get energy from the grass seeds it eats. But where does the grass get its energy? Grass doesn't eat food. It makes its own.

The Sun's energy warms your skin. Sunlight also falls on the animals in an ecosystem. But you can't use sunlight energy directly, and neither can the animals. Only plants can use sunlight directly.

Using a special green chemical called chlorophyll (klôr′ə fil), plants, seaweed, and many kinds of micro-scopic organisms capture energy from sunlight. They use this energy to build energy-rich sugars, starches, and fats from water, the gas carbon dioxide, and minerals in the soil.

How Energy Is Passed On

A mouse eating a seed can use some of the energy stored in the seed. If a gopher snake eats the mouse, it can use some of the energy stored in the mouse's muscles and fat. A red-tailed hawk eating the snake uses some of the energy stored in the snake's tissues.

So the stored energy moves from organism to organism. Each organism is connected to its food like links in a chain: a food chain. A **food chain** is the path energy takes from producers to consumers to decomposers. The red-tailed hawk doesn't eat plant food. However, it gets some of the Sun's energy that was originally stored in the grass because of the food chain.

In this example, the food chain starts when green grass captures some of the Sun's energy. It passes through each link, all the way up to the hawk. However, this is not the end of the

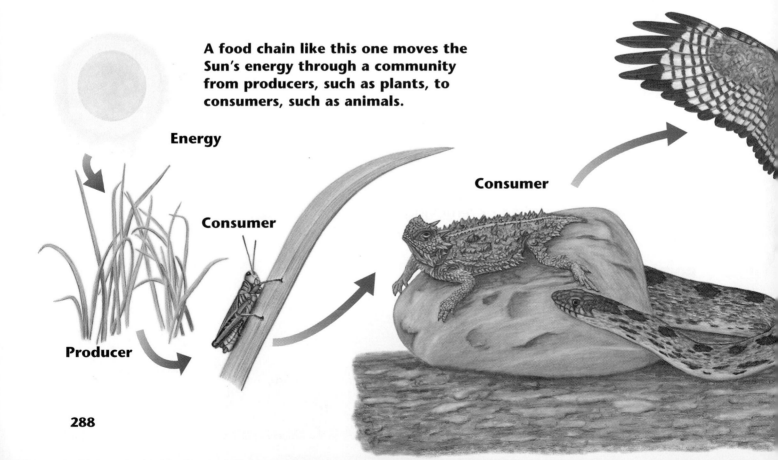

A food chain like this one moves the Sun's energy through a community from producers, such as plants, to consumers, such as animals.

Energy

Consumer

Consumer

Producer

process. Each animal makes droppings that contain some energy stored in chemicals, and each dies. The dead bodies contain energy stored in the chemicals making up their tissues. Finally, bacteria and fungi break down the matter in the droppings and dead bodies, forming simple chemicals again.

READING ∿ DIAGRAMS

1. **DISCUSS** There are many food chains in a community. List at least one animal that, along with the red-tailed hawk, occupies the top of a foothill food chain.

2. **WRITE** Describe two or more food chains whose top link might be the red-tailed hawk.

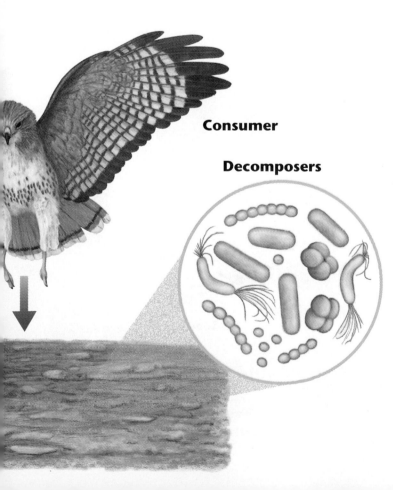

Consumer

Decomposers

Getting Food

HYPOTHESIZE What living things are in a community near your school or home? Which are producers? Consumers? Write a hypothesis in your *Science Journal.*

MATERIALS
- pencil
- *Science Journal*

PROCEDURES

1. Take a walk outdoors around your home or school. Chose a community to study. Make a list of the living things you see. Do not include people or domestic animals like dogs, cats, and farm animals. Remember that flower beds and even weed patches have communities, too.

2. **CLASSIFY** Organize the organisms into two groups—those that can make their own food (producers) and those that cannot (consumers). (Hint: Look at the color.)

CONCLUDE AND APPLY

1. **COMMUNICATE** Draw two or more food chains to show how energy moves through the community.

2. **INFER** Did your observations support your hypothesis? Explain.

What Are Food Webs?

Many small food chains actually overlap each other. A California ground squirrel eats green plants, seeds, nuts, mushrooms, fruits, berries, birds, eggs, and insects. The squirrel competes with the deer mouse for some of these foods. In turn, both the squirrels and mice become food for snakes, hawks, and coyotes.

Imagine arrows to each of these animals from each of their foods and arrows from each animal to each animal that eats it. You'd have something like a web.

A food chain shows how food energy flows from one kind of organism to another and another. A **food web** links all the different food chains in a community together. It shows how each population in a community relates to all the other populations.

Producers

All ecosystems contain organisms that make their own food: *producers*. The producers on land include grasses, trees, and all other organisms that use the Sun's energy to make their own food, including some bacteria. In the oceans, producers include large algae and many green one-celled organisms.

Eating Producers

Organisms that cannot make their own food are called *con-sumers*. Con-sumers get energy from the tissues of other organisms. Consumers can be grouped according to the type of food they eat. **Herbivores** (hûr′ bə vôrz′) eat producers. Both Earth's land and waters swarm with herbivores, animal that eat plants, algae, and other producers.

Eating Herbivores

Herbivores, in turn, are eaten by **carnivores** (kär′nə vôrz′)—animals that eat other animals. All cats, big and small, are carnivores. So are dogs, wolves, foxes, coyotes, and other sharp-toothed animals.

LAND FOOD WEB

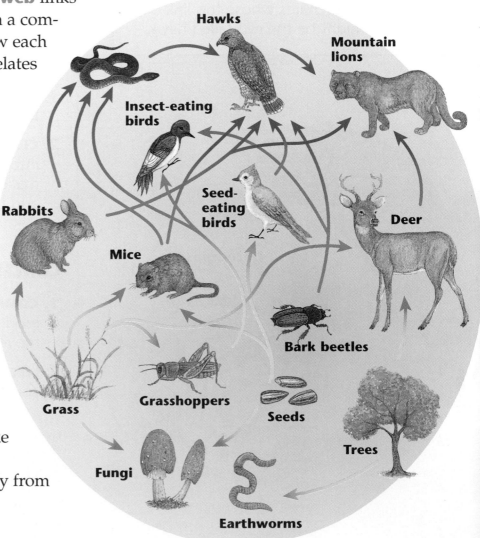

Hawks

Mountain lions

Insect-eating birds

Rabbits

Seed-eating birds

Deer

Mice

Bark beetles

Grass

Grasshoppers

Seeds

Trees

Fungi

Earthworms

MARINE FOOD WEB

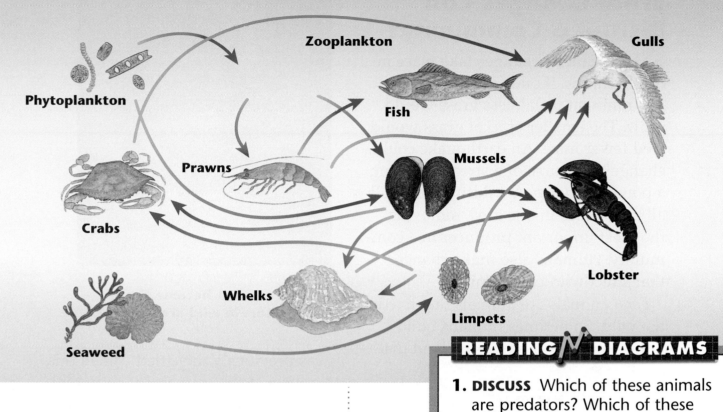

Phytoplankton, Zooplankton, Fish, Gulls, Prawns, Mussels, Crabs, Lobster, Whelks, Limpets, Seaweed

READING ⋀ DIAGRAMS

1. **DISCUSS** Which of these animals are predators? Which of these animals are prey?
2. **WRITE** Explain how scavengers differ from decomposers.

What Is a Predator?

Living things that hunt other living things for food are called **predators.** The animals predators hunt are called **prey.** The relationships between predators and prey are a key part of food webs.

Not all meat eaters are predators. Some animals eat meat but do not hunt it. Such meat eaters are called **scavengers.** They feed on the remains of dead animals. Have you ever seen vultures circling above a dead animal? Then you have seen scavengers. Crows are also scavengers. Many insects and worms also eat animal remains.

The sea is home to many scavengers. Crabs and lobsters eat the bodies of dying or dead animals. Many of the smallest sea creatures also feed on dead sea animals on the sea floor.

When an animal eats both animals and plants, it is called an **omnivore.** Humans are omnivores. Bears are omnivores, too, eating things ranging from berries to salmon.

Every food web has small animals that eat the remains of other animals and dead parts of plants. Some even eat animal droppings. Worms and insects help with this clean-up job.

Two other kinds of organisms break down dead tissues or droppings into simple chemicals that plants can use. These are the *decomposers:* bacteria and fungi. All organisms—even plants— carry on some decomposition, breaking food down into simple chemicals.

What Changes Can Disrupt a Community?

Many natural changes take place in communities. If one year had much less rain that usual, less grass would grow. The smaller crop of grass would feed fewer mice. An earthquake could change the course of a stream, causing a pond to dry up. A wildfire could kill all the bushes in one area, removing the most important producer in a community. Humans also make changes that affect wild communities.

Feral animals are animals that live in the wild. Sometimes humans build homes and communities on land that

Feral cats can become fierce predators in wild areas.

was previously unsettled. When this happens, feral animals living in that area are forced to relocate to other territories. When feral animals enter a new territory, they change the balance of the plant and animal life.

Change can also happen when new animals enter a community. One common example involves domestic cats. Cats that are introduced into a new territory can spell trouble for a wild community. Because cats make such good predators, they survive easily in the wild. In the wild they become feral. Feral cats can enter a community and become new—and very fierce—predators. If they breed and form a feral population, they can reduce the populations of rodents and birds.

But cats usually do not become the top predator in wild communities. In many wild areas, coyotes keep cats in check, by eating them and by chasing them away. In these areas, the coyotes are the top predators.

NATIONAL GEOGRAPHIC

FUNtastic Facts

When its food supply runs out, a walking catfish climbs out of the water and "walks" to a new pond. A spine on each front fin digs into the ground to support the fish as it zigzags across land. Special organs behind the gills work like lungs so the catfish can breathe air. How might the catfish affect the food web in the new pond?

What Happens to the Cats If the Coyotes Are Removed?

Coyotes need to live in a large wild area in order to find enough food. As humans build more homes, they bulldoze wild areas to build roads, houses, and schools. Coyotes are clever and adaptable. If coyotes cannot find enough food in wild areas, they may begin to raid garbage cans. Then people may try to get rid of the coyotes.

Building tends to cut wild areas into smaller wild "islands" in a sea of roads and houses. If these "islands" become too small, the coyotes may leave or die out. What does that mean for the feral cats? The cats become the top predator. With nothing to prey upon them, the cats will breed and their population will increase

Coyotes are the top predators in many Western wild areas.

unchecked. As a consequence, prey populations will decrease. Without coyotes, feral cats may reduce the populations of many bird species. As bird populations decrease, other bird predators may also begin to decrease in number.

In this example, feral cats entered a community and changed that community. Humans have introduced animals deliberately in many places throughout the world. Almost always, such introductions of predators have unexpected —and harmful — effects on the ecosystem.

How Is Energy Moved in a Community?

Plants capture energy from sunlight. They capture only a tiny bit of the light that falls on their green tissues. Only some of that energy ends up stored in leaves, stems, and seeds. When you eat a plant, how much of that energy ends up in your tissues? Not all of it. Some escapes as heat.

The pyramid diagram on this page illustrates how this energy loss affects a food chain. Energy is lost at each level as you move up the chain. As a result, at the higher levels the chain supports fewer and fewer animals. The higher the level, the smaller the population of each species.

Each consumer species stores energy gained from eating plants or animals from lower levels of the pyramid. Because the higher levels have smaller species populations, there is less stored energy at those levels. Energy decreases from the base to the top of an energy pyramid.

In an Antarctic community, algae and single-celled producers form the base. These organisms capture the Sun's energy and store it in their cells. Small fish eat some of these organisms. The organisms that are not eaten drift to the bottom, where they become part of a different food web. Also, only some of the energy the fish get is passed up to the next level. Some is used in swimming, and much is lost as heat.

ENERGY PYRAMID FOR A LAND FOOD CHAIN

Brain Power

What happens to the number of organisms at each level of the pyramid as you go from the base toward the top? Why do you think this happens?

What Happens to the Energy?

Penguins dive for small fish and eat as many as they can catch. Yet many fish get away. Nevertheless, the penguins have snared some energy-rich food. Some of the energy from the fish is stored in the penguins' tissues. Some of the energy is used to heat their bodies. A dip in the frigid water or a blast of icy air removes some of this heat from the penguins' bodies. Now they have less energy than they took in from the fish and must use more food energy to keep warm.

Rising from below, a leopard seal clamps its sharp teeth around a penguin and eats it. Does this predator get all the energy that was originally in the algae the fish ate? No. Energy has been lost at each level in the pyramid.

Kilogram for kilogram, there are fewer fish than algae. There are fewer penguins than fish. There are fewer leopard seals than penguins. That's because there is less food and energy available at each higher level in the energy pyramid. At each higher level, fewer living things can be supported.

How much energy is lost from one level of an energy pyramid to the next? Scientists have measured it. The figure is 90 percent! Of all the Sun's energy captured by the algae, the leopard seal gets only one-tenth of one percent.

ENERGY PYRAMID FOR AN OCEAN FOOD CHAIN

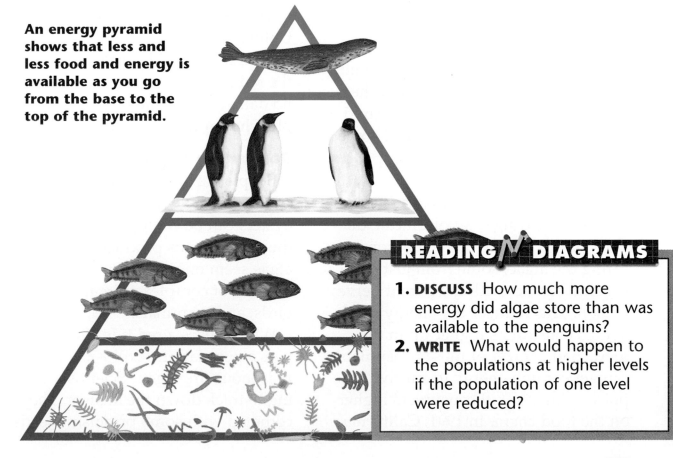

An energy pyramid shows that less and less food and energy is available as you go from the base to the top of the pyramid.

READING *N* DIAGRAMS

1. **DISCUSS** How much more energy did algae store than was available to the penguins?
2. **WRITE** What would happen to the populations at higher levels if the population of one level were reduced?

What Happens When There Is a Red Tide?

If you saw waves turn from their normal gray-blue to a reddish tint, you might be concerned. So would ecologists and fisheries experts in California, Texas, and Florida, where red tides are common.

Ocean water can become reddish brown when the population of certain kinds of microscopic ocean organisms shoots up. This population increase is called a *bloom*. When they bloom, millions of individuals (each a single cell) turn large patches of ocean red.

Many kinds of single-celled algae can bloom, but the ones that cause a red tide are called dinoflagellates. These tiny algae are some of the producers at the bottom of every ocean food web.

As producers, they also form part of the base of the ocean energy pyramid. They store the sun's energy, and the stored energy passes up the pyramid as food. However, in the case of some dinoflagellates, they also pass up deadly poisons!

In the sea, many organisms feed on the algae. The algae's poison can kill many kinds of fish. Some die from eating the algae, some from just coming into contact with the potent nerve poison. This reduces the energy available to consumers higher up in the food chain. Fewer of these consumers can get enough energy to survive. The poison can also kill consumers higher on the food chain. In 1991, California

Deadly red tides like this one occur when the ocean population of fire algae greatly increases.

pelicans began to die after eating anchovies that had eaten fire algae.

Clams, mussels, and oysters pose a special problem. These animals (and many others in the sea) eat by filtering sea water. As they pass the water through their filters, they catch microscopic algae and animals. Unfortunately, this allows them to concentrate red tide organisms and the red tide poison. The clams suffer no damage from the poison, but people who eat them may become sick.

Dangers to People

People are also affected by red tides. A person who eats poisoned clams or oysters can be come very sick or even die. The poisons produced by fire algae seem only to affect the nervous systems of complex animals like fish, birds, and mammals.

What causes a red tide? What triggers a populations explosion among poisonous fire algae? Scientists are trying to track down the answer. They've come up with some promising leads.

Fertilizing the Algae

One clue came from Hong Kong, across the Pacific Ocean. Between 1976 and 1986, the number of red tides increased from 2 a year to 18 a year. At the same time, the human population of Hong Kong went up six times. As the human population increased, so did the amount of fertilizers they used. Rain washes a lot of fertilizer into the sea. Sewage washing into the sea could also help fertilize algae. The nutrients in the fertilizers may have led to the blooms.

When the government of Japan created rules that reduced ocean pollution, the number of red tides in the less polluted water was cut in half. The evidence seems to point to the conclusion that at least one cause of red tides is human activity. Other scientists say high temperatures, little wind, and no rainfall may cause the problem.

Preserving food chains from damage is important for an ecosystem. If a food chain, food web, or energy pyramid changes, the result can affect humans. On farms a decrease in predators like insect-eating birds might lead to a population explosion of insects. If the insects are plant pests, crops may suffer, food prices may soar, and farmers may lose money. In an ocean chain, red tides may seriously affect the market in fresh oysters.

If there were no predators to eat these insects, what might happen to the crops?

REVIEW

1. What is the original source of energy in an ecosystem?

2. Explain why it is or is not possible to have a food chain that has only a producer and a decomposer.

3. **COMPARE AND CONTRAST** What is the relationship between a food chain and a food web?

4. Choose a meat product you eat, and construct a food chain that includes yourself as the final consumer.

5. **CRITICAL THINKING** *Analyze* Explain why there are fewer coyotes than mice in a prairie ecosystem.

WHY IT MATTERS THINK ABOUT IT
Think about a food web in your local ecosystem. What might happen if one of the plant populations died out?

WHY IT MATTERS WRITE ABOUT IT
Write a paragraph describing what might happen if the number of herbivores in your local ecosystem suddenly decreased.

BANKING ON SEEDS

Where do farmers get the corn seeds they plant each year? Before farmers knew about plant heredity, they just planted leftover seeds from the last year's crop. There were thousands of varieties of corn. Then farmers learned about hybrids.

Ears of corn from a hybrid all become ripe at the same time. They're the same size, so harvesting is easier. Today only six varieties make up 71 percent of all the corn grown in the United States.

Farmers can breed corn that thrives despite chemical pesticides and fertilizers. Many crops grow faster, produce more food, and store better.

That's the good news about farming. There's bad news, too. If farmers grow just one kind of plant, a disease or pest invasion can wipe out a whole crop.

That's what happened in Ireland during the 1840s. Almost every Irish farmer grew the same kind of potato. When a potato disease hit, it killed almost the entire Irish potato crop. There was a serious shortage of food, and many Irish people moved to the United States.

If farmers grow only a few kinds of plants, other plants become extinct. Then animals that depend on a specific kind of plant die out as well.

As hybrids became more common, people became alarmed by the number of plant types dying out. Consequently seeds were collected from existing plants and placed in seed banks. The banks preserve the seeds from plants that otherwise might become extinct. Farmers have also been encouraged to grow more varied crops.

Social Studies Link

In a field of hybrids, all the corn looks the same.

DISCUSSION STARTER

1. How did hybrids change the way farmers farmed?

2. Why were seed banks started?

To learn more about seed banks, visit *www.mhschool.com/science* and enter the keyword BANKS.

*inter***NET**
CONNECTION

WHY IT MATTERS

Organisms can help or hinder the survival of other organisms.

SCIENCE WORDS

limiting factor anything that controls the growth or survival of an organism or population

adaptation a characteristic that helps an organism survive in its environment

symbiosis a relationship between two kinds of organisms over time

mutualism a relationship between two kinds of organisms that benefits both

parasitism a relationship in which one kind of organism lives on or in another organism and may harm the organism

commensalism a relationship between two kinds of organisms that benefits one without affecting the other

Surviving in Ecosystems

What affects the size of a population? Some forests are so thick with trees and shrubs that you would have a tough time hiking through them. Yet hiking through other forests would be as easy as walking down a country road or the street in front of your house. That's because these forests have few trees or shrubs. Why?

EXPLORE

HYPOTHESIZE What kinds of things do organisms need in their environment in order to survive? What happens when these things are limited or unavailable? Write a hypothesis in your *Science Journal*. Test your ideas.

Investigate What Controls the Growth of Populations

Experiment to see how light and water can affect the growth and survival of seeds.

PROCEDURES

1. Label the cartons 1 to 4. Fill carton 1 and 2 with dry potting soil. Fill cartons 3 and 4 with moistened potting soil. Fill the cartons to within 2 cm of the top.

2. Plant ten seeds in each carton, and cover the seeds with 0.5 cm of soil.

3. **USE VARIABLES** Place cartons 1 and 3 in a well-lighted area. Place cartons 2 and 4 in a dark place. Label the cartons to show if they are wet or dry and in the light or in the dark.

4. **OBSERVE** Examine the cartons each day for four days. Keep the soil moist in cartons 3 and 4. Record your observations in your *Science Journal*.

5. **COMPARE** Observe the plants for two weeks after they sprout. Continue to keep the soil moist in the cartons, and record your observations in your *Science Journal*.

CONCLUDE AND APPLY

1. **COMMUNICATE** How many seeds sprouted in each carton?

2. **OBSERVE** After two weeks how many plants in each carton were still living?

3. **IDENTIFY** What factor is needed for seeds to sprout? What is needed for bean plants to grow? What evidence do you have to support your answer?

GOING FURTHER: Problem Solving

4. **CAUSE AND EFFECT** Why did some seeds sprout and then die?

MATERIALS

- 4 small, clean milk cartons with the tops removed
- 40 pinto bean seeds that have been soaked overnight
- soil
- water
- *Science Journal*

What Controls the Growth of Populations?

How much do living things depend on conditions in their environment in order to survive? As the Explore Activity showed, certain factors control the growth and survival of bean plants. What about other living things?

A dry wind howls across the prairie. The hot Sun bakes the ground below. No rain has fallen in days. Grasses have withered. Plant-eating insects have gone hungry.

High in the bright, cloudless sky, a hawk wheels one way and then another. Its sharp eyes sweep over the barren land below. An unsuspecting deer mouse scurries along the ground in search of an insect.

The mouse's tan fur blends in with the dusty soil, but its movement gives it away. The hawk tucks in its wings and dives like a falling rock. In a flash its talons grab the mouse.

Hidden in this story are clues to how the size of a population is limited.

Anything that controls the growth or survival of a population is called a **limiting factor**.

Some limiting factors are nonliving. In the story the sunlight, wind, water, and temperature were nonliving limiting factors. They controlled the population of grasses on the prairie.

The grasses, insects, deer mice, and hawks were living limiting factors. The grasses had withered. There was less food for plant-eating insects, so the number of insects living in the prairie decreased. That meant there was less food for the insect-eating deer mice. The deer mouse population was also limited by the hawks, which are predators.

Brain Power

Identify a population in your area. What limiting factors affect this population? What is the role of each limiting factor?

How Do Predators Compete?

Predators are the hunters. The hunted are the prey. The number of predators in an ecosystem affects the number of prey. The number of prey in an ecosystem can also determine how many predators the ecosystem can support. If there were few hawks, the deer mouse population might stay steady or even rise. More hawks, however, mean fewer deer mice.

Hawks also compete with other predators, like coyotes and raccoons. Coyotes and raccoons hunt many animals, including small rodents like deer mice.

Coyotes and raccoons also compete with each other for food, water, and places to live, and for a territory. The population that wins such competitions is likely to grow.

Yet even a growing population faces problems. Its size will soon limit its growth. The organisms in the population will become crowded. They will have to compete with one another for food, water, and shelter. Some will die. Eventually there will be enough for the number of organisms that remain.

Overcrowding limits the growth of any population.

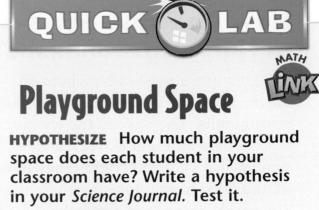

Playground Space

HYPOTHESIZE How much playground space does each student in your classroom have? Write a hypothesis in your *Science Journal.* Test it.

MATERIALS
- meterstick
- *Science Journal*

1. Working in groups use a meterstick to measure the length and width of your playground.

2. Multiply the length by the width to find the area in square meters.

3. Count the number of students in your class.

4. To find out how much space each student has, divide the area of the playground by the number of students.

CONCLUDE AND APPLY

1. **INFER** What would happen to the space each student had if the number of students doubled?

2. **INFER** Assume two other classes with the same number of students as yours used the playground at the same time as your class. What effect might this have on your class?

How Do Plants Survive in Harsh Environments?

Plants live almost everywhere on Earth. They live in deserts, where rain seldom falls. They live in the icy northland, where sunlight is weak and winters are long and frigid. They live on the floor of rain forests, where the Sun rarely shines and the soil has few nutrients.

Plants can survive in these conditions because they have developed special characteristics. Characteristics that help an organism survive in its environment are called **adaptations**.

One of the harshest areas for plant growth is a desert. What adaptations do desert plants have that allow them to live where less than 2 inches of rain falls each year? Most people in the United States live where that much rain might fall in a few hours.

The Sonoran Desert stretches from southern California to western Arizona. If you were to visit there, you would see the barrel cactus. The barrel cactus is very well adapted to desert conditions.

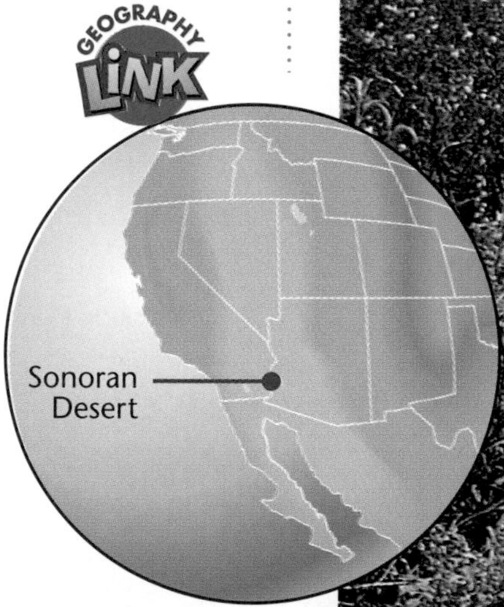

GEOGRAPHY
LINK

Sonoran Desert

The barrel cactus is adapted to the harsh conditions of the Sonoran Desert.

How Does the Barrel Cactus Survive?

The plant's roots are very shallow and grow only about 3 inches into the dry soil. There is an advantage to this. When rain does fall, the roots catch the rain and soak it up very quickly. However, during long dry spells, the fine ends of the roots fall off. What's the advantage? The lack of a fine network of root ends prevents water stored in the cactus from passing out into the soil.

The stem of the barrel cactus also helps it survive in the desert. It is folded and covered with needle-sharp spines. What are the advantages?

The stem stores water. The folds, which are deepest during dry spells, protect moist parts of the stem from hot, dry desert winds. Otherwise these winds would draw away water from the stem's surface. The spines keep away birds and small animals that try to get water from the stems of plants. If you have a small spiny cactus plant at home, you've probably learned two things—you don't have to water it often, and it is better not to touch it.

READING ∧ MAPS

WRITE Describe where in the United States the Sonoran Desert is.

How Do Different Kinds of Organisms Interact?

Different kinds of organisms interact with each other in a number of different ways. You have already seen that some organisms hunt others. Some organisms are predators. Some organisms are prey. You have also seen that different kinds of organisms may compete with each other for food or territory. Two different kinds of predators may hunt the same prey. However, there are also other kinds of relationships between different kinds of organisms. Some of these relationships are long lasting.

In nature a relationship between two kinds of organisms that lasts over a period of time is called **symbiosis**. There are different kinds of symbiosis. Sometimes both organisms benefit from the relationship. Sometimes one organism benefits while harming the other. Sometimes only one benefits, and the other is not affected. Let's take a closer look at each kind of symbiosis.

When a relationship between two kinds of organisms benefits both of them, it is called **mutualism**.

A strange-looking plant grows in the Mojave Desert of southern California. It's called a Joshua tree, or yucca plant.

When this tree's creamy flowers are in bloom, small gray shadows seem to dart from flower to flower. A more careful look reveals that the "shadows" are actually moths. These are yucca moths.

Yucca trees and yucca moths depend on each other for survival. Each helps the other reproduce. This relationship is called mutualism

Mojave Desert

How Do They Help Each Other?

Yucca moths cannot survive without yucca trees. The yucca trees would also quickly become extinct if the moths vanished. The yucca moths and the yucca trees benefit from each other and share a relationship of mutualism. How does this work?

At night a female yucca moth visits a yucca flower. Inside the flower the moth picks up pollen and rolls it up into a ball, which it holds gently in its mouth. Then the moth flutters over to another flower. There it makes a hole in the flower's ovary. The moth injects its eggs through the hole. Finally, it packs the sticky ball of pollen onto the flower's stigma. The stigma and ovary are female reproductive parts of a flower. Pollen holds male sex cells.

In protecting its eggs, the moth has also pollinated the yucca flower. The pollinated flower can then make seeds. Eventually some of the seeds will sprout into new yucca plants. This means yucca plants will continue to grow in the desert.

The moth's eggs and the tree's seeds develop at the same time. When the eggs hatch into larvae, the larvae will feed on some of the seeds. All this is happening inside the protective ovary wall. The larvae are not only getting needed food, they are also safe from predators.

IT'S MUTUAL

Leaf-cutter ants "farm" a type of fungus. They chew up leaves then they plant tufts of fungus on the leaves. The fungus cannot grow without the kinds of things the ants do for it. What do the ants get out of the relationship?

What is Parasitism?

A relationship in which one kind of organism lives on or in another organism and may harm that organism is called **parasitism** (par'ə sī tiz'əm). The organisms that live on or in other organisms are called *parasites* (par'ə sīts'). The organisms they feed on are called *hosts*. The parasites benefit from the relationship. The hosts are harmed by it.

Fleas are parasites of dogs and cats. The dogs and cats are hosts of the fleas. The fleas live off the blood of these pets and give nothing back but itching and irritation. Plants also have parasites, which often are other plants.

The bright orange dodder plant has little chlorophyll. This means that it can't make enough food to live on. Instead it winds around a plant that can make its own food. The dodder then sends tubes into the stem of the plant it is coiled around. Next, the dodder gets food from the plant through the tubes. Although the plant it lives on usually does not die, it is weakened, grows more slowly, and is not able to easily fight off diseases.

The coiling dodder plant, which can't make enough of its own food, draws food from other plants.

Flea

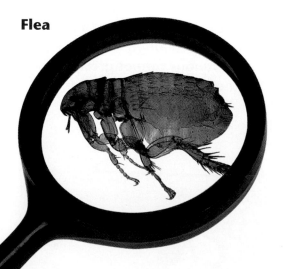

Mistletoe is another parasitic plant. It is an evergreen that grows on the trunk or branches of trees such as hawthorn, poplar, fir, or apple.

Some tropical fish are protected from predators by the poison in an anemone's tentacles.

Orchids benefit from their position on the trunks of trees.

What is Commensalism?

Few plants can grow on the floor of a rain forest. One reason is that the thick canopy above keeps light from reaching the ground. If plants could climb trees, they might overcome this. However, some plants, like orchids, attach themselves to the trunks of trees high above the rain forest floor. The orchids don't take anything from the trees. They simply use the trees to get needed sunlight. This relationship, in which one organism benefits from another without harming or helping it, is called **commensalism** (kə men′sə liz′əm).

Many animals also have this kind of relationship. Certain tropical fish live unharmed among the poisonous tentacles of sea anemones. The anemones provide safety for the fish. The fish neither harm nor help the anemones.

309

When Changes Come, What Survives?

About 18,000 years ago, great sheets of ice moved deep into the center of what is now the United States. Vast ice sheets also covered much of Europe and parts of South America. Sea levels dropped as more and more water froze. New land was exposed. Earth was a cold place.

Slowly Earth began to warm up. The ice melted. Sea levels rose. Coastal land became flooded.

These kinds of changes have occurred no less than seven times during the past 700,000 years. Scientists call these cold periods *ice ages*.

Earth has also changed in other ways. Over millions of years, continents have moved north and south, east and west. Huge mountain-sized rocks have crashed into Earth. Volcanoes have poured gases and dust into the air.

Each of these events has had an effect on living things. Some have died out, or become extinct. Others have survived. Why did some of these creatures vanish, while others survived?

Death of the Dinosaurs

Let's travel back in time to a day about 65 million years ago. Fossil evidence indicates that dinosaurs shared the land with many other animals. These animals included frogs, snails, insects, turtles, snakes, and some small furry mammals. Plants of all kinds grew everywhere. The seas were full of organisms like fish, sea urchins, clams, and algae.

Even today volcanoes fill the air with ash, dust, and soot.

Then an asteroid up to 10 kilometers (6 miles) in diameter roared in from outer space. It weighed perhaps 200,000 tons. It streaked downward at 16 to 21 kilometers (10 to 13 miles) a second, crashing into Earth on the coast north of Mexico's Yucatan Peninsula.

The impact created a tremendous explosion. It gouged out a crater 70 kilometers (43 miles) across and threw huge amounts of dust into the sky. The dust may have blanketed the sky for months, even years. Sunlight was probably blocked from reaching the ground.

Plants needing lots of sunlight may have died out. That means that the large plant-eating dinosaurs could not get enough food. They may have died out.

The large dinosaurs preying on plant eaters would have also died out. It may have been that every animal weighing more than about 121 kilograms (55 pounds) became extinct.

Yet many of the smaller animals could have survived. They needed less food to live. They could have moved more easily from habitat to habitat. They would no longer have been in competition with dinosaurs. They would have been free to grow in size and variety.

A world once ruled by dinosaurs became ruled by mammals. If not for such a catastrophe 65 million years ago, perhaps dinosaurs would still roam Earth today.

Scientific evidence suggests that about 65 million years ago, an asteroid from outer space may have struck Earth, killing off many animals and plants.

How Do People Change the Environment?

How do you affect your environment? About fifteen times a minute, you change the environment. That's the number of times you probably breathe in and out every 60 seconds. Each time you exhale, you add carbon dioxide and water to the air. Each time you inhale, you remove oxygen.

The amount of these substances you breathe in and out is small. Yet they change the environment around you and far away. That's because air circulates around Earth. Those molecules of carbon dioxide you exhaled might find their way into a local tree or a plant miles away. Oxygen that the plant gives off might be inhaled by an animal even farther from your home.

Although living thousands of miles from you, the ruffed lemur (above) and the spot-billed toucanet (left) are affected by what you and other people do.

Eventually some of the air you exhaled might go though several cycles. In the process that air might also travel around the world.

Some of that air might find its way into a jaborandi (zha′bə ran′dē′) tree in northern Brazil. Some of it might wind up in a periwinkle shrub in Madagascar. Madagascar is an island in the Indian Ocean off the east coast of Africa.

The plants use the carbon to build their stems, leaves, roots, and other parts. Some of these parts will be eaten by animals. They might be Madagascar's big-eyed ruffed lemurs or Brazil's many-colored spot-billed toucanets. Each of these animals seeks food and shelter among the plants of its environment.

But there's more to the story. There's a chapter that could someday affect you or someone you know.

Why Are These Plants Important to People?

The jaborandi tree produces a chemical called *pilocarpine* (pī′lə kär′pēn′). Doctors use this chemical to treat an eye disease called glaucoma. Glaucoma can cause blindness if it is not treated. The Madagascar periwinkle produces a chemical called *vincristine* (vin kris′tēn′). Vincristine is used to treat a cancer called childhood *leukemia* (lü kē′mē ə). These plants are important for our health and survival. Many others are, too.

Many kinds of plants are endangered by human activities. When people pollute the air and water, they may harm other living things that depend on that air and water. People can interfere with an ecosystem by damming up rivers, using pesticides, or cutting down trees. Yet people can also find ways to improve the environment by cleaning up polluted air and water and by reducing future sources of pollution. They can plant trees to replace those that are cut down or are destroyed by forest fires. Each person has an effect. The lives of all organisms are affected by other living things—and by nonliving things—in their environment.

With every breath you take, you are changing not only your environment but the world's

REVIEW

1. Identify two biotic and two abiotic limiting factors.

2. COMPARE AND CONTRAST How is mutualism like commensalism? How is it different?

3. Identify an organism and its adaptation that helps it survive in its environment.

4. CRITICAL THINKING *Analyze* Several species of whales are threatened with extinction. Propose two hypotheses that might account for the threat.

WHY IT MATTERS THINK ABOUT IT
How do you affect your environment? How does your community affect its environment?

WHY IT MATTERS WRITE ABOUT IT
Make a list of ways you and your community affect your environment. Suggest what could be done to make things better.

Yogurt to the Rescue!

Bacteria can be bad news. They spoil food, cause tooth decay, and can make you sick. Bacteria can be good news, too, because they help you digest food!

Bacteria can change milk into cheese or yogurt. How? First, the milk is heated to about 37°C (115°F). That's the temperature at which bacteria multiply best. Then, active yogurt cultures are put into the milk. (Active cultures contain live bacteria.) Before long the bacteria multiply and turn the milk into yogurt!

Did you know that the bacteria in yogurt can keep you healthy? It's true. Active yogurt cultures can live in your intestines and help you digest food.

The strains of bacteria in yogurt are just a few of the more than one million kinds of bacteria. Only about 200 cause diseases in humans.

Have some yogurt! Your digestive system will thank you. So will your taste buds!

Health Link

Antibiotics can kill bacteria that make people sick. Some antibiotics contain bacteria, too. Others are made from fungi.

However, antibiotics can kill useful bacteria in the body, too. When that happens you may have trouble digesting food. You may get stomach cramps or other problems. Let yogurt come to the rescue!

Live yogurt cultures move to the lining of your intestine. There they multiply and help restore your body's digestive balance. Therefore, if your doctor prescribes an antibiotic, pick up some yogurt, too!

DISCUSSION STARTER

1. What happens when active yogurt cultures are added to hot milk?

2. How can yogurt help if you're taking antibiotics?

To learn more about yogurt, visit *www.mhschool.com/science* and enter the keyword YOGURT.

*inter*NET
CONNECTION

315

WHY IT MATTERS

Animals play various roles in the water, carbon, and nitrogen cycles.

SCIENCE WORDS

water cycle the continuous movement of water between Earth's surface and the air, changing from liquid to gas to liquid

carbon cycle the continuous transfer of carbon between the atmosphere and living things

nitrogen cycle the transfer of nitrogen from the atmosphere to plants and back to the atmosphere and directly into plants again

Cycles of Life

In what order do you think the scenes on this page occurred? Could the scenes have happened in reverse order, too? Organisms require certain things to stay alive. Yet as they live, they use up these things. How can they, and the generations that follow them, continue to inhabit Earth?

EXPLORE

HYPOTHESIZE How can we, and all living things, keep using water every day and not use it all up? Write a hypothesis in your *Science Journal*. How would you experiment to test your ideas?

Investigate What Happens to Water

Use a model to see how water in the environment is recycled.

MATERIALS

- plastic food container with clear cover
- small bowl or cup filled with water
- small tray filled with dry soil
- 4-cm-square (1.6-in.-square) piece of paper towel
- 100-W lamp (if available)
- *Science Journal*

PROCEDURES

1. Place the dry paper towel, the dry soil, and the bowl of water in the plastic container. Close the container with the lid.

2. OBSERVE Place the container under a lamp or in direct sunlight. Observe every ten minutes for a class period. Record your observations in your *Science Journal*.

3. REPEAT Observe the container on the second day. Record your observations.

CONCLUDE AND APPLY

1. COMPARE AND CONTRAST What did you observe the first day? What did you observe the second day?

2. INFER What was the source of the water? What was the source of the energy that caused changes in the container?

GOING FURTHER: Apply

3. DRAW CONCLUSIONS What happened to the water?

4. INFER What parts of the water cycle does this model show?

317

What Happens to Water?

Does water get lost when it evaporates? The Explore Activity showed that water is not lost from an environment. It evaporates, condenses, and moves from one part of the environment to another. In other words the water is recycled.

This is what you saw happening in the photographs of the African water hole on page 316. The same thing happens on a much larger scale in nature. This process of naturally recycling water on Earth is called the **water cycle**. Here's how it works.

Condensation

Condensation As the moist air rises higher and higher, it cools. When cooled enough, water vapor condenses into tiny water droplets or changes from vapor to tiny ice crystals. If enough of them gather, they form a cloud. In clouds the droplets and ice crystals can grow larger and heavier. Water in the atmosphere represents only $\frac{1}{10,000}$ of Earth's water.

Flash flooding in an arroyo in Arizona

Evaporation

OCEAN

MOUNTAINS

RIVER

DESERT

Collection Some of the water flows into streams, lakes, and rivers. Some of it soaks into the ground. This stored water is called *groundwater*. Lots of this water slowly finds its way back into Earth's oceans. The oceans contain more than 97 percent of the world's water.

READING /\/ DIAGRAMS

1. **DISCUSS** Explain the differences between evaporation, condensation, and precipitation.
2. **WRITE** What is the difference between runoff and groundwater?

Precipitation

Eventually the droplets or ice crystals become so large and heavy that they can no longer stay up in the air. They fall to Earth's surface as precipitation—rain, snow, sleet, or hail.

Snow in a cold, northern region of the world

Precipitation

Evaporation
Heat from the Sun is absorbed by oceans, seas, lakes, streams, ponds, puddles, and even dew. This heat energy makes the water evaporate and rise into the air. The Sun's energy also evaporates water that collects on the leaves of plants.

Runoff
On land some of the rain seeps into the ground. However, some of the water flows downhill across the surface instead. This water becomes *runoff*. Rapidly melting snow, sleet, or hail can also become runoff.

Evaporation

LAKE

FOREST AND FIELDS

Runoff

Transpiration Transpiration Transpiration

Living Things
Organisms are also part of the water cycle. Plants remove water from the soil. Some of this water returns to the atmosphere through the plants' leaves. Animals also take in water. Some of this water returns to the environment through the skin or during breathing. Some returns as waste products.

EARTH
LINK
SCIENCE

Plants play an important role in the water cycle.

319

This dead tree is being decomposed by fungi, shown here, and microscopic bacteria.

What Happens to a Dead Tree?

How can a dead tree help living things? A wind howls through the night in a forest. Suddenly the darkness is filled with the sounds of snapping branches as an old tree begins to topple. Down the tree falls. The ground shivers as the huge trunk crashes down. A few animals shriek. Then only the wind whistles in the night.

Yet other things are beginning to happen. The tree, which was once part of one food web, is becoming part of another food web.

Even though the tree is now dead, it is being turned into substances other organisms need to survive. Some of these organisms are other trees. The dead tree is providing elements for living trees. When these trees die, they will provide elements that other trees

need. The cycling of matter is continuous. How does this happen?

An old, fallen tree is made of wood, bark, and other dead tree tissue. That tissue holds all sorts of complex chemical substances. Most of the chemicals are too complex to be used by most other living things. They need to be broken down into simpler chemicals.

How Decomposers Help

There are organisms that recycle matter in dead organisms. They're called decomposers. Worms, crickets, cockroaches, bacteria, and fungi are decomposers. These organisms can break down dead wood and other dead plant parts into *carbon dioxide* and

Brain Power

How else might a dead tree help living things?

320

ammonia. All living plants need carbon dioxide in order to make sugars. Ammonia is a simple substance that contains the element *nitrogen*. Nitrogen is extremely important for plants. No plant can live or grow without nitrogen. All organisms need nitrogen in order to make proteins.

Fertilizers

Nitrogen is a chemical found in plant *fertilizers*. Fertilizers are substances used to add minerals to the soil. Some fertilizers are natural. These are decaying plants and animals, and animal wastes. Other fertilizers are made in factories. Both natural and artificial fertilizers contain nitrogen. The next time you go to a store that sells fertilizers, read the labels. You're sure to find nitrogen as one of the ingredients.

As you'll soon discover, like water, nitrogen and carbon have their own cycles in nature. Earth, like the setup in the Explore Activity, is a closed system. With the exception of energy, almost nothing gets out or gets in. It is recycled.

Fertilizers sold in stores contain nitrogen. Nitrogen is an element plants need to grow and stay healthy.

10-10-10

FERTILIZER

5 LBS. NET WEIGHT

10-10-1

Guaranteed Analysis

Total Nitrogen (N) 10%
Available Phosphate (P_2O_5) 10%
Soluble Potash (K_2O) 10%
The Plant Foods used in Espoma Garden Food are Ammonium Sulfate, Triple Superphosphate and Potash. Also contained in Garden Food is the natural mineral limestone.

Food 10-10-10 is an agricultural

QUICK LAB

Soil Sample

HYPOTHESIZE How do nutrients get recycled in nature? Write a hypothesis in your *Science Journal*. Test it by examining a soil core.

MATERIALS
- empty can
- *Science Journal*

PROCEDURES

SAFETY Do not touch the sharp edges of the can.

1. Go to a wooded area in a park or other location near your school. Find a patch of soft, moist soil.

2. Press a can, open side down, into the soil to get a core sample. You might have to gently rotate the can so it cuts into the soil.

3. Carefully remove the core so it stays in one piece.

4. **OBSERVE** In your *Science Journal*, describe and draw the core.

CONCLUDE AND APPLY

1. **INFER** From top to bottom, what kind of matter does the core hold?

2. **INFER** In what order did the layers form?

3. **INFER** Which layer holds the most available nutrients? Explain.

321

How Is Carbon Recycled?

Sometimes simple activities can turn into a scientific investigation. Cooking a meal doesn't seem to have much in common with a scientific experiment. Yet what happens if a meal made of baked potatoes, steak, and toasted marshmallows is burned? What do you have?

The food may be ruined, but you can make an important scientific discovery. The burned food, which is made up of plant and animal products, is black and looks like charcoal. It contains the same black substance that makes up charcoal. That substance is *carbon*.

What scientific information is hidden in the ruined meal? One of the elements that make up all living things is carbon.

Nature recycles carbon, and it is used by all organisms. The recycling of this important substance is called the **carbon cycle**.

Nature recycles carbon in the carbon cycle. At the same time, oxygen is also being cycled through ecosystems.

Photosynthesis During photosynthesis plants use the carbon from carbon dioxide to make sugars, starches, and proteins.

Car exhaust

Decaying matter

Oil

Carbon Dioxide Carbon dioxide enters the air when plants and animals decay. It enters the air when animals breathe out. It enters the air when fossil fuels such as coal, oil, gasoline, and natural gas are burned. Forest fires also add carbon dioxide to the air.

1. **DISCUSS** When does carbon dioxide enter the air?
2. **WRITE** What happens to carbon when living things die?

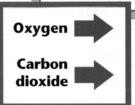

Oxygen ➡️

Carbon dioxide ➡️

Oxygen

Carbon dioxide

Plants Plants take in carbon dioxide and give off oxygen, which animals use

Animals Animals eat plant sugars, starches, proteins, and other substances. The carbon in these substances is used by animals to make their own body chemicals.

Death, Decay, Storage When living things die, decay releases the carbon compounds in their bodies. Some of it is turned into carbon dioxide by decomposers. Over millions of years, some of it turns into fossil fuels.

How Is Nitrogen Recycled?

What do you need nitrogen for? When you eat meat, fish, cereal, or vegetables, you are taking in the nutrients that your body needs to make *proteins*. Proteins are a part of your muscles and many cell structures.

Among other things proteins are rich in the element nitrogen. You need nitrogen to make parts of your body, such as muscles, nerves, skin, bones, blood, and digestive juices.

If you know something about Earth science, you might say: "Who needs to eat protein to get nitrogen? The air is 78 percent nitrogen." That's true. However, animals and plants cannot use the nitrogen that is in the air. Animals get nitrogen by eating proteins. Plants get nitrogen by absorbing it from the soil. Some plants even get nitrogen with the help of a special group of bacteria.

The way nitrogen moves between the air, soil, plants, and animals is called the nitrogen cycle. Here's how it works.

Air Air is made up of about 78 percent nitrogen gas.

Nitrogen-Fixing Bacteria Some bacteria that grow on pea and bean roots give those plants the nitrogen they need. The bacteria turn nitrogen gas in the air to nitrogen-containing substances the plants can use to make their proteins.

Decomposers When the plant dies, decomposers in the soil break down the plant proteins. One product is the nitrogen-containing substance ammonia. Soil bacteria change ammonia into nitrites.

Ammonia

READING N DIAGRAMS

1. DISCUSS Compare the different ways various kinds of bacteria help in the nitrogen cycle.

2. WRITE How do pea and bean plants get the nitrogen they need?

Denitrifying Bacteria Some soil bacteria turn nitrates back into nitrogen gas.

Animals Animals eat plant proteins, or they eat other animals that eat plant proteins. Animal wastes contain nitrogen compounds.

Plants Plants absorb nitrates dissolved in water through their roots. The nitrogen is then used by the plant to make proteins.

Nitrogen compounds

Nitrites   **Nitrates**

Nitrites and ammonia

Bacteria Certain bacteria can use nitrogen from the air to make nitrogen-containing substances called *nitrites*. Other bacteria can turn nitrites into *nitrates*—another group of nitrogen-containing substances.

325

Why Recycle?

Have you ever seen a paper bag with a symbol that says "Printed on recycled paper"? Why is this important?

The environment provides the materials people use to make products. Sunlight is an *inexhaustible resource*. The Sun will last for millions, if not billions, of years. Other resources, however, are not inexhaustible. The paper to make books, magazines, newspapers, and containers comes from the wood in trees. Metals mined from the ground are used to make cars, ships, pots and pans, appliances, and many other things. Glass is made from sand. Plastics are made from chemicals in oil found deep underground.

Wood, metals, sand, and oil are called *raw materials*. Raw materials are the building blocks of products.

Many raw materials, such as oil and metals, are *nonrenewable resources*. Earth's oil was formed millions of years ago. There's a limited amount of it. When it's gone, it's gone forever.

Certain other resources, such as wood, are *renewable resources*. If trees are cut down for lumber and paper, more can be planted to replace them. Even so, trees take years to grow. Recycling paper and other wood products can help keep forests from being destroyed. This can also help keep the animals in them from losing their homes and, perhaps, facing extinction.

MATH LINK

This graph shows the percent of different materials in garbage thrown away each day by each person in the United States. Study the graph and answer the questions.

READING N GRAPHS

1. **DISCUSS** Let's say there are 280,000,000 people in the United States. Each person throws away 1.8 kilograms (4 pounds) of garbage each day. How much garbage is thrown away by all the people each day?
2. **DISCUSS** How much of this is paper?
3. **WRITE** If a book has a mass of 2 kilograms (4.4 pounds), how many books would it take to make up the amount of paper thrown away?

How Are Recycled Products Used?

For all of these reasons, many people urge that we conserve raw materials by recycling them—just as nature recycles water, carbon, and nitrogen. Many communities have recycling programs. Glass products are collected in one set of bins, metal containers in another. Plastics are collected in still another. Papers are bundled up. Service stations save oil that is drained from car engines.

These materials are then sent to recycling centers. The manufacturers break them down into raw materials that can be used to make new products. What's the result? Less garbage piles up in our environment. Fewer raw materials are wasted. Less of Earth's valuable raw materials are used up.

The environment provides all the things you need. It provides food for you to eat, water for you to drink, and raw materials for the products you use. The environment will keep doing these things as long as we let it recycle the substances that make life possible and comfortable. People can either help or hinder this process.

REVIEW

1. By what process does water move from oceans, lakes, rivers, and streams into the air?

2. What organisms turn a dead tree into substances that can be used by living trees?

3. Describe three ways that carbon dioxide gets into the air.

4. **IDENTIFY** Name two substances that contain nitrogen.

5. **CRITICAL THINKING** *Apply* How can you and other people conserve trees?

WHY IT MATTERS THINK ABOUT IT
Why is it important to recycle cans, bottles, and paper?

WHY IT MATTERS WRITE ABOUT IT
Write a paragraph explaining the importance of using recycled materials.

READING SKILL
Look at the diagram on pages 322-323 Write a paragraph explaining what information you can get from reading this diagram.

The Human Touch

How do humans affect ecosystems? Sometimes in good ways, but other times humans can harm and change an ecosystem. Here are a few examples.

Thousands of years ago, people began irrigating crops, but not with fresh water. As irrigation water evaporated, it left salts behind. Over time the soil became poisoned. Crops that had once thrived in the fields stopped growing.

Today farmers use fertilizers containing nitrogen. Runoff carries the nitrogen into streams, lakes, and the ocean. Plants need some nitrogen to grow, but too much causes overgrowth. Water plants can grow so thick that they use up the oxygen and block the sunlight. Most water animals can't live in such conditions.

Gases in the exhausts from humans' cars are high in nitrogen compounds. So are gases from high-temperature burning in factories and power plants. The nitrogen pollutes the air and contributes to acid rain.

Acid rain can release poisonous aluminum compounds into the soil in forests. Trees begin to die. Living trees remove carbon from the air, while decaying or burnt trees release it.

When they burn fossil fuels, humans also increase the carbon dioxide in the air. Evidence suggests that this causes global warming—a rise in average air temperatures around the world.

Science, Technology, and Society

DISCUSSION STARTER

1. How have humans changed ecosystems?

2. What causes global warming?

Agricultural runoff has affected some fishing areas.

You can see the effects of acid rain on this forest.

To learn more about the consequences of human behavior, visit *www.mhschool.com/science* and enter the keyword PEOPLE.

*inter*NET
CONNECTION

WHY IT MATTERS

Ecosystems can change over time.

SCIENCE WORDS

ecological succession the gradual replacement of one community by another

pioneer species the first species living in an area

pioneer community the first community living in an area

climax community the final stage of succession in an area, unless a major change happens

How Ecosystems Change

Before May 18, 1980, the area around Mount Saint Helens in the state of Washington was decorated with beautiful groves of Douglas fir and western hemlock trees. Wildflowers sprouted from the soil. Animals of many kinds made their home here. Then the mountain exploded.

EXPLORE

HYPOTHESIZE Can different ecosystems affect each other when they change? How might an abandoned farm and a nearby forest affect each other? Write a hypothesis in your *Science Journal*. Test your ideas.

EXPLORE ACTIVITY

Investigate How Ecosystems Change

Compare what happened at Mount Saint Helens to what might happen to an abandoned farm at the edge of a forest.

PROCEDURES

1. OBSERVE Examine the photograph.

2. COMMUNICATE In your *Science Journal*, describe the two ecosystems that you see.

CONCLUDE AND APPLY

1. INFER How do the two ecosystems affect each other?

2. PREDICT If the land is not farmed for ten years, what would you expect the area to look like?

3. DRAW CONCLUSIONS How can one ecosystem be changed into another?

4. COMPARE AND CONTRAST Compare what you think will happen to the abandoned farm with what happened at Mount Saint Helens. In what ways would the changes in ecosystems be similar? In what ways would they be different?

GOING FURTHER: Apply

5. ANALYZE Think of another ecosystem that might be changed by nature. Think of another ecosystem that might be changed by humans. Describe how such ecosystems might continue to change over time.

How Do Ecosystems Change?

What happens when people abandon a city? Nature takes over. One example is the cities and temples of Angkor in Cambodia. They were built between 820 and about 1150. They are among the great wonders of the world. Many of their buildings still lie hidden under the vines and trees of the jungle. Yet it wasn't always that way. Once, hundreds of years ago, people cleared the land for their cities. Then about 600 years ago, the ancient cities were abandoned and the jungle crept over them.

Similar, if not so spectacular, changes happen everywhere on Earth. They can

After they were abandoned, the great cities of Angkor in Cambodia became covered by the jungle.

occur in your backyard. They can happen in an empty city lot or on one of its abandoned streets. They can occur in a suburb or on a farm. If given a chance, nature has a way of changing an ecosystem or producing a new one. How does nature change an abandoned farm's field into a flourishing forest?

From Farmland to Forest

Abandoned Farm—First Year
A community of crabgrass, insects, and mice invades the field where corn or another crop once grew.

Second and Third Years
Tall weeds, such as asters, ragweed, and goldenrod, and tall grasses grow among the crabgrass. The crabgrass can't easily survive in the shade cast by the taller weeds. It begins to die out. Rabbits and seed-eating birds move in.

Four to Six Years Later

The hot, dry field of tall weeds provides a perfect environment for pine seeds to sprout. Pine trees begin to grow and shade the weeds, which begin to die out. More birds join the community, as do small mammals like opossums and skunks.

Twenty-Five Years Later

A pine forest has replaced the old farm field. Yet the number of new pine seedlings drops because they can't grow in the shade. Seeds of deciduous trees such as maple, hickory, and oak sprout and take root. Larger animals like raccoons and foxes begin to visit.

One Hundred Years Later

The forest is now mostly deciduous trees. These trees are the habitats of many different kinds of birds and small animals, such as squirrels. Deer, raccoons, and foxes also live in the forest.

How Do Communities Change?

The abandoned farm field you just read about gave way to short crabgrass, then tall grasses and shrubs. Later, pine trees, and finally, deciduous trees grew there. Scientists call the gradual replacement of one community by another **ecological succession**.

Ecological succession can begin in two different kinds of places. It can begin where a community already exists—such as in an abandoned farm field. Ecological succession in a place where a community already exists is called *secondary succession*.

Ecological succession can also happen where there are few, if any, living things. This is called *primary succession*. Primary succession can begin where communities were wiped out. Such places would include land swept clean by a volcanic eruption or forest fire. It can also begin where communities never existed before, such as on a new island that rises out of the sea.

How do you explore this kind of succession? Explore what happened to Mount Saint Helens in the state of Washington shortly after May 18, 1980.

Mount Saint Helens had just erupted. The blast from the volcano knocked down thousands of trees. To make matters worse, the whole area was covered knee-deep with hot volcanic ash and finely smashed up rock.

The landscape was different shades of gray as far as you could see. No spot of green greeted your eyes, not even a blade of grass. If you didn't know better, you might think you were on the Moon.

A year after Mount Saint Helens erupted, the rose-purple flowers of fireweed announced that life was returning to the destroyed land. Just four years after Mount Saint Helens erupted, seedlings of Douglas fir trees began to take root in the rubble of the volcano.

How Does Mount Saint Helens Change?

A year passes. You return to the slopes of Mount Saint Helens expecting to see unbroken stretches of rock and stumps of dead trees. However, something has happened in the year you were gone. Wind and rain have cleared some of the ash and dust, especially from steep slopes. The wind has also blown in some seeds and fruits from nearby forests. You see a scattering of rose-purple objects among the charred and fallen tree trunks. As you come closer, you recognize the objects. They are the flowers of a plant called fireweed. It gets its name from the fact that it is often the first plant to grow after a forest fire.

Scientists would call the fireweed a **pioneer species**. That's because it is the first species to be living in an otherwise lifeless area. You notice that the blooming of fireweed has attracted animals such as insects and an occasional insect-eating bird. A new community, called a **pioneer community**, is beginning to thrive around Mount Saint Helens.

You return in 1984 and almost step on a little green shoot. You bend down and take a closer look. The shoot has little needlelike leaves. You recognize it. It is the sprout of a Douglas fir tree. Its seed was probably blown here from a forest miles away.

Now you can picture the land around Mount Saint Helens 100 or 200 years in the future. It is covered with a dense forest of evergreens. The forest is much like the one that spread around it before that explosive day in 1980.

**Fir trees grow tall
11 years after the blast.**

What Makes Up Pioneer Communities?

Are the first organisms in a pioneer community always plants? In some places the answer is no. This is usually the case in newly formed fiery volcanic islands that rise from the sea. Here the pioneer community is usually made up of bacteria, fungi, and algae. Over many years these organisms slowly break down the volcanic rock into soil.

On a continent far away from an ocean, succession might be starting in a rocky field. Lichens, tiny organisms composed of algae and fungi, start to grow on a rock. The rock gradually crumbles over time into soil.

What happens when there is enough soil, and other conditions are right for plants to grow? A seed blown to the island by the wind or dropped by a passing bird will take root. The new plant, and others like it, will gradually spread over the land.

During their life cycles, plants will die and further enrich the soil. Perhaps a coconut will drift ashore. When it germinates its roots will find a good supply of nutrients. A coconut palm will spring up, and a new island paradise will be born.

Finally, a Climax Community

More years will pass—perhaps hundreds of them. The climate of the island will remain pretty much unchanged. Its community will grow. Its populations will become balanced and stable. Few new animals and plants will arrive. Few will leave. Ecological succession will slow down or stop altogether. A scientist visiting the island will see a **climax community**. It is a final stage of succession. This community will stay largely unchanged unless some major event occurs.

A PIONEER COMMUNITY

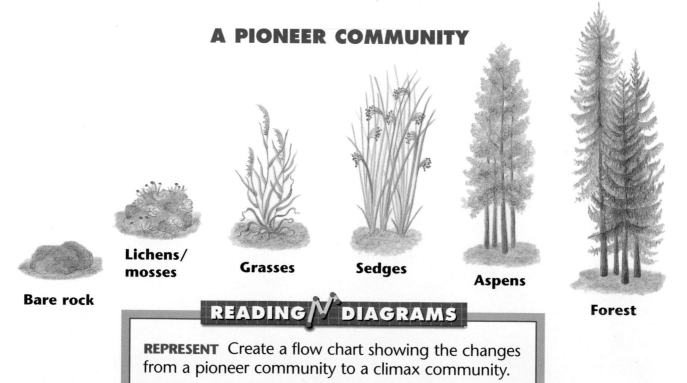

Bare rock

Lichens/ mosses

Grasses

Sedges

Aspens

Forest

READING DIAGRAMS

REPRESENT Create a flow chart showing the changes from a pioneer community to a climax community.

Events That Can Change an Entire Ecosystem

A hurricane may sweep across the island. The volcano that gave it birth might erupt again. People might come and build hotels or introduce new plants or animals. The climate might change. Then the processes of ecological succession would begin all over again. Another climax community would eventually develop. It might—or might not—be the same as the earlier climax community.

The volcano Kilauea erupting on the island of Hawaii

QUICK LAB

Predicting Succession

HYPOTHESIZE In what areas where you live do you think ecological succession may be taking place? Write a hypothesis in your *Science Journal*. Test it.

MATERIALS
• *Science Journal*

PROCEDURES

1. **OBSERVE** Identify an area near you where you think ecological succession is taking place.

2. **COMMUNICATE** Describe the area. List the evidence you have that indicates ecological succession is taking place.

CONCLUDE AND APPLY

1. **INFER** Do you think the succession will be primary or secondary? Explain.

2. **PREDICT** In what order do you think new species will colonize the area? Explain the reasons for your predictions.

3. **COMMUNICATE** Describe the climax community that you think will eventually live in the area. Give reasons for your conclusion.

What's Living on Surtsey?

HISTORY LINK

In 1963 the island of Surtsey, near Iceland, was formed from a volcano. Between 1963 and 1996, at least 45 types of plants were seen growing there. Several kinds of birds, such as snow buntings, were also found raising their young on the island.

Flying insects have also been found there. Scientists expect that more types of plants and birds will live on Surtsey in the future.

Surtsey, a volcanic island, rose from the sea near Iceland in 1963.

By 1996 many plants and birds lived on Surtsey.

Damage caused by the Soufriere Hills volcano on the island of Montserrat

Brain Power

In the 1990s the erupting Soufriere Hills volcano on the island of Montserrat covered over much of the island. What do you think it is like there today? How would you find out if you are correct?

SKILL BUILDER

Skills: Interpreting Data and Inferring

COMPARING ECOSYSTEMS IN VOLCANIC AREAS

In this activity you will collect and interpret data about the ecosystems of two volcanic areas.

Data are different kinds of facts. They might include observations, measurements, calculations, and other kinds of information. Scientists collect data about an event to better understand what caused it, what it will cause, and how it will affect other events.

What do these data tell the scientist? The scientist first organizes the data in some way—perhaps a table, chart, or graph. The scientist then studies the organized data and interprets it. *Interpret* means "draw a conclusion." In this case you will draw a conclusion about what determines which plants will return to a volcanic area.

MATERIALS
- research books
- Internet
- *Science Journal*

PROCEDURES

1. Collect data on two volcanic areas, Mount Saint Helens and the Soufriere Hills volcano on the island of Montserrat or the active volcanoes of Hawaii. Organize the data in your *Science Journal.*

2. **COMMUNICATE** Describe the sequence of events that has taken place.

3. **INTERPRET DATA** Draw a conclusion about why certain plants return when they do.

CONCLUDE AND APPLY

1. **COMPARE** In what ways is succession in the two areas alike? In what ways is it different?

2. **INFER** Why is the succession in these two areas similar or different?

3. **INFER** What abiotic factors must you consider when drawing conclusions? What biotic factors must you consider?

Why Do Some Organisms Survive While Others Don't?

Our planet is changing all the time. Its continents move north and south, east and west. Climates change from hot to cold, cold to hot, wet to dry, or dry to wet. As these changes occur, populations and communities change with them.

Take, for example, the following mystery and its solution.

Clues

- Scientists gathering fossils in Italy make a discovery. About six million years ago, fish and other sea creatures disappeared from the Mediterranean Sea.

- Other fossils from a slightly later period reveal that horselike animals from Africa arrived in Europe.

- The fossil of an ancient African hippopotamus is found on an island in the middle of the Mediterranean.

- Fossil palm trees of the same age are dug up in Switzerland.

- Then there is another surprising discovery. Five-million-year-old fossils of fish turn up in the Mediterranean area.

Scientists study fossils to discover how the Mediterranean area changed.

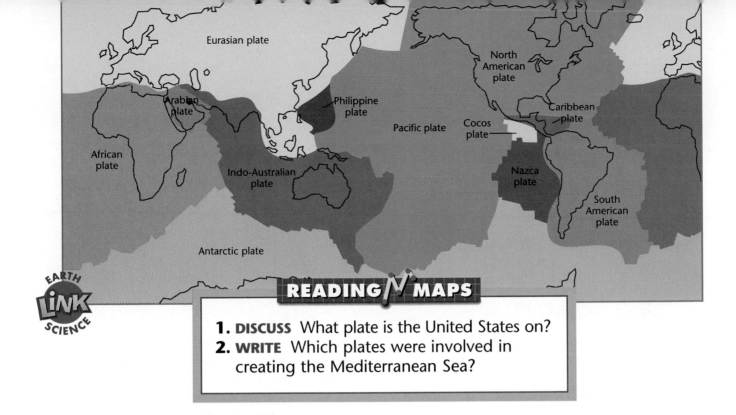

Eurasian plate

North American plate

Arabian plate

Philippine plate

Pacific plate

Cocos plate

Caribbean plate

African plate

Indo-Australian plate

Nazca plate

South American plate

Antarctic plate

READING 🔍 MAPS

1. **DISCUSS** What plate is the United States on?
2. **WRITE** Which plates were involved in creating the Mediterranean Sea?

EARTH LINK SCIENCE

6 million years ago

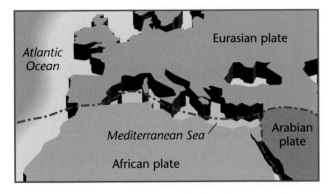

Atlantic Ocean

Eurasian plate

Mediterranean Sea

Arabian plate

African plate

Present day

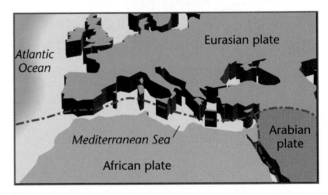

Atlantic Ocean

Eurasian plate

Mediterranean Sea

Arabian plate

African plate

What could have gone on back then to have these clues make sense? Scientists have developed hypotheses. Here's one.

About six million years ago, the continents of Africa and Europe bumped into each other. Earth's crust is made up of moving plates—pieces of crust. Two plates—the African and the Eurasian—collided back then. This happened at what is now the Strait of Gibraltar. This collision created a natural dam between the Atlantic Ocean and the Mediterranean Sea.

Without a source of water from the ocean, the sea dried up in perhaps as little as 1,000 years. The Mediterranean Sea became a desert. The sea's fish and other marine life died out. Animals from Africa migrated across the desert to Europe. Palm trees sprouted in Switzerland.

Then about five million years ago, the dam began to crumble. A gigantic waterfall poured water into the desert. It carried many kinds of marine life from the Atlantic Ocean. The Mediterranean became a sea again.

Where Have All the Metals Gone?

The soil under your feet looks brown. The rocks are mostly gray. Yet both hold a treasure chest of glittering colorful metals—gold, silver, aluminum, iron, copper, and many more.

People use these metals in many ways. Gold is made into jewelry and coins. Silver is, too. Silver is also in photographic film and tableware.

Fly in an airplane. Ride in an automobile. Open a soft drink can. Squeeze a toothpaste tube. Marvel at fireworks. For all these things, you can thank aluminum. It's in each of these products.

Every large building, bridge, ship, train, and piece of machinery has iron in it—usually as part of steel.

Turn on your TV, your home's lights, a CD player. Electricity flowing through copper wires gets them going.

Clearly metals play an important part in our modern society. Yet we pay a price for them—and not only in money. Since metal-containing rocks

The easiest way to mine metals that are near the surface is to scrape the surface away. However, this leaves the land barren and often covered with dangerous chemicals.

are buried in the ground, we must change the ground to get at them. If the rocks are near the surface, we simply carve away huge areas of land. This is called surface mining, open-pit mining, or strip mining.

In the United States alone, about 2,331 square kilometers (900 square miles) of land has been cleared for mining. That's about three-fourths of the area of the entire state of Rhode Island.

The Problem Continues

That's not the end of the problem. Surface-mined land is loaded with substances that are harmful to living things. Rainwater flows easily over this kind of land and carries pollutants into nearby streams, rivers, and lakes. The wind picks up dust, which pollutes the air. In both cases, living things are harmed.

One Solution

We need metals. However, we don't need pollution and ugly landscapes. What can be done? Abandoned surface mines can be reclaimed. That means people can try to restore them as they once were. They can try to turn them into useful ecosystems after secondary succession takes place. This process is difficult and expensive. The restored soil may be poisonous to plants. Also there may not be fertile topsoil to put on the reclaimed land. Therefore, it may be difficult to grow plants there.

Another Solution

Yet maybe there's another solution. Cut down on the mining of metals. How? Reduce how much we use them. How do we do that? We do that by reusing and recycling. Those are the "3 Rs" of conservation—reduce, reuse, recycle.

The activities and health of all living things on Earth are intertwined. What happens to one living thing and one ecosystem usually affects other living things and other ecosystems. To control the effects of changes in ecosystems, people must first understand how they work.

REVIEW

1. Describe how an abandoned farm field becomes a deciduous forest.

2. Give an example of a pioneer community and a climax community.

3. **INTERPRET DATA/INFER** List the evidence that supports the conclusion that the Mediterranean Sea once dried up.

4. Explain how a volcanic eruption might affect an ecosystem.

5. **CRITICAL THINKING** *Apply* Write a regulation that would protect your community from a specific kind of pollution without causing hardships to people, such as business owners.

WHY IT MATTERS THINK ABOUT IT
What things do you do every day that can affect the ecosystem you live in?

WHY IT MATTERS WRITE ABOUT IT
Write a paragraph explaining what you can do to help preserve the ecosystem you live in.

FIRE ECOLOGY

Until 100 years ago, wildfires burned freely in California. In many California ecosystems, fire is a natural part of ecological succession. Fire clears out brush and makes room for new plants. It also recycles nutrients into the forest floor.

Before there were people in California, lightning started most forest fires. Then, approximately 12,000 years ago, Native Americans began using fire to clear the land. By some estimates, Native Americans annually burned over a million acres of Western forest. But big blazes were rare. Fire destroyed thin-barked fir trees, brush, and small plants. Mature, thick-barked pines survived.

In the 1800s, settlers arriving from the East and from Europe prized forests for fuel and wood products to build ships, homes, mines, and entire cities. Fires were considered a wasteful loss of valuable wood. Now most forest fires are extinguished as soon as possible. With many people now living and working near forests, fires cannot be allowed to burn quite so freely.

But fire suppression has created new problems. Old brush, weak fire-prone trees, and tinder build up. The danger of superhot big blazes becomes greater every year as the fuel supply increases. These superhot fires sterilize the soil. Few new plants grow in the burned areas, and the soil erodes. One solution is controlled burning of small areas. Forests can also be selectively thinned to remove dead trees.

DISCUSSION STARTER
1. Why does fire suppression lead to bigger, hotter fires?
2. Why is fire a bigger concern today than 100 years ago?

To learn more about the role of fire in nature, visit *www.mhschool.com/science* and enter the keyword FIRE.

*inter*NET
CONNECTION

SCIENCE WORDS

adaptation p. 304

climax

  community p. 356

commensalism

  p. 309

herbivore p. 290

mutualism p. 306

parasitism p. 308

predator p. 291

prey p. 291

scavenger p. 291

symbiosis p. 306

USING SCIENCE WORDS

Number a paper from 1 to 10. Fill in 1 to 5 with words from the list above.

1. The relationship of ___?___ means that both populations benefit.

2. A relationship between two organisms in which one benefits while the other is harmed is called ___?___.

3. ___?___ is a living thing that is hunted for food.

4. An animal that eats plants is a(n) ___?___.

5. A relationship between two organisms that benefits one without affecting the other is called ___?___.

6–10. **Pick five words from the list above that were not used in 1 to 5, and use each in a sentence.**

UNDERSTANDING SCIENCE IDEAS

11. What is the difference between predators and prey?

12. Describe two ways food moves through a community.

13. How does the structure of a cactus enable it to survive in the desert?

14. Explain why carbon and nitrogen are always available to living things.

15. Describe the role of a vulture.

USING IDEAS AND SKILLS

16. What are two important characteristics of an energy pyramid?

17. What is the relationship between herbivores and carnivores?

18. **USE VARIABLES** Study the table below. Suggest a reason for the change in the eagle population.

ECOSYSTEM CHANGES

Year	Grasslands	Rabbits	Eagles
1960	26,418 km (10,200 mi)	101,000	1,050
1970	23,569 km (9,100 mi)	89,000	864
1980	21,238 km (8,200 mi)	78,000	782
1990	13,727 km (5,300 mi)	42,000	386
2000	13,313 km (5,140 mi)	41,900	378

19. **READING SKILL: SUMMARIZE** What are limiting factors and how do they control the growth of populations?

20. **THINKING LIKE A SCIENTIST** Plants need nitrogen, which is in the air. However, they can't take this nitrogen in. How do plants get nitrogen?

PROBLEMS and PUZZLES

Fire, Exit **SAFETY** Wear goggles. Carbon dioxide is a useful fire extinguisher. Pour about 2/3 cm (1/4 in.) of vinegar into a jar. Add a spoonful of baking soda. This mixture produces carbon dioxide gas, which causes bubbling. While the mixture is bubbling, use a pair of tongs to lower a lighted match into the glass. What happens?

USING SCIENCE WORDS

biotic factor p.245

climax
  community p.356

community p.249

desert p.263

food chain p.288

limiting
  factor p.302

niche p.250

nitrogen
  cycle p.324

omnivore p.291

parasitism p.308

pioneer

  species p.335

scavenger p.291

symbiosis p.306

tundra p.262

USING SCIENCE WORDS

Number a paper from 1 to 10. Beside each number write the word or words that best complete the sentence.

1. The role of a species in an ecosystem is called the species' ___?___.

2. The living parts of an ecosystem are known as ___?___.

3. Bears and people both eat meat and plants and are both ___?___.

4. The path of the energy in food from an insect to the bird that eats it is called a(n) ___?___.

5. Bacteria that grow in peas and bean roots play an important role in the ___?___.

6. The amount of available water can be a(n) ___?___ of the size of a population.

7. Mutualism is a form of ___?___ between two species.

8. The ground below the surface is always frozen in the biome called the ___?___.

9. The biome called the Sahara is a(n) ___?___.

10. The first living thing in an otherwise lifeless area is called a(n) ___?___.

UNDERSTANDING SCIENCE IDEAS

Write 11 to 15. For each number write the letter for the best answer. You may wish to use the hints provided.

11. All of the members of a species in an area make up a(n)
    a. community
    b. habitat
    c. abiotic factor
    d. population
    (Hint: Read page 249.)

12. Because elephants and rabbits eat only plants, they are both
    a. omnivores
    b. scavengers
    c. predators
    d. herbivores
    (Hint: Read page 290.)

13. A key ingredient in plant fertilizer is
    a. carbon
    b. nitrogen
    c. oxygen
    d. hydrogen
    (Hint: Read pages 320–321.)

14. Which biome has the most species of insects, reptiles, and amphibians?
    a. tropical rain forest
    b. deciduous forest
    c. taiga
    d. tundra
    (Hint: Read page 259.)

15. What is the best description of life on Mount Saint Helens today?
    a. no life, barren
    b. a pioneer community
    c. a climax community
    d. a deciduous forest
    (Hint: Read page 330.)

UNIT 4 REVIEW

USING IDEAS AND SKILLS

16. List five abiotic factors that plants and animals need.

17. Someone accidentally spills sugar next to an anthill. Describe what you think will happen to the ant population.

18. Explain why a seal in the food chain *algae → fish → penguin → seal* only gets about one-tenth of 1 percent of the algae's stored energy.

19. What material do decomposers convert dead trees into? What happens to the material?

20. Make a simplified diagram of the carbon cycle.

21. Why is the yucca moth *not* a parasite of the yucca tree?

22. What apparently killed the dinosaurs?

23. **USE VARIABLES** In many places there is an overpopulation of deer. What variable(s) do you think are responsible? How would you remedy this problem?

THINKING LIKE A SCIENTIST

24. **USE NUMBERS** Look at the chart of elk populations on page 252. From 1988 to 1989, the population increased by approximately 15 percent. About how many elk would there be in 1994 if the population increased by 15 percent over the 1993 total?

25. What is the difference between primary succession and secondary succession?

WRITING IN YOUR JOURNAL

SCIENCE IN YOUR LIFE
List four things that limit the number of people who can live in your area. Why are these things limiting factors?

PRODUCT ADS
Advertisements for some products claim that the products are environmentally friendly. What does that mean? What are examples of products that are environmentally friendly and products that are not?

HOW SCIENTISTS WORK
Scientists make observations and gather data to learn about living things and how they interact. How do scientists obtain data? Give four examples from this unit.

Design your own Experiment

What pioneer species live in your area? Design an experiment to find out. Check with your teacher before carrying out the experiment.

interNET CONNECTION

For help in reviewing this unit, visit *www.mhschool.com/science*

PROBLEMS and PUZZLES

Eco-Poems

Follow the directions below to write an eco-poem about an animal of your choice. On the first line, write the name of the animal. Follow the directions on each line after that. Use "The Frog" as your guide. Print your eco-poems on cards, and hang them from the ceiling.

> The Frog—
> Green like a lily pad
> Swimming fast, hopping, jumping
> Preying on flies, sticking out
> its long tongue
> Hiding underwater
> Among the leaves,
> Waiting.

1. Name of animal
2. Color or shape
3. How it moves
4. What it eats
5. Habitats
6. What it often does

School Community

Compare your school with a natural community. Instead of food your school community creates knowledge. Who are the producers of knowledge? The consumers? Does your school have primary and secondary consumers? What niches do different students, teachers, and other school workers fill? Draw a diagram to explain your knowledge community.

Biome Spinner Game

Play with two or more players. Take turns spinning the spinner. Name an animal or plant that lives in the biome that the spinner lands on. Score a point for each plant or animal you name. You may not use a plant or animal that has been used by another player.

Spinner sections: Taiga, Desert, Fresh Water, Tropical Rain Forest, Tundra, Salt Water, Temperate Forest, Grassland

My Dog Has Fleas

To dogs, pests and parasites can be serious problems. What if two new parasites are released into the dog community? One is a flea that irritates the dog but causes no major damage to its body. The other is a worm that kills its dog hosts. Which parasite has a greater chance of becoming a long-term pest for dogs? Explain your answer.

RESOURCES

CHAPTER 9

RESOURCES OF THE CRUST

Earth's crust provides us with minerals of many difrerent colors and shapes. We use them to make everything from concrete to jet aircraft. Some minerals, like gold, are very valuable. What other valuable minerals can you think of?

We also get rocks and soil from Earth's crust. How many different rocks can you name? What is each one used for? How does soil help provide all of the food you eat?

 In Chapter 9 you will have many opportunities to read diagrams for information.

WHY IT MATTERS

Minerals are used in many different ways.

SCIENCE WORDS

mineral a solid material of Earth's crust with a definite composition

luster the way light bounces off a mineral's surface

streak the color of the powder left when a mineral is rubbed against a hard, rough surface

hardness how well a mineral resists scratching

cleavage the tendency of a mineral to break along flat surfaces

ore a mineral containing a useful substance

gem a mineral valued for being rare and beautiful

nonrenewable resource a resource that cannot be replaced within a short period of time or at all

Minerals of Earth's Crust

How many substances do you think make up Earth's solid surface, the crust? Would you believe about 2,000?

The substances that make up Earth's crust are minerals. Here are two of them. One is pure gold. The other looks like gold ore, but isn't. It's nicknamed "fool's gold." Many of the miners who went to California in the 1800s could not tell real gold ore from fool's gold. Which of the two do you think is pure gold?

EXPLORE

HYPOTHESIZE How do you think people can tell minerals apart? Write a hypothesis in your *Science Journal.* Test your ideas.

Investigate How You Can Identify a Mineral

Compare properties of minerals to tell minerals apart.

PROCEDURES

1. COMMUNICATE Use tape and a marker to label each sample with a number. In your *Science Journal*, make a table with the column headings shown. Fill in numbers under "Mineral" to match your samples.

2. OBSERVE Use the table shown as a guide to collect data on each sample. Fill in the data in your table. Turn to the table on page 355 for more ideas to fill in "Other."

CONCLUDE AND APPLY

1. ANALYZE Use your data and the table below to identify your samples. Were you sure of all your samples? Explain.

2. MAKE DECISIONS Which observations were most helpful? Explain.

GOING FURTHER: Problem Solving

3. DRAW CONCLUSIONS How could you make a better Scratch (Hardness) test?

MATERIALS

- mineral samples
- clear tape
- red marker
- copper penny or wire
- streak plate
- porcelain tile
- hand lens
- mineral property table (page 355, or see *Science Journal*)
- nail
- *Science Journal*

Color = color of surface

Porcelain Plate Test = the color you see when you rub the sample gently on porcelain

Shiny Like a Metal = reflects light like a metal, such as aluminium foil or metal coins

Scratch (Hardness): Does it scratch copper? A piece of glass?

Other: Is it very dense? (Is a small piece heavy?) Has it got flat surfaces?

	Mineral	Color	Shiny Like a Metal (Yes/No)	Porcelain Plate Test	Scratch (Hardness)	Other
1. 2.						

What Are Minerals?

What do diamond rings, talcum powder, and aluminum foil have in common? They are made from **minerals**. So are copper wire, teeth fillings, china dishes, and table salt.

With so many differences in minerals, what can they have in common? Minerals are solid materials of Earth's crust. Like all matter they are made of elements. Some minerals, like gold, silver, copper, and carbon, are made of one element. Most minerals are made of compounds, that is, two or more elements joined together.

Whether it is an element or a compound, each mineral has a definite chemical composition. Scientists can identify minerals by checking out the elements or compounds inside.

As minerals form, their atoms and molecules get into fixed patterns. These patterns cause minerals to form geometric shapes, called *crystals*. Different patterns form different crystal shapes. You can see the six main crystal shapes on these pages.

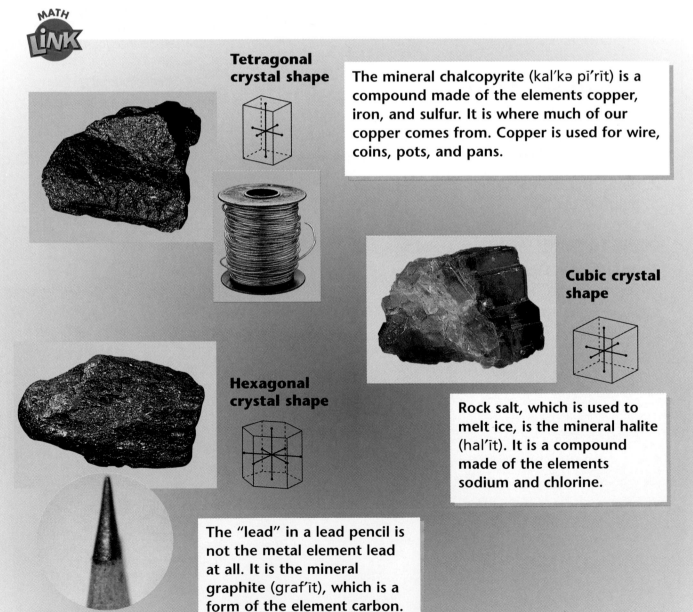

MATH LINK

Tetragonal crystal shape

The mineral chalcopyrite (kal′kə pī′rīt) is a compound made of the elements copper, iron, and sulfur. It is where much of our copper comes from. Copper is used for wire, coins, pots, and pans.

Cubic crystal shape

Hexagonal crystal shape

Rock salt, which is used to melt ice, is the mineral halite (hal′īt). It is a compound made of the elements sodium and chlorine.

The "lead" in a lead pencil is not the metal element lead at all. It is the mineral graphite (graf′īt), which is a form of the element carbon.

How Can You Identify a Mineral?

No two minerals are exactly alike. Each mineral has a different composition. Each has its own set of properties that you can use to tell them apart. Crystal shape is one property. However, telling the exact chemical composition of most minerals or their crystal shape isn't easy. This requires special instruments.

The Explore Activity introduced some simpler properties to use.

- The color of the outer surface of the mineral is the first thing you see. However, if a mineral is exposed to weather, it can become discolored.

Therefore, you should always observe color on a fresh surface. Color alone cannot be used to identify most minerals. Why not? Some minerals come in a variety of colors, and some colors are common to many minerals.

- **Luster** is the way light bounces off a mineral. Minerals with a metallic luster are shiny, like metals. Graphite has a metallic luster.

Minerals with a nonmetallic luster may look shiny or dull. Nonmetallic luster can be described as glassy, waxy, pearly, earthy, oily, or silky. Talc has a nonmetallic luster often described as oily.

Orthorhombic crystal shape

Topaz is a mineral used in many kinds of jewelry. It comes in many colors—pink, pale blue, and even yellow or white.

Brain Power

1. Which minerals on these pages have metallic luster?
2. Which have nonmetallic luster?

The mineral kaolinite (kā'ə lə nīt') is used in china plates and ceramic objects. It comes in many colors—red, white, reddish brown, and even black.

Monoclinic crystal shape

Talc is the mineral used in talcum powder. Talc comes in white and greenish colors.

Triclinic crystal shape

Hematite has a blackish color but a reddish streak.

Galena has three cleavage planes. It breaks into cubes.

Mica has one cleavage plane. It breaks into sheets.

MOHS SCALE OF HARDNESS

Hardness	Sample Mineral	Tool
1	Talc	
2	Gypsum	
		Fingernail
3	Calcite	
		Copper penny/wire
4	Fluorite	
		Iron nail
5	Apatite	
		Glass plate
6	Feldspar	
		Steel file
7	Quartz	
		Streak plate
8	Topaz	
9	Corundum	
10	Diamond	

READING N CHARTS

1. **DISCUSS** Which mineral is the softest? The hardest?
2. **WRITE** Which minerals does a fingernail scratch? Which does a glass plate scratch?

How Can Rubbing and Scratching Help?

Here are three other ways to identify a mineral.

- **Streak** is the color of the powder left when a mineral is rubbed against a hard, rough surface. Rub it against a porcelain streak plate. The streak is always the same for a given mineral, even if the mineral varies in color.

The streak may not be the color of the outer surface of the mineral. Fool's gold, pyrite, is brassy yellow, but it has a greenish black streak. Gold has a yellow streak. You would need a streak plate to tell that the real gold on page 414 is on the right.

- **Hardness** is a measure of how well a mineral resists scratching. Soft minerals are easily scratched. Mohs Scale of Hardness is a numbered list of minerals. Talc, number 1, is the softest mineral. It can be scratched with your fingernail! Any item on the list, including the tools, can scratch something above it. You can use the tools to help find the hardness.

- The way a mineral breaks is also helpful. Some minerals have **cleavage**. This property is the tendency of a mineral to break along flat surfaces. Cleavage is described by the number of directions, or planes, the mineral breaks in.

Many minerals do not break smoothly. They are said to have *fracture*. Quartz, for example, shows jagged edges when it breaks.

Some minerals have special proper-ties that help you identify them. Magnetite, for example, is attracted by a magnet. Some minerals are very dense—such as gold, silver, and galena. Even a small sample feels quite heavy.

PROPERTIES OF MINERALS

MINERAL	COLOR(S)	LUSTER (Shiny as metals)	PORCELAIN PLATE TEST (Streak)	CLEAVAGE (Number)	HARDNESS (Tools Scratched by)	DENSITY (Compared with water)
Gypsum	colorless, gray, white, brown	no	white	yes—1	2 (all five tools)	2.3
Quartz	colorless, various colors	no	none	no	7 (none)	2.6
Pyrite	brassy, yellow	yes	greenish black	no	6 (steel file, streak plate)	5.0
Calcite	colorless, white, pale blue	no	colorless, white	yes—3 (cubes)	3 (all but fingernail)	2.7
Galena	steel gray	yes	gray to black	yes—3 (cubes)	2.5 (all but fingernail)	7.5
Feldspar	gray, green, yellow, white	no	colorless	yes—2	6 (steel file, streak plate)	2.5
Mica	colorless, silvery, black	no	white	yes—1 (thin sheets)	3 (all but fingernail)	3.0
Hornblende	green to black	no	gray to white	yes—2	5–6 (steel file, streak plate)	3.4
Bauxite	gray, red, brown, white	no	gray	no	1–3 (all but fingernail)	2.0–2.5
Chalcopyrite	brassy to golden yellow	yes	greenish black	no	3.5–4 (glass, steel file, streak plate)	4.2
Hematite	black or red-brown	yes	red or red-brown	no	6 (steel file, streak plate)	5.3

A form of calcite shows double image because it refracts light twice as you look through it.

READING CHARTS

1. **WRITE** Which minerals would feel heaviest if you had equal-sized samples of all?
2. **DISCUSS** How is hornblende different from quartz? From feldspar? From mica?

The specks you see in this rock include minerals such as quartz, feldspar, hornblende, and mica. How would you tell them apart?

Quartz crystal

Granite quarry

How Do Minerals Form?

Where do you find minerals? The answer is simple—in the ground. Minerals make up the rocks of the crust. If you examine rocks with a hand lens, you can often find some of the most common rock-forming minerals in the rock.

How do minerals form? Many form when hot liquid rock, or magma, cools and hardens into a solid. Magma is very hot, and its molecules move very fast. When magma cools its molecules slow down and get closer together. Then they connect into a pattern, forming crystals. The longer it takes magma to cool, the more time the

crystals have to grow, and the larger they get. The huge quartz crystal shown here formed in magma that cooled very slowly.

Some of the rarest minerals form deep within Earth. The temperatures are high at great depths. The weight of rocks overhead presses down on rocks below, like a huge pressure cooker. The heat and pressure produce minerals such as diamonds. Movements of Earth's crust then bring the minerals near the surface, where they can be mined.

Diamond

How Do Minerals Form in Water?

Crystals can form from the cooling of hot water. Water heated by magma inside Earth is rich in dissolved minerals. Hot water can hold more dissolved minerals than cold water. As the water cools, it is able to hold less dissolved minerals. The minerals that can no longer stay dissolved form crystals. These crystals then slowly settle to the bottom of the water.

Minerals can also form from evaporation. Ocean water contains many dissolved substances. As the ocean water evaporates, the substances that were dissolved form crystals. Common table salt is mined in areas that were once covered with salt water. The salt is a mineral, halite. It was left behind when an ancient sea evaporated.

The piles of brightly colored minerals in this hot spring form when the heated water cools as it is exposed to the air.

QUICK LAB

Growing Crystals

HYPOTHESIZE How can you watch crystals grow? Write a hypothesis in your *Science Journal*.

MATERIALS
- foam cup half-filled with hot water
- granulated table salt
- 2 plastic spoons
- crystal of rock salt
- string (about 15 cm)
- pencil
- *Science Journal*

PROCEDURES

Your teacher will put a cup of hot water onto a counter for you.

SAFETY Use a kitchen mitt if you need to hold or move the cup. Don't touch the hot water.

1. Gradually add small amounts of salt to the water. Stir. Keep adding and stirring until no more will dissolve.

2. Tie one end of the string to a crystal of rock salt. Tie the other end to a pencil. Lay the pencil across the cup so that the crystal hangs in the hot salt water without touching the sides or bottom.

3. **OBSERVE** Observe the setup for several days. In your *Science Journal*, record what you see.

CONCLUDE AND APPLY

COMPARE AND CONTRAST Did any crystals grow? If so, did they have many shapes or just one? Explain your answer. If not, how would you change what you did if you tried again?

What Are Minerals Used For?

Can you find minerals being used at home or school? Minerals are used to make many products, from steel to electric light bulbs.

Some of the most useful minerals are called **ores** (ôrz). An ore is a mineral that contains a useful substance. Ores contain enough useful substances to make it valuable to mine them.

For example, iron comes from the mineral hematite (hē′mə tīt′). Iron is used to make nails, buildings, and even ships. Aluminum comes from the mineral bauxite. It is used for food-wrap foil, soft-drink cans, and pie tins, just to name a few uses.

The iron and aluminum that come from these two ores are *metals*. Metals have many useful properties. Many of them conduct electricity and can be stretched into wires. The metal copper, for example, comes from a mineral ore. It is used to make electrical wires.

Aluminum is lightweight and strong. It shares these properties with another metal that comes from an ore, magnesium. These metals are ideal for use in building jets and spacecraft.

If you look in a jewelry store window, you'll probably see some minerals called **gems**. Gems are minerals that are valued for being rare and beautiful. You may have seen diamond rings. Rubies and sapphires are other gemstones.

1 Gypsum is used in drywall, or wallboard, for construction of buildings.

2 Gemstones mark special occasions—such as weddings and birthdays. What is your birthstone? Birthstones are gemstones.

Do Minerals Last Forever?

A diamond ring may last centuries. However, Earth's supply of minerals is being used up.

Minerals are **nonrenewable resources**. They cannot be replaced, for example, as trees can be. They take so long to form that they cannot be replaced in your lifetime.

Because minerals are nonrenewable, they must be *conserved*. *To conserve* means "to use wisely or avoid waste." One way people can conserve minerals is by recycling them—finding ways to treat them and use them again. Researchers can also come up with substitutes to use in place of natural minerals. Many diamonds used in industry for cutting stone, for example, are not natural diamonds.

You use minerals all the time. Quartz is just one example. The most common kind of sand is bits of quartz. Quartz sand can be used to make concrete or glass.

Quartz contains the element silicon. This silicon can be removed and used to make computer chips. Quartz crystals, when a small electric current is added, vibrate and can keep time.

REVIEW

1. Which properties are most useful to identify a mineral—streak, color, luster? Explain your answer.

2. **IDENTIFY** What if you had two white samples of talc and gypsum? How would they be alike? How could you tell them apart in one step?

3. How does time affect crystals?

4. How useful are metallic ores? Give some ways you use one of them.

5. **CRITICAL THINKING** *Apply* How could you avoid the mistake that miners made, thinking fool's gold was real gold? What are all the observations you might make to tell them apart?

WHY IT MATTERS THINK ABOUT IT
Start with an empty room. As you decorate it, how might you be using minerals?

WHY IT MATTERS WRITE ABOUT IT
How many ways do you use glass in a typical day? How can you conserve glass? Other minerals?

Monuments to Minerals

The hotel's paint is peeling, but that doesn't matter. The last guest checked out years ago. Nobody lives in this town anymore. It's just one more ghost town in America's West.

Ghost towns were once busy places. Most were built soon after silver, copper, gold, or other minerals were discovered nearby. The towns were like a monument honoring the minerals!

In the late 1800s, hopeful miners and their families rushed to live in these new towns. They left just as quickly when the mines closed.

Jerome, Arizona, was built in 1882 on the steep sides of Cleopatra Hill. The town wasn't far from some new copper and gold mines. By the 1920s Jerome had a population of 15,000. Over time gravity and poor construction caused the town to slide down the hill. Its Sliding Jail moved 70 meters (230 feet)!

Soon Jerome faced bigger problems. By 1945 the copper and gold were gone, so the mines closed. By 1995 Jerome had a population of about 560.

Most ghost towns end up like Copper Hill, Arizona. Set up in 1908, the town had 500 residents, shops, a school, and a hospital by 1925. By 1933 Copper Hill was completely deserted. Can you guess why?

Some ghost towns have been preserved for others to enjoy.

DISCUSSION STARTER

1. What attracted people to places that later became ghost towns?

2. What caused people to leave Jerome and other ghost towns?

To learn more about mining, visit *www.mhschool.com/science* and enter the keyword MINES.

*inter*NET
CONNECTION

WHY IT MATTERS

Rocks come in many types and have many uses.

SCIENCE WORDS

igneous rock a rock that forms when hot, liquid rock material cools and hardens into a solid

sedimentary rock a rock that forms from pieces of other rocks that are squeezed or cemented together

metamorphic rock a rock that forms from another kind of rock that is changed by heat or pressure or by a chemical reaction

humus decayed plant or animal material in soil

pollution adding any harmful substance to Earth's land, water, or air

rock cycle rocks continually changing from one kind into another in a never-ending process

Earth's Rocks and Soil

What is happening here? You're watching solid rock forming before your very eyes. The red-hot material is molten rock that comes from below Earth's surface. At the surface it cools and hardens into solid rock.

Where do you see rocks around you? Have you ever wondered where a rock came from? What kinds of processes form rocks? A rock is like a history book. It was formed and it was changed by many processes. The rock you hold in your hand today may have a history that goes far back in time and place.

EXPLORE

HYPOTHESIZE Are all rocks alike? Are they different? If so, how? Write a hypothesis in your *Science Journal*. How would you test your ideas?

Basalt (bə sôlt′)

Andesite (an′də zīt′)

Coquina (kō kē′nə)

EXPLORE ACTIVITY

Design Your Own Experiment

HOW ARE ROCKS ALIKE AND DIFFERENT?

PROCEDURES

1. Use the tape to number each sample in a group of rocks.

2. CLASSIFY Find a way to sort the group into smaller groups. Determine what properties you will use. Group the rocks that share one or more properties. Record your results in your *Science Journal*.

3. COMPARE You might consider hardness, the ability to resist scratches. Your fingernail, the copper wire, and the edge of a streak plate are tools you might use. Scratch gently.

4. USE NUMBERS You might estimate the density of each sample. Use a balance to find the mass. Use a metric ruler to estimate the length, width, and height. **Length x width x height = volume Density = mass ÷ volume**

MATERIALS

- samples of rocks
- clear tape
- red marker
- hand lens
- copper wire
- streak plate
- balance
- metric ruler
- calculator
- *Science Journal*

CONCLUDE AND APPLY

1. DRAW CONCLUSIONS How were you able to make smaller groups? Give supporting details from the notes you recorded.

2. ANALYZE Could you find more than one way to sort the rocks into groups? Give examples of how rocks from two different smaller groups may have a property in common.

3. COMMUNICATE Share your results with others. Compare your systems for sorting the rocks.

GOING FURTHER: Problem Solving

4. EXPERIMENT If you could not easily measure your samples, how could you find their volume?

5. INFER How might some properties that you observed make a sample useful?

363

How Can You Tell Rocks Apart?

A rock is a mineral or mixture of minerals. Because most rocks are mixtures of things, they are not as easy to tell apart as individual minerals are. One way to identify a rock is by identifying the minerals it contains. Granite, for example, is made up of mica, quartz, feldspar, and hornblende.

Another way to tell rocks apart is by *texture*. The texture is the feel of the surface of the rock. It is based on the size and the shape of pieces of materials in the rock. A coarse rock feels scratchy. A *glassy* rock feels smooth.

Another way to tell rocks apart is by *structure*. The structure is the way the pieces of materials in the rock fit together. The structure may be crystalline (kris′tə lin). That is, the pieces may fit together to make one interlocking mass. Otherwise the structure may appear to be made of chunks or fragments stuck together.

A rock gets its properties from the way it forms. Rocks form from several basic processes. They are grouped by the way they form into three main groups. As you learn about them, look for their textures and structures.

TEXTURE AND STRUCTURE

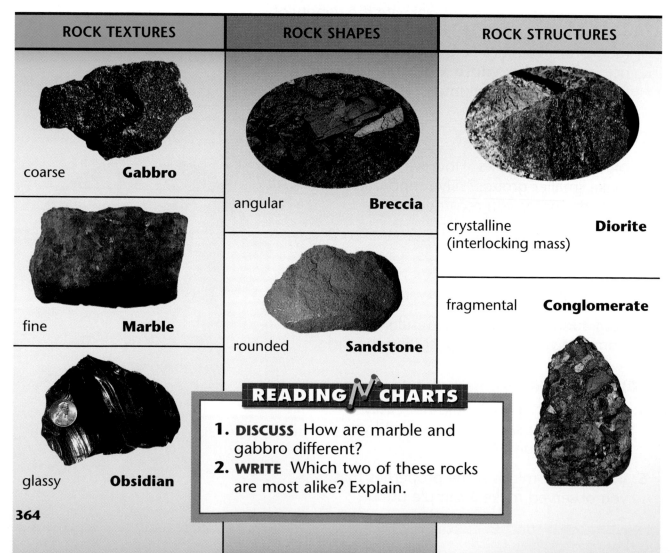

ROCK TEXTURES	ROCK SHAPES	ROCK STRUCTURES
coarse **Gabbro**	angular **Breccia**	crystalline (interlocking mass) **Diorite**
fine **Marble**	rounded **Sandstone**	fragmental **Conglomerate**
glassy **Obsidian**		

READING CHARTS

1. **DISCUSS** How are marble and gabbro different?
2. **WRITE** Which two of these rocks are most alike? Explain.

What Are Igneous Rocks?

The rock forming from molten material on page 362 is an example of an **igneous** (ig'nē əs) **rock**. Igneous rocks form when hot liquid rock material cools and hardens into solid. There are many kinds of igneous rocks. Some have a much coarser, rougher texture than others. The difference depends largely on where the rocks form.

Some igneous rocks form from magma. As it pushes its way up through cracks, it may become trapped. Surrounded by solid rocks, the magma cools slowly. It may take centuries to harden. During this long time, the igneous rocks form with large crystals that give the rocks a coarse texture.

CLASSIFYING IGNEOUS ROCKS

Intrusive: formed below the surface		
ROCK	TEXTURE	COLOR
Granite	coarse	light
Gabbro	coarse	dark

Extrusive: formed above the surface		
ROCK	TEXTURE	COLOR
Rhyolite	fine	light
Basalt	fine	dark
Obsidian	glassy	dark
Pumice	fine	light

READING TABLES

1. **WRITE** Use the table to describe each rock, based on its formation and properties.
2. **DISCUSS** Find another way to organize the table.

Igneous rocks that form underground are called *intrusive* rocks. The *in-* in *intrusive* is for "inside" Earth's crust.

Lava flow

Gabbro

Granite

Magma (trapped)

Igneous Rocks Form from Lava

Magma may reach all the way to Earth's surface before cooling and hardening. At Earth's surface the molten rock may flow from a volcano as *lava*. It may be hurled into the air when a volcano erupts suddenly.

At the surface lava is exposed to cooler temperatures. It cools and hardens quickly. There is not enough time for large crystals to form. These rocks have a fine texture. Some form so quickly, they look like solid glass.

Igneous rocks have different colors, depending on the minerals that make them up. These minerals differ in the magma or lava that produces the rocks.

How Do Sedimentary Rocks Form?

Did you know that a **sedimentary** (sed'ə men'tə rē) **rock** is bits and pieces of rocks clumped together?

Water and wind break down rocks into bits and pieces of sediment. The sediment, in turn, is carried away by wind, moving water, or other forces of erosion.

Eventually the sediment is dropped, or deposited, in a new location. Layers build up. The *pressure*, or weight over a given area, increases. The upper layers press sediment into a bottom layer. This can cause fine particles to squeeze together and harden into a layer of solid rock.

Rock salt, or halite, formed from the mineral calcite, which was dissolved in ocean water.

Many limestones are formed from a chemical process. They formed in the past in layers under seas oroceans. Many of these areas today are dry land.

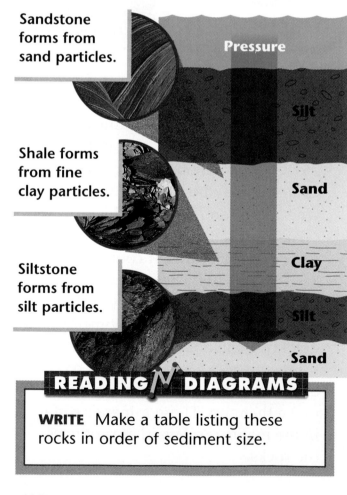

Sandstone forms from sand particles.

Shale forms from fine clay particles.

Siltstone forms from silt particles.

Pressure

Silt

Sand

Clay

Silt

Sand

READING ⚡ DIAGRAMS

WRITE Make a table listing these rocks in order of sediment size.

Rocks Formed from Mineral Crystals

Sedimentary rocks are formed not just by squeezing and compacting bits of sediment. For example, the sediment in some sedimentary rocks is mineral crystals. These rocks form when water dissolves minerals from other rocks. When the water dries up, the minerals are left behind as crystals.

Rocks Formed from Seashells

Some sedimentary rocks are made of sediment that was once part of or made by living things. Many limestones are made of what was once parts of living ocean animals, such as shells. The fragments of shells piled up into layers that became solid rock.

How Can Pressure and Heat Change Rocks?

As you have seen, rocks can have very complex histories. **Metamorphic** (met′ə môr′fik) **rocks** may top the history list. The word *metamorphic* means "change." A metamorphic rock was another kind of rock that "changed." The rocks start out as igneous rocks, sedimentary rocks, or even other *metamorphic rocks!* Then great heat, great pressure, and even chemical reactions change them. They become rocks with different properties.

Metamorphic rocks often form deep underground. Temperatures are high, and the pressure is great from rocks above. In some parts of the crust, rocks over a large area are exposed to great heat and pressure. This can happen along boundaries of colliding plates of the crust. As plates collide, rocks are crumpled and thrust deep underground. The result is metamorphic rocks.

Metamorphic rocks also form when rocks come in contact with hot magma or lava. As magma rises in the crust, layers of rock that it pushes through or against can change into metamorphic rock.

When a metamorphic rock forms, it does not melt. Melting would produce more magma. Instead changes occur in the structure and texture of the rock.

METAMORPHIC ROCK

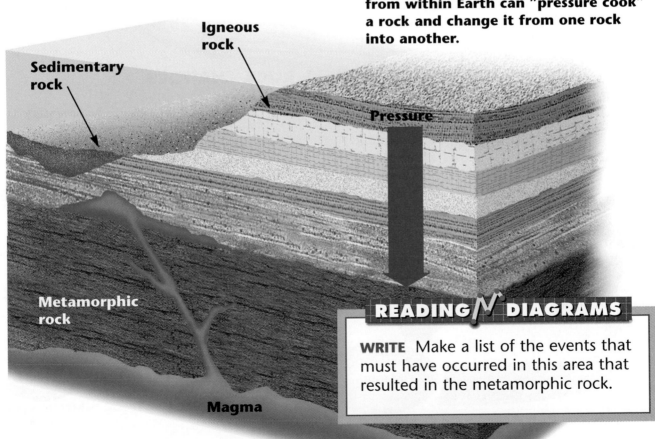

Pressure from overlying rock and heat from within Earth can "pressure cook" a rock and change it from one rock into another.

Sedimentary rock

Igneous rock

Pressure

Metamorphic rock

Magma

READING /N DIAGRAMS

WRITE Make a list of the events that must have occurred in this area that resulted in the metamorphic rock.

What Is Before? What Is After?

A metamorphic rock has undergone a tremendous facelift. Here are some examples of one rock changing into a metamorphic rock. Can you see a similarity from before and after?

One of the more visible effects of change is that you can often see layers form. Look at the layers in the gneiss, for instance. Sometimes, as in slate, you may not see the layers, but the rock breaks in layers. In other cases, such as marble or quartzite, no layers form at all.

EXAMPLES OF ROCK CHANGES

BEFORE | AFTER

Granite (igneous) → Gneiss (metamorphic)

Sandstone (sedimentary) → Quartzite (metamorphic)

Shale (sedimentary) → Slate (metamorphic)

FACTORS AFFECTING ROCK CHANGES

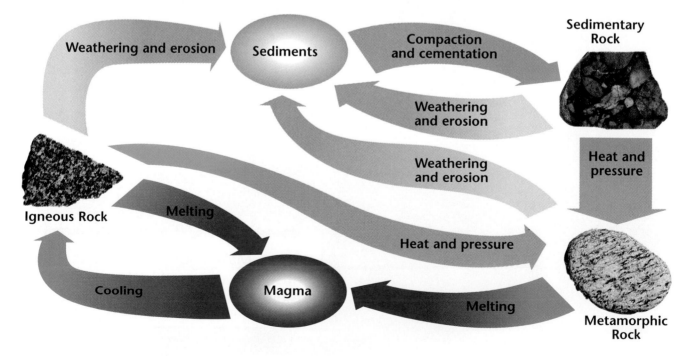

How Useful Are Makeovers?

Metamorphic rocks are "rock makeovers." In their remade form, these rocks have new properties that are very useful.

Slate, for example, breaks into thin sheets. The minerals in slate are so tightly packed together that water cannot seep through this rock. This makes slate useful as roofing shingles as well as stepping stones and outdoor floors.

Marble is often shiny. It often contains minerals that give it brilliant colors, from greenish to red. It is easy to carve. It's often a first choice for making statues, floors, countertops, and monuments.

One kind of coal is a metamorphic rock. It is called anthracite, or hard coal. Anthracite is formed from soft coal.

Anthracite, hard coal, burns cleaner and longer than soft coal, but does not provide as much energy.

THE STORY OF COAL

Millions of Years Ago					
300	280	220	150	10	Present
A forest swamp	Plants die and sink to the bottom.	A thick layer of peat, partly decayed plants, builds up.	The swamp dries up. Buried under layers of sediment, the peat changes to a sedimentary rock called lignite (lig'nĭt).	Buried by more and more layers of sediment, the lignite becomes more compacted. It forms bituminous coal.	Buried even deeper, bituminous coal is changed by great heat and pressure. It forms anthracite, a metamorphic rock.

Peat

Lignite

Bituminous (soft) coal (sedimentary rock)

Anthracite (hard) coal (metamorphic rock)

READING N DIAGRAMS

1. **DISCUSS** How is the position of the fuel layer changing from picture to picture?
2. **WRITE** How does this position affect what happens to the layer?

Skill: Defining Terms Based on Observations

DEFINING SOIL

Earth's crust is made up of rocks and minerals. However, to get to the rocks, you usually have to dig through layers of soil.

Soil looks different at different places. It has different properties. Soil can be sandy. It can be moist.

Just what is soil? Make some observations. Write a definition that fits your observations.

MATERIALS

- moist soil sample in plastic bag
- sand sample in plastic bag
- hand lens
- 2 cups
- 2 plastic spoons
- *Science Journal*

PROCEDURES

1. OBSERVE Use a hand lens to examine a sample of moist soil. What materials can you find? How do their sizes compare? Write a description in your *Science Journal*.

2. COMPARE Some soils are more like sand. How does a sample of sand compare with your moist soil sample?

3. USE VARIABLES Which sample absorbs water more quickly? Fill a cup halfway with sand and another with moist soil. Pour a spoonful of water in each at the same time.

4. EXPERIMENT Which absorbs more water? Make a prediction. Find a way to test your prediction.

5. EXPERIMENT Make any other observations. Look for other differences.

CONCLUDE AND APPLY

1. DRAW CONCLUSIONS Based on your observations, what is soil made up of?

2. DRAW CONCLUSIONS How did soils differ?

3. DEFINE Write a definition for *soil.* Take into account all your observations.

What Has Soil Got to Do with Rocks?

Under a hand lens, you can see that any soil shows that it is a mixture of many things. The main ingredient in soil is weathered rock. Soil may also contain water, air, bacteria, and *humus*. **Humus** is decayed plant or animal material.

Where does soil come from? A layer of solid rock weathers into chunks. The chunks weather into smaller pieces. Living things die and decay and form humus.

Gradually layers of soil, or soil horizons, develop. If you dig down through soil, you can see many layers and the solid rock, bedrock, beneath it. How do the horizons differ?

Soils differ in different locations. In polar deserts there is no A horizon at the top. However, grassland and forest soils can have very thick A horizons. Why do you think this is so? Some soils are very sandy. Why? How would they differ from soils in many farms?

Sometimes the materials in soil match the bedrock below it. Sometimes they do not match. Can you explain why?

Soil is Earth's greatest treasure. All rooted plants need soil to grow. Therefore, almost all living things depend on soil for food—and survival. One of the most important uses of soil is farming. All of the food you eat depends on soil.

SOIL HORIZONS

Brain Power

What is your favorite meal? Can you trace each food in this meal back to the soil?

A horizon

B horizon

C horizon

Bedrock

How Can People Ruin Soil?

People depend on soil. Would you believe people ruin and waste soil? That might include you! It may be people, in general, or industries—such as factories or farms. People often

- get rid of garbage and hazardous wastes by burying them in soil. Hazardous wastes are wastes that may be poisonous or cause diseases, such as cancer.

- spray chemicals on soil to kill unwanted animals and plants. These chemicals become a part of the soil.

- toss foam cups, plastic wrappers, and materials onto the ground, instead of using trash baskets. These materials may be carried by wind or water into the soil. They do not decay. They remain as wastes in the soil. They may build up and make the soil unusable.

All these materials add up to **pollution**. Pollution means adding any harmful substances to Earth's land, water, or air. The substances are called *pollutants*. When people add pollution, we say they *pollute* soil, water, or air.

Not only do people pollute soil, but they often waste it, too. For example, soil needs plants. When plants die and decay, they add valuable substances back into the soil. When a crop is harvested, the plants are removed. They do not decay and return nutrients back into the soil. Growing the same crop year after year uses up the nutrients in soil. Plants don't grow well in nutrient-poor soil.

Plant roots hold soil particles together. They protect soil from being blown or washed away by wind or water. If plants are removed or if weak, sickly plants are growing in an area, the soil is exposed to erosion by wind and rain.

Letting cattle graze in the same area for a long time also exposes soil. Cutting down forests for lumber exposes soil, too. As a result of any of these practices, soil that took centuries to form may be removed in weeks.

Each piece of garbage was thrown away by somebody. It takes people to make garbage. What are some ways to prevent this kind of pollution?

How Can People Protect the Soil?

Have you ever taken care of a pet? If so, what was it like? How did you have to protect your pet?

People also need to take care of soil. We have to protect it from being polluted and wasted. Farmers take care of soil by

- *adding fertilizers and humus.* After growing crops, farmers add these materials to replace minerals removed by crops.

- *rotating crops.* Each year farmers grow different crops. In this way the soil does not use up the same kinds of minerals year after year. Crops from one year may help replace minerals in the soil that are used up another year.

- *strip farming.* Many crops have stems spaced far apart. Rainwater can run off between the stems and wash soil away. In strip farming strips of tightly growing grasses are grown between more widely spaced crops. The grasses trap runoff and the soil it carries. The next year the position of the strips is switched.

- *contour plowing.* Farmers plow furrows across a slope rather than up and down a slope. Each furrow traps rainwater and keeps it from eroding the soil.

- *terracing.* A hillside is shaped into a series of steps. Runoff water and eroded soil get trapped on the steps

- *planting wind breaks.* Planting rows of trees to block the wind prevents soil from being blown away.

What can you do to prevent soil from being polluted or wasted? Think about what you toss away as garbage. Is there any way to throw it away to make sure it does not simply end up in the soil? Is there any way to keep from throwing as much away each day as you might?

Contour means "shape." How does contour plowing prevent water from running downhill?

By building terraces people in Bali have been able to farm steep hillsides.

How Do Rocks Get Made Over Again and Again?

Where do rocks and soil come from? Igneous rocks come from magma or lava. However, where did the magma and lava come from? Magma or lava, remember, is melted rock material.

Sedimentary rock is made of broken up pieces of rock. However, where did the pieces of rock come from?

You also learned that a rock had to exist in order to change into a metamorphic rock. Where do the existing rocks come from?

All rocks come from other rocks! Rocks are constantly changing from one rock into another. They change in a never-ending series of processes called the **rock cycle**. Part of this cycle is the weathering of rocks into bits and pieces—some of which may eventually become soil.

Rocks are constantly forming—one changing into another. However, any rock takes a really long time to form. When we dig up a deposit of sandstone or use up the coal in an area, it cannot be replaced. Rocks are a non-renewable resource.

Soil may take centuries to form. However, with care, people can prevent it from being wasted. Fertilizers and humus may replenish overused soil. In many ways soil is renewable—but only with care.

READING IN DIAGRAMS

1. **WRITE** Describe a way a sedimentary rock can become an igneous rock.
2. **DISCUSS** How might it become a metamorphic rock?
3. **DISCUSS** How might it become another sedimentary rock?

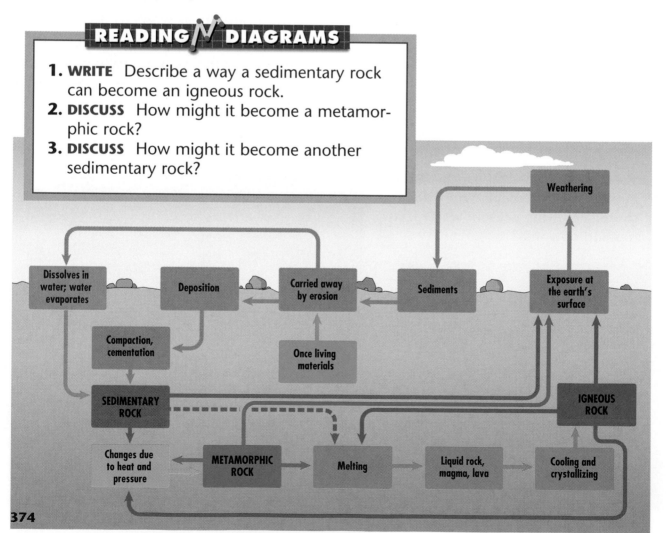

Can People Make Rocks?

The rock cycle diagram does not show how people get into the rock-making process.

Concrete is a rock material made out of water, sand, and chunks of gravel, held together with a binding mixture. The binding mixture is made of limestone and shale, crushed to a fine powder, mixed with gypsum and another mineral.

Some bathtubs are made from a human-made rock. Porcelain is clay that has been heated to a high temperature and then cooled. It contains mostly the mineral kaolinite.

Bricks are another artificial rock. Made mostly of clay, they can be shaped while soft and then baked in an oven to rock hardness. How many other human-made rocks can you find?

Concrete is made of sand and gravel, mixed with powdered limestone and shale, minerals, and water. Where is concrete used in your neighborhood?

It is important to be able to tell one type of rock from another. Just think of all the ways you use rocks. What would life be like without them? There would be no mountains to climb, no beaches to walk on. There would be no soil—so that means no food, or forests, or fields. There would be no metals, because metals come from mineral ores that are found in rocks. There would be no bricks, no concrete, no buildings, no . . .

REVIEW

1. **DEFINE** How can you tell rocks apart? Why are they different to identify than minerals?

2. How can you tell igneous rocks apart?

3. You pick up a rock. How can you tell if it is a sedimentary rock?

4. How are soils alike? How are they different?

5. **CRITICAL THINKING** *Synthesize* How can an igneous rock become a metamorphic rock? Think of three different ways.

WHY IT MATTERS THINK ABOUT IT
How are rocks a part of your life?

WHY IT MATTERS WRITE ABOUT IT
How do you depend on soil, even if you don't live anywhere near a farm?

Forest Resources: MORE THAN JUST TIMBER!

You might think of forests just as providers of wood, paper products, wildlife, and recreation. But forests actually do so much more! Forests supply water to a thirsty world. They clean the air and prevent soil from eroding. They even keep the climate from becoming too hot!

About 85 percent of California's water supply passes through forest soils. Good forest soil is like a sponge that absorbs water from rain and melting snow. The soil then releases this water gradually so that it flows gently into streams. Forest soils and tree roots also filter out pollutants. Healthy forest soils help protect California's almost 13,000 km (8,000 miles) of rivers from mud and pollutants. California has about 37 percent of its land area in forests. California harvests about $1 billion worth of pine, fir and other trees for lumber every year. Forests worldwide also supply us with $11 billion worth of nuts, medicines, oils and other products every year. Fortunately, people realize the value of trees. The United States now plants more trees every year than are cut down.

Forests also protect the air we breathe. Trees act like giant air filters. As trees grow, carbon dioxide and pollutants are absorbed from the air. The carbon in trees is recycled into the soil when trees decompose. This slows global warming. Trees also respire fresh oxygen into the air for us to breathe.

Stream

Life Science Link

CO₂

O₂

DISCUSSION STARTER

1. Why are forest soils good for the water supply?

2. How do forests help cleanse the air we breathe?

3. What is the most valuable function of forests?

Melting snow

Carbon

Water

To learn more about forest resources, visit *www.mhschool.com/science* and enter the keyword TREASURE.

*inter*NET
CONNECTION

377

WHY IT MATTERS

California's wealth of minerals, rocks, and soils is a valuable natural resource.

SCIENCE WORDS

lode a veinlike mineral deposit (often gold) in solid rock

prospector a person who searches for gold or other precious minerals

placer deposits particles of gold found in loose gravel

California's Soil, Rocks, and Minerals

Ever since the great 1848 Gold Rush, people have been coming to California to look for rocks and minerals. The state has one of the richest varieties of rocks in the nation. Can you name the kinds of rocks that are common in your area? Do you know what minerals are found in the state? What does the force of plate tectonics have to do with the rocks, minerals, and soils that exist in California?

EXPLORE

HYPOTHESIZE Gold and other valuable minerals have been found in California streambeds. What might be a simple way to separate the minerals from sand and gravel? Write a hypothesis in your *Science Journal*. Test your ideas.

Investigate How to Pan for Gold

Learn to pan for gold and other minerals.

MATERIALS
- small shallow aluminum pan about 15 cm (6 in.) in diameter
- larger pan to catch sand and water spillover
- water
- bucket full of silt, sand, fine gravel collected from a stream or other convenient source
- *Science Journal*

PROCEDURES

1. Fill the small pan half full with the silt, sand, and gravel mixture.

2. Add enough water to fill the pan almost to the brim. For the remaining steps, hold this pan over the larger catch basin.

3. Stir the mixture carefully to make sure it is wet. Tilt the pan slightly and swirl the mixture.

4. As the mixture moves, lighter materials will separate to the top of the mixture. Allow these to spill *slowly* out and into the catch basin.

5. Continue swirling slowly, until nearly all the sand mixture has been washed out. You may have to add water once or twice before you are finished.

6. Collect the remaining minerals from the bottom of the pan and examine closely.

CONCLUDE AND APPLY

1. OBSERVE What did you find in the bottom of your pan? Describe the size, shape, and color of the material.

2. COMPARE Compare material from the bottom of the pan with the materials in your catch basin.

GOING FURTHER: Problem Solving

3. HYPOTHESIZE What kind of stream would be best for panning for minerals?

Why Does California Have So Many Rocks and Minerals?

California is a paradise for *rock hounds*, people who collect rocks. A huge number of different rocks are found in the state. There are also more than 600 kinds of minerals. Fifty of these are found nowhere else. How did all these rocks and minerals get here?

The answer is plate tectonics. For millions of years, what is now California has been a meeting place of tectonic plates. Ocean plates have pushed toward the North American plate and descended beneath it. As they moved, these plates carried bits and pieces of crust from as far away as the Equator. These pieces of crust included many different kinds of rocks. Many of them ended up as part of California.

When ocean plates descended beneath California, volcanoes were formed. Lava flows created igneous rocks. Magma beneath the surface solidified into more masses of igneous rock. Heat and tectonic pressures created metamorphic rocks.

Much later, a different tectonic process began. A new ocean plate collided with North America. Instead of sliding beneath it, the new plate moved slantwise against it. The pressure crumpled the crust, forcing up mountain ranges. Rocks from deep below ground came to the surface. These rocks had formed at different times in different places. Some were igneous rocks formed from magma. Others were sedimentary rocks formed in ancient seabeds. This process is still continuing today. It is the reason for the variety of rocks and minerals in California.

Where tectonic plates collided, rocks from deep below ground have been pushed to the surface. [above] "Rock hounds" can find 600 different kinds of minerals in California.

SHEAR

Where Are the Oldest and Youngest Rocks?

Do you think that you could recognize California's oldest rocks? It is not easy to tell how old rocks are. Even geologists often need special electronic equipment to do the job.

In California, some rocks are very old and others are much younger. In parts of the state you find older rocks as you travel inland from the coast. That is because the land was formed by tectonic forces. Pieces of crust were jammed against North America one after another. The oldest rocks arrived first, and younger rocks were later jammed against them. The sedimentary rocks that were formed on the sea floor are also very old. These rocks were later pushed to the surface when tectonic forces created mountains. Good places to look for these very old rocks are in the Sierra Nevada or near Death Valley.

Rocks from the age of dinosaurs are common in California. Many of them contain the fossils of ancient sea creatures. That is because much of what is now California once lay beneath the sea. A good place to look for these rocks is in the Coast Ranges near San Francisco. Traces of land dinosaurs have been found in rocks of the eastern Mojave Desert.

California's youngest rocks are those formed by active volcanoes. As recently as the early 1900s, new rocks were formed by lava flows from Lassen Peak in the Cascade Range. In that area, the rock formation process is still going on.

For a geologist, rocks tell the story of events in Earth's history.

What Are California's Igneous Rocks?

Igneous rock is rock formed when melted rock material cools and hardens. Granite and basalt are two examples. Where would you expect to find igneous rock in California?

Erupted lava has formed igneous rocks in this volcanic landscape in northern California.

You are correct if you answered "near California's volcanoes." In northeastern California, near the active and recently active volcanoes, there is a lot of igneous rock. Much of it is dark-colored basalt. This basalt was formed from erupted lava. In some parts of this region, large areas are covered with shattered pieces of basaltic rock.

Igneous rock is found in other areas, too. In those parts of California, igneous rock was formed by magma. The magma cooled and hardened below ground. In eastern California, this process formed a gigantic underground block of granite. Much later, tectonic pressure caused the granite block to tilt upward. The tilting formed the high peaks of the Sierra Nevada range. These mountains are made largely of granite.

In other parts of California, very ancient igneous rocks have undergone "makeovers." Many of these rocks were originally formed by lava or magma far away. Some were once part of ancient island chains. Millions of years ago, tectonic plates carried the islands to California. The surface rocks were piled up along the California coast. Today, they are part of the Coast Ranges. Over time, the rocks became metamorphic rocks. But in many cases, they have kept their original shape. That is how geologists can tell that these were once igneous rocks.

What Are California's Sedimentary Rocks?

Sedimentary rock is rock made of bits of matter compacted together. There are many kinds of sedimentary rock in California. Most were formed when matter was deposited on ancient seabeds. The seabeds were later forced upward by tectonic pressure. Today, you can find sedimentary rock in many California mountain ranges.

One common sedimentary rock is sandstone. You can find it throughout California. It is particularly common in the Coast Ranges north of San Francisco. It is gray-brown and often contains bits and pieces of other rocks.

Shale is another common sedimentary rock in California. You often find shale together with sandstone. Shale is usually dark gray or black in color.

A third type of sedimentary rock is chert. It is formed from tiny marine organisms deposited on the floors of very deep ocean basins. Today, you can find chert in the Coast Ranges, the Transverse Ranges, and the Klamath Mountains. Chert can be black, brown, red, green, or white. It is very dense and hard. It can resist erosion when other nearby rocks are worn away. In landscapes near San Francisco, many hills are made of chert.

A fourth kind of sedimentary rock is limestone. Limestone is found on the San Francisco peninsula, where it is quarried to make cement and concrete. It is also found in some of the mountain ranges of California.

Look for layers of sedimentary rock where roads cut through a hillside.

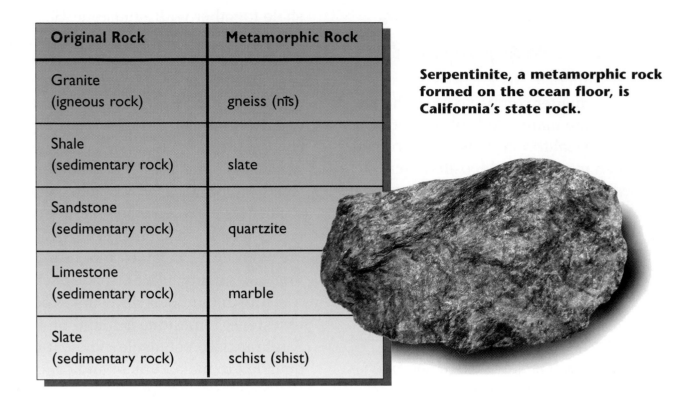

Original Rock	Metamorphic Rock
Granite (igneous rock)	gneiss (nīs)
Shale (sedimentary rock)	slate
Sandstone (sedimentary rock)	quartzite
Limestone (sedimentary rock)	marble
Slate (sedimentary rock)	schist (shist)

Serpentinite, a metamorphic rock formed on the ocean floor, is California's state rock.

What Are California's Metamorphic Rocks?

Metamorphic rocks are rocks formed under heat and pressure from some other kind of rock. In California, there are many types of metamorphic rock.

One common type is serpentinite. It was formed in the crust of an ocean plate deep beneath the bottom of the sea. There water seeped down into igneous rocks rising from the mantle. This process changed the rocks. They became smooth and shiny, with a green-and-white color pattern that looks like a snakeskin. Later, the ocean plate carried these rocks toward the North American coast. When the plate slid under North America, the rocks ended up jammed against the shore. Other pieces of crust followed.

Today, serpentinite is found as far inland as the Sierra Nevada. It is often found near faults, where deep rocks have been brought to the surface. Serpentinite is California's state rock.

Another common metamorphic rock in California is slate. It was originally shale or sandstone. You can find slate in the western foothills of the Sierra Nevada.

Schist is a metamorphic rock that is common in many mountain areas. In southern California, you can find it in the Santa Monica and San Gabriel mountains. In northern California, you can find it in the Klamath Mountains.

Marble, a valuable metamorphic rock, is rare in California. It is found only in the Sierra Nevada and in the Klamath Mountains. Marble is formed from limestone, a sedimentary rock.

What Minerals Are Found in California?

California is rich in many kinds of minerals. Once again, the reason is plate tectonics. Moving tectonic plates have brought many minerals to California. Tectonic forces have caused minerals to form deep within the Earth.

Common minerals in California include quartz, feldspars, mica, and hornblende. Hematite is visible in red-colored rocks in California's mountains. Calcite is found in marble and in sedimentary rocks.

California's most famous mineral is gold. It was first discovered in the Sierra Nevada in 1848. The rocks in which it was found are part of an ancient ocean plate. That ocean plate was the same one that brought serpentinite to California.

The plate collided with North America in the age of the dinosaurs. As the plate slid beneath North America, hot magma flowed upward to form granite. Some of the magma contained gold. When the magma came into contact with water, the gold dissolved out of the magma. The dissolved gold rose through cracks in the crust. As it cooled, it hardened into metal. Quartz crystals formed around the gold to create a **lode,** or veinlike mineral deposit. Much later, when the granite rose to form the Sierra Nevada, the gold-quartz deposits became part of the mountains too.

Starting in 1848, prospectors began looking for gold. **Prospectors** are people who search for precious minerals. They looked for gold-quartz lodes. They also looked for **placer deposits**, particles of gold found in loose gravel in stream beds. They learned that wherever they found serpentinite, they might find gold.

Today, most of California's lode gold is gone. But there is still a wealth of other minerals in California's rocks and soil.

Gold was mined in these Sierra Nevada foothills in the 1800s.

How Do People Use California's Rocks and Minerals?

Take a look around you for things made from minerals. Each American uses an average of 18,000 kg (40,000 pounds) of minerals each year for various purposes. Minerals are used to create concrete, cleaning supplies, tires, and even toothpaste. At least 30 different minerals are used to build a typical computer. More than 80 kinds of minerals are mined in California each year. Almost every part of the state has some useful mineral deposits.

Many of the minerals you are using right now probably came from California. There is a good chance that the sand, gravel, and cement in the sidewalk, streets, and buildings around you probably came from California quarries. Gypsum mined in California is used to make plaster and in constructing the walls of your house.

Mercury mined in California is used in thermometers and electrical switches. Zinc is coated on steel to prevent rust. Tungsten is added to steel to make it stronger. Copper is made into wire to conduct electricity.

Mines in California's southeastern deserts produce borax. This mineral is used to make enamel and certain cleaning materials. The first borax mines were near Death Valley. Today, the main borax mines are in the Mojave Desert.

Where did the freeways come from? California is a leading producer of the concrete used in sidewalks and streets.

What Is Special About California Soils?

The next time you take a walk, stop and look for patches of bare soil. What color is the soil? In California, chances are that you will find many different colors of soil along your walk.

Soil color is determined by the kind of rock from which the soil was formed. Different kinds of rock weather down into different-colored soils. Some California soils come from sandstone. Some come from sedimentary rock washed downstream as silt. Some are full of clay. Some have a red color that shows the presence of iron. California has a greater variety of soils than most other states because it has so many different kinds of rocks.

In the Central Valley, soil conditions are ideal for farming. Central Valley soils are made from sediment washed down by rivers from nearby mountains. The sediment has been deposited on a vast, flat floodplain. Plants have been growing on the floodplain surface for thousands of years. They have enriched the soil with organic material. Today, the Central Valley is one of America's most productive farming areas. Farmers take advantage of the mild climate to harvest as many as three or four crops each year.

In California's deserts, soil conditions are very different. Because there is so little rain, weathering and soil formation take place very slowly. Minerals coat the soil surface instead of dissolving into the ground. There is little vegetation to enrich the soil with organic material. There are few plants to hold the soil in place, so the wind often blows it away.

QUICK LAB

Identifying Soils in Your Neighborhood

HYPOTHESIZE How can you identify the different soils in your neighborhood? Write a hypothesis in your *Science Journal.*

MATERIALS
- 3 or 4 cups or plastic bags of soil samples
- water
- plastic spoon
- *Science Journal*

PROCEDURES

1. Add a few teaspoons of water to each soil sample. Add just enough water to make the soil sticky.

2. **OBSERVE** What color is each soil sample? What minerals do you think are in your soil? (See the list of minerals on page 355). Record what you see in your *Science Journal.*

3. Add a few teaspoons of water to each soil sample to wet the soil.

4. Feel the soil. Record your observations. Sandy soil feels gritty. Silt feels smooth and slippery. Clay feels sticky.

CONCLUDE AND APPLY

1. **DRAW CONCLUSIONS** Based on color, what rocks or minerals do you think the soil came from?

2. **DRAW CONCLUSIONS** Based on texture, what are your soils made up of: sand, silt, clay, or a mixture of the three?

What Are the Major Threats to California's Soils?

Can you guess what are the biggest threats to California's soils? One is the building of new towns and cities. Every year new homes and streets cover thousands of acres of California's farmlands. Soils that produced crops of fruits and vegetables are paved over and lost to farming. Today, however, many people recognize that farmland is worth protecting. Builders are encouraged to build on land that is not usable for farming. Steps are being taken to preserve farming areas and their soil resources.

Another threat to California's soils comes from irrigation. Many farms are irrigated because rainfall is scarce. The water dissolves certain minerals called salts in the soil. The dissolved salts are carried downward through the soil.

Under normal rainfall conditions, this process is very slow. However, irrigation water can quickly dissolve and carry large amounts of salts. In some areas, the downward flow is blocked by layers of clay. Where this happens, salt deposits build up in the soil. These deposits can harm or even kill crops growing in the soil.

Scientists estimate that about one-tenth of the soil in the Central Valley has been damaged by salt deposits. They are now looking for ways to solve the problem. One suggestion is to build drains beneath the fields to carry away the salty water. However, when this idea was tried, new problems arose. When the salty water was drained into a nearby reservoir, waterbirds in the area were harmed. Scientists are now seeking other ways to reduce salt buildup in Central Valley soils.

Soil problems like these do not happen only on farms. They can happen even in

In many areas, new streets and houses are covering land once used for farming.

your garden. Many California gardens contain plants that originally grew in a wetter climate. These plants require heavy watering, which can cause the same kind of soil problem as irrigation. One solution is to fill your garden with native California plants. These plants can survive without the extra watering that can damage soils.

Gardening with native plants can protect the soil.

You depend on rocks and soil for many things in your life. California is rich in these natural resources. Gold and other minerals were one of the main reasons people came to the state in the 1800s. Today, many of the things you use are made from California rocks and minerals. Many of the fruits and vegetables you eat are grown in California soils. Understanding and protecting these resources is important for your future.

REVIEW

1. What kind of rock is serpentinite?

2. Where can you find California's oldest and youngest rocks?

3. What mineral is often found where gold is found?

4. **COMPARE AND CONTRAST** How is Central Valley soil different from soil in the desert?

5. **CRITICAL THINKING** *Infer* Why might sedimentary rocks from a California mountain contain fossil sea creatures?

WHY IT MATTERS THINK ABOUT IT
Why does California have more kinds of rocks than most other states?

WHY IT MATTERS WRITE ABOUT IT
Do you live near a volcano, earthquake faultline, or the coast? How does your location affect which rocks, minerals, and soils you could collect?

SCIENCE MAGAZINE

STILL PANNING FOR GOLD

The greatest gold rush in United States history was the 1848 California Gold Rush. It all began with the discovery of gold at Sutter's Mill, in the Sierra Nevada foothills near Sacramento. It was a cool Monday morning in January as James Marshal walked along the stream. Something shiny attracted his attention. He reached down and picked up the shiny rock. "I think it's gold," he muttered.

News of the gold find in California spread quickly to the East Coast and around the world. During the next ten years, more than 150,000 people came to California. Some came looking for gold. Others came to start businesses to serve gold prospectors. Most people found very little of the precious metal. It is estimated that only one in 1,000 miners found enough gold to get rich.

Gold is still found in California today. Each year amateur and professional gold prospectors collect more than a million ounces of gold. Amateur collectors have the best chance of finding gold if they look in places where gold has been found before.

Gold can be found in two kinds of places. It can be found within solid rock called lode gold. Much of California's lode gold has been dug out. Gold can also be found in streams, trapped in the rocks, sands and silt. These stream deposits are called placer deposits. People have a better chance of finding gold in streams near known deposits.

What is the simplest method for amateur prospectors to collect gold? The answer is panning. Panning is used to separate the gold from the silt, sand, and gravel of the stream deposits. A wash basin or special pan is used to scoop up water, sand, and gravel from a stream. Gold is much heavier than the minerals that make up the sand and gravel. So when the pan is shaken and swirled, the grains and flakes of gold sink and collect on the bottom of the pan. As the lighter materials are separated from the gold, they can be removed from the pan. What is left is the the gold.

If you want to look for gold in California, keep these rules in mind. If you plan to prospect on private property, you must always get permission from the owner. Before prospecting on federal land, contact the United States Bureau of Land Management.

DISCUSSION STARTER

1. Where do you have the best chance of finding gold in California today?

2. Why does gold separate from sand and gravel during panning?

To learn more about gold, visit *www.mhschool.com/science* and enter the keyword GOLD.

*inter*NET
CONNECTION

SCIENCE WORDS

streak p. 354

igneous rock p. 365

lode p. 385

luster p. 353

metamorphic
  rock p. 367

mineral p. 352

ore p. 358

pollution p. 372

rock cycle p. 374

sedimentary rock
  p. 366

USING SCIENCE WORDS

**Number a paper from 1 to 10. Fill in
1 to 5 with words from the list above.**

1. Rock that changes due to heat and
pressure is __?__.

2. A veinlike mineral deposit in solid
rock is called a(n) __?__.

3. __?__ is the color of the powder left
when a mineral is rubbed against a
hard, rough surface.

4. The way light bounces off a mineral's
surface is called __?__.

5. A(n) __?__ is a mineral containing a
useful substance.

6–10. **Pick five words from the list
above that were not used in 1 to 5,
and use each in a sentence.**

UNDERSTANDING SCIENCE IDEAS

11. Describe the difference in the way
sedimentary and igneous rocks are
formed.

12. Explain the difference between
bituminous coal and anthracite.

13. Describe the rock cycle.

14. Describe two tests you can
use to determine what minerals a rock is made of.

15. What are two ways to tell
rocks apart?

USING IDEAS AND SKILLS

16. Describe two ways that farmers can
protect the soil.

17. Tension, compression, and shear
affect rock differently. Is this true or
false? Explain your answer.

18. **READING SKILL: READING
DIAGRAMS.** Examine the chart on
page 355. Of the minerals listed,
which one is densest compared with
water?

19. **DEFINE** You find a rock that is
made up of different-colored
layers. It seems to be made of differ-
ent-sized grains. Some of it looks as
though it is made of tiny seashells
glued together. What type of rock
is it?

20. **THINKING LIKE A SCIENTIST** Do you
think wet or dry sand warms up
faster in sunlight? Why? State and
explain your hypothesis. Describe
how you might test your idea.

PROBLEMS and PUZZLES

Not Just Dirt Where would you
expect to find more living things, in
soil from a desert of in soil from a
forest? Explain your answer.

CHAPTER 10
EARTH'S AIR, WATER, AND ENERGY

You can't drink ocean water. However, water from the oceans is part of a cycle that produces clouds, rain, and water for Earth's land— fresh water.

The oceans also provide food and, in some places, energy. Drilling into the ocean bottom at places off the coast provides a rich source of oil.

How else does planet Earth provide materials that make life possible?

In Chapter 10 you will read in order to practice drawing conclusions.

WHY IT MATTERS

Air pollution affects everyone and everything.

SCIENCE WORDS

renewable resource a resource that can be replaced in a short period of time

ozone layer a layer of ozone gas in the atmosphere that screens out much of the Sun's UV rays

fossil fuel a fuel formed from the decay of ancient forms of life

smog a mixture of smoke and fog

acid rain moisture that falls to Earth after being mixed with wastes from burned fossil fuels

Earth's Atmosphere

Every day American cars burn about 500 million gallons of gasoline. How do you think this affects the land, air, and water?

How can the air be different from day to day? The air may seem clear and clean on some days. If you live in or near a big city, you may have days when the air seems smoky, or "hazy." Why?

EXPLORE

HYPOTHESIZE What kinds of pollutants are in the air that can make it look as it does in the picture? Write a hypothesis in your *Science Journal*. Test your ideas.

EXPLORE ACTIVITY

Investigate What Makes Air Dirty

Try to collect pollutants to analyze them.

MATERIALS

- 12 cardboard strips, about 12 cm long
- petroleum jelly
- plastic knife
- transparent tape
- string
- hand lens
- metric ruler
- marker
- *Science Journal*

PROCEDURES

1. Make square "frames" by taping together the corners of four cardboard strips. Make three frames, and label them A, B, and C. Tie a 30-cm string to a corner of each frame.

2. Stretch and attach three strips of tape across each frame, with all sticky sides facing the same way. Use a plastic knife to spread a thin coat of petroleum jelly across each sticky side.

3. PREDICT Hang the frames in different places to try to collect pollutants. Decide on places indoors or outdoors. Be sure to tell a parent or teacher where.

4. OBSERVE Observe each frame over four days. Note the weather and air condition each day in your *Science Journal*.

5. USE NUMBERS Then collect the frames. Observe the sticky sides with a hand lens and a metric ruler to compare particles.

CONCLUDE AND APPLY

1. INTERPRET DATA How did the frames change over time? How did the hand lens and ruler help you describe any pollution?

2. COMMUNICATE Present your data in a graph to show differences in amounts.

GOING FURTHER: Problem Solving

3. PLAN What kinds of pollutants would your frames not collect? How might you design a collector for them?

4. PLAN How might you extend this activity over different periods of time?

395

How Do Living Things Use Air?

Why couldn't humans live on a planet that does not have an atmosphere as on Earth? Every minute of every day you need air.

Air is a mixture of nitrogen, oxygen, and a few traces of other gases, including water vapor. This mixture is a vital resource. It supports and protects life on Earth in many ways.

Almost all organisms need air to live. Actually, they need oxygen, one of the gases that is in air. On land, living things have structures that enable them to get oxygen directly from the air. Living things in water habitats take in oxygen that is dissolved in the water.

What is oxygen for? Living things take in oxygen for respiration. In this process oxygen is used to break down food so that energy can be gotten from it. As a result of this process, living things give off wastes, including the gas carbon dioxide.

Why doesn't the atmosphere fill up with carbon dioxide? Plants and other producers, living things that have the green substance chlorophyll, take in carbon dioxide. They use it for making food. In the presence of light, these organisms carry on the process called photosynthesis. In this process they make food and give off oxygen.

Producers range in size from green plants to one-celled algae. They replace oxygen in the atmosphere. This makes oxygen a naturally **renewable resource.** A renewable resource is one that can be replaced. It can be replaced in a short enough period of time, such as a human lifetime, to support life on Earth.

Brain Power

How do you take in oxygen? What are some structures that animals have to take in oxygen? How do plants take in oxygen?

HOW EARTH'S ATMOSPHERE SUPPORTS LIFE

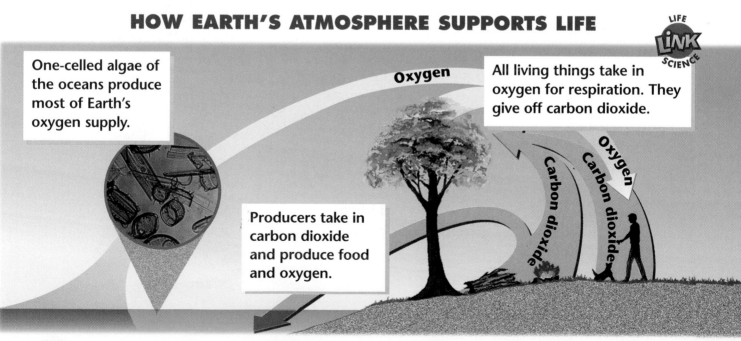

One-celled algae of the oceans produce most of Earth's oxygen supply.

Producers take in carbon dioxide and produce food and oxygen.

Oxygen

All living things take in oxygen for respiration. They give off carbon dioxide.

Oxygen

Carbon dioxide

Oxygen

Carbon dioxide

How Does Air Protect?

The atmosphere also acts as a protective shield. It shields Earth's surface from harmful energy that comes from the Sun. The atmosphere helps screen out harmful radiation, such as X rays, gamma rays, and most ultraviolet rays (UV rays) from the Sun. About 30 kilometers above your head is a layer of gas called ozone (ō′zōn). This **ozone layer** screens out from 95 to 99 percent of the Sun's UV rays.

The atmosphere also shields Earth from rocks from space. The "shooting stars" you see on a clear night are not stars. They are rocks from space that burn up due to friction with the air as they speed through the atmosphere.

The atmosphere also protects life from extremes of temperature. Clouds block sunlight during the day. At night they keep much of the heat from escaping into space, so that the planet does not "cool off." Whenever one part of the atmosphere gets hotter than another, the air moves or circulates in ways that spread the heat around.

Most of the air, about 78 percent, is nitrogen. Nitrogen is an important ingredient in food, namely proteins. How does it get into proteins? Nitrogen is taken from the air by certain kinds of bacteria. These bacteria change the nitrogen into a form that stays in the soil.

Plants use the changed form of nitrogen to make proteins. As living things eat the plants, nitrogen is passed along. It is returned to the air when living things die.

READING N DIAGRAMS

1. **DISCUSS** Do you see any cycles in this picture? Cycles are continuous processes, where one thing happens after another over and over in the same order.
2. **WRITE** Explain any cycles you see.

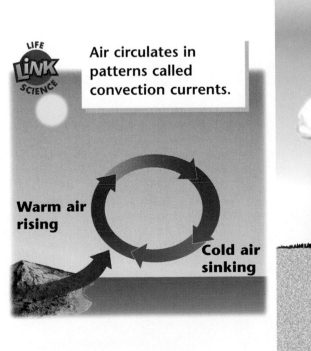

LIFE LINK SCIENCE

Air circulates in patterns called convection currents.

Warm air rising

Cold air sinking

Clouds at night prevent heat from escaping.

Nitrogen in air

Nitrogen goes from air to plants to all living things. When living things die, nitrogen is returned to the air.

What Makes Air Dirty?

Many of the things we humans do add pollution to the air. The Explore Activity on page 395 showed a way to collect and observe solid pollutants. In addition to solids, there are harmful gases and liquids in the air. Where do they come from?

Many pollutants get into the air from burning **fossil fuels**. These fuels were formed from the decay of ancient forms of life. Fossil fuels include coal, oil, natural gas, and gasoline. Cars, buses, trucks, and planes burn these fuels, as do many homes and power plants. The wastes from burning these fuels add pollution to the air.

Burning trash adds smoke to the air. Dust comes from plowed fields. It comes from construction sites and from mines. Factories add chemical wastes to the air.

Other events also add to air pollution. Volcanoes erupt and shoot gases and particles into the air. Forest fires and grass fires can spread smoke over great distances

All these pollutants can build up into thick clouds, called **smog**. Smog is a mixture of smoke and fog. It forms when smoke and fumes collect in moist, calm air. Smog irritates the eyes, nose, and throat. People with breathing problems have died from heavy smog.

Smog hangs like a brown cloud over many cities. Why do you think it is most common in big coastal cities like Los Angeles?

Sometimes ozone can form in smog. High up in the atmosphere, remember, ozone protects Earth from UV radiation. However, at ground level this gas can make people sick.

1 Natural events can add to air pollution.

2 Industries produce wastes that add to air pollution.

3 How can a mask help at times when smog is very heavy?

Can Rain Be Harmful?

What can destroy forests, kill animals and plants in lakes, and even eat away at buildings? Part of the answer comes from power plants that burn coal to produce energy. Another part comes from motor vehicles that burn gasoline.

Wastes that come from burning these fossil fuels travel into the air. In the air the wastes mix with moisture. They can form chemicals called acids in the moisture. The moisture with acids can eventually fall to Earth's surface as **acid rain**. This term includes all forms of precipitation—snow, hail, and sleet.

Acid rain can harm soil and water supplies. Some trees sicken and die if there is too much acid in the soil. Fish die in lakes whose waters contain too much acid. The acid weathers away statues and buildings. It can cause metal surfaces on cars to crumble.

④ **Trees yellow and die due to acid rain.**

Acids

PHYSICAL LINK SCIENCE

HYPOTHESIZE How can acid rain change a rock? Write a hypothesis in your *Science Journal*.

MATERIALS
- chalk
- limestone and other rock samples
- vinegar (a mild acid)
- plastic cups
- goggles
- plastic wrap
- rubber bands
- plastic knife
- *Science Journal*

PROCEDURES
SAFETY
Wear goggles.

1. **USE VARIABLES** Break a stick of chalk into smaller pieces. Place some small pieces in a plastic cup. Place each rock sample in its own cup. Slowly pour vinegar in each cup to cover each object.

2. **OBSERVE** Watch for any changes in the chalk and the rocks. Watch for several minutes and then at later times in the day. Record your observations in your *Science Journal*.

3. Cover each cup using plastic wrap and a rubber band to help keep the vinegar from evaporating.

CONCLUDE AND APPLY

1. **EXPLAIN** Vinegar is a mild acid. How did it change the chalk?

2. **COMPARE AND CONTRAST** Do all rocks change the same way? Explain based on your results.

How Can We Clean Up the Air?

Cleaning up the air is a job that takes all nations to work on. That is why the Congress of the United States passed laws to protect the air. It passed the Clean Air Act in 1967 and added more parts in 1970, 1977, and 1990.

There are a few common pollutants found all over the United States. The Clean Air Act has many programs designed to decrease air pollution. This list from a booklet called "Plain English Guide to the Clean Air Act" gives you some idea of its scope. Do you see a part that might affect you or your family?

Clean Air Resolutions

As a result of these laws, cars now have lowered the amounts of harmful wastes that are released. "Clean coal" methods were introduced to lower the amount of harmful wastes that result in acid rain. Power plants that burn coal can wash coal before burning it to remove sulfur. The sulfur can result in acid rain when the coal burns.

In 1970 the first Earth Day was celebrated. People were becoming very concerned about the health of planet Earth. That year the Environmental Protection Agency (EPA) was formed. The EPA is part of the United States government. It has the job of checking that laws are being followed. It investigates new dangers and offers solutions and guidelines.

Stop Damage Before It's Too Late

These photographs show "holes" in the ozone layer. The ozone layer, remember, is a layer high up in the atmosphere that protects Earth from harmful UV radiation. However, it seems we humans have poked holes in this layer. The holes are letting UV radiation through.

How did the holes get there? Scientists are not totally sure. Much evidence points to substances that people have been using a lot. These substances are called CFCs, which is short for chlorofluorocarbons (klôr′ō flür′ō kär′bənz). They are gases used in such things as refrigerators, freezers, and air conditioners. When the CFCs leak out from these appliances, they rise into the atmosphere. There they can affect the ozone layer.

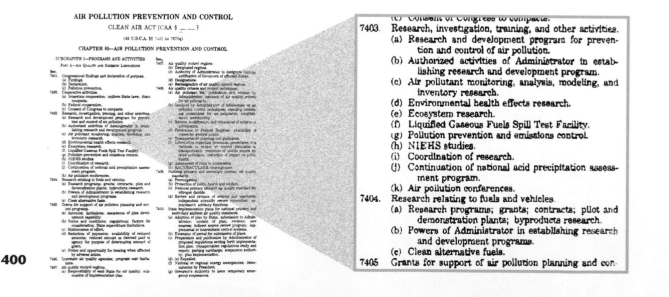

CFCs were also used in many aerosol spray cans. Spray paints, hair sprays, and even shaving foams released CFCs with each squeeze of the push button. Concern about the ozone layer changed that. In 1990 a group of representatives from around the world met in London. They signed an agreement to ban the use of CFCs worldwide in just ten years.

Aerosol spray cans now use substitutes. Just read the label on a spray can item and you can see for yourself.

These photographs show holes developing in the ozone layer.

WHY IT MATTERS

Air pollution harms trees, lakes, and buildings. It can also affect you directly. Air pollution can make people sick. It can make your eyes and nose feel like they are burning. It can make your throat feel itchy and irritated.

Laws help to protect the air. However, it takes people to save the air. The Clean Air Act can work only if people work together. For example, using less electricity can save fuel. Finding ways to cut down on using cars saves fuel, too. Cutting down on burning fuel lowers air pollution.

REVIEW

1. Why is air important to living things?

2. How does the atmosphere protect Earth?

3. How do people pollute the air?

4. CAUSE AND EFFECT What causes acid rain? How does acid rain affect land and water?

5. CRITICAL THINKING *Apply* How can using less electricity cut down on use of fossil fuels?

WHY IT MATTERS THINK ABOUT IT
How do you know when air is polluted?

WHY IT MATTERS WRITE ABOUT IT
How can you cut down on using electricity and fuel? Be specific. Think about things you, your family, and your friends can do.

Be Your Own Weather Forecaster

"What's the temperature going to be today?" That's the question we most often ask about the weather.

THERMOMETER
Air temperature is measured by a thermometer. The glass tube contains mercury or colored alcohol that expands (rises) or contracts (falls) with temperature changes.

BAROMETER
A barometer measures air pressure—the force on a given area by the weight of air. In this barometer, colored water indicates changes in air pressure. Changes in air pressure cause the water to rise and fall.

ANEMOMETER
Winds are described by the direction from which they blow—a north wind comes from the north. Wind vanes show wind direction. An anemometer measures wind speed by counting the revolutions of the cups in a given amount of time.

°F °C
120 50
100 40
80 30
60 20
40 10
FREEZE 0
20 10
0 20
20 30
40 40
60 50
60

Science, Technology, and Society

Warm air weighs less than cool air, so it forms low pressure areas, or lows, which usually mean cloudy skies. Cool air forms high pressure areas, or highs, which usually mean clear skies.

HYGROMETER

A hygrometer measures humidity, or the amount of water vapor in the air. It consists of two thermometers, one dry and one covered by a wet sack. The instrument is whirled in the air, and the wet thermometer records a lower temperature. Meteorologists use a chart to convert the difference in temperatures to relative humidity.

Different shapes and patterns of clouds can predict a cold front, a warm front, or even a thunderstorm! You can use a cup and ruler to measure precipitation!

DISCUSSION STARTER

1. Collect weather data from any instruments you have at home, and listen to weather reports on TV for five days. Record changes. Are there any patterns to these changes?

2. What are some of the reasons weather prediction is so important?

To learn more about weather forecasting, visit *www.mhschool.com/science* and select the keyword FORECAST.

403

*inter*NET
CONNECTION

Topic
EARTH SCIENCE
5

WHY IT MATTERS

Everyone must help save water and keep it clean.

SCIENCE WORDS

desalination getting fresh water from seawater

water cycle the continuous movement of water between Earth's surface and the air, changing from liquid to gas to liquid

groundwater water that seeps into the ground into spaces between bits of rock and soil

water table the top of the water-filled spaces in the ground

aquifer an underground layer of rock or soil filled with water

spring a place where groundwater seeps out of the ground

well a hole dug below the water table that water seeps into

reservoir a storage area for freshwater supplies

Earth's Water Supply

On the average an American uses about 660 liters (178 gallons) of water a day. Where do we get all that water?

Over 70 percent of Earth's surface is covered with water. However, most of this is not fresh water but salt water in Earth's oceans. People don't use salt water for drinking or cleaning. Where does our fresh water come from then? How might we change salt water into fresh water?

EXPLORE

HYPOTHESIZE How can water with something dissolved in it be changed into fresh water? Write a hypothesis in your *Science Journal*. Test your ideas.

Investigate How to Make Salt Water Usable

Decide how the water cycle can make salt water fresh.

MATERIALS

- tea bag
- deep pan
- plastic cup
- saucer (or petri dish)
- large, clear bowl or container
- water
- *Science Journal*

PROCEDURES

1. MAKE A MODEL Keep a tea bag in a cup of water until the water is orange.

2. MAKE A MODEL Place a pan where there is strong light (sunlight, if possible). Pour some tea water into the saucer. Put the saucer in the pan. Cover the saucer with a large bowl.

3. OBSERVE Look at the bowl and pan several times during the day and the next day. Note any water you see on the bowl or in the pan. Write your observations in your *Science Journal*.

CONCLUDE AND APPLY

1. COMPARE AND CONTRAST How was the water that collected in the bowl or pan different from the tea water?

2. INFER What do you think caused the water to collect in the bowl and pan?

3. DRAW CONCLUSIONS How does this model represent what might happen to salt water, the water of Earth's oceans?

GOING FURTHER: Problem Solving

4. USE VARIABLES How long did it take for water to collect in the bowl and pan? How might this process be speeded up?

5. EVALUATE Do you think this model shows a useful way of turning ocean water into fresh water? Explain.

How Do We Use Earth's Oceans?

If all the water in Earth's hydrosphere was represented by 100 cents, not even 3 cents would represent fresh water. Over 97 cents would be salt water. Salt water is water in the oceans as well as saltwater lakes and inland seas.

Much of the salt in salt water is halite, common rock salt. Salt water has seven times more salt than a person can stand. A person cannot survive drinking it. However, Earth's oceans and inland seas are still useful for the resources they contain.

- **Seafood** What kinds of seafood do you eat? Why are these foods healthful? The oceans support many forms of life. The water has dissolved gases, oxygen, and carbon dioxide, as well as minerals. Plants and other producers of the sea are able to get sunlight so that they can make food. They become food for other forms of sea life, which become food for us.

- **Minerals** Almost everything dissolves in water, at least a little. A pail of seawater contains almost every known element. It contains more minerals than just rock salt.

Hot water bubbling out of underwater volcanoes is especially mineral rich. It leaves rich deposits of minerals on the sea floor. Nodules, or lumps, of minerals can be picked up from the sea floor. They contain manganese and iron. Metals such as tin and gold are also found on the sea floor.

- **Fossil fuels** Offshore rigs pump oil and natural gas from beneath the ocean floor in many places around the globe. This fuel is worth more than all other resources taken from the oceans.

MATH LINK

WATER IN THE HYDROSPHERE

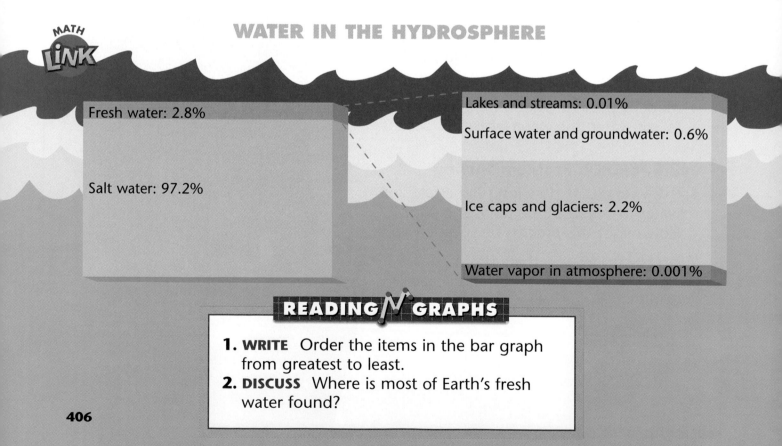

Fresh water: 2.8%

Salt water: 97.2%

Lakes and streams: 0.01%

Surface water and groundwater: 0.6%

Ice caps and glaciers: 2.2%

Water vapor in atmosphere: 0.001%

READING GRAPHS

1. **WRITE** Order the items in the bar graph from greatest to least.
2. **DISCUSS** Where is most of Earth's fresh water found?

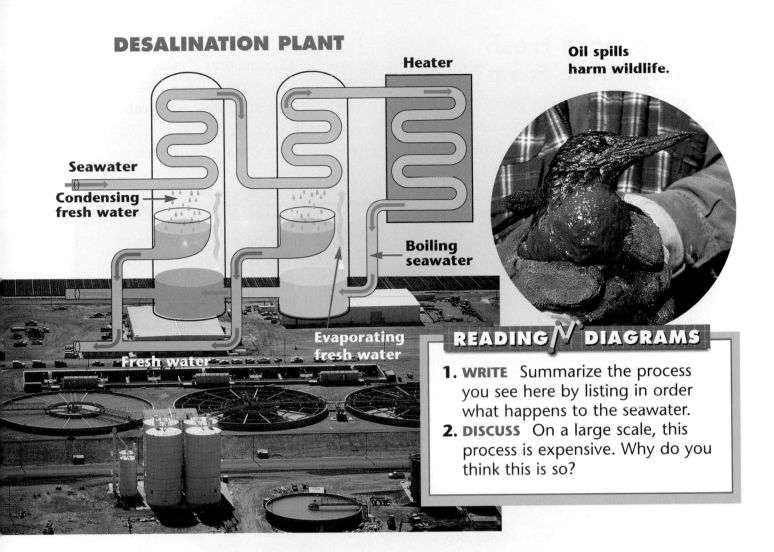

DESALINATION PLANT

Heater

Seawater

Condensing fresh water

Boiling seawater

Evaporating fresh water

Fresh water

Oil spills harm wildlife.

How Can We Make Salt Water Usable?

You can't drink seawater or use it to water plants. You need fresh water. Your fresh water comes mostly from freshwater lakes and rivers.

Some areas have very little fresh water available. The islands of Malta, for example, are surrounded by oceans. However, they have no permanent lakes or rivers. Over two-thirds of the water used by the people is gotten from seawater.

Getting fresh water from seawater takes a process called **desalination** (dē sal'ə nā'shən). The Explore Activity introduced this process.

Seawater contains dissolved rock salt and other materials. As water evaporates it leaves the dissolved materials behind. The liquid water that collects at the end of the process is free of dissolved materials.

What else is in seawater that can make it harmful? In the past barges loaded with garbage and poisonous wastes would sail out every day to dump their loads at sea. Sometimes accidents such as oil spills from tankers poured huge amounts of oil into the oceans.

Pollution in the ocean does not go away. It builds up. Eventually it can kill sea life. It ruins our seafood supplies in certain parts of the oceans.

Where Does Fresh Water Come From?

Only a tiny fraction of Earth's water is usable fresh water. People use so much fresh water each day, you might wonder why it doesn't run out. Fresh water doesn't run out because it is constantly renewed by the **water cycle**.

In the water cycle, water is on the move—as a liquid that changes to a gas (water vapor) and back to liquid. When water evaporates, remember, it leaves behind the material it contained. The water vapor is not salt water.

Brain Power

Do you think the water that falls to Earth's surface is always "clean"? Does this cycle provide water for every place on Earth? Explain your answers.

WATER CYCLE

3 Water vapor in the air cools and condenses into tiny droplets. Bunches of tiny droplets collect into clouds.

1 The main source of water in the water cycle is the oceans. Every day trillions of liters of water evaporate from the oceans.

4 Water from clouds falls back to Earth's surface as precipitation. Rain and snow are the main sources of fresh water on land.

2 Water also evaporates from rivers, lakes, and other sources on land. Plants give off water vapor as well.

Water vapor in the atmosphere

Ice caps and glaciers

Lakes and streams

Drainage basins

5 When water reaches the ground, three things happen to it. Some water seeps into the ground. Some runs downhill over the surface. Some evaporates back into the air.

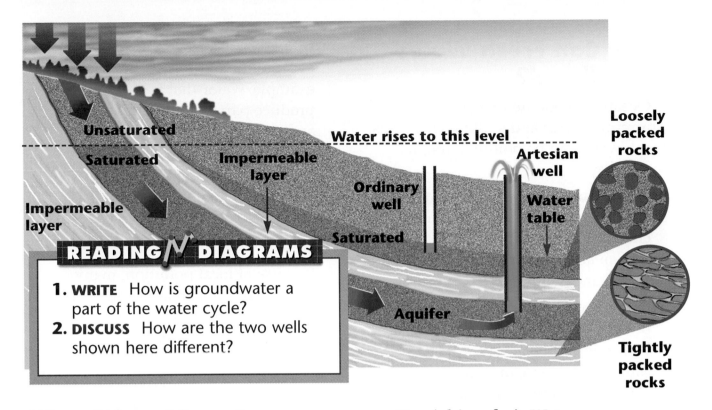

Unsaturated

Saturated

Impermeable layer

Impermeable layer

Water rises to this level

Ordinary well

Saturated

Artesian well

Water table

Aquifer

Loosely packed rocks

Tightly packed rocks

READING ∧ DIAGRAMS

1. **WRITE** How is groundwater a part of the water cycle?
2. **DISCUSS** How are the two wells shown here different?

Where Rain and Snow Go

When water falls back to Earth, where does it go? Some water seeps into the ground. It becomes **groundwater**. Groundwater seeps into the spaces between bits of rock and soil. It seeps downward until it is blocked by a kind of rock that is so tightly packed that it has few spaces.

Then the water starts to back up and fill the spaces in the soil and rocks above. The top of the water-filled spaces is called the **water table**. If the water table reaches above the surface, a pond, a lake, or a stream forms.

Ponds and lakes are still bodies of water. They form where water fills up low-lying places. Streams, however, are flowing downhill. As they flow they join with other streams and become larger, a river. Eventually rivers reach the ocean or some other large bodies of water.

An underground layer of rock or soil that is filled with water is called an **aquifer** (ak′wə fər). Water can move through an aquifer for great distances.

Some groundwater seeps out of the ground in what is called a **spring**. Springs occur where the water table meets the surface. They can feed water into streams and lakes long after it stops raining.

Long ago people learned to tap into groundwater by digging **wells**. Wells are holes dug below the water table. The water seeps into the hole. In some wells people get the water out of the hole with pumps. Wells can also be dug deep into aquifers that are sandwiched between tightly packed layers of rock. Water spouts up in these wells because it is being squeezed by the rock layers.

Most supplies of fresh water for large towns and cities come from **reservoirs** (rez′ər vwärz′). Reservoirs are storage areas for freshwater supplies. They may be human-made or natural lakes or ponds. Pipelines transport the water from reservoirs.

How Can Fresh Water Be Polluted?

Oceans are polluted by people dumping wastes and spilling chemicals. Fresh water can be polluted, too, in many ways.

- **Precipitation** Rain or snow may pick up pollutants from the air. Some chemicals in the air make the rain turn into an acid. Acid rain harms living things and property.

- **Runoff water** Fresh water also gets polluted as it runs off over the land. Water that runs over dumped garbage can end up in streams and lakes. In some cases garbage is dumped into rivers.

- **Groundwater** As water soaks down through the soil, it can pick up chemicals, such as pesticides.

- **Industry** Water used by industry gets polluted as it is used. For example, water that is used to help produce paper is filled with fibers and chemicals.

- You pollute water, too. Every time you flush the toilet, take a bath, brush your teeth, or wash dishes or clothes, water is polluted with wastes. Where do you think this water ends up?

Because of local pollution, many families use water-treatment devices in their faucets. Some families have to use bottled water for cooking and drinking.

PURE

Glacier Water

Skill: Forming a Hypothesis

HOW DO WASTES FROM LAND GET INTO LAKES AND RIVERS?

In seeking an answer to a question, the first thing you might do is find out as much as possible. You make observations. You might look up information.

Next, you would think of an explanation for these observations. That explanation is a hypothesis. It may be stated as an "If . . . then" sentence. "If water runs over land where garbage is dumped, then . . ." Sometimes you can test a hypothesis by making and observing a model.

MATERIALS

- soil
- food color
- foam bits
- 2 deep pans
- 1 L (2 c) of water
- 2 textbooks
- *Science Journal*

PROCEDURES

1. FORM A HYPOTHESIS Write a hypothesis to answer the question above.

2. MAKE A MODEL Pack moist soil to fill one-half (one side) of one pan. As you pack the soil, add 10–20 drops of food color to the soil just below the surface. Sprinkle crumbled bits of foam over the top.

3. EXPERIMENT Use two books to tilt the pan with the soil side up. Place the lower edge of the soil-filled pan in the other pan. Pour water over the uppermost edge of the pan. In your *Science Journal*, describe what happens. Let your model stand for some time and observe it again.

CONCLUDE AND APPLY

1. EXPLAIN How does this model represent wastes on land?

2. DRAW CONCLUSIONS Based on the model, how do wastes from land get into water? Does the model support your hypothesis? Explain.

3. FORM A HYPOTHESIS How can some wastes be removed from water? Form a hypothesis, and test your ideas.

How Can We Solve Water Problems?

Can polluted water be cleaned up? Yes, it can be—in many ways. For example, the water cycle helps clean water. Remember that when water evaporates, it leaves behind materials it contained. The water vapor and eventually the rain that forms no longer contain those materials.

When water seeps into the ground, the ground acts as a fine screen, or filter. Most dirt particles in water are trapped, or filtered out, as water seeps down through the ground. As a result a well that is dug down deep in the ground collects water that has been filtered.

Freshwater supplies for large areas can be cleaned on a large scale. Follow the steps in the process.

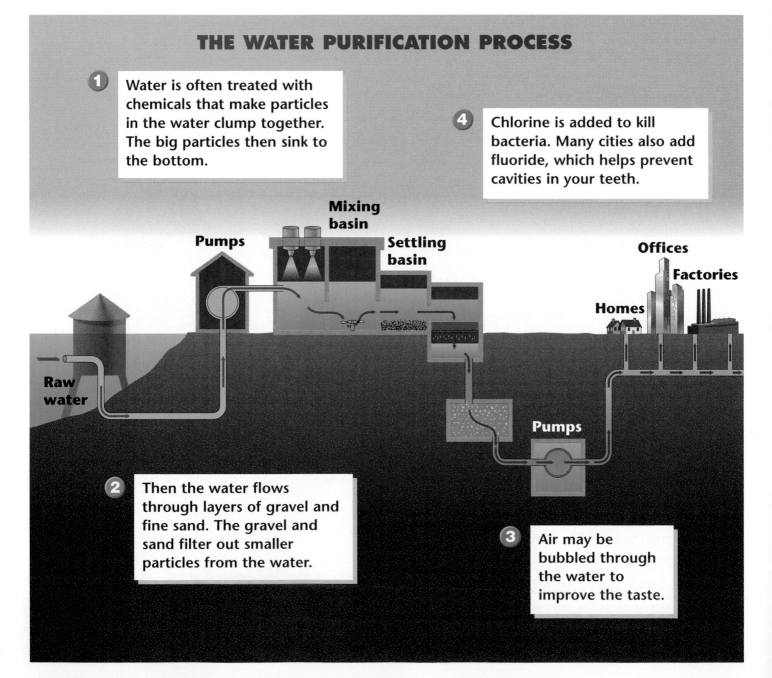

THE WATER PURIFICATION PROCESS

1. Water is often treated with chemicals that make particles in the water clump together. The big particles then sink to the bottom.

4. Chlorine is added to kill bacteria. Many cities also add fluoride, which helps prevent cavities in your teeth.

Mixing basin

Pumps

Settling basin

Offices

Factories

Homes

Raw water

Pumps

2. Then the water flows through layers of gravel and fine sand. The gravel and sand filter out smaller particles from the water.

3. Air may be bubbled through the water to improve the taste.

What Can You Do?

People waste fresh water more than they realize. Often water can be safely reused. At times when the rainfall is low, water supplies may be very low. You may live in a part of the country where water supplies are low much of the time. No matter where you live, saving and recycling water should be part of your daily routine.

DAILY USES OF WATER

Activity	Amount of Water Used
Flushing a toilet	16–24 liters
Washing dishes	32–80 liters
Taking a shower	80–120 liters
Taking a bath	120–160 liters

READING *N* CHARTS

1. **REPRESENT** How could you make a graph to represent these numbers?
2. **WRITE** How does taking a shower help save water?

The United States Congress has passed laws such as the Safe Drinking Water Act and the Clean Water Act. These laws set standards for water purity. The Environmental Protection Agency (EPA) checks that these laws are being followed.

Laws are important. However, it takes people—like you—to help save water and keep it clean.

How does a sprinkler attached to a hydrant help save water?

REVIEW

1. How do you depend on the oceans, even if you don't live near one?

2. **HYPOTHESIZE** How does the Sun help provide you with freshwater supplies?

3. How do wastes get into ocean water? Fresh water?

4. How can freshwater supplies be cleaned up?

5. **CRITICAL THINKING** *Evaluate* How can you tell the amount of water wasted in a day by a leaky faucet? Find a way to tell without wasting any.

WHY IT MATTERS THINK ABOUT IT
How would you add to the table above to include other ways you use water? To include other ways water is used in your neighborhood or town?

WHY IT MATTERS WRITE ABOUT IT
How can you help keep water clean? How can you save water?

413

WATER WORKS!

California is a large and thirsty state. There are more than 30 million people in California. Most live or farm far from water supplies. A system of aqueducts brings water to crops and people.

The oldest aqueduct in California is the Los Angeles Aqueduct. It opened in 1913. The Los Angeles Aqueduct transports water 388 km (241 miles) from the Owens Valley to Los Angeles. The Owens Valley is 1200 meters (3937 feet) above sea level. The water flows downhill to Los Angeles. Little pumping is needed. This is energy efficient.

Los Angeles recently reduced water imports from the Los Angeles Aqueduct. This was done to allow water levels to rise in distant Mono Lake. Southern California must also reduce water imports from the Colorado River. This is because neighboring states need more water. But California's population is still growing. Something must be done to prevent a future water shortage. Water conservation means making better use of existing water supplies. Wastewater can be recycled and reused by farms and industry. Water banking adds to groundwater supplies during wet years. During dry years banked groundwater is withdrawn. Cities can also buy water from farmers. Farmers use 80% of California's water. They would have to grow fewer crops. Some cities are converting seawater into fresh water. But this is expensive.

To protect the fragile environment of Mono Lake, Los Angeles has reduced water imports from the Los Angeles Aqueduct.

Geography Link

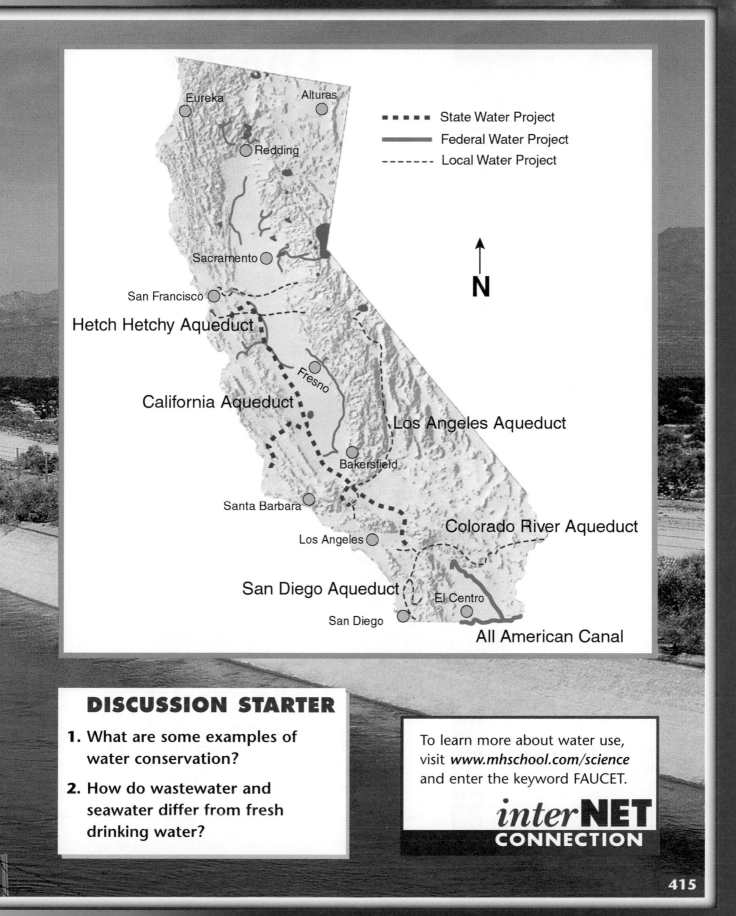

State Water Project

Federal Water Project

Local Water Project

Eureka

Alturas

Redding

Sacramento

San Francisco

Hetch Hetchy Aqueduct

Fresno

California Aqueduct

Los Angeles Aqueduct

Bakersfield

Santa Barbara

Colorado River Aqueduct

Los Angeles

San Diego Aqueduct

El Centro

San Diego

All American Canal

N

DISCUSSION STARTER

1. What are some examples of water conservation?

2. How do wastewater and seawater differ from fresh drinking water?

To learn more about water use, visit *www.mhschool.com/science* and enter the keyword FAUCET.

*inter*NET
CONNECTION

WHY IT MATTERS

Fossil fuels will not last forever. We should use them wisely.

SCIENCE WORDS

solar cell a device that generates an electric current from sunlight

biomass conversion getting energy from plant and animal materials by changing them into high-quality fuels

nuclear fission the splitting of a nucleus with a large mass into two nuclei with smaller masses

chain reaction a reaction that is kept going by products of the reaction

nuclear fusion the merging of nuclei with smaller masses into a nucleus with a larger mass

hydroelectricity the use of flowing water to generate electricity

thermal pollution the excess heating of the environment

Sources of Energy

How many kinds of energy do you use each day? How much energy do you use? How might you tell?

Where does all the energy you use each day come from? One way or another, most of our energy supplies come from sunlight. How is this home using sunlight directly as a source of heat?

EXPLORE

HYPOTHESIZE How can you use the Sun's energy for useful purposes, such as to cook food? Write a hypothesis in your *Science Journal*. Test your ideas.

Investigate How to Use Energy from the Sun

See how well sunlight can heat food.

PROCEDURES

1. In your *Science Journal*, plan your steps. Place the aluminum foil on top of the white construction paper. The shiny side of the foil should be facing up.

2. Roll the paper and foil into a cone with the bottom narrow enough to fit into the paper cup. Tape the cone so that the cone keeps its shape.

3. Line the inside of one paper cup with black construction paper.

4. Insert the second paper cup into the first. The black construction paper should now be between the two cups.

5. Place small pieces of peeled apple on the bottom of the second cup.

6. Insert the cone, narrow end first, into the second cup and tape it in place.

7. Place the cone in direct sunlight for two hours. Also place small pieces of peeled apple in direct sunlight, next to the cup.

MATERIALS

- white construction paper
- black construction paper
- unwaxed paper cups
- aluminum foil
- transparent tape
- a peeled apple
- *Science Journal*

CONCLUDE AND APPLY

1. OBSERVE Look at the pieces of apple every half-hour for two hours. Compare the apple pieces inside the cup and the apple pieces next to the cup.

2. ANALYZE What caused the differences you observed? How do you think the cone works?

GOING FURTHER: Problem Solving

3. PLAN Would other food items show the same results? Write a hypothesis. How would you test it?

How Can the Sun's Energy Be Used?

Where do you get your daily energy supply from? Most of the living things on Earth obtain their energy directly or indirectly from the Sun. Plants convert the Sun's energy into chemical energy stored in compounds called carbohy-drates. Animals then feed on the plants or eat other animals that feed on plants.

Humans, too, consume "solar energy" by eating plants and animals. Humans also build devices to capture energy from the Sun and put it to practical use. As shown below, there are two basic types of solar heating systems.

AN ACTIVE SOLAR HEATING SYSTEM

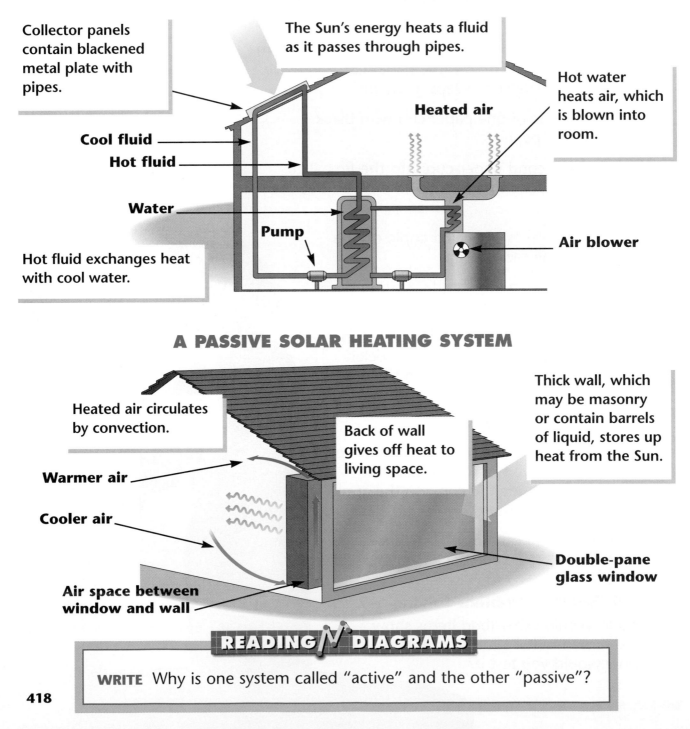

Collector panels contain blackened metal plate with pipes.

The Sun's energy heats a fluid as it passes through pipes.

Hot water heats air, which is blown into room.

Heated air

Cool fluid

Hot fluid

Water

Pump

Hot fluid exchanges heat with cool water.

Air blower

A PASSIVE SOLAR HEATING SYSTEM

Heated air circulates by convection.

Warmer air

Cooler air

Air space between window and wall

Back of wall gives off heat to living space.

Thick wall, which may be masonry or contain barrels of liquid, stores up heat from the Sun.

Double-pane glass window

READING *N* DIAGRAMS

WRITE Why is one system called "active" and the other "passive"?

A single solar cell

An experimental electric car powered by many solar cells connected together

These mirrors focus the Sun's rays onto the top of the 300-foot tower at the center of Solar Two. There molten salt is heated to temperatures greater than 1,000°F.

How Can Sunlight Be Turned into Electricity?

Scientists have developed materials made mainly of silicon that can produce electrons when struck by light. When layered properly these materials can be made into **solar cells**. Solar cells generate an electric current from sunlight. The electricity can be used to charge batteries or run motors. Solar cells can power an electric vehicle. Solar cells can also be positioned on rooftops to provide electricity for buildings.

In some locations engineers have built large power plants that use many mirrors to focus the Sun's rays onto a central collector. The focused rays heat water to boiling or melt salt at high temperatures in the collector. The heat energy is used to make steam, which in turn spins a turbine and generates electricity.

One such power plant is located at Daggett, California. Called Solar Two, this facility began operating in 1996. It has nearly 2,000 mirrors and can provide 10,000 homes with electricity.

This is a close-up view of the mirrors used in Solar Two. The mirrors automatically follow the Sun as it moves across the sky.

Scientists predict that billions of years from now, the Sun will burn out. Until then, however, it will produce a steady supply of energy. You might describe the Sun's energy as inexhaustible, meaning it will always be there for us to use.

This well pumps crude oil out of the ground. The oil is thick, like syrup.

An ancient swamp—where today's coal supplies started

Bituminous, or "soft," coal

Why Are Fossil Fuels Called Fossil Fuels?

EARTH
LINK
SCIENCE

The scene is a swamp far back in Earth's history. Scientists believe that the plants in such swamps became buried as they died. Over time the plants' remains were covered by sand or other mineral matter. Eventually heat and pressure converted the plant remains into a mineral called coal.

In a similar manner, the remains of tiny ocean-dwelling plants and animals became buried under mud and sand on the ocean bottom millions of years ago. As time passed, the organisms' remains were squeezed by the weight of the mineral layers over

them into a thick liquid called crude oil. In many cases part of the remains was also changed into a gas called natural gas.

Coal, oil, and natural gas all give off large amounts of heat when burned, so they are very good fuels. Because these materials all formed from ancient plants and animals, we call them fossil fuels. Presently the United States obtains about 79 percent of its yearly energy supply from fossil fuels.

Because fossil fuels take millions of years to form, they are examples of *nonrenewable* resources. *Nonrenewable* means that once we use the resources, we can't get them back.

Kelp, a kind of seaweed, grows rapidly in the ocean. It can be used as biomass for bacteria that produce methane.

Can Modern Plant and Animal Matter Give Us Energy?

Fossil fuels were once living plants and animals. Can matter from plants and animals living today produce energy and help to conserve fossil fuels?

In fact farmers have used animal wastes as a fuel for centuries. When dried in sunlight, cow and horse manure burns readily. However, new methods allow us to change both plant and animal materials into high-quality fuels. We refer to this kind of change as **biomass conversion** (bī'ō mas' kən vûr'zhən).

In one method, grains are mixed in a large container with yeast cells. The yeast cells change the sugar in the grains into ethyl alcohol (ethanol) and carbon dioxide. Both ethyl alcohol and methyl alcohol can be added to unleaded gasoline to form gasohol.

Through biomass conversion fuels can be made from plants and other living things.

In another method bacteria are used to digest the biomass in conditions where air is lacking. Garbage buried deep in landfills or plant matter placed in airtight tanks provide the proper conditions. The bacteria produce methane gas, which is the main ingredient of natural gas.

The fuels from biomass conversion are examples of *renewable* resources. *Renewable* means that we can make more of the resources and use them again and again.

WARNING: Do not use in standard gasoline engines Use only in methanol designated vehicles

THIS SALE

GALLONS

Methanol

102

California Energy Commission

The sugar in an ear of corn can be turned into methanol, a fuel that mixes well with gasoline.

Brain Power

Why might it be important for the United States to develop new energy sources, like biomass conversion?

How Can Atomic Nuclei Produce Energy by Splitting?

In a nuclear reaction, the number of protons in the nuclei of atoms often changes. Since the identity of any atom is determined by the number of protons it has, a change in the number of protons produces an atom with a different identity.

One type of nuclear reaction is called **nuclear fission** (nü′klē ər fish′ən). Nuclear fission is the splitting of a nucleus into two pieces. The nucleus can be split when struck with a slow-moving neutron. Neutrons and energy are also produced by nuclear fission.

If enough large nuclei are present, the neutrons released by one splitting atom can strike additional nuclei and make them split. These nuclei then release several more neutrons, which can split even more nuclei. Much as a single match can start a large fire, a single neutron can start a large nuclear reaction. We say that the first neutron starts a **chain reaction** of splitting nuclei. In a chain reaction, products of the reaction keep the reaction going.

Because the forces in an atomic nucleus are very strong, the energy released is much greater than the energy produced by chemical reactions. Allowing the atoms in about 0.25 gram of uranium to split, for example, yields as much energy as burning half a ton of coal!

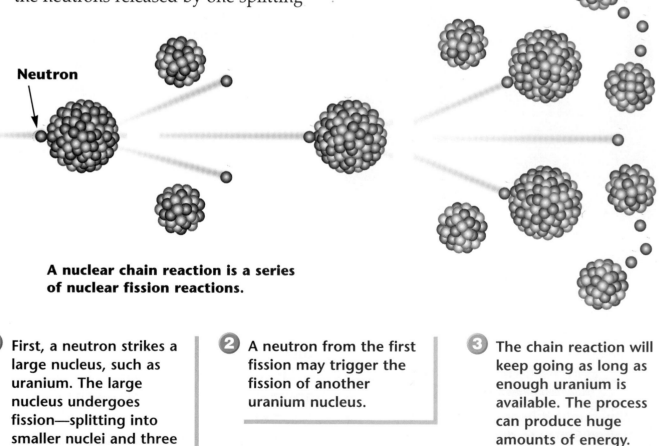

Neutron

A nuclear chain reaction is a series of nuclear fission reactions.

1 First, a neutron strikes a large nucleus, such as uranium. The large nucleus undergoes fission—splitting into smaller nuclei and three neutrons.

2 A neutron from the first fission may trigger the fission of another uranium nucleus.

3 The chain reaction will keep going as long as enough uranium is available. The process can produce huge amounts of energy.

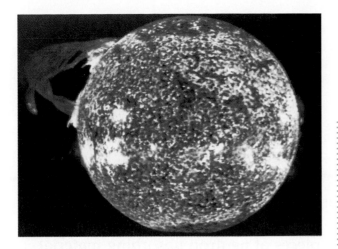

How Can Atomic Nuclei Produce Energy by Merging?

You've seen how nuclei of heavy atoms can split into medium-sized nuclei and release energy. Energy can also be released when nuclei with smaller masses merge to make a nucleus with a larger mass. This process is called **nuclear fusion** (nü′klē ər fū′zhən).

During the fusion reactions in the diagram, some of the mass of the particles seems to disappear—the helium nucleus at the end has less mass than the particles from which it was made. Scientists have learned that the missing mass gets turned into a large amount of energy. It may seem odd that matter can change into energy. It was not until 1905 that Albert Einstein predicted that this could happen.

Nuclear fusion reactions occur only at very high temperatures. The nuclei that must merge have a positive charge and repel one another. The nuclei must be traveling at high speeds to be able to get close enough to fuse. In nature, temperatures great enough for nuclear fusion to happen are found in the cores of stars. There nuclear fusion reactions produce vast amounts of energy and allow stars to shine brightly for billions of years.

1 If two nuclei are traveling extremely fast, they may have enough energy to collide.

2 When the nuclei combine, a tiny amount of their mass is changed into energy.

Tritium (hydrogen with two neutrons)

Deuterium (hydrogen with one neutron)

Helium

READING *N* DIAGRAMS

WRITE Does the diagram show fission or fusion?

A Chain Reaction

HYPOTHESIZE How can you use everyday materials to model a nuclear chain reaction? Write a hypothesis in your *Science Journal*.

MATERIALS
- everyday materials
- *Science Journal*

PROCEDURES

1. PLAN Decide on everyday materials that you can use. You might choose foam balls, dried beans, or squares of colored paper to model the nuclei and neutrons. You could present your model on a poster, in a diorama, or as an activity involving your classmates.

2. MAKE A MODEL With your teacher's approval, build your model. Your teacher may ask you to write an explanation of the model or to discuss the model with the class.

CONCLUDE AND APPLY

EVALUATE In what ways was your model successful? In what ways was it not successful?

How Can We Use Nuclear Fission to Make Electricity?

Neutrons can start a chain reaction of nuclear fission. To control the amount of energy released by the chain reaction, two things can be done. First, the nuclear fuel used must not contain too many nuclei that can split. Second, pieces of neutron-absorbing material can be put around the nuclear fuel. These pieces "soak up" some of the neutrons from splitting nuclei and prevent the neutrons from causing too much fission.

A large number of power plants have been built around the world that use a fission chain reaction to produce electricity. Most of these plants use uranium as a nuclear fuel. Uranium ore from mines naturally contains a very small amount of a form of uranium that can undergo fission. Special processing increases the amount of the fissionable uranium to the point that there are enough nuclei to support a safe chain reaction.

The core of a nuclear power plant

Which Is Better— Fission or Fusion?

Today, nuclear fission reactors produce electricity across the United States, in Europe, and in many other places on Earth. These reactors are quiet, do not pollute the atmosphere, and help conserve fossil fuels.

However, these reactors cause problems. Their most serious problem is the waste products of nuclear fission, which stay highly radioactive for thousands of years. These wastes must be stored safely for a very long time.

A nuclear fusion reactor would not have these problems. Nuclear fusion produces far less radioactive waste than nuclear fission. Also the fuels for nuclear fusion are special forms of hydrogen called deuterium and tritium. Both of these forms are safe and easily obtained from nature.

Unfortunately researchers have not yet succeeded in developing a working fusion reactor. The problem is that temperatures greater than 100 million degrees are needed to keep the fusion going. Ordinary materials cannot withstand such high temperatures.

Researchers are trying to use magnetic fields to confine the reaction. The tokamak design, shown below, uses a donut-shaped magnetic field to hold the heated deuterium and tritium fuel. Scientists are hopeful that nuclear fusion reactors like the tokamak may become practical by the middle of the 21st century.

This illustration shows how a tokamak reactor would confine a white-hot mixture of fusing deuterium and tritium.

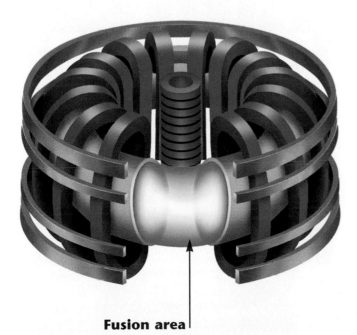

Fusion area

Nuclear fission reactors produce waste that stays radioactive for thousands of years. This waste is dangerous to living things. One way scientists have dealt with this problem has been to store the waste underground in shielded containers. Why would this help protect living things?

How Can We Capture Energy from Wind?

It may surprise you to know that wind is a form of solar energy. Wind is caused by uneven heating of Earth's surface by the Sun—air moves from colder areas into warmer areas and produces wind.

Capturing the energy in wind is not a new idea. For centuries farmers have used windmills to grind grain. In America windmills have been used for over 100 years to pump water on farms, as shown. Also many small wind-driven electric generators were put in service between 1930 and 1960, especially in remote areas. By 1960 electric companies had strung wires to most parts of the United States, and the need for wind-driven generators lessened greatly.

However, the growing demand for energy in America has recently led to a renewed interest in wind energy. Manufacturers have developed large wind turbines that can convert wind into electricity.

California has most of the wind turbines in the United States About 1 percent of this state's electricity comes from wind turbines, many of them on wind farms. While wind power is clean and will never be used up, some people object to the noise and appearance of the large turbines.

A windmill on a farm

This wind turbine is 50 meters tall. In a 28-mile-per-hour wind, it produces about one-thousandth the electricity of a medium-sized fossil-fuel electric power plant.

Thousands of wind turbines can be assembled to make wind farms like this one in California.

Flowing water causes this wheel to turn.

How Can Falling Water Give Us Energy?

What can falling water be used for? The kinetic energy of falling water can be captured and used to turn a wheel. This principle can be used to generate electricity. The dam shown here has large turbines at its base. Water from the lake behind the dam can be made to flow through the turbines, causing them to spin and drive electric generators. When electricity is produced by flowing water in this fashion, it is called **hydroelectricity**.

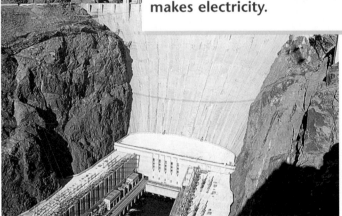

Hoover Dam creates Lake Mead. Lake water rushing through the turbines below the dam structure makes electricity.

Like wind power hydroelectricity is really a form of solar energy. The Sun warms water in oceans and lakes, causing it to evaporate. The water vapor rises high in the atmosphere and can fall as precipitation at high elevations. As the water from the precipitation runs downhill due to gravity, it gains kinetic energy. This is the energy that can be tapped for hydroelectricity.

Presently the United States gets about 15 percent of its electricity from hydroelectricity. The good things about hydroelectricity are that it causes little pollution and it will always be available as long as it rains or snows. But hydroelectricity does present problems. The number of sites where more large dams can be built is limited. Building such dams can be damaging to the environment. It takes very careful planning to make sure animal and plant species are not harmed in some way by dams.

Dams in the Pacific Northwest could stop salmon from migrating upstream. Fish ladders, shown below, allow fish to get past dams.

427

How Can Fossil Fuels Be Used to Make Electricity?

Fossil fuels are really a form of solar energy. They contain chemical energy that was originally light from the Sun used by ancient plants for growth.

Fossil fuels are composed mainly of carbon and hydrogen. When they are burned, they combine with oxygen in the air to make water, carbon dioxide, and heat. Study the diagram to see how this heat is used to make electricity that is sent to homes, offices, and factories.

HOW FOSSIL FUEL ENERGY BECOMES ELECTRICITY

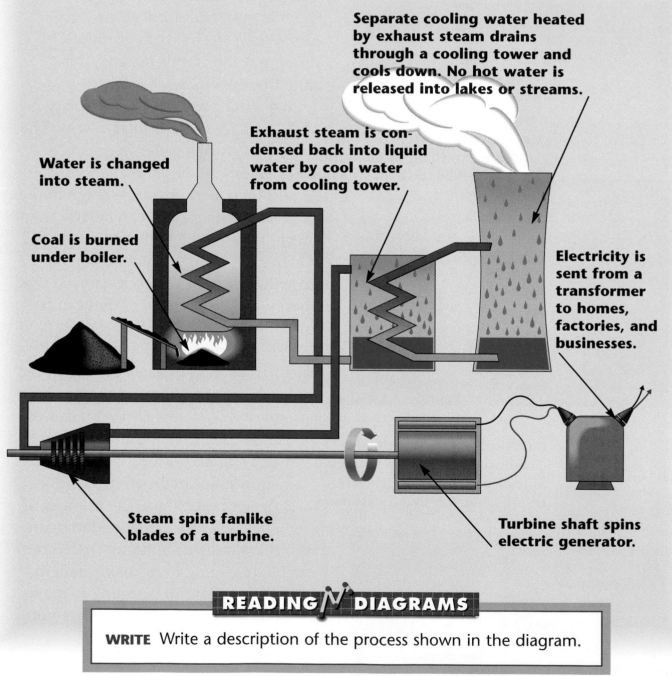

Separate cooling water heated by exhaust steam drains through a cooling tower and cools down. No hot water is released into lakes or streams.

Water is changed into steam.

Exhaust steam is condensed back into liquid water by cool water from cooling tower.

Coal is burned under boiler.

Electricity is sent from a transformer to homes, factories, and businesses.

Steam spins fanlike blades of a turbine.

Turbine shaft spins electric generator.

READING /N/ DIAGRAMS

WRITE Write a description of the process shown in the diagram.

How Do Electric Power Plants Control Pollution?

At an electric power plant, separate cooling water is used to condense the exhaust steam from the turbines. This water warms up as it cools the steam. If the warmed water were to be released into a river or lake, the increase in temperature could harm water-dwelling plants and animals. This problem is known as **thermal pollution**, the excess heating of the environment.

Thermal pollution from power plants can be controlled with cooling towers, as in the photograph. The warm water that has been used to condense exhaust steam is allowed to trickle down over several decks in the tower. The water cools as it comes into contact with the air. By the time it reaches the bottom of the tower, it is cool enough to once again condense exhaust steam.

A cooling tower at an electric power plant.

WHY IT MATTERS

Studies show that our demand for energy is steadily increasing. However, the supplies of oil and other fossil fuels will not last forever. One of the most important things each of us can do is to avoid wasting our precious energy. How many ways can you think of to conserve energy in your daily activities?

REVIEW

1. How can energy from the Sun be captured directly and used?

2. Why are coal, oil, and natural gas called fossil fuels?

3. What is the difference between nuclear fission and nuclear fusion?

4. **SEQUENCE** How does energy from a power plant reach your home?

5. **CRITICAL THINKING** *Analyze* Why can hydroelectricity be thought of as a form of solar energy?

WHY IT MATTERS THINK ABOUT IT
How do you use fossil fuels each day—either directly or indirectly?

WHY IT MATTERS WRITE ABOUT IT
How can turning off the lights in an empty room help to save fossil fuels? How else can you save fossil fuels?

Nuclear... or Not?

Nuclear energy can be used to power a submarine, explode a bomb, or run a power plant. Today nuclear power costs about the same as coal power. Which is best to use?

Small amounts of uranium can run a nuclear power plant for years. Coal-fired plants use tons of coal daily, and someday we'll run out of coal.

Coal smoke adds to air pollution and global warming. Nuclear plants release only water vapor.

Both nuclear and coal plants can be damaged. In 1986 a nuclear plant in the Soviet Union exploded.

Radioactive fallout spread all over northern Europe. Coal-fired plants have burned down, but damage was limited to the plant.

Both nuclear and coal wastes have leaked. Nuclear wastes can be radioactive for thousands of years. Coal ash can contaminate water supplies.

DISCUSSION STARTER

1. What is a disadvantage of nuclear power? Of coal power?

2. Is nuclear or coal power better for the environment? Why?

This submarines runs on nuclear power.

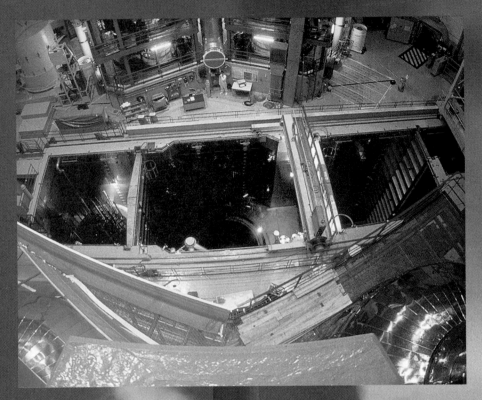

The United States has more than 100 nuclear plants. They produce about one-tenth of our electricity.

To learn more about nuclear energy, visit *www.mhschool.com/science* and enter the keyword NUCLEAR.

*inter*NET CONNECTION

Topic
EARTH SCIENCE
7

WHY IT MATTERS

Water, energy, and clean air are vital to your future in California.

SCIENCE WORDS

refining separating crude oil mainly into gasoline and heating oil

irrigation supplying cropland with water by artificial means

flash distillation process in which water evaporates below its normal boiling temperature

California's Air, Water, and Energy

Today in California, large cities have been built in what was once a nearly waterless desert. Freeways carry millions of cars that burn fuel and emit exhaust. Nearby mountains can trap dirty air over cities, making it hard to breathe. Huge amounts of energy are needed to power homes, factories, and cars.

What can be done to make sure that there is enough drinking water for all Californians? What can be done to improve California's air and keep it fresh and clean? How can energy be used wisely and resources conserved for the future?

EXPLORE

HYPOTHESIZE How does burning gasoline cause air pollution? Write a hypothesis in your *Science Journal*. How could you test your idea?

Investigate How Fossil Fuels Make Air Dirty

See how coal and petroleum cause pollution.

PROCEDURES

 SAFETY Wear goggles.

1. Place a few chips of coal in a test tube.

2. Loosely stuff a small amount of glass wool into the top of the test tube.

3. Gently and slowly warm the bottom of the test tube by holding it above the flame of a Bunsen burner for several minutes.

4. **OBSERVE** Place the hot test tube in the test tube stand. Look for signs of pollution on the test tube and glass wool. Record your observations in your *Science Journal*.

5. **OBSERVE** Put a few drops of petroleum into a second test tube. Add glass wool, and heat as before. Look for signs of pollution. Record your observations.

CONCLUDE AND APPLY

1. **INFER** Did you observe any material deposited on the glass wool? Where would that material be now, if you had not put the glass wool in the test tube?

2. **DRAW CONCLUSIONS** What does this experiment have to do with air pollution in California?

GOING FURTHER: Problem Solving

4. **HYPOTHESIZE** When wood is burned, it gives off carbon dioxide. Coal and oil are fossilized wood. Might they give off the same gas? Form a hypothesis. Then describe an experiment you could do to test your hypothesis.

MATERIALS

- Bunsen burner
- 2 Pyrex or Kimax test tubes
- test tube holder
- test tube rack
- glass wool
- small chips of soft coal
- small amount of petroleum
- goggles
- *Science Journal*

433

What Makes California's Air Clean or Dirty?

Clean air flows into California from the Pacific Ocean and also sometimes from the eastern deserts. People make California's air dirty by burning fossil fuels in cars as well as in homes, office buildings, and factories.

On some days, smoke from burning fossil fuels mixes with fog rolling in from the ocean. The result is a combination called *smog*. Smoggy air often gets trapped in inland valleys. On smoggy days, many people have difficulty breathing. Some people may find that their eyes begin to hurt.

There are also other sources of air pollution in California. Burning trash, whether in an open area or in a wire container, makes the air dirty. So does dust from plowed fields and construction sites. Chemical wastes from factories also cause dirty air.

Among the worst pollutants are wastes from refining petroleum. **Refining** is the process of separating crude oil mainly into gasoline and heating oil. It is carried on in large factories called refineries. Many refineries are located near cities and towns where large numbers of people live.

Still another source of air pollution is forest fires. During some seasons,

2 Refineries produce gasoline from crude oil. Some also produce air pollution.

1 Pollution from automobiles can mix with fog to create smog in the air over California cities.

forest fires and brush fires may burn very large areas. Many fires are started by lightning or by hikers who are not careful to put out their campfires. Still others, unfortunately, are deliberately set. Some fires may continue burning for many days.

Forest fires send large amounts of solid and gaseous pollutants into the air. These pollutants may drift in the air over area that are far from the fires. Efforts to put out the fires may involve hundreds of people. Planes drop special chemicals on the fires to put them out.

Many people in California are working to clean up the air, but there is no easy way to do it. Factories and office buildings cannot be closed just to reduce air pollution. People still need cars, and new homes must be built and heated. In fact, as more and more people come to California, more homes, more factories, more office buildings, and more cars will be needed. So scientists, engineers, lawmakers, and all of us need to find other ways to protect the air. Cleaner air is important to everyone who lives in California.

Brain Power

Burning fuel to heat homes can increase air pollution. How can the use of air conditioning also lead to increased air pollution?

3 **Forest fires in California can cause air pollution even in cities many miles away.**

How Can We Protect California's Air?

If you walk around outside after a long, steady rain, you notice right away that the air is clear. It smells clean. The rain has washed the pollution away—for a while. How can the air be kept clean all the time?

One way to clean up the air is to find other fuels besides gasoline to power cars. Scientists have now developed cars and buses that run on electricity or on natural gas. These cars and buses do not produce the same pollutants as gasoline-powered cars. The number of electric and natural gas-powered cars on California roads is expected to increase.

Another way to clean up the air is to find ways to reduce pollution from burning gasoline. Today, all new cars shipped into California must have special exhaust systems to reduce air pollution. Also, every two years every car owner must get a "smog certificate." The certificate is issued only if a car meets clean-air standards.

Protecting California's indoor air from the smoke and ash of cigarette smoking is important, too. The state taxes cigarettes, making them more expensive to buy. The aim is to reduce smoking, especially among teenagers.

"Second-hand smoke" is the smoke nonsmokers inhale when they are around smokers. It is believed to kill many people each year. To reduce second-hand smoke, laws now forbid smoking in most restaurants in California. Many buildings are also cigarette-free. The only way people in the building can smoke is to go outside.

Cars in California must be inspected every two years in order to meet clean-air standards.

Does California Have Enough Water?

Most of California has a dry climate. But in California's higher mountains, there is a large amount of precipitation. The reason is that the mountains force moist Pacific air to rise and cool. When the air cools, water vapor condenses as rain or snow. Unfortunately, this rain and snow falls far from where most Californians live.

Many parts of California, particularly southern California, do not have enough drinking water. These areas must get their water from elsewhere, often from places that are hundreds of miles away. Water also must be transported for growing crops.

To bring water to California's cities and towns, people have built a huge system of aqueducts. An *aqueduct* is an above-ground structure for carrying large amounts of flowing water. Aqueducts carry water to southern California from the Sierra Nevada mountains in the northern and eastern part of the state. Other aqueducts bring water from the Colorado River, which flows along the California-Arizona border.

Hoover Dam on the Colorado River was built by the United States government to create a large water reservoir behind it. This reservoir, called Lake Mead, is an important source of drinking water for many cities in southern California.

QUICK LAB

Dew Point

HYPOTHESIZE What happens to water vapor in the air as the air is cooled? Write a hypothesis that you can test by using these materials.

MATERIALS
- large metal can
- water
- ice cubes
- thermometer
- wooden or plastic stirrer
- *Science Journal*

PROCEDURES

1. Remove the paper label from a large can. Clean the can, dry it, and fill it halfway with room temperature water.

2. **PLAN** How can you use these materials to gradually lower the air temperature, so you can observe what happens to water vapor in the air? (Hint: Observe the outside of the can.)

3. **EXPERIMENT** With your teacher's approval, carry out your plan.

4. **OBSERVE** Watch carefully what happens as your experiment proceeds. Record your observations.

CONCLUDE AND APPLY

1. **EVALUATE** Did your observations support your hypothesis? Explain.

2. **DEFINE** The temperature you measured is called the *dew point*. Write a definition of dew point, based on your observations.

How Can We Protect California's Water?

Because water is scarce in those parts of California where most people live, it must be conserved and protected. It also needs to be guarded against pollution.

Water is important for domestic, agricultural, and industrial purposes. In homes, water is used for drinking, bathing, washing, and flushing toilets. In agriculture, water is used mainly for irrigation. **Irrigation** is a way of supplying dry land with water by artificial means. In industry, the amount of water used varies with the product being produced.

There are a number of things that can be done to protect and conserve California's water supply. In homes, people can take short showers rather than baths, because they use less water. New toilets can be installed, which use less than the usual 15–27 L (4–7 gallons) of water per flush.

Farmers can conserve water in two main ways. First, they can plant rows of vegetables and fruits in ways that prevent runoff. Rows of crops should be planted around a hill, not up and down.

Second, farmers can use irrigation water wisely. Water can be carried by underground pipelines, which reduce evaporation. Drip and sprinkler irrigation systems conserve water. Lined trenches prevent water seepage.

Industries can reuse water, especially the water used for cooling. Factories must also dispose of waste without dumping it into streams.

Another way to meet California's water needs would be to make use of seawater. Seawater cannot be used directly because of the salt it contains. So methods are used to *desalinate* the water, or remove the salt from it.

CONSERVING CALIFORNIA'S WATER

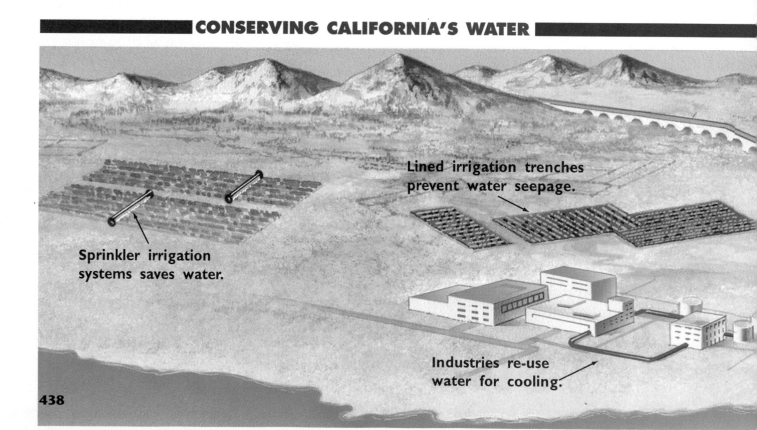

Sprinkler irrigation systems saves water.

Lined irrigation trenches prevent water seepage.

Industries re-use water for cooling.

Flash distillation is a process in which water evaporates below its normal boiling temperature. In a desalination plant, seawater is put through this process in a series of chambers. The very salty water that remains is returned to the ocean. The fresh water enters our water supply.

The energy cost for flash distillation is very high. However, the cost can be reduced if desalination plans can be linked with nuclear power plants located in coastal areas. A better solution might be to develop solar-powered desalination plants. There are currently desalination plants in California at Monterey on the central coast, on Catalina Island, and at Port Hueneme.

Seawater is turned into drinking water at this California desalination plant.

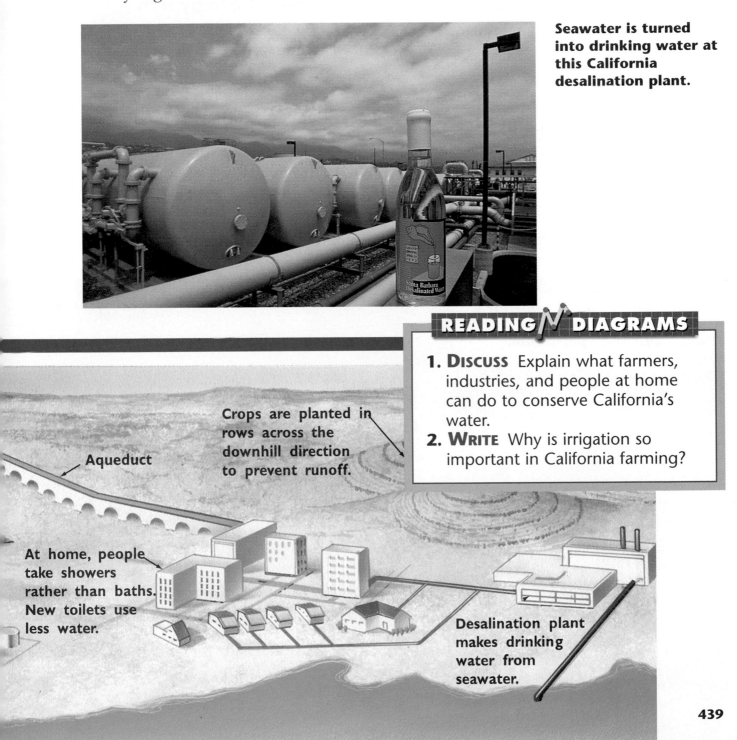

Aqueduct

Crops are planted in rows across the downhill direction to prevent runoff.

At home, people take showers rather than baths. New toilets use less water.

Desalination plant makes drinking water from seawater.

READING DIAGRAMS

1. **DISCUSS** Explain what farmers, industries, and people at home can do to conserve California's water.
2. **WRITE** Why is irrigation so important in California farming?

What Are California's Energy Resources?

California is rich in energy resources. There are large deposits of fossil fuels, especially petroleum. However, burning petroleum can cause air pollution. Three other sources of natural energy are also available. These are solar energy, wind energy, and geothermal energy. None of them pollute the air. In addition, energy is also available from several nuclear power plants in the state.

Fossil Fuels

Californians use huge quantities of fossil fuels. Petroleum is used to generate electrcicity and to fuel cars. The state has almost no coal, but it does have many oil wells. Many of them are located near Bakersfield in the Central Valley. Even so, California does not produce nearly enough oil to meet all its needs. Today, many new wells are being drilled on the continental shelf off the California coast. Offshore oilwells account for a growing share of California's oil production.

Solar Energy

Much solar energy falls directly on forests and croplands. Solar energy is used to produce electricity at an unusual plant in Barstow, California. Dozens of mirror-like reflectors focus solar rays onto a boiler mounted on a central tower. Steam in the tower moves through a turbine to produce electricity.

Wind Energy

Wind energy is obtained by using a special kind of windmill called a wind turbine. In the mountain passes just

1 Offshore oil wells provide a growing share of California's petroleum.

2 The solar energy being produced at this plant is a clean alternative to fossil fuels.

outside of Palm Springs, California, there are hundreds of wind turbines. These "wind farms" require little care, and they produce no air pollution. Today, they supply about one percent of California's energy. This amount is expected to increase in the future as wind turbine technology improves.

Geothermal Energy

Heat from inside Earth is called *geothermal energy*. The heat comes from underground magma. The magma heats water in the ground to create steam or hot water springs. The world's largest geothermal power station is at The Geysers in Sonoma County, California. At The Geysers, the average temperature of the steam is about 250°C (480°F).

In other parts of the world, geothermal energy heats homes and large buildings. Perhaps California will soon use geothermal energy in the same way.

Nuclear Energy

Several nuclear power plants around the state generate electricity from nuclear energy. Inside the plant, a nuclear chain reaction generates heat, which produces steam. The steam drives turbines to produce electricity. One kilogram of nuclear fuel can produce as much energy as 45 to 65 million pounds of coal. As a method of generating electricity, nuclear power is much cleaner than burning fossil fuels. But nuclear energy presents other environmental problems.

Brain Power

Nuclear energy will probably not be used as a source of power for cars. Give at least two reasons why.

③ "Wind farms" with wind turbines like these supply about one percent of California's energy.

④ The San Onofre nuclear power plant at San Clemente generates electricity for southern California.

How Can We Conserve California's Energy?

Although rich in energy resources, California does not produce all of its own energy. A large share must be purchased from other places. So it makes sense to use energy wisely and to conserve it when possible. Another good reason to reduce energy consumption is to avoid burning fossil fuels that pollute the air.

Use Less Gasoline

One way to conserve energy is to drive cars that burn less gasoline. Car buyers can choose car models that get more mileage from a tankful of gas. Homes and factories can also be designed to use less fossil fuel.

Take Mass Transit

Another way to conserve energy is to make more use of mass transit. San Francisco and Los Angeles have built underground mass-transit rail systems in an effort to reduce automobile traffic. San Diego and other cities have built ground-level light-rail mass transit systems for the same purpose. By reducing traffic and gasoline consumption, mass transit can also make the air cleaner in California's cities.

Above: The new Los Angeles subway is designed to reduce automobile traffic and improve the city's air quality.

Right: San Diego is using a light-rail mass transit system to reduce automobile traffic.

Use Solar Energy

In the sunny California climate, fossil fuels can be replaced with solar power for many uses. In some parts of California, almost 90 percent of the available solar energy reaches the ground. By contrast, in the northern part of the United States, only about 60 percent of the available solar energy reaches the ground. That is why for many Californians, it pays to make use of solar energy.

Solar energy in California is used chiefly to heat homes. Many Californians live in passive solar-heated houses. The houses are heated as sunlight passes through double, insulated glass windows.

Still other Californians live in active solar-heated houses, which have rooftop solar energy collectors. Many schools and offices are also heated with solar energy. Are there houses or other buildings in your community that are heated in this way?

Use Nuclear Energy

Another way to avoid burning fossil fuels is to make use of nuclear energy. Currently, nuclear power plants use a process called fission to produce energy. In the future, it may also be possible to produce energy from a different process called nuclear fusion. Scientists at the Lawrence Livermore Laboratory of the University of California are working to develop practical nuclear fusion generators. The raw materials needed can be found in ordinary seawater. If the process is ever perfected, California will have a nearly limitless supply of nuclear fuel in the Pacific Ocean.

Tremendous amounts of energy are needed to bring power to Los Angeles and other large California cities. Managing energy wisely is important to everyone.

California's growing population is increasing demands on the state's natural resources. [inset] The water needs of California's farms must be balanced against those of its cities.

Are California's Resource Needs Growing?

California's population and economy both continue to grow at a rapid rate. More people and more activities make more and more demands on the state's resources. That is why it is more important than ever to manage the state's air, water, and energy wisely. Only in that way can we make sure that California continues to be a wonderful place to live or visit.

More and more cars and trucks travel California's freeways and local roads. The growing traffic continues to threaten the quality of California's air. Nevertheless, statewide controls on car exhaust emissions are reducing smog and other types of air pollution. Goals have been set to make California's air even cleaner in the future.

Having more people also means making more demands on California's water resources. Distant new sources may have to be found to provide water for growing cities. New aqueducts may have to be built to transport the water. In addition, farmers need water to irrigate their farms. Their needs must be

444

balanced against those of thirsty city dwellers. New arrangements may have to be made with neighboring states about how best to share scarce water supplies.

More energy is also needed to heat and light California's homes. It is also needed to power the state's expanding economy. Supplying this energy—and doing so without increasing air pollution from burning fossil fuels—is a challenge that must be met.

Wise, careful management of California's air, water, and energy resources is a job for everyone.

You and millions of other people live in California. Millions more visit the state every year. People are attracted by California's beautiful natural scenery, pleasant climate, and quality of life. But the millions who live here also drive cars that pollute the air. They build towns and cities in waterless areas and have to import scarce drinking water from far away. They use huge amounts of energy to power homes and factories.

For the sake of your future in California, it makes sense to try to preserve the state's resources and natural environment.

REVIEW

1. How is smog formed?

2. Why is irrigation so important to California?

3. How could the Pacific Ocean be a resource for nuclear fusion?

4. **CAUSE AND EFFECT** How do electric cars and cars using natural gas reduce air pollution?

5. **CRITICAL THINKING** *Analyze* Why are solar-heated houses ideal for the climate of southern California?

WHY IT MATTERS **THINK ABOUT IT**
Why are Hoover Dam and Lake Mead so important to southern California?

WHY IT MATTERS **WRITE ABOUT IT**
Explain ways in which you can help to conserve water and make California's air clearer.

SIERRA SNOWPACK

Where does California's drinking water spend the winter? The answer is in the snowpack that coats the Sierra Nevada. Of all the precipitation that falls on the state each year, the largest share winds up in the snowpack. In winter the snowpack is more than 500 miles long and 65 miles wide. Its yearly growth and springtime melting have enormous effects on the whole state.

Meltwater from the snowpack supplies water to most of California's 33 million people. It supplies one-third of the water used by over 16 million people in southern California.

The snowpack changes greatly in size from year to year. These changes are important. They determine how much water will be available in the coming year and what it will cost. That in turn determines what kinds of crops get planted, how much farmers can expect to earn—and even the number of striped bass and salmon in the rivers.

Each winter scientists measure the amount of water in the snowpack. Their measurements answer many important questions. Will spring bring a drought or a flood? Can the reservoirs hold all the runoff, or will they overflow? How much hydroelectric power will be generated by the dams of northern and central California?

DISCUSSION STARTER

1. What determines the amount of drinking water and irrigation water for California

2. How does the size of the snowpack determine what crops farmers will plant in the spring?

Next year's drinking water lies frozen in the Sierra Nevada snowpack.

To learn more about snow, visit **www.mhschool.com/science** and enter the keyword SNOW.

SCIENCE WORDS

acid rain p. 399

aquifer p. 409

desalination p. 407

fossil fuel p. 398

groundwater p. 409

ozone layer p. 397

renewable resource p. 396

reservoir p. 409

smog p. 398

water table p. 409

USING SCIENCE WORDS

Number a paper from 1 to 10. Fill in 1 to 5 with words from the list above.

1. Solar power is a(n) __?__.

2. A(n) __?__ is an underground layer of rock or soil filled with water.

3. Precipitation mixed with wastes from burned fossil fuels is called __?__.

4. __?__ is a mix of smoke and fog in the air.

5. Natural gas is a(n) __?__.

6–10. **Pick five words from the list above that were not used in 1 to 5, and use each in a sentence.**

UNDERSTANDING SCIENCE IDEAS

11. What is the difference between renewable and nonrenewable energy sources?

12. How were fossil fuels formed?

13. Where does geothermal energy come from?

14. What are springs and where do they occur?

15. Explain how to turn salt water into fresh water.

USING IDEAS AND SKILLS

16. How does smog form?

17. **READING SKILL: DRAW CONCLUSIONS** All electricity is made by burning fossil fuels. Is this true or false? Explain your answer.

18. **USE NUMBERS** Suppose the costs of two heating systems were as follows:

    solar energy $5/day

    oil burner $10/day

On sunny days, you can run your solar heating system. On cloudy days, you must run your oil burner. How much would it cost to heat your home for a week if two days were cloudy? If four days were cloudy?

19. **HYPOTHESIZE** Does rain remove pollutant particles from the air? What could you do to test your hypothesis?

20. **THINKING LIKE A SCIENTIST** Does filtering water remove all impurities? Explain your answer. How would you prove your answer?

PROBLEMS and PUZZLES

Saving Soil How do growing plants help conserve soil? Grow some grass seeds in a tray. In a second tray, lay down some soil. Tilt both trays, and use a watering can to produce "rain" over them. Which tray loses more soil?

UNIT 5 REVIEW

acid rain p. 399

desalination p. 407

geothermal energy p. 441

humus p. 371

metamorphic rock p. 387

mineral p. 352

ozone layer p. 397

renewable resource p. 396

solar cell p. 419

spring p. 409

USING SCIENCE WORDS

Number a paper from 1 to 10. Beside each number write the word or words that best complete the sentence.

1. Moisture that falls to Earth after mixing with wastes from burned fossil fuels is __?__.

2. __?__ is decayed plant or animal material in soil.

3. A __?__ is a device that generates an electric current from sunlight.

4. Streak, luster, hardness, and cleavage are properties of __?__.

5. Marble, formed by the action of heat and pressure on limestone, is a(n) __?__.

6. Oxygen that is given off by plants is an example of a(n) __?__.

7. The gas layer in the atmosphere that screens out UV (ultraviolet) rays from the Sun is the __?__.

8. Groundwater seeps out of the ground at places called __?__.

9. Fresh water can be produced from seawater by a process called __?__.

10. Energy from geysers is an example of __?__.

UNDERSTANDING SCIENCE IDEAS

Write 11 to 15. For each number write the letter for the best answer. You may wish to use the hints provided.

11. Which of the following is a nonrenewable resource?
    a. hydroelectricity
    b. natural gas
    c. wind power
    d. biomass conversion fuels
    (Hint: Read page 420.)

12. Which of the following can be scratched by glass?
    a. steel plate
    b. diamond
    c. chalk
    d. topaz
    (Hint: Read page 354.)

13. Which of the following pollutes the air?
    a. sulfur
    b. calcium
    c. water
    d. oxygen
    (Hint: Read page 400.)

14. Most fresh water is found in
    a. groundwater
    b. ice caps and glaciers
    c. oceans
    d. lakes and streams
    (Hint: Read page 406.)

15. The fuel used in most nuclear power plants is
    a. tritium
    b. carbon dioxide
    c. uranium
    d. ethanol
    (Hint: Read page 424.)

USING IDEAS AND SKILLS

16. Describe how "active" solar heating works.

17. Explain how irrigation can sometimes harm soils.

18. What are two problems with building more hydroelectric dams?

19. **DEFINE** How is hardness defined for minerals?

20. What are the two types of coal? How are they related?

21. Explain what a renewable resource is. Give an example.

22. How does burning coal cause acid rain?

23. Where does the fresh water found in glaciers and rivers come from?

THINKING LIKE A SCIENTIST

24. **HYPOTHESIZE** Explain why you might have to use a model to test a hypothesis.

25. **HYPOTHESIZE** A natural spring in your area has dried up. What do you think has happened to the water table? How might you test your idea?

interNET CONNECTION

For help in reviewing this unit, visit *www.mhschool.com/science*

WRITING IN YOUR JOURNAL

SCIENCE IN YOUR LIFE
Describe two ways you use water each day and two ways businesses or farms use water. Explain how these uses might pollute water.

PRODUCT ADS
More and more ads are appearing for electric cars (EVs) that run on electricity rather than gasoline. Why do you think companies are starting to make such cars?

HOW SCIENTISTS WORK
Scientists routinely organize information in tables and graphs. Use two examples from this unit to tell why this is useful.

Design your own Experiment

Form a hypothesis about how much garbage is produced in your school. Design an experiment to test your hypothesis. Think safety first. Review your experiment with your teacher before you attempt it.

PROBLEMS and PUZZLES

Artificial Atmosphere

Moon Colony I is being built under a huge greenhouse dome designed to hold an atmosphere like that of Earth. Your job is to create and maintain this artificial atmosphere. Of the following four items, which two would you take to the Moon to help you get the job done?

- A cloud-generating machine

- An ozone-generating machine

- A wind machine to generate convection currents

- Green plants

Explain your choices.

Garbage to the Moon

Each year each person in the United States creates a 15-foot-tall pile of garbage. If stacked end to end, could all of the garbage piles created by 260 million Americans reach the Moon? Could it reach the Sun? Use the data in the figure to find the answer. Explain how close or how far the garbage would reach.

Earth–Moon 240,000 miles

Earth–Sun 93,000,000 miles

Soil: A Close-Up View

Fill a tall glass jar one-third full with soil. Add water to make the jar two-thirds full. Add a capful of water softener, if available. Then analyze your soil.

1. Shake the mixture well. Then let it settle for 15 to 20 minutes, until layers form.

2. Which layer settles first? Second? Third? Hold a sheet of paper next to the jar. Draw each layer that you see.

3. Compare your soil to the soil shown in the diagram. Is your soil sandy, silty, or high in clay?

4. Which kind of soil do you think is best for growing plants? Plant some seeds, and see if you are right.

3 Clay: The lightest, finest particles are clay. Some stay suspended in the water.

2 Silt: The silt layer is made of the small, heavy particles. Silt settles after the sand.

1 Sand: Sand settles first. The sand layer is made of the large, heavy particles.

REFERENCE SECTION

DIAGRAM BUILDERS

Building a Topographic Map

A topographic map uses **contour lines** to show the shape of the land. A contour line is drawn through points of a given height, or elevation, above or below sea level. **How do contour lines show the shape of the land?**

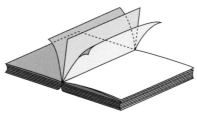

BASE

To find out, look at the map on the facing page. Lift up all the plastic overlays (1, 2, 3), and look at the base. You see an area of land as if you were looking down from an airplane.
Do you see the landforms?

OVERLAY 1

1 Now drop overlay 1 onto the base. From one contour line to the next is a difference of 1,000 meters in elevation. That difference is not a measure of how far apart the lines are. To tell that, measure the distance between any two lines and compare the distance to the map scale.
Do the contour lines help you see any landforms or the shape of the land? How?

OVERLAY 2

2 Now drop overlay 2 onto overlay 1. The contour lines are now drawn for every 500 meters.
Can you see the shape of the land better than with just overlay 1? Explain.

OVERLAY 3

3 Now drop overlay 3 onto overlay 2.
What details are added? How do they complete the picture?

SUMMARIZE

How do the lines of a contour map help you tell which places are steeper than others?

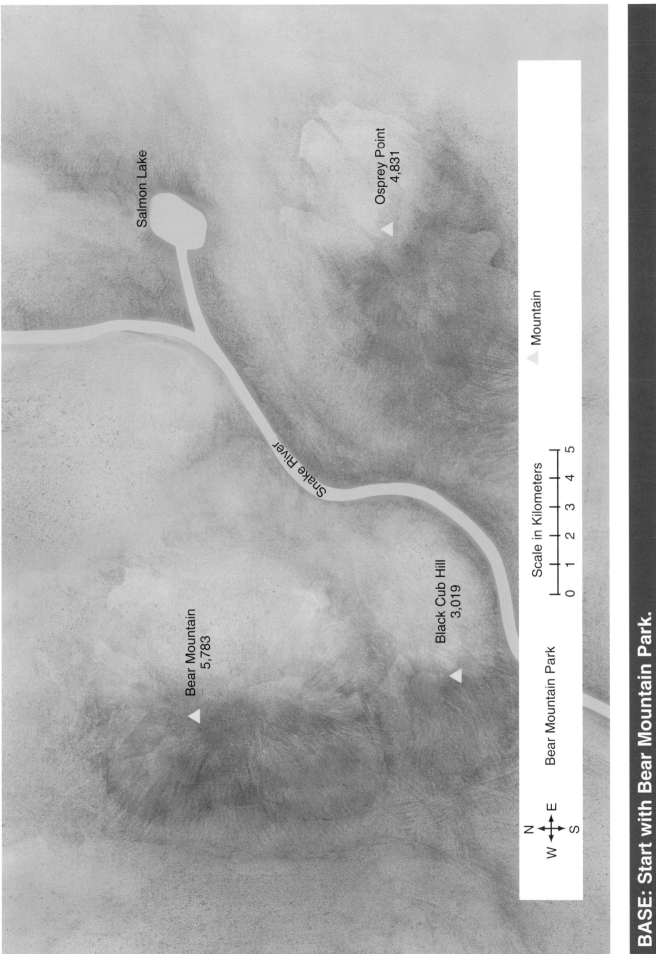

BASE: Start with Bear Mountain Park.

DIAGRAM BUILDERS
Activities

1 Make a Map

You need: compass, graph paper, meterstick or tape measure

Make a map of a room, your school playground, or any small area. Use the compass to tell what the direction of each corner is. Measure the sides. Decide how many squares of a graph paper grid you would need to show the area. What real length would each side of a graph paper square represent?

2 Make Observations

You need: washers, string, ruler

Hang a heavy weight, like a bunch of washers, on a string to make what is called a plumb line. Tie the free end of the string to the end of a ruler. Hold the free end of the ruler down onto your shoulder so that the string and weight are hanging alongside your body. How can you use this string and weight to tell if you are walking along a level surface or you are going up or down a slanted surface? Explain.

3 Write About a Main Idea

How can a contour map help you study changes in an area? Think of an area, for example, along a shoreline that is hit by strong waves or an area that has frequent earthquakes.

REFERENCE SECTION

MEASUREMENTS

This bottle of juice has a volume of 1 liter.

That is a little more than 1 quart.

She can walk 20 meters in 5 seconds.

That means her speed is 4 meters per second.

Table of Measurements

SI (INTERNATIONAL SYSTEM) OF UNITS

Temperature

Water freezes at 0°C and boils at 100°C.

Length and Distance

1,000 meters = 1 kilometer
100 centimeters = 1 meter
10 millimeters = 1 centimeter

Volume

1,000 milliliters = 1 liter
1 cubic centimeter = 1 milliliter

Mass

1,000 grams = 1 kilogram

ENGLISH SYSTEM OF UNITS

Temperature

Water freezes at 32°F and boils at 212°F.

Length and Distance

5,280 feet = 1 mile
3 feet = 1 yard
12 inches = 1 foot

Volume of Fluids

4 quarts = 1 gallon
2 pints = 1 quart
2 cups = 1 pint
8 fluid ounces = 1 cup

Weight

2,000 pounds = 1 ton
16 ounces = 1 pound

In the Classroom

The most important part of doing any experiment is doing it safely. You can be safe by paying attention to your teacher and doing your work carefully. Here are some other ways to stay safe while you do experiments.

Before the Experiment

- Read all of the directions. Make sure you understand them. When you see ▨ be sure to follow the safety rule.

- Listen to your teacher for special safety directions. If you don't understand something, ask for help.

During the Experiment

- Wear safety goggles when your teacher tells you to wear them and whenever you see 🥽.
- Wear a safety apron if you work with anything messy or anything that might spill.
- If you spill something, wipe it up right away or ask your teacher for help.
- Tell your teacher if something breaks. If glass breaks do not clean it up yourself.

- Keep your hair and clothes away from open flames. Tie back long hair and roll up long sleeves.
- Be careful around a hot plate. Know when it is on and when it is off. Remember that the plate stays hot for a few minutes after you turn it off.
- Keep your hands dry around electrical equipment.
- Don't eat or drink anything during the experiment.

After the Experiment

- Put equipment back the way your teacher tells you.
- Dispose of things the way your teacher tells you.
- Clean up your work area and wash your hands.

In the Field

■ Always be accompanied by a trusted adult—like your teacher or a parent or guardian.
■ Never touch animals or plants without the adult's approval. The animal might bite. The plant might be poison ivy or another dangerous plant.

Responsibility

Acting safely is one way to be responsible. You can also be responsible by treating animals, the environment, and each other with respect in the class and in the field.

Treat Living Things with Respect

■ If you have animals in the classroom, keep their homes clean. Change the water in fish tanks and clean out cages.
■ Feed classroom animals the right amount of food.
■ Give your classroom animals enough space.
■ When you observe animals, don't hurt them or disturb their homes.
■ Find a way to care for animals while school is on vacation.

Treat the Environment with Respect

■ Do not pick flowers.
■ Do not litter, including gum and food.
■ If you see litter, ask your teacher if you can pick it up.
■ Recycle materials used in experiments. Ask your teacher what materials can be recycled instead of thrown away. These might include plastics, aluminum, and newspapers.

Treat Each Other with Respect

■ Use materials carefully around others so that people don't get hurt or get stains on their clothes.
■ Be careful not to bump people when they are doing experiments. Do not disturb or damage their experiments.
■ If you see that people are having trouble with an experiment, help them.

Use a Hand Lens

One of the most important things you do in science is something that you do every day—make observations. You make an observation every time you use your senses to learn about the world around you. Whether you are watching a bird build a nest, listening to the rumble of distant thunder, or feeling the pull of a refrigerator magnet, you are using your senses to learn.

Sometimes your senses need a little help, especially during experiments. A hand lens, for example, magnifies an object, or makes the object look larger. With a hand lens, you can see details that would be hard to see otherwise.

Magnify a Piece of Cereal

1. Place a piece of your favorite cereal on a flat surface. Look at the cereal carefully. Draw a picture of it.
2. Look at the cereal through the large lens of a hand lens. Move the lens toward or away from the cereal until it looks larger and in focus. Draw a picture of the cereal as you see it through the hand lens. Fill in details that you did not see before.
3. Look at the cereal through the smaller lens, which will magnify the cereal even more. If you notice more details, add them to your drawing.
4. Repeat this activity using objects you are studying in science. It might be a rock, some soil, or a seed.

Observe Mold in a Petri Dish

A petri dish is a shallow, clear, round dish with a cover. It's useful for growing microscopic organisms such as mold.

1. Place a piece of bread about the size of your palm in a petri dish. It is best if the bread is a few days old and not made with preservatives.
2. Wet the bread by sprinkling water on it. Put the lid on the petri dish, and place the dish in a warm place.
3. After a few days, mold will start to grow on the bread. Use a hand lens to observe the mold through the clear petri dish. Draw what you see. Do not remove the cover from the dish.

Use a Microscope

Hand lenses make objects look several times larger. A microscope, however, can magnify an object to look hundreds of times larger.

Examine Salt Grains

1. Look at the photograph to learn the different parts of your microscope.
2. Place the microscope on a flat surface. Always carry a microscope with both hands. Hold the arm with one hand, and put your other hand beneath the base.
3. Move the mirror so that it reflects light up toward the stage. Never point the mirror directly at the Sun or a bright light.
4. Place a few grains of salt on the slide. Put the slide under the stage clips. Be sure that the salt grains you are going to examine are over the hole in the stage.
5. Look through the eyepiece. Turn the focusing knob slowly until the salt grains come into focus.
6. Draw what the grains look like through the microscope.
7. Look at other objects through the microscope. Try a piece of leaf, a human hair, or a pencil mark.

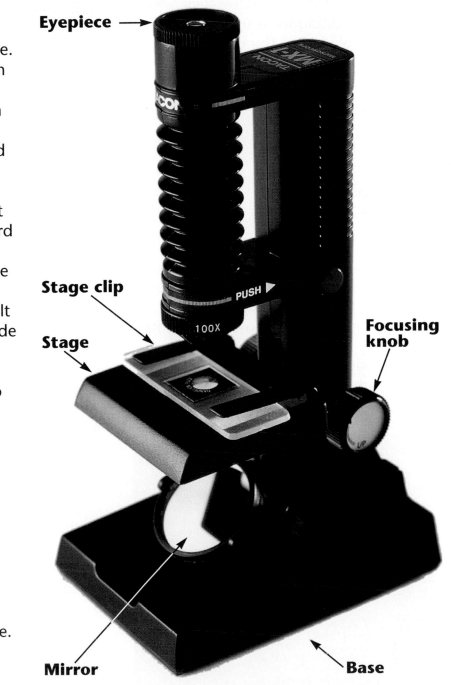

Eyepiece →

Stage clip

Stage

Focusing knob

Mirror

Base

Use a Collecting Net

You can use a collecting net to catch insects and observe them. You can try catching an insect in midair, but you might have better luck waiting for it to land on a plant. Put the net over the whole plant. Then you can place the insect in a jar with holes in the lid.

Use a Compass

You use a compass to find directions. A compass is a small, thin magnet that swings freely, like a spinner in a board game. One end of the magnet always points north. This end is the magnet's north pole. How does a compass work?

1. Place the compass on a surface that is not made of magnetic material, such as a wooden table or a sidewalk.

2. Find the magnet's north pole. The north pole is marked in some way, usually with a color or an arrowhead.
3. Notice the letters N, E, S, and W on the compass. These letters stand for the directions north, east, south, and west. When the magnet stops swinging, turn the compass so that the N lines up with the north pole of the magnet.
4. Face to the north. Then face to the east, to the south, and to the west.
5. Repeat this activity by holding the compass in your hand and then at different places indoors and outdoors.

Use a Telescope

You make most observations for science class during the day. Some things are observed best at night—like the Moon and the stars.

You can observe the Moon and the stars simply by looking up into a clear night sky. However, it's hard to see much detail on the Moon, such as craters and mountains. Also you can see only a tiny fraction of the stars and other objects that are actually in the sky. A telescope improves those observations.

A telescope uses lenses or mirrors to gather light and magnify objects. You can see much greater detail of the Moon's surface with a telescope than with just your eyes. A telescope gathers light better than your eyes can. With a telescope you can see stars that are too faint to see with just your eyes. See for yourself how a telescope can improve your observations.

1. Look at the Moon in the night sky, and draw a picture of what you see. Draw as many details as you can.
2. Point a telescope toward the Moon. Look through the eyepiece of the telescope. Move the telescope until you see the Moon. Turn the knob until the Moon comes into focus.

3. Draw a picture of what you see, including as many details as you can. Compare your two pictures.
4. Find the brightest star in the sky. Notice if there are any other stars near it.
5. Point a telescope toward the bright star. Look through the eyepiece and turn the knob until the stars come into focus. Move the telescope until you find the bright star.
6. Can you see stars through the telescope that you cannot see with just your eyes?

Objective lens

Eyepiece lens
Focusing knob

R9

Use a Camera, Tape Recorder, Map, and Compass

Camera

You can use a camera to record what you observe in nature. When taking photographs keep these tips in mind.

1. Hold the camera steady. Gently press the shutter button so that you do not jerk the camera.
2. Try to take pictures with the Sun at your back. Then your pictures will be bright and clear.
3. Don't get too close to the subject. Without a special lens, the picture could turn out blurry.
4. Be patient. If you are taking a picture of an animal, you may have to wait for the animal to appear.

Tape Recorder

You can record observations on a tape recorder. This is sometimes better than writing notes because, with a tape recorder, you can record your observations at the exact time you are making them. Later you can listen to the tape and write down your observations.

Use a Map and a Compass

When you are busy observing nature, it might be easy to get lost. You can use a map of the area and a compass to find your way. Here are some tips.

1. Lightly mark on the map your starting place. It might be the place where the bus parked.
2. Always know where you are on the map compared to your starting place. Watch for landmarks on the map, such as a river, a pond, trails, or buildings.
3. Use the map and compass to find special places to observe, such as a pond. Look at the map to see what direction the place is from you. Hold the compass to see where that direction is.
4. Use your map and compass with a friend.

Length

Find Length with a Ruler

1. Look at this section of a ruler. Each centimeter is divided into 10 milli-meters. How long is the paper clip?
2. The length of the paper clip is 3 cen-timeters plus 2 millimeters. You can write this length as 3.2 centimeters.
3. Place the ruler on your desk. Lay a pencil against the ruler so that one end of the pencil lines up with the left edge of the ruler. Record the length of the pencil.
4. Trade your pencil with a classmate. Measure and record the length of each other's pencil. Compare your answers.

1 centimeter = 10 millimeters

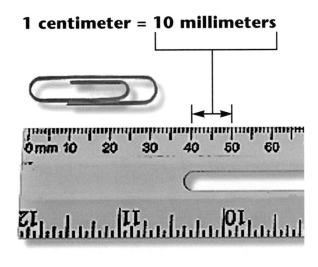

Find Length with a Meterstick

1. Line up the meterstick with the left edge of the chalkboard. Make a chalk mark on the board at the right end of the meterstick.
2. Move the meterstick so that the left edge lines up with the chalk mark. Keep the stick level. Make another mark on the board at the right end of the meterstick.
3. Continue to move the meterstick and make chalk marks until the meterstick meets or overlaps the right edge of the board.
4. Record the length of the chalkboard in centimeters by adding all the measure-ments you've made. Remember, a meterstick has 100 centimeters.

Measuring Area

Area is the amount of surface something covers. To find the area of a rectangle, multiply the rectangle's length by its width. For example, the rectangle here is 3 centimeters long and 2 centimeters wide. Its area is 3 cm x 2 cm = 6 square centimeters. You write the area as 6 cm^2.

1. Find the area of your science book. Measure the book's length to the nearest centimeter. Measure its width.
2. Multiply the book's length by its width. Remember to put the answer in cm^2.

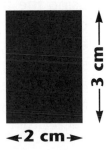

3 cm
◄2 cm►

Time

You use timing devices to measure how long something takes to happen. Some timing devices you use in science are a clock with a second hand and a stopwatch. Which one is more accurate?

Comparing a Clock and Stopwatch

1. Look at a clock with a second hand. The second hand is the hand that you can see moving. It measures seconds.
2. Get an egg timer with falling sand or some device like a wind-up toy that runs down after a certain length of time. When the second hand of the clock points to 12, tell your partner to start the egg timer. Watch the clock while the sand in the egg timer is falling.
3. When the sand stops falling, count how many seconds it took. Record this measurement. Repeat the activity, and compare the two measurements.
4. Switch roles with your partner.
5. Look at a stopwatch. Click the button on the top right. This starts the time. Click the button again. This stops the time. Click the button on the top left. This sets the stopwatch back to zero. Notice that the stopwatch tells time in minutes, seconds, and hundredths of a second.
6. Repeat the activity in steps 1–3, using the stopwatch instead of a clock. Make sure the stopwatch is set to zero. Click the top right button to start timing the reading. Click it again when the sand stops falling. Make sure you and your partner time each other twice.

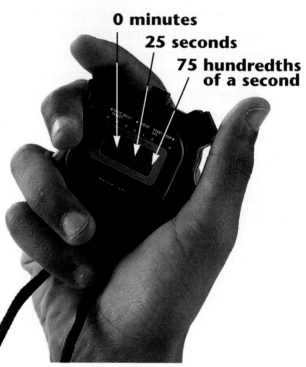

0 minutes
25 seconds
75 hundredths of a second

More About Time

1. Use the stopwatch to time how long it takes an ice cube to melt under cold running water. How long does an ice cube take to melt under warm running water?
2. Match each of these times with the action you think took that amount of time.

a. 0:00:14:55
b. 0:24:39:45
c. 2:10:23:00

1. A Little League baseball game
2. Saying the Pledge of Allegiance
3. Recess

HANDBOOK

Volume

Volume is the amount of space something takes up. If you've ever helped bake a cake or do other cooking, you might have measured the volume of water, vegetable oil, or melted butter. In science you usually measure the volume of liquids by using beakers and graduated cylinders. These containers are marked in milliliters (mL).

Measure the Volume of a Liquid

1. Look at the beaker and at the graduated cylinder. The beaker has marks for each 25 mL up to 200 mL. The graduated cylinder has marks for each 1 mL up to 100 mL.

2. The surface of the water in the graduated cylinder curves up at the sides. You measure the volume by reading the height of the water at the flat part. What is the volume of water in the graduated cylinder? How much water is in the beaker? They both contain 75 mL of water.

3. Pour 50 mL of water from a pitcher into a graduated cylinder. The water should be at the 50-mL mark on the graduated cylinder. If you go over the mark, pour a little water back into the pitcher.

4. Pour the 50 mL of water into a beaker.

5. Repeat steps 3 and 4 using 30 mL, 45 mL, and 25 mL of water.

6. Measure the volume of water you have in the beaker. Do you have about the same amount of water as your classmates?

Mass

Mass is the amount of matter an object has. You use a balance to measure mass. To find the mass of an object, you balance it with objects whose masses you know. Let's find the mass of a box of crayons.

Measure the Mass of a Box of Crayons

1. Place the balance on a flat, level surface. Check that the two pans are empty and clean.
2. Make sure the empty pans are balanced with each other. The pointer should point to the middle mark. If it does not, move the slider a little to the right or left to balance the pans.
3. Gently place a box of crayons on the left pan. This pan will drop lower.
4. Add masses to the right pan until the pans are balanced.
5. Add the numbers on the masses that are in the right pan. The total is the mass of the box of crayons, in grams. Record this number. After the number write a *g* for "grams."

HANDBOOK

Predict the Mass of More Crayons

1. Leave the box of crayons and the masses on the balance.
2. Get two more crayons. If you put them in the pan with the box of crayons, what do you think the mass of all the crayons will be? Record what you predict the total mass will be.
3. Check your prediction. Gently place the two crayons in the left pan. Add masses to the right pan until the pans are balanced.
4. Add the numbers on the masses as you did before. Record this number. How close is it to your prediction?

More About Mass

What was the mass of all your crayons? It was probably less than 100 grams. What would happen if you replaced the crayons with a pineapple? You may not have enough masses to balance the pineapple. It has a mass of about 1,000 grams. That's the same as 1 kilogram because *kilo* means "1,000."

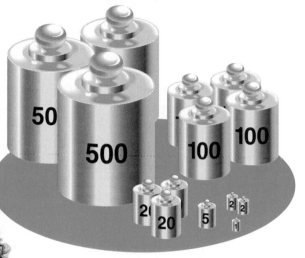

1. How many kilograms do all these masses add up to?
2. Which of these objects have a mass greater than 1 kilogram?
   a. large dog
   b. robin
   c. desktop computer
   d. calculator
   e. whole watermelon

HANDBOOK

Weight/Force

You use a spring scale to measure weight. An object has weight because the force of gravity pulls down on the object. Therefore, weight is a force. Weight is measured in newtons (N) like all forces.

Measure the Weight of an Object

1. Look at your spring scale to see how many newtons it measures. See how the measurements are divided. The spring scale shown here measures up to 5 N. It has a mark for every 0.1 N.
2. Hold the spring scale by the top loop. Put the object to be measured on the bottom hook. If the object will not stay on the hook, place it in a net bag. Then hang the bag from the hook.
3. Let go of the object slowly. It will pull down on a spring inside the scale. The spring is connected to a pointer. The pointer on the spring scale shown here is a small bar.
4. Wait for the pointer to stop moving. Read the number of newtons next to the pointer. This is the object's weight. The mug in the picture weighs 4 N.

More About Spring Scales

You probably weigh yourself by standing on a bathroom scale. This is a spring scale. The force of your body stretches a spring inside the scale. The dial on the scale is probably marked in pounds—the English unit of weight. One pound is equal to about 4.5 newtons.

Here are some other spring scales you may have seen.

Temperature

You use a thermometer to measure temperature—how hot or cold something is. A thermometer is made of a thin tube with colored liquid inside. When the liquid gets warmer, it expands and moves up the tube. When the liquid gets cooler, it contracts and moves down the tube. You may have seen most temperatures measured in degrees Fahrenheit (°F). Scientists measure temperature in degrees Celsius (°C).

Read a Thermometer

1. Look at the thermometer shown here. It has two scales—a Fahrenheit scale and a Celsius scale. Every 20 degrees on the Fahrenheit scale has a number. Every 10 degrees on the Celsius scale has a number.
2. What is the temperature shown on the thermometer? At what temperature does water freeze? Give your answers in °F and in °C.

What Is Convection?

1. Fill a large beaker about two-thirds full of cool water. Find the temperature of the water by holding a thermometer in the water. Do not let the bulb at the bottom of the thermometer touch the sides or bottom of the beaker.
2. Keep the thermometer in the water until the liquid in the tube stops moving— about a minute. Read and record the temperature in °C.

3. Sprinkle a little fish food on the surface of the water in the beaker. Do not knock the beaker, and most of the food will stay on top.
4. Carefully place the beaker on a hot plate. A hot plate is a small electric stove. Plug in the hot plate, and turn the control knob to a middle setting.
5. After a minute measure the temperature of water near the bottom of the beaker. At the same time, a classmate should measure the temperature of water near the top of the beaker. Record these temperatures. Is water near the bottom of the beaker heating up faster than near the top?
6. As the water heats up, notice what happens to the fish food. How do you know that warmer water at the bottom of the beaker rises and cooler water at the top sinks?

Water boils

Room temperature

Water freezes

°F   °C

Weather

What information is included in a weather report? You might think of temperature, cloud cover, wind speed, amount of rainfall, and so on. Various instruments are used to measure these parts of the weather. Some of them are shown here.

Barometer

A barometer measures air pressure. Most barometers are like the one shown here. It contains a flat metal can with most of the air removed. When air pressure increases (rises), the air pushes more on the can. A pointer that is attached to the can moves toward a higher number on the scale. When air pressure decreases (falls), the air pushes less on the can. The pointer moves toward a lower number on the scale.

29.73 inches ⟶

Notice that the barometer above measures air pressure in inches and in centimeters. The long arrow points to the current air pressure, which is 29.73 inches of mercury. That means the air pushing down on liquid mercury in a dish would force the mercury 29.73 inches up a tube, as the drawing shows. What is the air pressure in centimeters?

Follow these steps when you use a barometer.

1. Look at the current air pressure reading marked by the long arrow.
2. Turn the knob on the front of the barometer so the short arrow points to the current pressure reading.
3. Check the barometer several times a day to see if the pressure is rising, falling, or staying the same.

Rain Gauge

A rain gauge measures how much rain falls. This instrument is simply a container that collects water. It has one or more scales for measuring the amount of rain.

The rain gauge shown here has been collecting rain throughout the day. How much rain fell in inches? In centimeters?

Weather Vane

A weather vane measures wind direction. A weather vane is basically an arrow that is free to spin on a pole. Wind pushes on the widest part of the arrow—the tail—so that the arrow points to the direction that the wind is coming from. Letters on the weather vane show directions. If the vane doesn't have letters, you can tell direction with a compass. What direction is the wind coming from in the picture?

Windsock

A windsock also measures wind direction. You may have seen windsocks at airports. Windsocks are usually large and bright orange so that pilots can easily see which way the wind is blowing. The large opening of the windsock faces the wind. The narrow part of the windsock points in the direction that the wind is blowing. Which way is the wind blowing in the picture?

Anemometer

An anemometer measures wind speed. It is usually made of three shallow cones, or cups, that spin on an axle. The wind makes the cups and axle spin. The axle is attached to a dial that indicates wind speed. The faster the wind blows, the faster the cups turn.

Computer

A computer has many uses. The Internet connects your computer to many other computers around the world, so you can collect all kinds of information. You can use a computer to show this information and write reports. Best of all you can use a computer to explore, discover, and learn.

You can also get information from CD-ROMs. They are computer disks that can hold large amounts of information. You can fit a whole encyclopedia on one CD-ROM.

Use Computers for a Project

Here is how one group of students uses computers as they work on a weather project.

1. The students use instruments to measure temperature, wind speed, wind direction, and other parts of the weather. They input this information, or data, into the computer. The students keep the data in a table. This helps them compare the data from one day to the next.

2. The teacher finds out that another group of students in a town 200 kilometers to the west is also doing a weather project. The two groups use the Internet to talk to each other and share data. When a storm happens in the town to the west, that group tells the other group that it's coming its way.

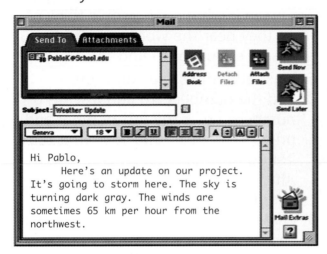

3. The students want to find out more. They decide to stay on the Internet and send questions to a local TV weather forecaster. She has a Web site and answers questions from students every day.

4. Meanwhile some students go to the library to gather more information from a CD-ROM disk. The CD-ROM has an encyclopedia that includes movie clips with sound. The clips give examples of different kinds of storms.

5. The students have kept all their information in a folder called Weather Project. Now they use that information to write a report about the weather. On the computer they can move around paragraphs, add words, take out words, put in diagrams, and draw their own weather maps. Then they print the report in color.

Calculator

Sometimes after you make measurements, you have to analyze your data to see what it means. This might involve doing calculations with your data. A calculator helps you do time-consuming calculations.

Find an Average

After you collect a set of measurements, you may want to get an idea of a typical measurement in that set. What if, for example, you are doing a weather project? As part of the project, you are studying rainfall data of a nearby town. The table shows how much rain fell in that town each week during the summer.

Week	Rain (cm)
1	2.0
2	1.4
3	0.0
4	0.5
5	1.2
6	2.5
7	1.8
8	1.4
9	2.4
10	8.6
11	7.5

What if you want to get an idea of how much rain fell during a typical week in the summer? In other words you want to find the average for the set of data. There are three kinds of averages— mean, median, and mode. Does it matter which one you use?

Find the Mean

The mean is what most people think of when they hear the word *average*. You can use a calculator to find the mean.

1. Make sure the calculator is on.
2. Add the numbers. To add a series of numbers, enter the first number and press ⊞. Repeat until you enter the last number. See the hints below. After your last number, press ⊟. Your total should be 29.3.
3. While entering so many numbers, it's easy to make a mistake and hit the wrong key. If you make a mistake, correct it by pressing the clear entry key, CE. Then continue entering the rest of the numbers.
4. Find the mean by dividing your total by the number of weeks. If 29.3 is displayed, press ÷ 1 1 =. Rounded up to one decimal point, your mean should be 2.7.

Hints:

- If the only number to the right of the decimal point is 0, you don't have to enter it into the calculator. To enter 2.0, just press 2.
- If the only number to the left of the decimal point is 0, you don't have to enter it into the calculator. To enter 0.5, just press · 5.

Find the Median

The median is the middle number when the numbers are arranged in order of size. When the rainfall measurements are arranged in order of size, they look like this.

0.0
0.5
1.2   The median is
1.4   1.8. This number
1.4   is in the middle;
1.8 ←—there are five
2.0   numbers above
2.4   it and five
2.5   numbers below it.
7.5
8.6

Find the Mode

The mode is the number that occurs most frequently. From the ranked set of data above, you can see that the most frequent number is 1.4. It occurs twice. Here are your three different averages from the same set of data.

Average Weekly Rainfall (cm)

Mean	**2.7**
Median	**1.8**
Mode	**1.4**

Why is the mean so much higher than the median or mode? The mean is affected greatly by the last two weeks when it rained a lot. A typical week for that summer was much drier than either of those last two weeks. The median or mode gives a better idea of rainfall for a typical week.

Find the Mean, Median, and Mode

The table shows the length of 15 peanuts. Find the mean, median, and mode for this set of data. Which do you think best represents a typical peanut?

Peanut	Length (mm)
1	32
2	29
3	30
4	31
5	33
6	26
7	28
8	27
9	29
10	29
11	32
12	31
13	23
14	36
15	31

Find the Percent

Sometimes numbers are given as percents (%). *Percent* literally means "per hundred." For example, 28% means 28 out of 100. What if there are about 14,000 trees in the forest and 28% are over 50 years old? How many of them are over 50 years old? Use your calculator. You want to find 28% of 14,000. Press ⬜1 ⬜4 ⬜0 ⬜0 ⬜0 ⬜× ⬜2 ⬜8 ⬜%. The answer should be 3,920.

Make Graphs to Organize Data

When you do an experiment in science, you collect information. To find out what your information means, you can organize it into graphs. There are many kinds of graphs.

Circle Graphs

A circle graph is helpful to show how a complete set of data is divided into parts. The circle graph here shows how water is used in the United States. What is the single largest use of water?

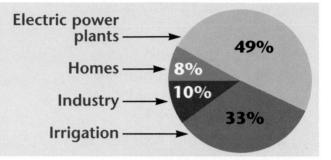

Electric power plants → 49%
Homes → 8%
Industry → 10%
Irrigation → 33%

Bar Graphs

A bar graph uses bars to show information. For example, what if you wrap wire around a nail and connect the ends to a battery? The nail becomes a magnet that can pick up paper clips. The graph shows that the more you wrap the wire around the nail, the more paper clips it picks up.

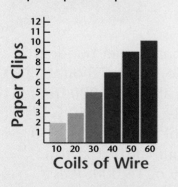

How many paper clips did the nail with 20 coils pick up? With 50 coils?

Line Graphs

A line graph shows information by connecting dots plotted on the graph. For example, what if you are growing a plant? Every week you measure how high the plant has grown. The line graph below organizes the measurements.

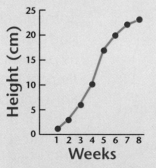

1. Between which two weeks did the plant grow most?
2. When did plant growth begin to level off?

Make a Graph

What if you collect information about how much water your family uses each day?

Activity	Water Used (L)
Drinking	10
Showering	180
Bathing	240
Brushing teeth	80
Washing dishes	140
Washing hands	30
Washing clothes	280
Flushing toilet	90

Decide what type of graph would best organize such data. Collect the information, and make your graph. Compare it with those of classmates.

Make Maps to Show Information

Locate Places

A map is a drawing that shows an area from above. Most maps have coordinates—numbers and letters along the top and side. Coordinates help you find places easily. For example, what if you wanted to find the library on the map? It is located at B4. Place a finger on the letter B at the top of the map and another finger on the number 4 along the side. Then move your fingers straight across and down the map until they meet. The library is located where the coordinates B and 4 meet, or very nearby.

1. What color building is located at F6?
2. The hospital is located three blocks north and two blocks east of the library. What are its coordinates?
3. Make a map of an area in your community. It might be a park or the area between your home and school. Include coordinates. Use a compass to find north, and mark north on your map. Exchange maps with classmates, and answer each other's questions.

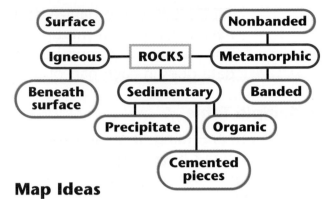

Map Ideas

The map shows how places are connected to each other. Idea maps, on the other hand, show how ideas are connected to each other. Idea maps help you organize information about a topic.

The idea map above connects ideas about rocks. This map shows that there are three major types of rock—igneous, sedimentary, and metamorphic. Connections to each rock type provide further information. For example, this map reminds you that igneous rocks are classified into those that form at Earth's surface and far beneath it.

Make an idea map about a topic you are learning in science. Your map can include words, phrases, or even sentences. Arrange your map in a way that makes sense to you and helps you understand the ideas.

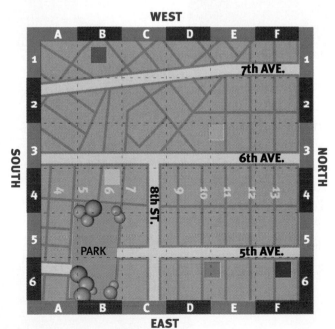

Make Tables and Charts to Organize Information

Tables help you organize data during experiments. Most tables have columns that run up and down, and rows that run across. The columns and rows have headings that tell you what kind of data goes in each part of the table.

A Sample Table

What if you are going to do an experiment to find out how long different kinds of seeds take to sprout? Before you begin the experiment, you should set up your table. Follow these steps.

1. In this experiment you will plant 20 radish seeds, 20 bean seeds, and 20 corn seeds. Your table must show how many radish seeds, bean seeds, and corn seeds sprouted on days 1, 2, 3, 4, and 5.

2. Make your table with columns, rows, and headings. You might use a computer to make a table. Some computer programs let you build a table with just the click of a mouse. You can delete or add columns and rows if you need to.

3. Give your table a title. Your table could look like the one here.

Make a Table

Now what if you are going to do an experiment to find out how temperature affects the sprouting of seeds? You will plant 20 bean seeds in each of two trays. You will keep each tray at a different temperature, as shown below, and observe the trays for seven days. Make a table you can use for this experiment.

Make a Chart

A chart is simply a table with pictures as well as words to label the rows or columns.

GLOSSARY

This Glossary will help you to pronounce and understand the meanings of the Science Words introduced in this book. The page number at the end of the definition tells where the word appears.

A

abiotic factor (ā′bī ot′ik fak′tər) A nonliving part of an ecosystem. (p. 244)

abrasion (ə brā′zhən) A process in which rocks rub against each other and break down into pebbles and sand. (p. CA11)

acid rain (as′id rān′) Moisture that falls to Earth after being mixed with wastes from burned fossil fuels. (p. 399)

active fault (ak′tiv fōlt′) A crack in Earth's surface where earthquakes take place. (p. 52)

adaptation (ad′əp tā′shən) A characteristic that enables a living thing to survive in its environment. (pp. 86, 304)

aftershock (af′tər shok′) Shaking of the crust after the initial shaking of an earthquake. (p. 20)

alpine tundra (al′pīn tun′drə) A cold, dry windy ecosystem found on mountaintops. (p. 272)

aquifer (ak′wə fər) An underground layer of rock or soil filled with water. (p. 409)

arroyo (ə rô yō) A deep canyon carved by water in a desert mountainside. (p. 118)

atmosphere (at′məs fîr′) The blanket of gases that surrounds Earth. (pp. 104, 395)

atom (at′əm) The smallest unit of an element that retains the properties of that element.

B

beach drift (bēch′drift) The motion of sand carried along the beach by the ocean waves. (p. 125)

benthos (ben′thos) Organisms that live on the bottom in aquatic ecosystems. (p. 266)

biodiversity (bī′ō di vûr′si tē) The wide variety of life on Earth. (p. 161)

biomass conversion (bī′ō mas′ kən vûr′zhən) Getting energy from plant and animal materials by changing them into high-quality fuels. (p. 421)

biome (bī′ōm) One of Earth's large ecosystems, with its own kind of climate, soil, plants, and animals. (p. 258)

biotic factor (bī ot′ik fak′tər) A living part of an ecosystem. (p. 245)

blind fault (blīnd fōlt′) A crack in Earth's surface that is not visible on the surface. (p. 52)

brushfire (brush′fīr) A wildfire in an area with mixed trees, shrubs, and grasses. (p. 150)

C

carbon cycle (kär′bən sī′kəl) The continuous exchange of carbon dioxide and oxygen among living things. (p. 322)

carnivore (kär′nə vôr′) An animal that eats another animal. (p. 290)

chain reaction (chān rē ak′shən) A reaction that is kept going by products of the reaction. (p. 422)

PRONUNCIATION KEY

The following symbols are used throughout the McGraw-Hill Science 2000 Glossaries.

a	at	e	end	o	hot	u	up	hw	white	ə	about
ā	ape	ē	me	ō	old	ū	use	ng	song		taken
ä	far	i	it	ô	fork	ü	rule	th	thin		pencil
âr	care	ī	ice	oi	oil	u̇	pull	th	this		lemon
		îr	pierce	ou	out	ûr	turn	zh	measure		circus

′ = *primary accent; shows which syllable takes the main stress, such as* **kil** *in* **kilogram** (kil′ə gram′)
′ = *secondary accent; shows which syllables take the lighter stresses, such as* **gram** *in* **kilogram**

chemical weathering (kem′i kəl weth′ər ing) The breaking down of rocks by oxidation or the dissolving action of acids. (p. 87)

cinder-cone volcano (sin′dər kōn vol kā′nō) A steep-sided cone that forms from explosive eruptions of hot rocks, ranging from particles to boulders. (p. 36)

cirrus cloud (sir′əs kloud) A high-altitude cloud with a featherlike shape, made of ice crystals. (p. 228)

cleavage (klē′vij) The tendency of a mineral to break along flat surfaces. (p. 354)

climate (klī′mit) The average weather pattern of a region. (p. 215)

climax community (klī′maks kə mū′ni tē) The final stage of succession in an area, unless a major change happens. (p. 356)

colonization (kol′əni zā′shən) The process that brings new plants and animals into an area (p. 147)

commensalism (kə men′sə liz′əm) A relationship between two kinds of organisms that benefits one without affecting the other. (p. 309)

community (kə mū′ni tē) All the populations living in an area. (p. 249)

composite volcano (kəm poz′it vol kā′nō) A cone formed from explosive eruptions of hot rocks followed by a flow of lava, over and over. (pp. CA3,36)

compression (kəm presh′ən) A movement of plates that presses together or squeezes Earth's crust. (p. 195)

condensation (kon′den sā′shən) The changing of a gas into a liquid. (p. 226)

conduction (kən duk′shən) The transfer of energy by the direct contact of molecules. (p. 181)

consumer (kən sü′mər) Any animal that eats plants or eats other plant-eating animals. (p. 245)

continental drift (kon′tə nen′təl drift) The idea that a supercontinent split apart into pieces, the continents, which drifted in time to their present locations. (p. 5)

contour interval (kon′tu̇r in′tər vəl) The difference in elevation between side-by-side contour lines on a topographic map. (p. 67)

contour line (kon′tu̇r līn′) A line on a topographic map that connects points with the same elevation. (p. 66)

convection (kən vek′shən) The flow of heat through a material, causing hot parts to rise and cooler parts to sink. (p. 181)

convection cell (kən vek′shən sel) A circular pattern of air rising, air sinking, and wind. (p. 216)

convection current (kən vek′shən ku̇r′ənt) The rising of warm matter and sinking of cooled matter. (p. 227)

convergent boundary (kən vûr′jənt boun′də rē) A place where tectonic plates are colliding. (p. 10)

core (kôr) The center of Earth, lying below the mantle. (p. 194)

crater (krā′tər) A cuplike hollow that forms at the top of a volcano around the vent. (p. 35)

crude oil (krüd′ oil) Oil that contains substances that need to be removed before the oil is useful. (p. CA25)

crust (krust) The rocky surface that makes up the top of the lithosphere and includes the continents and the ocean floor. (p. 4)

cumulus cloud (kū′myə ləs kloud) A puffy cloud that appears to rise up from a flat bottom. (p. 228)

D

debris flow (də brē′ flō) A wet mix of rocks, soil, and water that moves quickly. (p. 142)

deciduous forest (di sij′ü əs fôr′ist) A forest biome with many kinds of trees that lose their leaves each autumn. (p. 264)

decomposer (dē′kəm pō′zər) Any of the fungi or bacteria that break down dead plants and animals into useful things like minerals and rich soil. (p. 245)

delta (del′tə) A fan-shaped area of sediment deposited at the mouth of a river. (p. 114)

density (den′si tē) A measure of how tightly packed the matter in an object is. (p. 192)

deposition (dep′ə zish′ən) The dropping off of bits of eroded rock. (p. 96)

derrick (dâr′ik) A framework or tower built over an oil well. (p. CA26)

desalination (dē sal'ə nā'shən) Getting fresh water from seawater by removing salt. (p. 407)

desert (dez'ərt) A sandy or rocky biome with little precipitation and little plant life. (p. 263)

divergent boundary (di vûr'jənt boun'də rē) A place where tectonic plates are moving apart. (p. 10)

dormant volcano (dôr'mənt vol kā'nō) A volcano that has not been active for a long time but has erupted before. (p. 38)

dune (dün) A mound of sand created by blowing winds. (p. 59)

ecological succession (ek'ə loj'i kəl sək sesh'ən) The gradual replacement of one community by another. (p. 334)

ecology (ē kol'ə jē) The study of how living things and their environment interact. (p. 244)

ecosystem (ek'ō sis'təm) All the living and nonliving things in an area and their interactions with each other. (p. 244)

electromagnetic spectrum (i lek'trō mag net'ik spek'trəm) All the wavelengths of visible and invisible light in order, from short (gamma rays) to long (radio). (p. 167)

electromagnetism (i lek'trō mag'ni tiz'əm) The production of magnetism by electricity (and the production of electricity by magnets). (p. 166)

element (el'ə mənt) Pure substances that cannot be broken down into any simpler substances. (p. 308)

elevation (el'ə vā'shən) How high a place is above sea level. (p. 64)

El Niño (el nēn yō) A periodic warming in the tropical Pacific Ocean that affects weather in many parts of the world. (p. 152)

epicenter (ep'i sen'tər) The point on Earth's surface directly above the focus of an earthquake. (p. 20)

erosion (i rō'zhən) Picking up and carrying away pieces of rocks. (p. 85)

estuary (es'tū âr'ē) An arm of the sea at the mouth of a river. (p. 133)

evaporation (i vap'ə rā'shən) The changing of a liquid into a gas. (p. 224)

fault (fôlt) A crack in the crust whose sides show evidence of motion. (p. 19)

fault-block mountain (fôlt'blok moun'tən) A mountain formed by blocks of Earth's crust moving along a fault. (p. 84)

flash distillation (flash dis'tə lā'shən) A process in which water evaporates below its normal boiling temperature. (p. 439)

floodplain (flud'plān) The flat area above a river bank formed by flooding. (p. 141)

focus (fō'kəs) The point where an earthquake starts as rocks begin to slide past each other. (p. 20)

fog (fôg) A cloud that forms at ground level. (p. 228)

fold mountain (fōld' moun'tən) A mountain made up mostly of rock layers folded by being squeezed together. (p. 84)

food chain (füd chān) The path of the energy in food from one organism to another. (p. 288)

food web (füd web) The overlapping food chains in an ecosystem. (p. 290)

fossil fuel (fos'əl fū'əl) A fuel formed from the decay of ancient forms of life. (pp. CA25, 398)

friction (frik'shən) A force that opposes motion of one object in contact with another. (p. 192)

frond (frond) A leaflike plant structure. (p. 282)

fumarole (fū'mə rōl') A vent in the ground that releases volcanic gases and steam. (p. CA3)

gem (jem) A mineral valued for being rare and beautiful. (p. 358)

PRONUNCIATION KEY

a at; ā ape; ä far; âr care; e end; ē me; i it; ī ice; îr pierce; o hot; ō old; ô fork; oi oil; ou out; u up; ū use; ü rule; ù pull; ûr turn; hw white; ng song; th thin; <u>th</u> this; zh measure; ə about, taken, pencil, lemon, circus

geologic map (jē'ə log' ik map') A map that shows the types and positions of rocks at and below Earth's surface. (p. 74)

geologist (jē ōl'ə jist') A scientist who studies Earth. (p. 4)

geothermal energy (jē'ō thûr'məl en'ər jē) Earth's internal energy. (p. 199)

glacier (glā'shər) A huge sheet of ice and snow that moves slowly over the land. (p. 100)

gradient (grā'dē ənt) A difference in air pressure. (p. CA15)

grassland (gras'land') A biome where grasses, not trees, are the main plant life. Prairies are one kind of grassland region. (p. 260)

gravity (grav'i tē) A force of attraction, or pull, between any object and any other objects around it. Gravity is a property of all matter. (p. 196)

greenhouse effect (grēn'hous' i fekt') The ability of the atmosphere to let in sunlight but not to let heat escape. (p. 214)

greenhouse gases (grēn'hous' gas'əz) Chemicals in the atmosphere that act like greenhouse glass, reflecting infrared radiation back toward Earth. (p. 214)

groundwater (ground wô'tər) Water that seeps into the ground into spaces between bits of rock and soil. (p. 90)

gusher (gush'ər) An oil well in which the oil is pushed up out of the ground forcefully by natural underground pressures. (p. CA25)

H

habitat (hab'i tat') The place where a population lives. (p. 250)

hardness (härd'nis) How well a mineral resists scratching. (p. 354)

heat (hēt) Energy that flows between objects that have different temperatures. (p. 179)

herbivore (hûr'bə vōr') An animal that eats plants, algae, and other producers. (p. 290)

holdfast (hōld' fast) A rootlike structure that holds kelp tightly to the ocean floor. (pp. CA19, 279)

hot spot (hot' spot) A very hot part of the mantle, where magma can melt through a plate moving above it. (p. 34)

humidity (hū mid'i tē) The amount of water vapor in the air. (p. 224)

humus (hū'məs) Decayed plant or animal material in soil. (pp. 91, 371)

hydroelectricity (hī'drō i lek tris'i tē) The use of flowing water to generate electricity. (p. 427)

hydrothermal activity (hī'drō thûr'məl ak tiv ə tē) The action of underground water that is heated by magma. (p.CA3)

I–K

igneous rock (ig'nē əs rok') A rock formed when melted rock material cools and hardens. (p. 365)

insolation (in'sō lā'shən) The amount of the Sun's energy that reaches Earth at a given time and place. *Insolation* is short for *in*coming *sol*ar radia-*tion*. (p. 208)

insulation (in'sə lā'shən) The process of preventing heat from flowing in or out of a material. (p. 184)

insulator (in'sə lā'tər) A material that conducts heat poorly. (p. 194)

intertidal zone (in'tər ti'dəl zōn) The shallowest section of the marine, or ocean, ecosystem, where the ocean floor is covered and uncovered as the tide goes in and out. (p. 280)

kelp (kelp) Large marine algae or seaweed. (p. CA18)

kinetic energy (ki net'ik en'ər jē) The energy of any moving object. (p. 177)

L

lahar (lähär) A mudflow that results from volcanic activity (p. CA4)

lava (lä'və) Magma that reaches Earth's surface. (p. 35)

levee (lev'ē) A wall or ridge made of soil or concrete to keep a river from overflowing (p. 117)

light ray (līt' rā) A straight-line beam of light as it travels outward from its source. (p. 239)

light wave (līt' wāv) An electromagnetic wave that can travel without matter or through matter. (p. 166)

limiting factor (lim'ə ting fak'tər) Anything that controls the growth or survival of a population. (p. 302)

lode (lōd) A veinlike mineral deposit (often gold) in solid rock. (p. 385)

luster (lus'tər) The way light bounces off a mineral's surface. (p. 353)

M

magma (mag'mə) Hot, molten rock deep below Earth's surface. (p. 6)

magnitude (mag'ni tüd') The amount of energy released by an earthquake. (p. 24)

mantle (man'təl) The thickest layer of Earth, lying just under the crust. (p. 9)

map legend (map' lej'ənd) A table of symbols used on a map. (p.69)

map scale (map' scāl) A line on a map that compares a distance on the map with the distance on Earth's surface. (p. 70)

marine terrace (mə rēn'ter'əs) A steplike formation above a coast that was once an ancient shoreline. (p. 130)

mass (mas) A measure of the amount of matter in an object. (p. 196)

mass wasting (mas wās'ting) The downhill movement of Earth material caused by gravity. (p. 96)

matter (ma'tər) Anything that has mass and takes up space. (p. 164)

mechanical weathering (mə kan'i kəl weth'ər ing) The breaking down of rock by physical changes. (p. 86)

metamorphic rock (met'ə môr'fik rok') A rock formed under heat and pressure from another kind of rock. (p. 367)

meteorite (mē'tē ə rīt') A chunk of rock from space that strikes a surface (such as Earth or the Moon). (p. 202)

mineral (min'ər əl) A solid material of Earth's crust with a definite composition. (p. 352)

moraine (mə rān') A deposit of sediment in front of or along the sides of a glacier. (p. 102)

mutualism (mū'chü ə liz'əm) A relationship between two kinds of organisms that benefits both. (p. 306)

N

nekton (nek'ton) Organisms that swim through the water in aquatic ecosystems. (p. 266)

niche (nich) The role an organism has in its ecosystem. (p. 250)

nitrogen (nī'trə jən) An element that plants need to grow and stay healthy, and that all organisms need to make proteins. (p. 321)

nitrogen cycle (nī'trə jən sī'kəl) The continuous trapping of nitrogen gas into compounds in the soil and its return to the air. (p. 324)

nonrenewable resource (non'ri nü'ə bəl rē'sôrs') A resource that cannot be replaced within a short period of time or at all. (p. 359)

nuclear fission (nü'klē ər fish'ən) The splitting of a nucleus with a large mass into two nuclei with smaller masses. (p. 422)

nuclear fusion (nü'klē ər fü'zhən) The merging of nuclei with smaller masses into a nucleus with a larger mass. (p. 423)

O

omnivore (om'nə vôr') An animal that eats both plants and animals. (p. 291)

ore (ôr) A mineral containing a useful substance. (p. 358)

original horizontality (ə rij'ə nəl hôr'ə zän'ta'lə tē) The idea that many kinds of rocks form flat, horizontal layers. (p. 4)

ozone layer (ō'zōn lā'ər) A layer of ozone gas in the atmosphere that screens out much of the Sun's UV (ultraviolet) rays. (p. 397)

P

parasitism (par'ə sī tiz'əm) A relationship in which one kind of organism lives on and may harm another. (p. 308)

photon (fō'ton) The tiny bundles of energy by means of which light travels. (p. 167)

PRONUNCIATION KEY

a at; ā ape; ä far; âr care; e end; ē me; i it; ī ice; îr pierce; o hot; ō old; ô fork; oi oil; ou out; u up; ū use; ü rule; u̇ pull; ûr turn; hw white; ng song; th thin; th this; zh measure; ə about, taken, pencil, lemon, circus

GLOSSARY

pioneer community (pī'ə nīr' kə mū'ni tē) The first community thriving in a once lifeless area. (p. 335)

pioneer species (pī'ə nîr' spē'shēz) The first species living in an otherwise lifeless area. (p. 335)

placer deposits (plā' sər di poz' its) particles of gold found in loose gravel. (p. 385)

plankton (plangk'tən) Organisms that float on the water in aquatic ecosystems. (p. 266)

plateau (pla tō') A large area of flat land of high elevation that was created by crustal movement. (p. 85)

plate tectonics (plāt' tek ton'iks) The idea that Earth's surface is broken into plates that slide slowly across the mantle. (p. 9)

pollution (pə lü'shən) Adding any harmful substances to Earth's land, water, or air. (p. 372)

population (pop'yə lā'shən) All the members of one species in an area. (p. 249)

potential energy (pə ten'shəl en'ər jē) Stored energy. (p. 177)

precipitation (pri sip'i tā'shən) Any form of water particles that falls from the atmosphere and reaches the ground. (p. 230)

predator (pred'ə tər) A living thing that hunts other living things for food. (p. 291)

prey (prā) A living thing that is hunted for food. (p. 291)

primary wave (prī'mâr ē wāv') One of the back-and-forth vibrations of rocks in an earthquake, called *P waves* for short. They travel faster than secondary waves. (p. 21)

producer (prə dü'sər) Any of the plants and algae that produce oxygen and food that animals need. (p. 245)

prospector (pros' pek tər) A person who searches for gold or other precious minerals. (p. 385)

pyroclastic materials (pī'rə klas'tik mə tîr ē əls) the rocks and ash that violently erupt from a volcano. (p. CA3)

Q-R

radiation (rā'dē a'shən) The giving off of infrared rays through space. (p. 180)

radioactive decay (rā'dē ō ak'tiv di kā') A process in which some atoms break down into smaller atoms and release energy. (p. 193)

rain shadow (rān' sha'dō) The effect created when mountains block moist air from reaching areas beyond them. (p. 58)

refining (ri fī'ning) Separating crude oil mainly into gasoline and heating oil. (p. 434)

reflection (ri flek'shən) The bouncing of a sound wave off a surface. (p. 200)

refraction (ri frak'shən) The bending of light rays as they pass from one substance into another. (p. 200)

relative humidity (rel'ə tiv hū mid'i tē) A comparison between the actual amount of water vapor in the air and the amount the air can hold at a given temperature. (p. 225)

relief (ri lēf') The three-dimensional shape of the land. (p. 112)

renewable resource (ri nü'ə bəl rē'sôrs') A resource that can be replaced in a short period of time. (p. 396)

reservoir (rez'ər vwär') A storage area for freshwater supplies. (p. 409)

rock (rok) A naturally formed solid in the crust made up of one or more minerals. (p. 364)

rock cycle (rok' sī'kəl) Rocks changing from one form into another in a never-ending series of processes. (p. 374)

runoff (run'ôf) Precipitation that falls into rivers and streams. (p. 232)

S

scarp (skärp) A steep, sharp break in the ground at the top of some landslides. (p. 142)

scavenger (skav'ən jər) A meat-eating animal that feeds on the remains of dead animals. (p. 291)

sea-floor spreading (sē flōr spred'ing) The idea that new crust is forming at ridges in the sea floor, spreading apart the crust on either side of the ridges. (p. 6)

secondary wave (sek'ən dâr'ē wāv') One of the up-and-down vibrations of rocks in an earthquake, called *S waves* for short. They travel more slowly than primary waves. (p. 21)

sedimentary rock (sed'ə men'tə rē rok') A rock made of bits of matter joined together. (p. 366)

seismic-safe (sīz'mik sāf) The design of buildings and highways to keep them from collapsing in an earthquake. (p. 28)

seismic wave (sīz'mik wāv') A vibration that spreads out away from a focus when an earthquake happens. (p. 20)

seismograph (sīz'mə graf') A sensitive device that detects the shaking of Earth's crust during an earthquake. (p. 22)

shaded relief map (shā'dəd ri lef' map) A map that shows elevations of Earth's surface by shadows and colors. (p. 65)

shear (shîr) A movement of plates that twists, tears, or pushes one part of Earth's crust past another. (p. 195)

shield volcano (shēld' vol kā'nō) A wide, gently sloped cone that forms from flows of lava. (pp. CA3,36)

smog (smog) A mixture of smoke and fog. (p. 398)

soil (soil) A mixture of weathered rock, decayed plant and animal matter, living things, air, and water. (p. 88)

soil horizon (soil hə rī'zən) Any of the layers of soil from the surface to the bedrock. (p. 89)

solar cell (sō'lər sel) A device that generates an electric current from sunlight. (p. 419)

sound wave (sound' wāv') A vibration that spreads away from a vibrating object. (p. 163)

spring (spring) A place where groundwater seeps out of the ground. (p. 409)

stratus cloud (strā'təs kloud) A cloud that forms in a blanketlike layer. (p. 228)

streak (strēk) The color of the powder left when a mineral is rubbed against a hard, rough surface. (p. 354)

subduction (səb duk'shən) The sliding of a denser ocean plate under another plate when they collide. (p. 12)

surface wave (sûr'fis wāv) One of the wavelike vibrations of an earthquake that cause much of the damage to structures on Earth's surface. (p. 21)

symbiosis (sim'bi ō'sis) A relationship between two kinds of organisms over time. (p. 306)

taiga (tī'gə) A cool, forest biome of conifers in the upper Northern Hemisphere. (p. 261)

temperature (tem'pər ə chər) The average kinetic energy of the molecules in a material. (p. 178)

tension (ten'shən) A movement of plates that stretches or pulls apart Earth's crust. (p. 195)

thermal pollution (thûr'məl pə lü'shən) The excess heating of the environment. (p. 429)

tidepools (tīd' pülz) Small pools of water that remain at low tide on rocky seashores. (p. 275)

till (til) A jumble of many sizes of sediment deposited by a glacier. (p. 102)

timberline (tim'bər līn') The region on mountain slopes above which trees cannot grow. (p. 272)

topographic map (top'ə gra fik map) A map that shows features of Earth's surface as a pattern of lines. (p. 66)

transform fault (trans'fôrm' fôlt) Boundaries where tectonic plates slide past each other. (p. 11)

tropical rain forest (trop'i kəl rān fôr'ist) A hot, humid biome near the equator, with much rainfall and a wide variety of life. (p. 265)

tundra (tun'drə) A cold, treeless biome of the far north, marked by spongy topsoil. (p. 262)

upwelling (up wel' ing) The rising of cold water from the ocean's depths to replace warmer surface water that was driven offshore. (p. CA19)

vacuum (vak'ū əm) A space through which sound waves cannot travel because it contains no matter. (p. 164)

PRONUNCIATION KEY

a at; ā ape; ä far; âr care; e end; ē me; i it; ī ice; îr pierce; o hot; ō old; ô fork; oi oil; ou out; u up; ū use; ü rule; ù pull; ûr turn; hw white; ng song; th thin; th this; zh measure; ə about, taken, pencil, lemon, circus

vent (vent) The central opening in a volcanic area through which magma may escape. (p. 35)

vibration (vī brā'shən) A back-and-forth motion. (p. 162)

W

water cycle (wô'tər sī'kəl) The continuous movement of water between Earth's surface and the air, changing from liquid to gas to liquid. (p. 233)

water table (wô'tər tā'bəl) The top of the water-filled spaces in the ground. (p. 409)

water vapor (wô'tər vā'pər) Water in the form of a gas. (p. 224)

wavelength (wāv'lengkth') The distance from one peak to the next on a wave. (p. 166)

wave refraction (wāv'ri frak'shun) The process in which waves meeting a curving shore tend to bend and lose energy. (p. CA9)

wave (wāv) 1. A movement of energy through a body of water, such as the ocean. 2. A motion that carries energy. (pp. CA9, 160)

weather (weth'ər) What the lower atmosphere is like at any given place and time. (p. 215)

weathering (weth'ər ing) Breaking down rocks into smaller pieces. (p. 85)

well (wel) A hole dug below the water table that water seeps into. (p. 409)

INDEX

*Indicates an activity related to this topic.

INDEX

*Indicates an activity related to this topic.

CREDITS

Cover: printed from digital image ©1996 CORBIS

Maps: Geosystems

Transvisions: Richard Hutchings Photography (photography, TP1); Guy Porfirio (illustration)

Illustrations: Denny Bond: 324–325; Ka Botzis: 290–291; Dan Clifford: 318–319; Paul Dempsey: 88–90, 220; Drew-Brook-Cormack: CA31, 226, 229; Robert Frank: 310–311, 322–323; Thomas Gagliano: 22, 23, 125, 128, 145, 160, 210; Virge Kask: 147, 248, 288–289, 294–295; George Kelvin: CA25, CA30, 92–93, 104–105, 114–115, 140–141, 166, 181, 186, 194, 199, 212, 214, 218, 369, 371, 380, 396–397, 408–409, 422, 438–439; Katie Lee: 244–245, 332–333, 336; Joe LeMonnier: CA32, 7, 9, 38, 65, 84, 87, 98–99, 111, 148; Mowry Graphics: 232; Saul Rosenbaum: CA3, CA28, 151, 161, 195–196, 201, 209, 225, 231, 376–377; Steve Stankiewicz: CA2, CA8, CA14, 4, 17, 19, 20, 21, 22, 28, 40–41, 48, 50, 52, 54, 58, 85, 173, 179, 197, 211, 225, 258, 341, 352–353, 366, 374, 402–403, 407, 412, 418, 428; Art Thompson: 6, 10 12, 35–36, 39, 47, 58, 67, 74, 102, 142–143, 149, 185, 193, 216–217, 236, 247, 272, 274, 365, 367, 415, 425

Photography Credits: All photographs are by Richard Hutchings Photography and McGraw-Hill School Division except as noted below:

CA3: l. Index Stock Photography. CA4: *b.* Martin Miller; *t.* Stephen Frisch/Stock, Boston. CA5: *b.* Tom Myers; *b.r. inset* Mark E. Gibson. CA6: *b.l.* David L. Brown/The Stock Market; *t.r.* Mark E. Gibson. CA9: *b.* Michael J. Howell/Index Stock Photography, Inc. CA10: *b.* Jeff Myers; *t.* Sally Myers. CA11: *l.* Stephen Trimble/DRK Photo; *r.* Superstock. CA12: *t.r.* Mark E. Gibson; *b.* Mark E. Gibson. CA15: *b.* Craig J. Brown/Index Stock Photography. CA16: *b.* Kathy Merrifield/Photo Researchers, Inc.; *t.* James Marshall/The Image Works. CA18: *b.* Lawrence Naylor/Photo Researchers, Inc. CA19: *t.l.* Kevin McDonnell/Photo 20-20; *t.r.* Peter Hughes/Index Stock Photography, Inc. CA20: *b.m. inset* Randy Morse/Animals Animals; *b.* Sanford/Agliolo/The Stock Market. CA21: *t.* Bob Daemmrich/The Images Works; *t.r. inset* Jeff Myers. CA22: *b.l.* Jeff Greenberg/The Images Works; *b.r. inset* Joe Sohm/The Image Works. CA24: *b.* Vince Streano/Corbis. CA25: *t.r.* Science/Visuals Unlimited. CA26: *b.* Tom Myers. iii: NASA/Digital Stock. iv: Digital Stock. v: NASA/Digital Stock. vi: ©John D. Cunningham/VU. vii: Lee F. Snyder/Photo Researchers, Inc. S2–S3: ©David M. Sanders. S4: *l.* Lambert/Archive Photos; *m.* ©Jack Zehrt; *b.l.* ©Reuters/Scott Olson/Archive Photos. S6: *m.l.* ©Wernher Krutein. S7: *t.r.* ©NASA. S8: Scala/Art Resource, NY. S9: *b.r.* ©Bruce Caines. S10: *t.* John Bova/Photo Researchers, Inc.; *b.* Corbis/James L. Amos. S11: *t.r.* Frank Rossotto. S12: *m.l.* Robert Essel; *b.m.* Telegraph Colour Library. S13: *t.l.* ©Bruce Caines; *b.r.* ©Frank A. Cezus. S14: *b.l.* The Granger Collection, New York. S15: Scott Goldsmith. S16: *t.m.* ©NASA; *b.* ©Telegraph Colour Library. S17: *t.r.* Frank Rossotto; *m.l.* Bruce Forster. **Unit 1** 1: *full bkgnd.* Tom Bean; *b.r. inset* Mark Downey/Gamma Liaison; 3: *m.l.* Walter H. Hodge/Peter Arnold, Inc. 13: *m.r.* ©John Manno/Still Life Stock, Inc. 14: *c. inset* Chris McLaughlin/Animals Animals. 14–15: *bkgnd. spread* Anna E. Zuckerman/Photo Edit. 15: *r. inset* Tom Bean. 16: *b.* Culver Pictures, Inc.; *m.r. inset* Culver Pictures, Inc. 19: *t.* ©Georg Gerster/Photo Researchers, Inc. 21: *c.* Robert Yager/Tony Stone Images. 24: *b.* Index Stock Photography, Inc. 25: *b.* Mark Richards/Peter Arnold, Inc. 26: *l.* William S. Helsel/Tony Stone Images. 27: *t.* David Young-Wolff/Photo Edit. 28: *t.r.* ©James Stanfield/National Geographic; *m.r.* ©Stephen Saks/Photo Researchers, Inc. 32: *m.* ©Catherine Ursillo/Photo Researchers, Inc. 33: *b.r.* ©Josef Beck/FPG International LLC. 36: *b.l.* ©John D. Cunningham/Visuals Unlimited; *b.r.* ©C. Falco/Photo Researchers, Inc. 37: *b.l.* ©Krafft Explorer/Photo Researchers, Inc. 40: *b.r.* ©Richard Thom/Visuals Unlimited. 42: *b.* John V. Christiansen/Earth Images; *m.* Bill Ingallis/NASA. 42–43 *bkgnd. spread* Superstock. 45: *full bkgnd.* John Elk III/Stock, Boston: *b.r. inset* Larry Ulrich/DRK Photo. 46: *b.* R. G. K. Photography/Tony Stone Images. 48: *b.* Mark E. Gibson. 49: *t.* David Welling/Earth Scenes. 50: *b.* Ken Biggs/Photo Researchers, Inc. 51: *t.* Tom Myers. 52: *l.* William E. Ferguson. 53: *b.* George Olson/Gamma-Liaison. 54: *b.* Thomas Del Brase/Tony Stone Images. 55: *b.* Tom Bean/DRK Photo. 56: *r.* Charles Thatcher/Tony Stone Images. 57 *t.* Will & Deni McIntyre/Tony Stone Images. 59: *b.* Jyron Joriorian/Tony Stone Images. 60–61: *bkgnd. spread* David Parker/SPL/Photo Researchers, Inc. 61: *b.l. inset* Bruce Watkins/Earth Scenes. 62: *r.* David Muench/Tony Stone Images; *l. inset* Tom Bean. 64: *b.r.* Dennis Flaherty/Photo Researchers, Inc.; *t.l.* Kent & Donna Dannen/Photo Researchers, Inc. 66: *t.l.* Boberto Soncin Gerometta/Photo 20-20. 72: *r.* L. Linkhart/Visuals Unlimited. 73: *l.* Mark E. Gibson. 75: *b.* Fred Hischmann. **Unit 2** 81: *bkgnd.* Nathan Bilow/TSI; *inset* Nathan Bilow/TSI. 82 *m.r. inset* ©William J. Weber/Visuals Unlimited; *m.* ©William J. Weber/Visuals Unlimited. 84: *b.m.* ©Joel Arrington/Visuals Unlimited. 86: *b.r.* ©Ken Wagner/Visuals Unlimited. 88: *m.l.* ©Science/Visuals Unlimited. 90: *m.l.* ©Ross Frid/Visuals Unlimited; *b.r.* ©Ross Frid/Visuals Unlimited. 91: *m.r.* ©Science/Visuals Unlimited. 94: *b.r.* M. Richards/PhotoEdit. 96: *t.l.* Cesar Llacuna; *t.r.* ©John D. Cunningham/Visuals Unlimited. 97: *t.* ©Martin G. Miller/Visuals Unlimited; *t.m. inset* ©Martin G. Miller/Visuals Unlimited. 98: *b.l.* B. R. Roberts/Omni Photo. 99: *t.r.* Altitude/Peter Arnold, Inc.; *b.l.* Valmik Thalpar/Peter Arnold, Inc. 100: *t.r. inset* ©Jeanette Thomas/Visuals Unlimited; *b.* ©L. Linkhart/Visuals Unlimited; *m.l.* *inset* ©John Gerlach/Visuals Unlimited. 101: *b.* ©Bill Kamin/Visuals Unlimited; *b.l. inset* ©Martin G. Miller/Visuals Unlimited. 102: *m.r.* ©Steve McCutcheon/Visuals Unlimited. 103: *l.* Science/Visuals Unlimited. 104–105: *b.* PhotoDisc, Inc. 107: *full bkgnd.* Martin G. Miller/Visuals Unlimited; *b.r. inset* Gerald & Buff Corsi/Visuals Unlimited. 108: *b.* George Herben/Visuals Unlimited. 110: *b.* Mark E. Gibson/Visuals Unlimited. 112: *b.* Ted Streshinsky/Photo 20-20. 113: *t.* Tom Myers. 115: *t.* Tom Myers. 116: *b.* D. Cavagnaro/DRK Photo. 117: *t.* Mark E. Gibson. 118: *b.* Ted Levin/Animals Animals; *l. inset* Wernher Krutein/Liaison International. 119: *m.* John Eastcott/Yva Momatiuk/DRK Photo. 120: *b.* John D. Cunningham/Visuals Unlimited. 120–121: *bkgnd.* Runk/Schoenberger/Grant Heileman Photography. 121: *l.* Jacques Janqoux/Photo Researchers, Inc.; *r.* Science/Visuals Unlimited. 122: *b.* Mark E. Gibson/Visuals Unlimited. 124: *t.* Will & Deni McIntyre/Photo Researchers, Inc. 126: *r.* Spencer Grant/Photo Researchers, Inc.; *l.* Mark E. Gibson. 127: *b.* Arthur Morris/Visuals Unlimited. 129: *t.* James R. McCullagh/Visuals Unlimited. 130: *t.* Gerald Brimac/Liaison International. 131: *b.* D. Newman/Visuals Unlimited. 132: *b.* Greg Gawlowski/Photo 20-20. 133: *b.* Brooking Tatum/Visuals Unlimited. 134: *b.* Tom Bean. 135: *b.* Stephen J. Krasemann/DRK Photo. 136: *b.* Melvin B. Zucker/Visuals Unlimited. 138: *b.* Stan Skaggs/Visuals Unlimited. 140: *b.l.* Jack Wilburn/Earth Scenes. 142: *b.l.* Vince Streano/Tony Stone Images. 144: *b.* Sylvain Grandadam. 146: *t.l.* Breck P. Kent/Earth Scenes; *t.r.* Pat and Tom Leeson/Photo Reseaches, Inc. 148: *b.r.* David Wentraub/Photo Researchers, Inc. 150: *b.l.* Tom Benoit/Tony Stone Images; *b.r.* Tom Bean/DRK Photo. 151: *b.* Tom Benoit/Tony Stone Images. 152: *b.* A. Ramey/Photo Edit; *t.* Paul Sequeira/Photo Researchers, Inc. **Unit 3** 157: *bkgnd.* ©Yoav Levy/PhotoTake; *inset* ©1998 PhotoDisc. 158: *b.r. inset* Charles D. Winters/Photo Researchers, Inc.; *b.* Gary Braasch/Tony Stone Images. 162: *t.* Bob Daemmrich/The Image Works. 165: *l.* Ken Fisher/TSI. 168: *b.* Science/Visuals Unlimited. 170: *b.* Tom Bean/DRK Photo. 172: *l.* Science Photo Library/Photo Researchers, Inc.; *r.* North Wind; *bkgnd.* Wolfgang Kaehler/Corbis. 173: *l.* The Queens Borough Public Library, Long Island Division, Latimer Family Papers; *r.* Hall of Electrical History, Schenectady Museum, Schenectady, New York. 174: *m.* Tony Freeman/PhotoEdit. 176: *b.* Cesar Llacuna. 177: *b.l.* Jeff Greenberg/PhotoEdit. 178: *t.l.* ©Tony Freeman/PhotoEdit; *m.r.* Spencer Grant/PhotoEdit. 180: *t.m.* Tony Freeman/PhotoEdit; *b.r.* Dr. E. R. Degginger. 183: *t.l.* Myrleen Ferguson/PhotoEdit. 184: *t.r.* Dr. E. R. Degginger; *b.l.* Cesar Llacuna. 186–187: *bkgnd. spread* Michael Newman/Photo Edit. 189: *bkgnd.* Ezio Geneletti/The Image Bank; *inset* Ezio Geneletti/The Image Bank. 190: *b.* Ted Clutter/Photo Researchers, Inc. 192: *b.r.* Stephan Meyers/Earth Scenes. 198: *b.* G. Brad Lewis/Liaison International. 199: *t.* Joseph Sohm/Photo Researchers, Inc. 200: *l.* Sovfoto/Eastfoto/PNI. 202: *b.* NASA/SPL/Photo Researchers, Inc. 203: *r.* PhotoDisc, Inc. 204: *b.r.* Kraft/Explorer/Science Source/Photo Researchers, Inc. 205: *t.r. inset* Martin G. Miller. 206: *b.* Richard Kaylin/Tony Stone Images. 206–207: *r.* Carson Baldwin, Jr./Animals Animals. 208: *b.* Gary R. Zahm/DRK Photo. 215: *b.* Georg Gerster/Photo Researchers, Inc. 217: *b.* Gary A. Conner/Photo Edit. 218: *t.* Larry Ulrich/Tony Stone Images. 222: *l.* Superstock, Inc. 228: *t.* A. J. Copley/Visuals Unlimited; *m.* Henry W. Robison/Visuals Unlimited; *b.* Mark A. Schneider/Visuals Unlimited. 231: *b.* Peter Turnley/Corbis. 234: *t.l.* Runk/Schoenberger/Grant Heilman. 235: *m.* ©The Stock Market/Aaron Rezney. **Unit 4** 241: *bkgnd.* ©Ken Wagner/PhotoTake/PNI; *inset* Steve Hopkin/Masterfile. 242: *r.* ©Danilo G. Donadoni/Bruce Coleman, Inc.; *l.* ©J. McDonald/Bruce Coleman, Inc. 246: *b.l.* Michael Javorka/Tony Stone Images; *l. inset* Larry Ulrich/DRK Photo. 247: *b.* Tom Bean; *t.r. inset* Jeff Foott/DRK Photo. 249: *t.* Cindy Charles/Photo Edit. 250: *b.* Brian Milne/Animals Animals. 251: *t.* Paul A. Zahl/The National Geographic Image Collection. 252: *m.* Tom & Pat Leeson/DRK Photo; *c.* Dean Krakel II/Photo Researchers, Inc. 253: *m.* Inga Spence/Visuals Unlimited. 254: *m.* Gordon Wiltsie: *b.* Maria Stenzel. 256: *r.* ©Ken Graham/Bruce Coleman, Inc.; *l.* Patti Murray/Bruce Coleman, Inc. 258: *m.* ©Lee Rentz/Bruce Coleman, Inc.; *t.* Breck P. Kent/Earth Scenes; *b.* Nigel J. H. Smith/Earth Scenes. 259: *t.l.* ©J. C. Carton/Bruce Coleman, Inc.; *b.* ©M. Timothy O'Keefe/Bruce Coleman, Inc.; *r.* Eastcott/Momatiuk/Earth Scenes. 260: *t.* A. & M. Shah/Animals Animals. 261: *b.* Eastcott/Momatiuk/Earth Scenes. 262: *t.* ©Joe McDonald/Bruce Coleman, Inc. 263: *b.* ©Jen & Des Bartlett/Bruce Coleman, Inc.; *t.* ©Joy Spurr/Bruce Coleman, Inc. 264: *b.* ©Jeff Foott/Bruce Coleman, Inc.; *t.* ©John Shaw/Bruce Coleman, Inc. 265: *t.* Jim Tuten/Animals Animals; *b.* ©E&P Bauer/Bruce Coleman, Inc. 266: *l.* images copyright ©1998 PhotoDisc, Inc. 268: *l.* ©John D. Cunningham/Visuals Unlimited. 270: *b.* Larry Ulrich/DRK Photo. 272: *b.* Visuals Unlimited. 273: *t.* Verna R. Johnston/Photo Researchers, Inc.; *b.* Mark Newman/Photo Researchers, Inc. 274: *t.* T. A. Wiewandt/DRK Photo; *b.* A. & L. Sinibaldi/Tony Stone Images. 275: *t.l.* Frans Lanting/Photo Researchers, Inc.; *b.* Joe Munroe/Photo Researchers, Inc.; *t.r. inset* Mark E. Gibson/Visuals Unlimited. 276: *b.* Kevin & Betty Collins/Visuals Unlimited; *t.* R. G. K. Photography/Tony Stone; *t.l. inset* Tom J. Ulrich/Visuals Unlimited. 277: *l.* Liz Hymans/Tony Stone Images; *b.r.* Darrell Gulin/DRK Photo. 278: *b.l. inset* E. R. Degginger/Photo Researchers, Inc.; *b.r. inset* E. R. Degginger/Photo Researchers, Inc.; *t.r.* Stephen Krasemann/DRK Photo; *t.l.* Kennan Ward/DRK Photo. 279: *b.* Lewis Kemper/DRK Photo; *t.* Norbert Wu/DRK Photo. 280: *b.r.* Jeff Foott/DRK Photo; *t.l.* R. J. Erwin/DRK Photo. 281: *c.* Steve Kaufman/DRK Photo. 282: *b.l.* Stephen J. Krasemann/DRK Photo. 282–283: *bkgnd. spread* Randy Morse/Animals Animals. 285: *bkgnd.* The Stock Market/Zefa Germany; *b.* ©John Elk/Bruce Coleman, Inc. 286: *b.* Breck P. Kent/Animals Animals. 289: *b.r.* Derrick Ditchburn/Visuals Unlimited; *t.* Anthony Mercieca/Photo Researchers, Inc. 292: *t.r.* S. Nielsen/DRK Photo. 293: *b.* Paul Berquist/Animals Animals. 296: *r.* Carson Baldwin, Jr./Animals Animals. 297: *m.* Zig Leszczynski/Animals Animals. 300: *b.*

B&C Calhoun/Bruce Coleman, Inc. 303: *b.l.* ©Jeff Foott/Bruce Coleman, Inc. 304–305: *c. spread* Patti Murray/Earth Scenes. 305: *m.* Linda Bailery/Earth Scenes; *m.l.* Linda Bailery/Earth Scenes. 306–307: *b.* ©Mark Newman/Bruce Coleman, Inc. 307: *m.l.* ©M.P.L. Fogden/Bruce Coleman, Inc. 308: *t.* ©David Overcash/Bruce Coleman, Inc.; *b.l.* ©John Shaw/Bruce Coleman, Inc. 309: *t.* Gregory Brown/Animals Animals; *b.* ©D&M Plage/Bruce Coleman, Inc. 310: *t.r.* ©D&M Plage/Bruce Coleman, Inc. 312: *b.l.* Kevin Schafer/Corbis; *t.r.* ©Rod Williams/Bruce Coleman, Inc. 313: *b.l.* ©David Madison/Bruce Coleman, Inc. 314: *l.* Mary Steinbacher/PhotoEdit. 315: *b.r.* Cesar Llacuna. 316: *t.* ©Bill Ruth/Bruce Coleman, Inc.; *b.* ©John S. Flannery/Bruce Coleman, Inc. 318: *m.* Jack W. Dyking/Bruce Coleman, Inc. 319: *t.* Zig Leszczynski/Earth Scenes; *b.* Breck P. Kent/Earth Scenes. 320: *t.* E. R. Degginger/Earth Scenes. 321: *b.l.* Cesar Llacuna. 327: *r.* Peter Beck/The Stock Market. 328–329: *bkgnd.* Photo Library International/ESA/Photo Researchers, Inc. 329: *t.l.* Lowell Georgia/Photo Researchers, Inc.; *b.r.* Runk/Schoenberger/Grant Heilman Photography, Inc. 330: *b.r.* Jim Sugar Photography/Corbis. 331: *b.r.* Breck P. Kent/Earth Scenes. 332: *l.* Patti Murray/Earth Scenes. 334: *l.* Patti Murray/Earth Scenes; *r.* ©David Falconer/Bruce Coleman, Inc. 335: *b.* John Lemker/Earth Scenes. 337: *l.* E. R. Degginger/Earth Scenes; *t.r.* PhotoDisc, Inc. 338: *t.r.* ©S. Jonasson/Bruce Coleman, Inc.; *m.* ©S. Jonasson/Bruce Coleman, Inc.; *b.* Krafft/Explorer/Photo Researchers, Inc. 340: *b.* images copyright ©1998 PhotoDisc, Inc. 342: *t.* ©John H. Hoffman/Bruce Coleman, Inc.; *m.* Jeff Greenberg/Photo Researchers, Inc. 344: *r.* John Barr/Gamma Liaison. 348: *b.* PhotoDisc, Inc. **Unit 5** 349: *full bkgnd.* E. R. Degginger/Photo Researchers, Inc.; *b.r. inset* E. R. Degginger/Photo Researchers, Inc. 350: *l.* Joyce Photographics/Photo Researchers, Inc.; *r.* Tom McHugh/Photo Researchers, Inc. 352: *t.l.* Joyce Photographics/Photo Researchers, Inc.; *r.* George Whiteley/Photo Researchers, Inc.; *m.l.* E. R. Degginger/Photo Researchers, Inc.; *b.l.* Cesar Llacuna; *m.* Charles D. Winters/Photo Researchers, Inc. 353: *t.l.* Roberto De Guglielmo/Science Library/Photo Researchers, Inc.; *m.l.* Kaj R. Svensson/Science Library/Photo Researchers, Inc.; *m.r.* J. H. Robinson/Photo Researchers, Inc.; *b.r.* Cesar Llacuna; *b.l.* Cesar Llacuna. 354: *t.l.* ©John D. Cunningham/Visuals Unlimited; *m.* ©Mark A. Schneider/Visuals Unlimited; *b.l.* Tom Pantages/Photo Take. 355: *b.l.* ©A. J. Cunningham/Visuals Unlimited. 356: *t.* Joyce Photographics/Photo Researchers, Inc.; *t.l. inset* ©Ross Frid/Korner Gems, Traverse City, MI/Visuals Unlimited; *t.r. inset* Joyce Photographics/Photo Researchers, Inc.; *b.* ©A. J. Copley/Visuals Unlimited. 357: *b.l.* Peter Aitken/Photo Researchers, Inc. 358: *t.l.* ©LINK/Visuals Unlimited; *b.l.* ©A. J. Copley/Visuals Unlimited; *t.r.* Richard T. Nowitz/Photo Researchers, Inc.; *b.r.* ©Zale Corporation. 359: *r.* Michael W. Davidson/Photo Researchers, Inc. 360: *b.l.* ©Ron Sanford/TSI; *bkgnd.* Hulton Getty/Liaison Agency. 360–361: *b.r.* Hulton Getty/Liaison Agency. 361: *b.* ©Jim Simmen/TSI; *t.* Dave G. Houser/Corbis. 362: *l.* ©Dick Keen/Visuals Unlimited; *r.* E. R Degginger/Photo Researchers, Inc.; *b.m.* ©D. Cavagnaro/Visuals Unlimited; *m.l.* ©Beth Davidow/Visuals Unlimited; *b.r.* ©Gerald Corsi/Visuals Unlimited. 364: *bkgnd.* Owen Franken/Corbis; *c.l.* E. R. Degginger/Photo Researchers, Inc.; *r.* Biophoto/Photo Researchers, Inc.; *t.l.* E. R. Degginger/Photo Researchers, Inc.; *t.l. of b.* ©A. J. Copley/Visuals Unlimited; *m.l. of b.* ©A. J. Copley/Visuals Unlimited; *b.l. of b.* ©A. J. Copley/Visuals Unlimited; *t.m. of b.* ©Doug Sokell/Visuals Unlimited; *m. of b.* ©A. J. Copley/Visuals Unlimited; *t.r. of b.* ©McKutcheon/Visuals Unlimited; *b.r. of b.* ©Arthur R. Hill/Visuals Unlimited. 365: *t.l.* Andrew J. Martinez/Photo Researchers, Inc.; *t.r.* ©Doug Sokell/Visuals Unlimited; *b.* Andrew J. Martinez/Photo Researchers, Inc.; *b.l. of b.* ©A. J. Copley/Visuals Unlimited; *b.l. of b.r.* ©A. J. Copley/Visuals Unlimited. 366: *t.* Andrew J. Martinez/Photo Researchers, Inc.; *b.* ©A. J. Copley/Visuals Unlimited; *m.* ©Martin G. Miller/Visuals Unlimited; *b.m.* Joyce Photographics/Photo Researchers, Inc.; *t.m.* Andrew J. Martinez/Photo Researchers, Inc.; *b.l. of b.* ©Mark Newman/Visuals Unlimited; *t.l. of b.r.* ©John Solden/Visuals Unlimited; *m.l. of b.r.* ©S. Callahan/Visuals Unlimited; *t.r. of b.* ©John D. Cunningham/Visuals Unlimited; *m.l. of b.* S. J. Krasemann/Peter Arnold, Inc. 367: *r.* ©John D. Cunningham/Visuals Unlimited; *b.l.* Joyce Photographics/Photo Researchers, Inc.; *t.l.* Kjell B. Sandved/Photo Researchers, Inc. 368: *t.l.* ©John D. Cunningham/Visuals Unlimited; *t.m.l.* ©A. J. Copley/Visuals Unlimited; *b.m.r.* ©Henry W. Robinson/Visuals Unlimited; *t.r.* ©Martin G. Miller/Visuals Unlimited; *t.m.r.* ©John Solden/Visuals Unlimited; *m.r.* Corbis/Charles Mauzy; *b.l.* ©Joyce Photographics/Photo Researchers, Inc.; *b.m.r.* ©Joyce Photographics/Photo Researchers, Inc.; *b.r.* ©Joyce Photographics/Photo Researchers, Inc. 369: *t.* Michael P. Gadomski/Photo Researchers, Inc. 370: *t.* Joyce Photographics/Photo Researchers, Inc.; *b.* Joyce Photographics/Photo Researchers, Inc. 372: *b.* G. Byttner Naturbild/OKAPIA/Photo Researchers, Inc. 373: *l.* ©Ron Spomer/Visuals Unlimited; *r.* Christian Grzimek/OKAPIA/Photo Researchers, Inc. 375: *r.* Spencer Grant/Photo Researchers, Inc. 376: *t.r. inset* Barbara Gerlach/DRK Photo. 378: *b.* Superstock. 380: *r.* David Young-Wolff/Photo Edit. 381: *b.* John Buitenkant/Photo Researchers, Inc. 382: *l.* Mark E. Gibson. 383: *b.* Tom Myers. 384: *t.* Breck P. Kent/Earth Scenes; *t.* Tom Myers. 385: *b.* Mark E. Gibson. 386: *b.* Sam Sargent/Liaison International. 388: *b.* Paul Conklin/Photo Edit. 389: *m.* Erwin C. (Bud) Nielsen Images International/Visuals Unlimited. 390: *l.* Richard T. Nowitz/Photo Researchers, Inc. 390–391: *bkgnd. spread* California State Library/Tom Meyers. 393: *bkgnd.* ©Terry Vine/Tony Stone International; *inset* ©Keith Wood/Tony Stone International. 394: *r.* Tom McHugh/Photo Researchers, Inc.; *l.* Will & Deni McIntyre/Photo Researchers, Inc. 396: *b.l.* images copyright ©1998 PhotoDisc, Inc. 398: *bkgnd.* ©Gary Withey/Bruce Coleman, Inc.; *l.* Phil Degginger/Color-Pic, Inc.; *m.* Hattie Young/Science Photo Library/Photo Researchers, Inc. 399: *b.l.* Simon Fraser/Science Photo Library/Photo Researchers, Inc. 401: *m.* NASA/Science Photo Library/Photo Researchers, Inc. 402: *b.* JPL/NASA. 403: *t.l.* NASA. 404: *b.* IFA/Peter Arnold, Inc. 407: *l.* Calvin Larsen/Photo Researchers,

Inc.; *r.* Simon Fraser/Science Photo Library/Photo Researchers, Inc. 410: *b.* Simon Fraser/Science Photo Library/Photo Researchers, Inc. 413: *m.* David M. Grossman/Photo Researchers, Inc. 414: *c. inset* Rolf Hicker/Tony Stone Images. 415–416: *bkgnd. spread* Tom Bean. 416: *m.* ©A. M. Copley. 419: *t.l.* ©Rosenfeld Images Ltd./Photo Researchers, Inc.; *t.r.* ©Dana White/PhotoEdit; *m.r.* Tony Freeman/PhotoEdit; *b.r.* ©Ken Lucas/Visuals Unlimited. 420: *t.r. inset* ©Derrick Ditchburn/Visuals Unlimited; *t.m.* ©Arthur Hill/Visuals Unlimited. 421: *m.* Tony Freeman/PhotoEdit; *b.l.* ©Larry Lefever/Grant Heilman Photography, Inc.; *t.r.* ©Hal Beral/VU/Tony Stone Images. 423: *t.* Calvin Hamilton/NASA. 424: *t.* images copyright ©1999 PhotoDisc, Inc.; *b.* ©Science Visuals Unlimited. 426: *t.r.* ©Inga Spence/Visuals Unlimited; *b.r.* ©Ken Lucas/Visuals Unlimited; *m.r.* ©Inga Spence/Visuals Unlimited. 427: *t.l.* ©Jerry Irwin/Photo Researchers, Inc.; *m.l.* Bachmann/PhotoEdit; *b.l.* ©R. Calentine/Visuals Unlimited. 429: *m.r.* ©John Solden/Visuals Unlimited. 430: *bkgnd.* Grant Heilman Photography, Inc.; *b.l. inset* Calvin Larsen/Photo Researchers, Inc. 430–431: *bkgnd. spread* Martin Bond/SPL/Photo Researchers, Inc. 431: *r. inset* Sylvain Coffie/Tony Stone Images. 432: *b.* PhotoDisc, Inc. 434: *l. inset* Baron Wolman/Tony Stone Images; *b.* Richard During/Tony Stone Images. 435: *b.* Brian Hamer/Photo Edit. 436: *b.* Tony Freeman/Photo Edit. 439: *m.* R. Rolle/Gamma Liaison. 440: *b.* Bob Thomason/Tony Stone Images; *b.r. inset* Tony Freeman/Photo Edit. 441: *b.* Russell D. Curtis/Photo Researchers, Inc.; *b.r. inset* Beverly Anderson/Photo 20-20. 442: *m.* David Young-Wolff/Photo Edit; *b. inset* Miriam Agron/Earth Scenes. 443: *b.* Ken Biggs/Tony Stone Images. 444: *t.* Stephen Krasemann/Photo Researchers, Inc.; *r. inset* Inga Spence/Visuals Unlimited. 445: *b.* Peter Hughes/Index Stock Photography, Inc. 446: *c. boxed bkgnd.* Larry Ulrich/DRK Photo; *r. inset* Mark E. Gibson/Visuals Unlimited. R9: *r.* NASA/Digital Stock. R10: *t. bkgnd., b.l., b.r.* images copyright ©1999 PhotoDisc, Inc. R16: *r.* Jim Harrison/Stock Boston/PNI. R20: *b.l. bkgnd.* images copyright ©1988 PhotoDisc, Inc.; *b.l. inset* G. R. Roberts/Photo Researchers, Inc. R21: *t. inset* images copyright ©1999 PhotoDisc, Inc.; *b. inset* ©1998 AccuWeather.

PERIODIC TABLE OF THE ELEMENTS

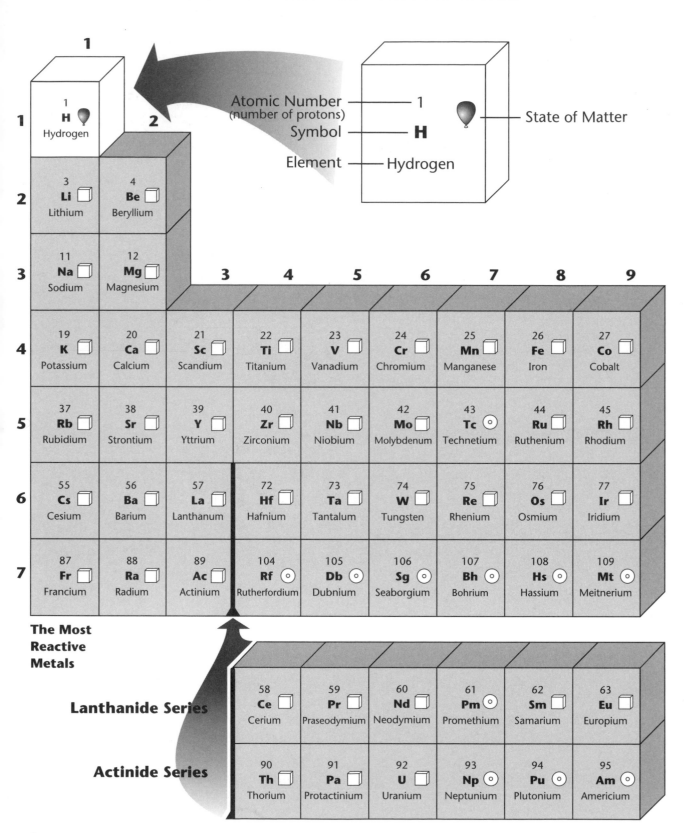

Atomic Number (number of protons) — 1

Symbol — **H**

Element — Hydrogen

State of Matter

1	2	3	4	5	6	7	8	9
1 **H** Hydrogen								
3 **Li** Lithium	4 **Be** Beryllium							
11 **Na** Sodium	12 **Mg** Magnesium							
19 **K** Potassium	20 **Ca** Calcium	21 **Sc** Scandium	22 **Ti** Titanium	23 **V** Vanadium	24 **Cr** Chromium	25 **Mn** Manganese	26 **Fe** Iron	27 **Co** Cobalt
37 **Rb** Rubidium	38 **Sr** Strontium	39 **Y** Yttrium	40 **Zr** Zirconium	41 **Nb** Niobium	42 **Mo** Molybdenum	43 **Tc** Technetium	44 **Ru** Ruthenium	45 **Rh** Rhodium
55 **Cs** Cesium	56 **Ba** Barium	57 **La** Lanthanum	72 **Hf** Hafnium	73 **Ta** Tantalum	74 **W** Tungsten	75 **Re** Rhenium	76 **Os** Osmium	77 **Ir** Iridium
87 **Fr** Francium	88 **Ra** Radium	89 **Ac** Actinium	104 **Rf** Rutherfordium	105 **Db** Dubnium	106 **Sg** Seaborgium	107 **Bh** Bohrium	108 **Hs** Hassium	109 **Mt** Meitnerium

The Most Reactive Metals

Lanthanide Series

58 **Ce** Cerium	59 **Pr** Praseodymium	60 **Nd** Neodymium	61 **Pm** Promethium	62 **Sm** Samarium	63 **Eu** Europium

Actinide Series

90 **Th** Thorium	91 **Pa** Protactinium	92 **U** Uranium	93 **Np** Neptunium	94 **Pu** Plutonium	95 **Am** Americium